GUIDE TO BUSINESS GAMING and EXPERIENTIAL LEARNING

GUIDE TO BUSINESS GAMING and EXPERIENTIAL LEARNING

Association for Business Simulation and Experiential Learning (ABSEL)

Edited by James W. Gentry

Nichols/GP Publishing, East Brunswick / Kogan Page, London

Library of Congress Cataloging-in-Publication Data

Guide to business gaming and experiential learning / Association for
  Business Simulation and Experiential Learning ; James W. Gentry, editor.
    p.   cm.
  Includes bibliographical references.
  ISBN 0-89397-369-6
  1. Management games. I. Gentry, James W., 1947–
II. Association for Business Simulation and Experiential Learning.
  HD30.26.G85   1990
658.4'0353—dc20   90-32561
                                           CIP

British Library Cataloguing-in-Publication Data

Guide to Business Gaming and Experiential Learning, edited by
James Gentry.
Higher education institutions. Curriculum subjects. Business games.
Management games.
658.0078
E-UK—

ISBN 0-74940-092-7

Printed in the United States of America.

The Association for Business Simulation and Experiential Learning dedicates this guide to its founder, J. Bernard Keys.

The editor also dedicates the guide to one of his mentors, Ralph L. Day, who was the third president of ABSEL, and to his parents, Donald and Carolyn Gentry.

PREFACE

OVERVIEW

Everyone learns from experience. This is as true in teaching as it is in any other area. In many instances, the first attempts to use or administer a new pedagogy result in a somewhat painful learning experience for the instructor. Determining where to start can be difficult and, once determined, the start-up costs are frequently quite high. What specific approach should be used? If one is considering a game or an experiential exercise, whose should be used? Should a new one be developed? What problems are associated with existing tools? What difficulties are encountered when developing one's own exercise or game? How does one handle the situation if the game breaks down or if the results do not make any sense? What if students make decisions that are completely outside the expected realm? And worse yet, what if those decisions yield good results? Do these approaches have any educational benefit?

This *Guide* is intended to provide practical insight into these problems and into their expedient handling. This guidance is based on the trial and (all-too-frequent) error learning that a number of us in the Association for Business Simulation and Experiential Learning (ABSEL) have obtained. Further, we will review the available evidence on the effectiveness of the various approaches.

BACKGROUND

The Association for Business Simulation and Experiential Learning was started in 1974 with the sponsorship of a conference on business gaming and experiential learning by J. Bernard Keys and Howard Leftwich of Oklahoma Christian College in Oklahoma City. ABSEL has developed into a professional association whose membership consists predominantly of business faculty. Currently there are approximately 150–200 members. The organizational goals are as follows:

1. The expansion of the use of simulations and other experiential learning techniques for business education in both current and evolving applications.

2. The provision of a forum for those currently using or developing simulations and experiential learning techniques and tools for business education.
3. The provision of an outlet for the generation of empirical studies in business gaming and experiential exercises.
4. The maintenance of a viable organization that employs a challenging yet supportive presentational style.

Chapter 1 will provide more discussion of ABSEL, in addition to discussing other organizations sharing somewhat similar purposes.

THE *GUIDE'S* ORGANIZATION

The *Guide* is divided into six parts. Part 1 provides an introduction to the area, with the first chapter discussing the sources available should one want to participate in organizations involved in experiential learning. Chapter 2 grapples with the question of what is meant by the term "experiential learning."

Part 2 provides an introduction to simulation gaming, with four chapters that discuss how to select games, usage trends for games, specific games currently available, and administrative issues involved in successful gaming experiences.

Part 3 deals with issues involved when one endeavors to develop one's own game. One chapter provides an overview of the problems faced, while the other deals with one specific issue that is critical in nearly all business games: the development of a realistic and robust demand function.

Part 4 deals with the next generation of simulation games, with one chapter on real time simulation and another on open systems simulation.

Part 5 of the *Guide* moves from simulation gaming to other experiential approaches. Chapter 11 provides an introduction to experiential exercises and discusses several vivid examples. The next chapter offers very practical guidance as to how to administer experiential exercises. Chapters 13 and 14 deal with the "live case," in which students are to work closely with an organization as part of the class requirements. The first of these chapters gives an overview, while the second offers insight into how the instructor can provide a theoretical structure to a largely unstructured process. The last chapter in this section discusses a general structure of experiential exercises, as well as some of the changing forms which we will be seeing.

The sixth and final part of the book covers the effectiveness of the various approaches. The first chapter discusses the vast array of concerns that need to be dealt with in order to conduct reasonably sound experimental studies in this area. The last two chapters evaluate the findings from the areas of simulation gaming and experiential learning.

CONTENTS

AUTHOR BIOGRAPHIES

Theodore C. Alex served on the marketing faculty at Wayne State University and is currently in business in the Detroit area.

William D. Biggs is department chairman of management at Beaver College, where he previously served as dean of Continuing Education. Bill is a past president of ABSEL.

Alvin C. Burns is on the marketing faculty at Louisiana State University, having returned from a stint as department chairman at Central Florida University. Al is a past president of ABSEL.

Hugh M. Cannon is on the marketing faculty at Wayne State University, having taught previously at Northwestern University. Hugh is currently the executive director of ABSEL.

Newell E. Chiesl is on the marketing faculty at Indiana State University, and is currently writing a Promotions textbook.

Richard V. Cotter is on the management faculty at the University of Nevada–Reno, and has run one of the longest running collegiate simulation game competitions in the United States.

Anthony J. Faria is the marketing department head at the University of Windsor, and is the co-author of two of the leading simulation games (*COMPETE* and *LAPTOP*) in marketing.

David J. Fritzsche is on the marketing faculty at the University of Portland after having taught at the University of Nevada–Reno, Illinois State University, and the Rochester Institute of Technology. Dave is a past president of ABSEL.

James W. Gentry is on the marketing faculty at the University of Nebraska–Lincoln, having taught previously at the University of Wisconsin–Madison, Oklahoma State University, and Kansas State University. Jim is a past president of ABSEL.

Steven C. Gold is on the economics faculty at the Rochester Institute of Technology. He is the author of the *ASTUTE* simulation game.

Jerry Gosenpud is on the management faculty at the University of Wisconsin–Whitewater. Jerry formerly was editor of the ABSEL *Newsletter* and is now a co-editor of the ABSEL *Proceedings*.

Lee A. Graf is on the management faculty at Illinois State University, and has served as president of ABSEL.

Calvin E. Kellogg is on the management faculty at the University of Mississippi, after having served on the faculty at Illinois State University and the University of Arkansas. He is currently the editor of the ABSEL *Newsletter.*

J. Bernard Keys is the Fuller E. Calloway Professor of Business at Georgia Southern College. Bernie is the founder of ABSEL, and was its first president. He is currently director of the Center for Business Simulation in the School of Business at Georgia Southern.

R. Bruce McAfee is on the management faculty at Old Dominion University, and has developed a series of intriguing experiential exercises over his career.

Alan L. Patz is on the management faculty at the University of Southern California, and specializes in the business policy area.

Thomas F. Pray is on the decision sciences faculty at the Rochester Institute of Technology, and is president-elect of ABSEL.

James W. Schreier is in private consulting with his own firm, Far Cliffs Consulting of Milwaukee, after serving as associate dean in the College of Business at Marquette University. Jim is a past president of ABSEL.

Richard D. Teach is on the marketing faculty at the Georgia Institute of Technology, and has been concerned with issues in simulation game design for many years.

Joseph Wolfe is on the management faculty at the University of Tulsa, currently on leave teaching in Hungary. Joe is a former president of ABSEL.

PART 1

INTRODUCTION

The first section provides an introduction to experiential learning. The first chapter by J. Bernard Keys provides background as to organizations in North America and Europe which stress experiential learning and simulation gaming. Included is a short history of the Association of Business Simulation and Experiential Learning, which has compiled this Guide. The second chapter by James W. Gentry attempts to clarify the domain of experiential learning pedagogies.

Chapter 1: Organizations Advancing Business Simulation and Experiential Learning, by J. Bernard Keys

Chapter 2: What Is Experiential Learning?, by James W. Gentry

CHAPTER 1

ORGANIZATIONS ADVANCING BUSINESS SIMULATION AND EXPERIENTIAL LEARNING

J. Bernard Keys

This chapter will discuss several organizations which serve to advance the areas of business simulation and experiential learning. Since this *Guide* is being written by the Association for Business Simulation and Experiential Learning, we will start with a discussion of ABSEL.

THE ASSOCIATION FOR BUSINESS SIMULATION AND EXPERIENTIAL LEARNING

ABSEL is a national association of professors of business and related disciplines and business trainers who are interested in business simulations and games and experiential teaching and learning. It was organized in 1974 at a conference in Oklahoma City, hosted by Bernard Keys and Howard Leftwich and the Oklahoma Christian College. ABSEL hosts an annual conference, usually in early spring, and publishes the proceedings of the conference. The 1990 Conference will be in Honolulu, the 1991 conference in Nashville, and the 1992 conference in Las Vegas. Members of ABSEL receive a biannual newsletter and a subscription to the international journal *Simulation and Games*.

For the annual conference, papers are solicited by a call for papers and, once received, are blind reviewed by three reviewers to determine whether

---

The author thanks Bill Biggs, Alan Cudworth, and Dick Teach for their inputs on some of the organizations discussed in this chapter.

they are of the quality to be presented at the annual meeting. The conference *Proceedings* is distributed at the conference, and discussants critique the papers and provide suggestions for further improvement before participants submit their papers to various journals for possible publication.

At the annual meeting of ABSEL, a game room is provided to allow members to demonstrate games and computerized exercises. The general tone of the conference is a quite relaxed one. One night during the conference the group as a whole visits a local attraction such as Sea World or a cruise ship. Textbook publishers often attend the meeting and provide displays of new experiential texts and business games. In order to extend familiarity with business games, a faculty business game competition is conducted each year with a conclusion to the game coinciding with the ABSEL annual meeting.

For a number of years, members of ABSEL have hosted intercollegiate business games in which undergraduate student teams compete and then attend a playoff for national awards. Competitions have been at Emory University and at the University of Nevada-Reno. Another such competition was co-hosted by ABSEL and Tennessee Tech University and later continued for two years at Georgia Southern College. The Emory competition has been suspended, but the University of Nevada-Reno competition continues (for further information, contact Richard V. Cotter in the College of Business Administration) and plans are underway to reinstate the Georgia Southern competition (contact Robert Wells in the College of Administration there for more information).

The most recent call for papers for an ABSEL conference invites paper submissions, symposia, and demonstrations which deal with business gaming and simulation development, research, evaluation and application, experiential exercises, and business teaching methods and evaluations. Submissions which include interactive participation of conference attendees are encouraged. The topics suggested for the next meeting include:

Evaluation of learning in simulation, games, and exercises

Development of simulations, games, and cases

Application of expert systems and decision support systems in business simulations and games

Innovative business teaching methods

Organization applications of simulations and exercises

Developing and using simulations and exercises for corporate education programs

International applications of cases, simulations, and experiential activities

Anyone interested in obtaining more information about ABSEL or in joining should contact Hugh Cannon in the College of Business Administration, Wayne State University, 5201 Cass Avenue, Detroit, MI 48202.

THE CENTER FOR THE ADVANCEMENT OF BUSINESS SIMULATION AND EXPERIENTIAL LEARNING (CABSEL)

CABSEL was founded in 1985 at Georgia Southern College by Bernard Keys. The center houses a business game library and archives for ABSEL, and provides a permanent center for contacts about business games and related research. Frequent contacts with CABSEL are made by persons throughout the world interested in business games and simulation. International visitors to the center are common and presently Huang Jiarong, a professor and visiting scholar from the People's Republic of China, is spending a year at CABSEL translating business games for use in his home country.

The primary purpose of CABSEL is to provide information about business games and simulations and to provide continuity of information about research conducted by ABSEL members and other associates. For this reason, the center maintains an extensive bibliography on business games and related research and makes the bibliography available at a nominal charge. The CABSEL business game bibliography also includes the table of contents of all ABSEL *Proceedings*. Copies of any ABSEL papers can be obtained by writing CABSEL. Also available from CABSEL is an annotated bibliography of experiential exercises from ABSEL conferences which was compiled by Calvin Kellogg.

CABSEL associates are engaged in ongoing research and in the development of business games and simulations. Large scale game development projects have been developed for Fortune 500 companies. Interested callers are often referred to the many business game experts in ABSEL.

CABSEL frequently hosts intercollegiate business game competitions. Two national competitions have been hosted for undergraduate students in cooperation with the ABSEL organization and plans are underway to continue with the competitions.

Presently CABSEL is funded by Georgia Southern College and by the publishers and clients of Bernard Keys, including MCB Publications, the publishers of the *Journal of Management Development* and *Executive Development,* international journals which publish articles about management development and for which Keys serves as co-editor.

Publishers of business games and authors of published research are encouraged to share copies of their publications with CABSEL, so that they can be included in the CABSEL archives and in the CABSEL bibliography.

To contact CABSEL, write or call Bernard Keys, Center for Business Simulation, Georgia Southern College, Statesboro, GA 30460-8127, phone: 912-681-5457, fax: 912-681-0292.

OTHER PRIMARILY U S ORGANIZATIONS

North American Simulation and Gaming Association (NASAGA)

NASAGA is the North American Simulation and Gaming Association. NASAGA began as the East Coast War Games Council, and war gaming was precisely the subject matter with which it dealt. Later other aspects of simulation gaming were featured, and the name was changed to the National Gaming Council. The emphasis shifted to business and economic gaming and then later shifted to the broader field of social science. For the last few years, leaders in the organization have attempted to regain the participation of simulation gamers coming from such areas as war gaming and business. A number of simulation games in the social sciences are available from NASAGA.

NASAGA sponsors an annual meeting with papers and workshops. The national office of NASAGA is located at the Community Systems Foundation, 1130 Hill Street, Ann Arbor, MI, 48104, phone: 313-761-1368. The Director is Fred Goodman.

The Organizational Behavior Teaching Society (OBTS)

OBTS is an organization dedicated to exchanging ideas, learning new methods, and examining the fundamental issues involved in teaching the organizational disciplines. The organization's primary activity is a three-day annual conference during which participants stay at a host university campus, live in dormitory rooms, and take their meals together. The annual meeting, held in late spring, consists of a series of concurrent workshop presentations of varying length on a wide variety of teaching-related topics. There are no formal paper presentations.

Registration at the annual meeting includes a subscription to a newsletter and a subscription to the *Organizational Behavior Teaching Review*. For information about the Society, contact Larry Michaelsen, Center for Economic and Management Research, College of Business Administration, University of Oklahoma, 307 West Brooks, Room 4, Norman, OK 73019.

Eastern Academy of Management Experiential Learning Group

There is an ad hoc subgroup of the Eastern Academy of Management which focuses on the development and dissemination of experiential exercises. In recent years, the group has sponsored sessions at the annual Eastern

Academy of Management conferences, with approximately 18 papers or exercises being presented. Some of the sessions are participatory in nature. One joins by joining the Eastern Academy of Management (dues were $15 as of 1989). For further information, you are encouraged to contact Joe Seltzer at LaSalle University.

INTERNATIONAL EXPERIENTIAL ORGANIZATIONS

ISAGA: The International Simulation and Gaming Association

ISAGA is a worldwide, but primarily European, organization whose members are interested in the use of simulation gaming as a pedagogical tool. ISAGA was found in Birmingham, England, with the purpose of creating an international forum for the exchange of ideas on simulation and games. The main objective is to promote the use of simulation and gaming as learning, training, and research approaches. Like ABSEL, ISAGA has adopted *Simulation and Games,* a Sage publication, as their official journal. Their interests are much broader than ABSEL's and their primary membership consists of scholars from the Social Sciences and Humanites and practitioners from a wide variety of businesses and governments. Those interested in business simulations make up a minority of its membership. The organization acts as the titular head of a wide group of national simulation associations such as SAGSET (Great Britain), NASAGA (North America), ADSEGA (Australia), as well as groups in Argentina, the Philippines, Poland, East and West Germany, and elsewhere.

ISAGA conferences take place in the summer. In the past the meetings have largely taken place in Europe, but future conferences will take place on other continents as well. Their meetings are informal and, in many of their three hour sessions, the attendees take part and play a simulation. The sessions are primarily in English, with only a few sessions held in the language of the host country. Annual dues for ISAGA in 1989 are US $25.

For further information about ISAGA contact the President, Dr. S. H. Gernert, Humboldt University, University of Architecture and Civil Engineering, Berlin or David Crookall, 4901 Seminary Road, Number 1122, Alexandria, VA 22311, USA, phone: 703-998-2329.

SAGSET: The Society for the Advancement of Games and Simulations in Education and Training

SAGSET was formed in 1969 in Great Britain to enable practitioners to publish, correspond, meet, discuss, and try out games and simulations. The interests of its members have spanned the whole range of education and training from primary school to university and from trade union to senior management. The Society has over 500 individual members and 150 institutional members throughout the world. Each member receives (1) the quarterly journal *Simulation/Games for Learning,* (2) *SAGSET News,* providing information about courses, conferences, and new publications and references, and (3) Resource Lists giving references and simulation games for a wide variety of applications. The Society holds an annual conference in Great Britain. Formal papers are not presented, but each delegate has a number of interesting workshops from which to choose. Most allow the individual to participate in the games or simulations. For example, at the 1989 conference the delegates participated in a cross-country "walk", in which they were subjected to a number of management training exercises. Membership fees in 1989 were 20 pounds per annum for overseas members. Further information can be obtained from Membership Secretary, SAGSET, Centre for Extension Studies, University of Technology, Loughborough, Leicestershire, LE11 3TU, United Kingdom.

Europaisches Planspiel Forum

The Europaisches Planspiel Forum is a German-speaking, three-day conference held in the late fall in Bad Neuenahr, Germany, covering business gaming and simulation. It is sponsored by the Deutsche Planspiel Zentrale (a German gaming and simulation center). The conference coordinator is Walter E. Rohn, D–5600 Wuppertal 12, Vonkein 51, Federal Republic of Germany.

Participants at the yearly conference represent a 50–50 mix of academics and practitioners from Germany, Austria, and The Netherlands. The conference is similar to a ABSEL conference as far as the topics are concerned, but more business and industrial training situations and applications are included. The typical session is more formal than those of ABSEL and the discussions are frequently quite technical, reflecting the more sophisticated and complex nature of the games being discussed. The sessions start after breakfast and continue until about 9:00 P.M.

CHAPTER 2

WHAT IS EXPERIENTIAL LEARNING?

James W. Gentry

Members of ABSEL are dedicated to the proposition that students can learn from experience. Most people adhere to the notion of "trial and error" learning. Various ABSEL participants have used the following quote, attributed to Confucius, to express their conviction that experiential learning is effective:

> I HEAR AND I FORGET
> I SEE AND I REMEMBER
> I DO AND I UNDERSTAND.[1]

Others have cited Sophocles' quote from 400 B.C., "One must learn by doing the thing, for though you think you know it—you have no certainty, until you try." Or, one could quote George Santayana, "The great difficulty of education is to get experience out of ideas."

It is hard to argue that experience will not lead to learning under the right conditions. However, it will be argued that the resultant learning can be in error unless care is taken to assure that those conditions occur. The purpose of this chapter is to delineate the components of "experiential learning" so that the necessary conditions for "proper" learning can be specified. While most pedagogies allow students to learn experientially to some extent, an attempt will be made to distinguish those approaches which would be more likely to facilitate experiential learning.

While the title of the chapter implies a focus on learning (the student perspective), to a large extent the chapter actually focuses on the structuring of the experience (the teacher perspective). What the student takes away from a particular experience is often idiosyncratic to his/her perceptions of the experience, and is somewhat outside the control of the instructor. The

---

[1] The AACSB Memorandum (Carter et al. 1986) used a slightly different version: Tell me and I'll forget. Show me and I'll remember. Involve me and I'll understand.

instructor is responsible for providing the experiential stimulus, and the quality of that stimulus will vary greatly depending upon the pedagogical approach used. Thus, much of the chapter will deal with the issue of which approaches facilitate experiential learning.

DEFINITION OF EXPERIENTIAL LEARNING

Various terms have been used to label the process of learning from experience. John Dewey (Dewey and Dewey 1915) discussed "learning by doing," while Wolfe and Byrne (1975) used the term "experienced-based learning." The term "trial and error" learning is used to explain inductive learning processes. The AACSB Task Force (1986) used the term "applied experiential learning," combining the learning from the "real-world" situation with the necessary condition of the application of concepts, ideas and theories to the interactive setting. The term "experiential learning" will be used here, but it is intended to cover the same domains as the other terms.

The AACSB Task Force (1986, p. 3) defined applied experiential learning as:

> A business curriculum-related endeavor which is interactive (other than between teacher and pupil) and is characterized by variability and uncertainty.

Most discussions of the concept by ABSEL participants have referred to the original (to ABSEL) definitional work by Hoover (1974) at the first ABSEL conference. He drew upon the work of Rogers (1969, p. 5), who defined the essence of experiential learning as:

> It has a quality of personal involvement—the whole-person in both his feeling and cognitive aspects being in the learning event.

Using this definition as a springboard, Hoover (1974) made the point that experiential learning involves more than just the cognitive learning generally stressed by management education. In addition to the affective domain mentioned by Rogers, Hoover also stressed the learning of behaviors. In a subsequent paper (Hoover and Whitehead 1975, p. 25), the following definition of experiential learning was given:

> Experiential learning exists when a personally responsible participant cognitively, affectively, and behaviorally processes knowledge, skills, and/or attitudes in a learning situation characterized by a high level of active involvement.

Discussion leading to Hoover's definitions used phrases such as "participative," "contact with the environment," "[an] attempt to combine the processes of learning with the content of learning," and emphasis on "the 'how' as well as the 'what' of the instruction or training."

Comparison of the AACSB definition and that by Hoover and Whitehead shows that neither is comprehensive. Before discussing the components involved in either or both definitions, it will be beneficial to discuss the overall experiential learning task structure proposed by Wolfe and Byrne (1975). They state that experientially-based approaches involve four phases: design, conduct, evaluation, and feedback.

Design. This phase involves the upfront efforts by the instructor to set the stage for the experience. Included in this phase are the specification of learning objectives, the production or selection of activities for participants, the identification of factors affecting student learning, and the creation of a scheme for implementation. Thus, this phase is critical for the "applied" part of the AACSB's applied experiential learning; the theoretical base is laid so that the participant can view the experience in the desired context.

Conduct. This phase involves maintaining and controlling the design. The design phase may include the creation of a timetable for the experience, but the conduct phase involves the altering of the original timetable and activities to sustain a favorable learning environment. The important implication of this phase is that the experience is a structured and closely-monitored one.

Evaluation. To be sure, evaluation is conducted by the instructor. But the emphasis here by Wolfe and Byrne is on the provision of opportunities for students to evaluate the experience. Participants should be able to articulate and demonstrate specific learning gained from the design and conduct of the experience.

Feedback. Wolfe and Byrne point out that feedback should be an almost continuous process from the pre-experience introduction through the final debriefing. Included is the monitoring of the process by the instructor in order to foster positive aspects and eliminate those features that are negative. One possible concern in this phase is whether students should have the opportunity to fail. To the extent that we learn from our errors, the freedom to fail may be encouraged. On the other hand, if the experiential exercise involves a business client (such as in a small business case), failure can affect the business school's reputation negatively.

Learning will be best facilitated when all four phases (design, conduct, evaluation, and feedback) are present and repeated over time. Such a process would resemble that in Figure 2-1. This process-oriented approach is somewhat similar in nature to those proposed by Kolb (1984) and Lewin (1951).

FIGURE 2-1
Process-Oriented Version of the Wolfe and Byrne Model

CRITICAL COMPONENTS TO EXPERIENTIAL LEARNING

Contrasting the AACSB and the Hoover and Whitehead definitions while considering the Wolfe and Byrne framework, one can begin to delineate the components of "experiential learning." This section will provide a discussion of them.

Business curriculum-related. Clearly the business discipline has no monopoly on the use of experiential learning. Given that AACSB administers collegiate schools of business and that the majority of ABSEL members are business faculty, the emphasis on business curricula is appropriate. As pointed out by the AACSB Task Force, business is an applied discipline: "Business education involves studying applications of mathematics, economics and behavioral sciences to problems in the production and distribution of goods and services" [Carter et al., 1986, p. 6]. Thus, the applied nature of business education might be a more appropriate discipline for the use of experiential learning pedagogies than one with a stronger theoretical orientation.

One should note in passing that experiential learning approaches are not used solely by universities, but also by corporate trainers. The emphasis of this volume is on the university classroom; consequently, topics such as grading may be largely irrelevant to corporate trainers. However, the vast majority of the discussion herein should be of value in any application of experiential learning (corporate or university; business discipline or behavioral science discipline).

One interesting point raised in the AACSB Task Force Memorandum is that, as an alternative or possibly a supplement to an increased use of experiential learning in the business curriculum, business schools should emphasize the benefits of the extracurricular activities of students. Clearly, such activities offer a small subset of the student body a chance to develop their leadership skills experientially. The Memorandum suggests that business schools actively encourage student clubs to promote activities which involve student participation so that their speaking, discussion, interpersonal, and goal-setting abilities are developed.

Applied. As presented by Wolfe and Byrne (1975), the design phase of the experience is critical. Experiences occurring without guidance and adequate academic preparation may yield little insight into the general processes taking place. The Task Force stated that experiences will not qualify as applied experiential learning without having the expected educational outcomes articulated and related to the curriculum.

Participative. The student must be involved in the process. Experiential learning is active rather than passive. Rather than just listening to a lecture, students do role plays, or make decisions (as in a simulation game), or perform an analysis of a firm's problems (as in a small business case project).

Interactive. As specified by the Task Force, the interaction involves more than just the instructor/student dyad. Student/student, student/client, or student/environment interaction is also required. Example interactions include group decision-making in a simulation game, presentations to clients in small business case projects, and conducting survey research of local households for a marketing research course project.

Whole-person emphasis. Experiential learning can involve learning on the behavioral and affective dimensions as well as the cognitive dimension. Given the problem-solving orientation of most management education, there is a natural tendency among business faculty to emphasize the cognitive dimension. Given the importance of "people skills" and "technical skills" though, the broader horizons offered by experiential learning approaches (as compared to more traditional teaching methods such as lectures and class discussion) may be very beneficial. While the AACSB definition does not mention the whole-person concept, the Task Force did acknowledge the development of a student's interpersonal and other non-cognitive skills as one of the major expected benefits from experiential learning.

Contact with the Environment. The term "experience" implies a real world contact (or at least a "real-world-like") contact. Some forms of experiential learning (such as simulation games, role-playing exercises, and case discussions) do not involve actual real world contact and were labeled as "surrogate" applied experiential learning by the AACSB Task Force.

Business internships may involve actual work experience, but most types of experiential learning will fall short of giving students actual decision-making authority. Nonetheless, the simulated environments are intended to be analogous to the real situations which students will face later.

The real or simulated experience makes possible learning through interaction with one's environment. The person X situation interaction is itself crucial. Students should be provided with a variety of situations. Also it should be noted that different students will react quite differently to the same situational cue, and that the interaction process should be monitored closely.

Variability and Uncertainty. The use of these terms in the AACSB Task Force definition may have been for the purpose of placing added emphasis on the real-world environment. One of the benefits which they cite for experiential learning is that students get a feel for the "messiness" and ambiguity associated with real-world situations. It may be enlightening to a student to listen to a lecture on organizational conflict; however, when it is encountered in the team play of a simulation game and there is no one with the authority to reconcile the opposing views, the messiness associated with organizational conflict becomes very real.

A divide and conquer approach is used in most lecture-based courses, as the topic being covered is broken down into its components which are then dealt with separately. This process sometimes obscures the complexity that occurs when the various parts are integrated into the whole. The systems aspects may become clearer to students when they have to handle tradeoffs in a large-scale simulation game.

Structured Exercise. The experience should be structured and monitored. If there is insufficient autonomy, the willingness to participate may be greatly stifled. On the other hand, if there is no guidance provided, the experience may be largely meaningless in terms of the specific content area for which the instructor is responsible. Faculty time commitments to teaching usually increase (and increase substantially) rather than decrease when students become more participative in and out of class. An "experience" by itself will not insure learning; the instructor has to insure that it is a quality experience.

Student Evaluation of the Experience. Students need to have the opportunity to articulate their thoughts and feelings as to what the experience is involving. Even though the instructor is monitoring the experience, the important perceptions of what is happening reside within the student. Accordingly these perceptions must be understood and articulated by the student. The design of even highly structured experiential exercises such as simulation games and role plays is often dynamic in nature, as the designer modifies the exercise upon receiving feedback as to what is perceived by the participant to be happening as opposed to what the designer "objectively" perceives to be happening. A good measure of students' ability to integrate content and process is to have them critique the experience by specifying what should have occurred in the experience as opposed to what was actually involved.

Feedback. We do not always learn well from experience. George Bernard Shaw once stated that "we learn from experience that we never learn from experience." To the extent that we learn by "trial and error," the learning is essentially inductive in nature. We experience certain situations and we generalize rules to explain what happened. Or as Kelly (1955) described the process:

> The person who merely stands agog at each emerging event may experience a series of interesting surprises, but if he makes no attempt to discover the recurrent themes, his experience does not amount to much. It is when man begins to see the orderliness in a sequence of events that he begins to experience them. . . . From the standpoint of the psychology of personal constructs, it is the learning which constitutes experience.

Most learning occurs through outcome feedback—an action is taken and we observe the outcome. In many cases, we judge the quality of the decision by the favorableness of the outcome. Phrases such as "we reward productivity, not effort" and "bottom-line management" indicate emphasis on outcomes. Decision theorists (one example is Emery and Tuggle, 1976) have frequently pointed out that outcomes frequently depend on factors outside the control of decision makers, and that we should evaluate the decision process rather than the outcome. In the long run, a good decision process should result in more profit, but this may not be true in the short run.

This emphasis on process rather than outcome feedback has found its way into our approaches to teaching. When we grade cases, we often state that the final recommendation is not as critical as the logical and empirical support that precedes it. In simulation games, we do not weight the entire game grade on the game results, but rather place quite a bit of emphasis on the students' discussion of their game strategies and their justifications for the specific decisions. On the other hand, it is simpler to observe their game-end profit or their recommended case solution than it is to delineate the process used to bring about these outcomes. Further, far less effort is required to critique the outcomes than to critique the process.

Even if we as instructors provide process feedback, students may concentrate on the outcome feedback (grade) and ignore the process feedback (written comments). Most students have come to expect consistency between the two types of feedback, and they are not easily placated when distinctions between the two are made.

Students are not alone in finding the distinction between good/bad decisions and good/bad outcomes to be counter intuitive. Most people do. After all, we have a lifetime of experience in learning from outcomes. Outcomes are visible, available, and often unambiguous; the process, however, often must be inferred on the part of the instructor. In many business contexts, process feedback is almost impossible. For example, salespersons perform most of their duties outside the home firm's environment; consequently, the sales manager must evaluate outcomes (total sales) rather than process. Those process variables which are available (such as the number of sales calls) often do not provide much insight into the sales process.

Unfortunately, most of our learning based on outcome feedback is based on a very small sample size. Frazer (1986) discussed the possibility of indoctrinating students as to the importance of certain variables (such as price or salesforce) given the nature of the particular demand function used in a simulation game. To the extent that students carry such an artificially developed view of the importance of variables away from the game as the lesson learned, the experience may be more harmful than helpful in future decision-making.

Even when sufficient outcome feedback is available to provide a systematic view of possible relationships among variables, problems still may occur. Because of the way feedback occurs and the methods that humans use to test rules via experience, positive reinforcement can occur even for incorrect rules (Wason 1960). More specifically, representation of outcomes in memory is thought to be often of categorical form—successes and failures, rather than absolute levels of the criterion (Estes 1976). Further research (Jenkins and Ward 1965; Smedslund 1963; Ward and Jenkins 1965) indicates that people tend to focus on positive outcomes. In studies measuring subjects' ability to judge the contingency between variables x and y from information in a 2×2 table such as Figure 2–2, people were found to judge the strengths of the relationship by the frequency of positive hits while generally ignoring the other three cells. The implication of this finding is that people do not use all available outcome feedback even when it is presented systematically. An additional implication is that people have a tendency to focus on positive feedback more than on negative feedback.

Einhorn and Hogarth (1981) conclude that one must pay attention to nonoccurrences of the event as well as occurrences in order to develop a correct decision process. Without the search for disconfirming evidence, the development of decision processes will be based on the more visible and more memorable successes.

FIGURE 2–2
2 × 2 Table Format

	x	$\bar{x}$
y	positive hit	false positive
$\bar{y}$	false negative	negative hit

In summary, feedback is critical for proper learning to take place after an experience. The student should not be allowed to conclude what was learned without receiving feedback; there is too much evidence that human beings do not do this properly. The debriefing session is crucial. Students need to articulate their perception of what was learned, and the instructor needs to put things into a broader perspective. If the students correctly uncover what the key variables are in the present exercise, discussion should probe whether those variables are also dominant in other situations.

Second, process feedback is much more valuable than outcome feedback. The bottom line in many games is a less-than-perfect representation of the quality of the decisions for several possible reasons: (1) a high degree of randomization in the generation of the results, (2) unequal starting points, (3) different levels of competition, (4) competitive dynamics which yield different levels of performance across groups, or (5) a poorly structured model. Process feedback requires much more monitoring by the instructor, but it is the decision process used that needs to be applauded or critiqued.

WHICH PEDAGOGIES FACILITATE EXPERIENTIAL LEARNING?

Given that the components of experiential learning are specified in the previous section, it may be possible to dichotomize pedagogies as involving experiential learning or as not. An earlier attempt (Gentry 1981) to do so in the ABSEL Newsletter was criticized (Goosen 1981) for being somewhat narrow in its scope. Perhaps a superior approach to dichotomization is the one taken by the AACSB Task Force, which essentially presented a continuum of pedagogies. At the low end (those with little or no experiential learning potential) were the basic lecture, the seminar discussion, and a library research paper. Those approaches with some experiential learning potential were problem solving, laboratory and experiential exercises, case discussions, study group discussions, and individual case write-ups. Pedagogies with increasing experiential learning potential were group case assignments, simulation games, descriptive/analytic field projects, and consultative field projects. Over the years, ABSEL (through its acceptance of conference papers) has indicated that the following approaches may involve experiential learning: assessment centers, forums, group discussions, panel meetings, live cases, writing experiences, student-written textbooks, computer-assisted instruction, COMPUSTAT tape usage, communication workshops, Delphi forecasting, time management sessions, game show formats, learning cooperatives (where students take the responsibility for teaching themselves), internship programs, job search preparation, on-the-job training, field trips, and cases. Applying the criteria developed earlier, it is clear that a number of these may not qualify for having strong experiential learning potential. Three of the more prominent pedagogies will be evaluated as examples.

Internships. Internships meet most criteria easily: participative, interactive, contact with environment, and variability/uncertainty. Given that most interns have at least completed their junior year, a theoretical base of sorts should have been presented. Similarly, in order to get credit for the internship, most students must provide a written evaluation of the experience. The two criteria presenting problems are the structured exercise and feedback components. Since the internship takes place completely outside the university environment, it is nearly impossible to structure the experience for the student. Consequently the internship experience tends to vary greatly, from one that actually has negative learning (poor work attitudes, for example) to extremely positive experiences. Controlling the nature of the experience requires extremely good university/business relations and a great deal of effort on the part of the faculty in charge. As programs become successful, size problems often make them unsuccessful as administrative burnout occurs. Given the distance problem cited earlier, process feedback is difficult. It is possible to require interim reports, but it is often difficult to monitor the student's learning as it takes place. Giamartino and van Aalst (1986) provide a somewhat labor intensive model which indicates how to incorporate process and outcome feedback for secondary school educators. Thus, while internships are extremely high on the experiential, the quality of the learning involved may be suspect. Clearly there are those for whom the increased external validity of the experience is more than sufficient to compensate for control problems. These issues are discussed at greater length in Gentry and Giamartino (1989).

Computer-Assisted Instruction. At the other extreme may be an approach such as computer-assisted instruction. It may well be applied, since its focus is on content. Also, it is usually highly controlled, so it is high on structure. Similarly, feedback is very likely; in fact, continuous monitoring by the computer is possible. It does require more activity than the standard lecture format, and many such applications are self-paced. On the other hand, it may be weak on many criteria: interactive, contact with the environment, variability/uncertainty, and the whole-person perspective. It concentrates on the cognitive dimension, it involves communication with a static program (most commonly), there is no real-world environment, and there is usually no variability nor uncertainty involved in the process. In general, such an approach should be classified as being very low in experiential learning potential.

Live Case. An approach which meets the criteria well is the live case approach. This may take the form of a small business case, a marketing survey research project for a local business, or the development of an advertising campaign for a firm. A survey research project will be used as the specific example. In most situations, the students are doing this as part of the course requirements or as a follow-up course to a marketing research class. In either case, prior or concurrent coursework has provided the theory base. The typical project requires the students to determine the information needs, obtain background information, develop a questionnaire, pretest it, develop a sampling plan, collect the data, code them, enter them in the computer, analyze the data, write a report, and present it to the client. Participation and interaction are thus very prominent in the process, as is contact with the environment. The learning taking place involves the cognitive (especially in the questionnaire design and analysis stages), the affective (especially in the data collection stage), and the behavioral (in several stages) dimensions. The variability/uncertainty criterion is very much present, especially in the early stages when the students are trying to understand the nature of the problem being investigated. Guidance from the instructor is crucial, both in the form of deadlines that insure the completion of the project by the end of the semester and in the teaching of content which will shortly be used in the research process. Students provide feedback at various stages, but especially at the data collection stage. Most learn about themselves as they contact time-pressured individuals who do not want to be bothered; rarely does a project take place without students wishing to share horror stories. Relating such stories to the lecture material on differential response rates by various groups is straightforward. The nature of the research process (questionnaire design, sampling, analysis) presents ample opportunity for the instructor to monitor the progress of the project. Moreover, such monitoring is crucial in order to assure that the client gets something of value at the end. Thus, the live case pedagogy would be classified as being very high in experiential learning potential.

SUMMARY

This chapter has delineated several criteria which can be used to help evaluate whether a particular teaching methodology can be classified as facilitating experiential learning. Experiential learning is participative, interactive, and applied. It allows contact with the environment, and exposure to processes that are highly variable and uncertain. It involves the whole-person; learning takes place on the affective and behavioral dimensions as well as on the cognitive dimension. The experience needs to be structured to some degree; relevant learning objectives need to be specified and the conduct of the experience needs to be monitored. Students need to evaluate the experience in light of theory and in light of their own feelings. And, process feedback needs to be provided to the student to complement (and possibly supersede) the outcome feedback received by the student. A wide variety of pedagogies have been labeled as involving experiential learning; the use of the criteria can help evaluate their experiential learning potential. Approaches such as computer-assisted instruction may fall short on the "experience" criteria (contact with environment, variability/ uncertainty, interactive, etc.). On the other hand, approaches such as internships are strong on the experience criteria but may yield highly variable learning due to the lack of structure and to the difficulty associated with providing process feedback. Approaches such as live cases would appear to meet most of the criteria easily.

PART 2

INTRODUCTION TO SIMULATION GAMING

This section emphasizes simulation gaming, and the likely problems encountered by first time users. Chapter three by William D. Biggs introduces novices to the use of business simulation games. The fourth chapter, by Anthony J. Faria, covers the usage level of business games in the United States. Faria surveyed business deans, business faculty, and business trainers in order to ascertain the current level of game use and the expected trends. Chapter five by J. Bernard Keys and William D. Biggs provides a comprehensive review of large-scale business policy games and of functional games. It should be helpful to the novice in terms of selecting a game consistent with one's teaching philosophy and objectives. The sixth chapter by David J. Fritzsche and Richard V. Cotter provides insight into the role which the game administrator plays in developing a good learning environment. Issues such as game introduction, trial runs, decision entry, results dissemination, and debriefing will be covered.

Chapter 3: Introduction to Computerized Business Management Simulations, by William D. Biggs

Chapter 4: Business Simulation Games After Thirty Years: Current Usage Levels in the United States, by Anthony J. Faria

Chapter 5: A Review of Business Games, by J. Bernard Keys and William D. Biggs

Chapter 6: Guidelines for Administering Business Games, by David J. Fritzsche and Richard V. Cotter

CHAPTER 3

INTRODUCTION TO COMPUTERIZED BUSINESS MANAGEMENT SIMULATIONS

William D. Biggs

The purpose of this chapter is to provide general information about computerized business management simulations, the so-called business games. The chapter is divided into five sections. In the first section, historical information is provided along with sources of information about business games. The primary focus of the second section is on what constitutes a business game and how games are classified. The third and fourth sections deal with issues involved in selecting and using computerized business games, respectively. In the final section, a bibliography of a large number of the games currently available is provided.

BACKGROUND

It has now been more than a quarter of a century since the first practical business game was introduced by the American Management Association in 1956 (Meier, Newell, and Pazer, 1969). Rapid growth in interest in computerized business games during this 30 plus years can be documented in at least three ways. First, the number of games available has increased dramatically. The most recent edition of *The Guide to Simulations/Games for Education and Training* (Horn and Cleaves, 1980), for example, lists hundreds of such games. Second, a number of organizations and journals devoted to business games have come into existence. Third, in the most extensive research to date, Faria (1987), documents the increase in the number of users of computerized business games. His research, which is included in revised

---

This Chapter represents a revision of the article "Computerized Business Management Simulations for Tyros," which appeared in the 1986 ABSEL Proceedings.

form as the next chapter in this guide, is particularly noteworthy because it covered both usage in academia and business.

Given the rapid growth one might assume that the educational merits of business games are well established. The fact is, however, that their educational merits have been subject to considerable debate. There are studies which indicate that other forms of pedagogy are just as effective or more effective than business games, while other studies find the reverse to be true. Individuals who are interested in reading about learning in business games are referred to the articles by Greenlaw and Wyman (1973), Keys (1976), and Wolfe (1985), which review the more rigorous of the studies dealing with learning in business games. The Wolfe (1985) study is particularly useful since it is a 10-year update of the Greenlaw and Wyman (1973) study and therefore makes comparisons to the earlier study. In addition, the chapter in this guide by Wolfe should be reviewed. Finally, for information about learning in business games as well as for other information about business games the proceedings of the Association for Business Simulation and Experiential Learning (ABSEL), which began in 1974, should be reviewed. To simplify the review of the ABSEL Proceedings, consult *A Comprehensive Guide to ABSEL'S Conference Proceedings (1974–1981)* by Goosen (1982). The *Journal of Experiential Learning and Simulation,* which was published from 1979 through 1981, and *Simulation & Games,* which began in 1970, are also useful sources of information.

THE NATURE OF COMPUTERIZED BUSINESS GAMES

In computerized business games, game players (participants, students) assume the role of decision-makers in organizations. Frequently, the complexity of the game is such that the participants are grouped into teams of three or more members. The teams' decision areas may cover the total firm or a functional unit of a firm, depending on the focus of the simulation. The participants are provided with a player's manual which presents the "rules of the game," describes the environment, and gives a starting point for the firm. The starting point is usually the same for each firm in the industry. The participants submit a set of decisions for their firm to the game administrator (the instructor or trainer or his/her designee). Each set of decisions usually represents a quarter of a year or a year of operation of the firm. The game's administrator, using the computer, processes the decisions and returns the results to the participants. The participants, given their current situation, prepare another set of decisions which are then processed by the game administrator. The fact that participants make decisions for a number of decision periods forces them to live with the consequences of their previous decisions.

The output (results) received by participants generally consists of at least a balance sheet and an income statement. Frequently, at least one page of supplemental output is provided each firm and in some instances a great many pages are provided.

Business games may be classified on a number of dimensions. First, as alluded to earlier, business games may be classified by subject matter as functional or total enterprise. A functional business game is one which is designed to "focus specifically on problems of decision-making as seen in one particular functional area" (Cohen and Rhenman, 1961, p. 140). In contrast, a total enterprise game is one "designed to give people experience in making decisions at a top executive level and in which decisions from one functional area interact with those made in other areas of the firm" (Cohen and Rhenman, 1961, p. 140). Total enterprise games would be used in courses or training programs which are designed to give an overview of business management, such as the senior or graduate level business policy course, the freshmen level introduction to business course, or a management development program on strategic management. While this range from freshmen to senior to graduate to business executive may seem broad, the fact is that the level of complexity and expectations can be set so that even a single game may be used for diverse audiences.

A second way in which business games have been classified is as competitive or non-competitive. The primary basis for this distinction has been whether the decisions of players influence the results of one another (competitive) or not (non-competitive). For example, in a competitive game, if all else is equal, and Firm 1 charges a lower price than Firm 2, Firm 1 will sell more than Firm 2. In a non-competitive game, on the other hand, the participants are competing against the computer model or an environment rather than one another. As Thavikulwat (1988) has recently argued, however, the use of the terms competitive and non-competitive to describe the nature of the market in business games is ambiguous because such terms may have other meanings than whether the decisions of the players influence the results of one another. He suggests, for example, that a game could be seen as competitive depending upon the nature of the relationships the game user establishes between players. For example, a grading scheme which causes one's performance evaluation to vary depending on the performance of another could create a competitive environment, even when decisions of participants do not influence the game results of one another. For this reason Thavikulwat (1988) suggests that the phrases "dependent-across-firms" or "independent-across-firms" be used to describe the nature of the market in a game. Thus, games in which the demand for individual firms depends on the decisions of the other firms in the game would be "dependent-across-firms" while those in which demand for individual firms is not dependent on the decisions of other firms in the game would be "independent-across-firms." While Thavikulwat's (1988) suggested classification scheme focuses on demand, it would appear that it could apply to other factors which could be used to create competition among firms in a game. For example, the supply of labor or raw materials could be fixed so that firms must compete for them, thereby creating a competitive environment which is a function of supply not demand conditions.

Thavikulwat's (1988) conceptualization clearly has improved upon an earlier classification scheme. As we write about games in the future we need to carefully describe the types of competition, if any, which exist in games as designed or which were created by actions of the game user.

A third classification of business games of interactive or noninteractive refers to how participants interact with the computer. In an interactive game, participants play the game at a computer terminal or, more frequently today, at a microcomputer. Participants respond to questions at the terminal, receive an immediate response, and then submit additional decisions. In noninteractive games, decisions are submitted to the game administrator, run through the program, and the results are returned later. A recent combination of interactive and noninteractive has come into being as a result of the advent of microcomputers. A number of games, for example (Jensen and Cherrington, 1984; Scott and Strickland, 1985), now provide for the student to work at a computer terminal or microcomputer with an interactive program to put their decisions on a disk which they turn in to the game administrator. The game administrator then merges the disks of all participants and runs the simulation in a noninteractive fashion. Currently, demand-dependent-across-firms games are handled in a noninteractive mode since the decisions of the players influence the results of one another and therefore must be processed by the computer concurrently. The reader will note from the chapters in this guide by Patz and Chiesl that this type of constraint may change in the future.

A fourth classification of business games is on a continuum from industry specific to generic, depending upon whether or not a specific industry is being simulated. In an industry specific game, the authors attempt to replicate very closely the actual industry whereas in the generic games only general business relationships, such as the downward sloping demand curve, are replicated. In between industry-specific and generic games are those games which identify the specific product, such as electronics, but which do not attempt to replicate the industry closely. A fifth dimension along which business games may be classified is whether they are designed to be played by individuals or teams. Although many games can be played by individuals, the complexity frequently is such that team play is highly recommended. In addition, group play is sometimes recommended for behavioral reasons since the participants learn to work in groups, deal with conflict, communicate with and motivate others, and exercise leadership. On the other hand, some games are recommended for individual play because the game is seen as relatively simple or so that individual performance can be assessed. Sixth, computerized business games can be classified as being basically deterministic or stochastic, depending upon the extent to which random events occur. Seventh, a relatively new basis for classifying business games is in terms of the type of computer on which the game is to be run. Are we using a mainframe (including minicomputers) or are we using a microcomputer? This category may be further subdivided in the future as researchers compare games which were written directly for the microcomputer versus those which were originally written for mainframe computers and then were adapted to the micrcomputer.

Eighth, business games may be classified according to degree of complexity. As has been noted by Keys (1977), there are two dimensions of complexity in business games—game variable complexity and computer model complexity. According to Keys (1977, p. 5) the best measure of game complexity is "the number of individual decisions inputs per round of game play (a decision set)." The issue of game variable complexity also has been addressed by Butler, Pray, and Strang (1979), Raia (1966), and Wolfe (1978). An issue closely related to game variable complexity of how much information is needed for effective game play has been addressed by Biggs and Greenlaw (1976). The complexity of the computer model deals with items such as the program language, number of lines or pages of output, memory required, etc. Thus, this aspect of complexity is more concerned with computer hardware and software issues. A final way in which business games could be classified is according to the time period simulated. Does each decision set cover one day, one week, one quarter of a year, a year, etc? The time period simulated is important since it indicates whether participants are to focus on short term operating decisions, longer term strategic decisions, or both. Given this background information and dimensions along which business games may be classified, we will now turn our attention to selecting the simulation.

SELECTING A COMPUTERIZED BUSINESS GAME

When selecting a business game, the user must first identify the learning objectives for the course involved and decide whether a business game would help to meet the objectives. What is to be accomplished? If the stated objective in the business policy course is to expose the student to a variety of industries, leadership styles, decision-making styles, and managerial problems, then a set of case studies should be used rather than a business game. If, on the other hand, the objective is to provide the students with an opportunity to make decisions in a dynamic environment in which they will be required to use previously learned tools, to integrate the various business functional areas, and to live with their prior decisions, then one might well decide to use a general management simulation.

With the objectives firmly in mind you are now ready to identify the game characteristics along the dimensions previously cited. Since the dimensions are mutually exclusive, you may select any combination desired. For example you could select a general management, competitive, noninteractive, nonindustry, team-oriented, somewhat stochastic, and mainframe game for the business policy course. Within a specific game you will frequently find that there is some discretion concerning these dimensions. For example in the functional game *FINANSIM: A Financial Management Simulation* (Greenlaw and Frey, 1967), which is nonindustry, noncompetitive, noninteractive, recommended for team play and somewhat stochastic, the user can have the student input decisions and receive results right at the terminal to give an interactive effect. Further, the game could be played by individuals and the stochastic nature reduced by providing players with demand figures.

Further complicating the users' decisions along these dimensions is the fact that each dimension has certain advantages and disadvantages. For example, industry games add a degree of realism not found in generic games, but one runs the risk that participants will make decisions based upon what actually happened in the industry rather than through careful analysis of the game environment. Or, in a competitive game, a single firm may make irrational decisions which disrupt the game for other participants.

Once you have established what it is you are looking for, you can begin to identify games which are available which will meet your needs. As a starting point review, *The Guide to Simulations/Games for Education and Training* (Horn and Cleaves, 1980) provides descriptive information for hundreds of games. It covers such things as characteristics of the game, equipment needed, publisher, estimated playing time, etc. Next, review the publishers' lists of available books to see what they have, and contact the publishers' representatives to see if anything new is available. Incidentally, because simulations are a relatively new market for the publishers, the representatives are frequently not well-informed and therefore are often not a good first source of information. Finally, consult members of organizations such as ABSEL and colleagues at other institutions to see what is being used.

Having identified the simulations in which you are interested, you should obtain the student and instructor manuals, and the computer center manual, if there is one. It should be pointed out here that microcomputers have changed the way in which instructor and computer center manuals become available. A number of microcomputer simulations now include the instructor and computer center manuals on the disk with the program. With the disk you receive a brief set of instructions on how to load the disk and print out the manuals. Review the students' manual carefully to be sure the game does what you want and also for readability. Some of the most widely used simulations have student manuals which are very unclear, which creates problems for the students in their decision-making. For example, one simulation in the second edition kept references to rules which were not being used in the second version of the game. An unclear manual will contribute to poor decisions on the part of the students and will require a great deal of classroom time. In reading the student manual, check how complex the game is. How many decisions do students have to make per round of game play? In *FINANSIM: A Financial Management Simulation* (Greenlaw and Frey, 1967), there are 12 decisions per decision set; in *Tempomatic IV: A Management Simulation* (Scott and Strickland, 1984) about 50; and, in the *Carnegie Tech Management Game* about 300. What is the nature of the output the students will receive? In one general management game, the students receive not only an income statement and balance sheet but a complete production and sales analysis, and a cash flow statement. In addition, they receive estimated cash flow, production capacity, etc. for the next quarter. In some simulations, however, the student will have to calculate these figures. Again, what are your objectives?

It is also important to assess what output the game administrator receives. Such information can range from none to summary data to grade indices. Read the instructor's manual to gain additional insight into how the game operates to identify how much control you have over the simulation. For example, can it be tailored to replicate a specific industry or changed from one semester to the next?

Frequently information on actually running the simulation is given in the instructor's manual rather than a separate computer center manual, and you will need someone to read this information unless you possess the appropriate computer knowledge. The person with the computer expertise does not have to be a member of the computer center staff however. This writer has had success in operationalizing simulations by having undergraduate student assistants do the work. In some instances they have been paid, while in other instances an independent study was set up. In one instance, an undergraduate student developed a procedure for adapting games designed for mainframe computers to minicomputers (Biggs and Smith, 1982). In another instance (Biggs and Slocum, 1976), a student who agreed to get 10 simulations up and running on our system one summer actually operationalized 50 simulations. Total cost of the project, including purchasing the simulation packages, was under $1500.

This shotgun approach to having simulations available, rather than the more procedural rifle method which is being suggested here, is useful if one wishes to involve a number of faculty in using computerized business games, since the ease of availability may cause reluctant faculty to give games a try. In the case just cited, the ease of availability did result in rapid adoption and, within two years, we had a problem. In one year we were using six different simulations in seven different courses—introduction to business, business policy, principles of accounting, principles of marketing, principles of finance, advanced finance, and investments. One should pity the poor student who in one semester was playing and therefore learning the rules of three different simulations. You can appreciate his problem when you know that at one point he decided to dominate the industry in one of the simulations and therefore put $100,000 into advertising. Imagine his horror when the results came back and he had done very poorly because in that simulation he needed $1,000,000 not $100,000. He had mixed the rules of two of the simulations. You need to keep the student in mind when multiple simulations are being used in your institutions.

A criterion in selecting a simulation about which people frequently worry is the cost. As my early comment points out, however, the cost of the simulation is frequently minimal. While it is true that some simulations cost $10,000 or more, most of the simulations available from publishers can be obtained for the cost of the tape (card deck at one point) or disk, $5 to $20, and in most instances for free. You should be aware however, that some publishers will tell you that the program is free but is only available to adopters. When you receive such notification write a letter to the publisher which indicates that you would not consider adopting a simulation which you had not had an opportunity to test on your system. In fairness to the publishers, however, you are obligated to have done your homework before you request the program. You should not have students purchase manuals for a game until you know it will run. Also note that tapes or disks are available from the publisher; you do not have to punch the program into the computer.

Finally, before you make the final selection decision, do at least one trial run on your system. Many of the simulations today provide you with a trial run data deck and a copy of what the output from the trial run should look like. Do the trial run and check the student output carefully. You should also check the history output which will be used as part of the next period's input to be certain it looks okay and also to become more familiar with the simulation.

It is strongly recommended that you take the output from the trial run, add a set of dummy decisions, and do an additional run. You should do this to make sure that the successful trial run was not a fluke, to test the rules of the simulation, and to try to blow the simulation up. The successful trial run could be a fluke because of differences between your computer and the computer on which the simulation was developed. For example, the trial run for *PORTSTRAT: A Portfolio Strategy Simulation* (Gitman, Robana and Biggs, 1980) ran beautifully on many machines. Because the simulation was developed on a 32-bit machine, however, the random number generator fails on a 16-bit machine. Since the random number generator does not have to be used in the trial run, the problem does not show up until the next run. It should be pointed out that the 16 versus 32 problem was known to the authors and therefore they provided instructions in the instructor's manual on how to modify the simulation. They also provided a way to by-pass the random number generator to give the game administrator greater control and as an alternative to modifying the program. You should look for such information in the instructor's manual.

The trial runs should also be used to test the rules of the simulation and to try to blow it up in order to find where the holes are. A few examples will point out the types of problems encountered. In one simulation the author accidentally put in an upward sloping demand curve. Fortunately, this error was caught before the simulation became available. In another simulation it was possible to fire more salespeople than your firm employed. The effect was that cash flow and profit improved because the expense per salesperson was now a positive value and the salesperson expense was treated as a receipt. In one simulation a change in one variable caused demand for the industry to go negative (i.e., customers in that quarter returned more than they bought). A more subtle error exists in one simulation which has a penalty payment for early bond retirement. The penalty is assessed when the last payment is made, even though it should not be. Even harder to detect was the situation in one simulation which provided for the production decision to be limited by raw materials, workers, or plant capacity, whichever was lower. In fact, if you violated all three constraints your decision would be implemented. In another instance the sales per team were calculated and allocated before the number of salespersons available was checked. Later, the number of salespersons for which the team was charged was reduced to the number of salespersons available, but the market share calculation was based on the number assigned. Thus, you could get the benefit without the cost.

Before turning to the decisions associated with using business simulations, you should know that it is possible to get programs which have been pre-tested and evaluated; however, you must pay for the service. The organization which evaluates and debugs programs is known as *CONDUIT* (Helper, 1977).

USING A COMPUTERIZED BUSINESS GAME

You have now selected your simulation and it is running perfectly, so your troubles are over. Wrong! You now have a whole new set of decisions to make. First, are you going to use the simulation as written or is there something you wish to modify? Here are two examples of why you might want to modify a simulation. In one simulation, as originally written, if you stockout in an area, you lose one salesperson. There is no recognition of the magnitude of the stockout; a stockout of one unit or 10,000 units results in the loss of a salesperson. In this same simulation plant capacity never wears out; therefore, depending upon the demand schedule, students may be able to play the game and never be faced with the plant capacity decision. It is recommended that you use the simulation once before making any modifications, however.

A second decision you need to make is what other activities you are going to package around the simulation. Are you going to require reports and/or calculations? For example, in the business policy course in which three years are simulated, one could require a strategy report and management reports after each simulated year of operation. In addition, the students could make oral presentations to a board of directors. There are instructors who require students to keep a log in which they must record the rationale for each set of decisions and others who require students to submit pro forma statements with each set of decisions. Some instructors have labor negotiations take place during the game. The list of activities with which you can surround a game is virtually unlimited. A few words of caution are in order, however. First, don't try to introduce too many activities. Second, remember that each semester you have a new group of students. You know the simulation but they do not. If you add in a new activity, ask yourself if something else should be dropped. An example of an extra activity which illustrates the increasing complexity being put into simulation is the fact that at least two games (Jensen and Cherrington, 1984; Scott and Strickland, 1984) now have separate management information systems available to supplement the simulation. Again, be careful that you do not overload the student.

A third decision you need to make is when during the semester the simulation should be introduced. While there are no hard and fast rules, this writer's personal experience and belief in distributed learning suggest that the simulation should be introduced early in the semester. Initially there should be more time between decision due dates than later in the semester. As the decision-making progresses, the time needed tends to decline at an exponential rate, so it is not uncommon to find teams which spent six to eight hours on their first set of decisions making their last sets in 30 to 45 minutes.

The creation of the teams is a fourth decision you must make. If you are going to organize the students into teams, you have to decide on team size and on how to create the teams. The literature would suggest that for moderately complex games teams are best, and that teams of three to five are optimal (Wolfe and Chacko, 1982). This writer's experience with moderately complex total enterprise games suggests three is the optimal number. With more than three, one individual frequently gets a free ride. Functional simulations can often be handled by individuals. As with all these decision areas, however, your objectives are important. If you really wish to create a hierarchy and have a great deal of interpersonal behavior, then you would have larger teams. Some writers argue that instructors should create teams by random assignment or by forced assignment to balance team skills. For example, a good balance might be a finance major, a marketing major, and a production management major. Others suggest that students should create their own teams for pragmatic reasons—they have to be able to meet outside of class (Wilson, 1974)—and because students prefer to create their own teams (Sugges, 1983). Offsetting the need to match schedules, however, is the fact that students may not be the best judges of who should be on a team. In some instances, they pick on the basis of friendship only to find out that they do not work well together. In some instances, when students create their own teams, all the stronger students are together and all the weaker students are together. It is interesting to note, however, that the strong teams do not necessarily perform well if they are composed of strong-willed individuals who will not compromise. Overriding these problems, however, is the fact that students must get together outside of class, an increasingly difficult problem as we deal with part-time students who are working full-time. The issue of the effect of team cohesion on game performance has been addressed by Wolfe and Box (1988).

A fifth decision you will need to make is how you will grade performance in the game. Some simulations have grading packages built into the simulation. For example, one package uses seven variables (Sales, NI, ROS, ROE, ROA, EPS, and Stock Price). The instructor can weigh these variables. For each period an index is calculated for each team by finding the top team for each variable, giving that team 100%, dividing each of the other teams by the top team, multiplying by the weights, and summing the weighted percentage score for each team. Such an index should never be used as the only basis for assigning a grade. Rather, the instructor should also look at the decisions in terms of reasonableness. What has been argued is that the instructor should use multiple variables, both qualitative and quantitative measures, and should look at both input and output measures. Interestingly, Sugges (1983) found that the majority of students preferred that the instructor set quantitative criteria to evaluate company performance. This writer recommends that the performance grade be at least 20% to create an incentive to perform, but not more than 25% when team play is involved so that a non-participant does not get a good grade as the result of the work of others. The reader who wishes more information concerning grading performance in business games should refer to Biggs (1978), Butler and Parasuraman (1975), Hand and Sims (1975), and Sims and Hand (1975).

You will also find that you need to make decisions while the students are playing the game as unanticipated events take place. What do you do when a team member comes to you and says, "I am doing all the work?" Peer evaluations at the end may help alleviate this problem as will a provision that a team member may be fired. In fact peer evaluations at various times throughout the semester appear to be superior to end of game peer evaluations alone (Anderson and Lawton, 1988). What do you do if you find out in a competitive simulation that collusion is taking place? What do you do if someone posts a notice, which appears to be from you, which indicates that demand in the next period will drop 30%, and one team believes it? What do you do if a student finds a loop hole in the simulation and takes advantage of it? What do you do if there is an input error? If the students input their own decisions, you can say "too bad" but if you or your assistant have put the decisions in incorrectly you rerun. Be sure to leave adequate time between decision deadlines. These comments are not meant to exhaust everything one needs to consider when using a simulation. The reader is referred to the chapter by Fritzsche and Cotter elsewhere in this book for other considerations, as well as additional comments on items discussed in this chapter.

SIMULATION BIBLIOGRAPHY

It is hoped that the above comments have pointed out to you that statements such as, "Use a computerized simulation in your course, it's easy," or, "Computerized business simulations don't require any work on the instructors part; they run themselves," are foolish and fall in the same category as the statements: "Look why don't you take our old baby crib? We won't be needing it any more," or, "You'd be crazy not to claim it as a deduction."

It is also hoped, however, that the comments have illustrated that by drawing upon research, careful planning, putting forth some effort, and experimenting, one can incorporate computerized business simulations into a wide variety of courses successfully. Such games can efficiently contribute to learning effectiveness.

As a final attempt to help the reader in the search for appropriate simulations, a list of some of the business games currently on the market is provided in the Appendix. The simulations listed in the Appendix are presented in Table 3–1 according to whether they are of a general management or functional nature and also by whether they are for the mainframe, micro, or both types of computers. A number of these simulations are evaluated in the chapter in this guide by Keys and Biggs.

TABLE 3-1
Computerized Business Games Listed by Author

Mainframe Computer	Micro Computer	Mainframe & Micro Computer
General Management Games		
Babb 1979	Aronson, Gekoski 1984	Cotter, Fritzsche 1986
Barton 1974	Cotter, Fritzsche 1985	Edge, Keys, Remus
Darden, Lucas 1969	Cretien, Jennings 1988	1985
Eldredge, Bates 1984	Eldredge 1984	Henshaw, Jackson 1986
Frazer, 1975 1977	Funk, Smith 1985	Jensen, Cherrington
Gupta, Hammon 1974	Hinton, Smith 1985	1984
Keys, Leftwich 1977	Infoware 1984	C. Scott, Strickland
McFarlan, McKenney,	Keys 1988	1984
Seiler 1970	Jensen (due out) 1989	T. Scott, Strickland 1985
Meredith 1977	Mills, McDowell 1985	J. R. Smith 1987a
Nichols, Schott 1972	Ness 1987	
Smith, Estey, Vines	Penderghast 1988	
1974	Pettit 1985	
Strang, Pray 1981	Pitta, Sewell 1988	
Thorelli, Graves 1964	Priesmeyer 1987	
	Reality Technologies 1986, 1988	
	J. R. Smith 1985	
	Smith, Golden 1987a, 1987b,	
	due out 1989	
	Wilson, Hickman 1982	
Functional Games		
Boone, Hackleman	Beutell, Schuler 1986	Faria, Nulsen, Roussos
1971	Boudreau, Milkovich 1988	1984
Boone, Kurtz, Braden	Carrell, Smith 1988	Gitman, Robana, Biggs
(due out 1989)	Chapman 1988	1981
Brobst, Bush 1982	Cosenza, Boone, Kurtz 1988	Ness, Day 1984
Brooks 1987	Cretien 1989	
Goosen 1973	Day, Dalrymple 1985	
Greenlaw, Frey, Vernon	Faria, Dickinson 1987	
1979	Fisk, Fisk 1984	
Greenlaw, Hottenstein	Galloway, Evans 1987	
1969	Gates 1986	
Greenlaw, Kniffen 1964	Larreche, Weinstein 1988	
Johnson, Hendrick	Low 1985	
1984	Mason, Perreault 1987	
Keiser, Lupul 1977	Schnaars 1985	
	G. N. Smith 1983	
	J. R. Smith 1987b	
	Sprenger, Werdkamp,	
	Burns 1987a, 1987b	
	Zocco 1987	

With the exception of the Scott and Strickland simulations, the simulations which are usable on both mainframe and microcomputers have the same title and publication date. One additional comment regarding the bibliography is of interest. Five years ago the list would not have included simulations for service industries, whereas today there are an increasing number of such simulations available. Likewise, five years ago there would have been very few games available for the introduction to business course.

CHAPTER 4

BUSINESS SIMULATION GAMES AFTER THIRTY YEARS: CURRENT USAGE LEVELS IN THE UNITED STATES

Anthony J. Faria

Almost one third of a century has passed since the first business simulation games were played. In the early years of business gaming (1955–1957), only one or two new games appeared each year. After this relatively slow beginning, however, the number and variety of business games expanded enormously. Interest in the teaching and learning possibilities of business games has also grown among business educators. The growing number of organizations and publications devoted to simulation gaming also attests to the widespread interest in business games.

A large and growing body of research on business gaming exists. Hundreds of papers and journal articles examining conditions of business game usage and its merits relative to other teaching methods have been published. This research stream is certainly necessary to understand better the benefits offered by business games and the most appropriate environments for their use.

While a wide variety of research exists on the learning environment of business games, little has been published on the extent of business game usage. At an ABSEL meeting over ten years ago, Goosen (1977, p. 208) stated, "No studies have been made to ascertain the number of business simulation users in the United States." To rectify this situation, a survey was undertaken to determine the number of business game users in academia and in the business community.

Parts of this chapter are from Anthony J. Faria, "A Survey of the Use of Business Games in Academia and Business," *Simulations & Games*, Vol. 18, No. 2, pp. 207–225. Copyright 1987 by *Simulations & Games*. Reprinted by permision of Sage Publications, Inc.

BACKGROUND

The origin of the business simulation game dates back to 1955. In that year, the Rand Corporation developed a simulation exercise called *Monopologs* which focused on U.S. Air Force logistics (Jackson, 1959). *Monopologs* required its participants to perform as inventory managers in a simulated Air Force supply system, thus providing decision-making experience without the risks associated with the consequences of a wrong decision. The Air Force continued the use of *Monopologs* for many years and reported it to be a highly successful training device.

The success of *Monopologs* spurred the early growth of business games. The first practical and successful business game, *Top Management Decision Simulation,* was developed by the American Management Association in 1956 and was used in numerous management development seminars attended by academicians and business managers (Meier, Newell and Pazer, 1969). The consulting firm of McKinsey & Company developed the *Business Management Game* in 1957 for use in its management seminars (Andlinger, 1958) and the University of Washington became the first university classroom user of a business game when a simulation developed by Schreiber was used in a business policy course in 1957 (Watson, 1981).

A rapid growth in the number of business games occurred over the years from 1958 to 1961. One source estimated that by 1961 over 100 business games were in existence and had been played by more than 30,000 business executives (Kibbee, Craft and Nanus, 1961). The *Business Games Handbook* published in 1969 (Graham and Gray) listed nearly 200 games while the most recent edition of *The Guide to Simulations/Games for Education and Training* (Horn and Cleaves, 1980) provides descriptions of 228 business simulation games.

The growing number of business games and attendance at gaming conferences would certainly imply that business game usage is large and growing. Little, however, has been published on the extent of business game usage. Biggs (1979) examined adoption levels for selected business games, Faria and Schumacher (1984) surveyed a small sample of business firms regarding simulation usage in management training programs, and several studies have examined business game usage in selected courses (e.g., Williams, 1987; Dale and Klassen, 1964; Day, 1968; Hegarty, 1976; and Summers and Boyd, 1985). However, no attempt had been made to estimate overall business game usage.

DATA GATHERING

A mail survey was undertaken to estimate the current usage level of business simulation games among both academics and business firms. To supplement the data gathered through the mail survey, a thorough literature review and selected telephone contacts were also undertaken.

The mail survey involved four separate questionnaires directed to the following groups: (1) deans and directors of business schools or departments, (2) business school faculty, (3) business firm training and development managers, and (4) consulting firms that supply simulation games to industry for management training programs. A total of more than 1,700 questionnaires were mailed to samples selected from the above groups.

From the four groups surveyed, all consulting firms supplying business games to industry were contacted. As the remaining groups were very large only a sample was drawn from each. The sampling specifics for each of the groups surveyed will be presented in the following discussion.

BUSINESS SCHOOL USAGE

The University of Washington, in 1957, became the first school to use a business simulation game as part of a regular university class (Watson, 1981). Many other schools quickly followed as several surveys of AACSB member schools would indicate.

In the earliest study of this type, Dale and Klassen (1962) surveyed 107 AACSB member schools and found that 71.1% of the responding schools were using business games in at least one course. Two surveys undertaken in 1967 reported that 91% (Graham and Gray, 1969) and 94% (Day, 1968) of sampled AACSB schools were using simulation games. Finally, in order to gauge usage level changes, Roberts and Strauss (1975) resurveyed the same schools that Dale and Klassen had surveyed in 1962. Simulation game usage at these schools had increased to 94.5% in 1975 from 71.1% in 1962.

Survey of Deans and Directors

As previous research has shown, business game use at AACSB schools exceeded 90% of surveyed schools by the late 1960's and continued at this level into the mid-1970's. However, a problem with the reported research is that samples were small and the surveys involved only AACSB schools.

To rectify these shortcomings, a listing of all 2,013 four year degree granting schools in the United States offering a business program was obtained from the U.S. National Center for Education Statistics. From this listing, after determining a random starting point, every third school was selected for a total sample size of 671. A cover letter explaining the purpose of the survey and a questionnaire were sent to the head of the business program at each of the sampled schools. Each mailing was personally addressed using the name of the business school head, and the cover letter stressed the importance of responding.

A total of 410 returns were received for a response rate of 61.1%. The returns alone represent over 20% of all four year schools in the U.S. The results obtained from this survey, along with the results from two earlier surveys, are shown in Table 4-1.

TABLE 4-1
Usage of Business Games at Four Year Schools

	Dale and Klasson (1962)		Roberts and Strauss (1975)		Current Study	
	Number	Percent	Number	Percent	Number	Percent
Yes	64	71.1%	69	94.5%	353	86.1%
No	26	28.9	4	5.5	49	11.9
Not Sure	—	—	—	—	8	2.0
	90	100.0%	73	100.0%	410	100.0%

The present study findings show a lower business game usage level than the 1975 Roberts and Strauss study. The difference can be explained, of course, by the fact that the current study included all schools offering a business program while the Roberts and Strauss study included only AACSB schools. As such, the present study included much smaller business programs. For more direct comparison purposes, a sub-sample from the present survey can be viewed. If only the AACSB member responding schools are examined, 95.1% of this group are simulation game users. This compares very favorably with the 94.5% reported in the Roberts and Strauss study.

Projecting the 86.1% usage rate found in this survey to all 2,013 four year degree granting schools results in an estimate of 1,733 schools in which business games are currently being used.

Other issues addressed in the present survey revealed that business games are more likely to be used at the undergraduate level and that usage varies by type of course. Of the schools using simulations, 81.7% are using business games in undergraduate courses and 57.9% at the graduate level. Usage by course area is shown in Table 4-2.

As Table 4-2 identifies, business game usage is highest in the policy and marketing areas. The results reported here for the policy area (47.6%) are slightly higher than, but in line with, the results reported by Williams (1987). Williams reported that 41.1% of the surveyed business policy instructors use business games in their policy courses.

A study by Ahern, Bonanni, Ellis, McWhorten, Potter and Whelan (1968) reported that the typical business school was using two separate simulation

TABLE 4–2
Simulation Usage by Course Area

	Percent of Responding Schools Offering Course
Policy	47.6%
Marketing	46.3
Finance	21.8
Management	15.7
Accounting	6.9
Other	13.2

games. The present study found an average usage level of 2.2 games per using school. Projecting this to the estimated 1,733 schools using business games results in an estimate of 3,813 courses in which business games are being used.

In terms of usage trends, 65.1% of the responding business school heads indicated that simulation game usage within their faculties had increased over the past five years. Only 10.7% reported a decrease in usage while 24.2% reported no change in usage. Nearly 95% of the business school heads expected simulation game usage to increase or remain the same at their schools over the next five years.

Using the sub-sample of AACSB responding schools, 31.3% of the deans indicated that their schools participate in intercollegiate simulation competitions and 44.9% indicated that simulation exercises are used in executive development programs at their schools. Finally, the business school heads were asked to rate the effectiveness of lectures, cases, business games, and readings as teaching methods using a one (low effectiveness) to ten (high effectiveness) scale. The averages of the responses on this issue are shown in Table 4–3.

TABLE 4–3
Rating of Teaching Method Effectiveness by Business School Heads

	Rating
Cases	8.3
Business Games	7.9
Lectures	7.3
Readings	6.8

Cases were perceived by business school heads to be slightly more effective than business games which, in turn, were felt to be more effective teaching tools than lectures and reading assignments.

Survey of Business School Instructors

Several surveys have reported business game usage among specific teacher groups, such as policy teachers (e.g., Williams, 1987, and Summers and Boyd, 1985) and marketing teachers (e.g., Faria and Nulsen, 1979, and McGraith and Goeldner, 1962). However, large surveys across a sample of business instructors not restricted to a specific discipline are lacking.

A mailing list from a major publisher of business textbooks was obtained. This listing of 50,607 names included all business instructors at four year degree granting schools known to the publisher. After determining a random starting point on the list, every one-hundredth name was selected until a sample of 500 was generated. Each business instructor was sent a personally addressed cover letter and questionnaire. A total of 283 returns were received for a response rate of 56.6%.

Table 4–4 provides the survey results with regard to current and past usage of business games.

TABLE 4–4
Current and Past Business Game Usage of Business Instructors

	Number	Percent
Currently Use	48	16.9%
Have Used in Past	29	10.3
Have Never Used	206	72.8
	283	100.0%

Projecting the 16.9% current simulation game users to the approximately 50,607 instructors at four year degree granting schools, results in an estimate of 8,553 current business game users. This number would imply an average of over four simulation users at each of the 1,733 degree granting schools in the U.S. that are using business games.

The percentage of class time devoted to simulation games among current users ranged from 5% to 100% and averaged to 29% of class time. The average grade weighting for the simulation competition was 25% of the final course mark. Nearly 90% of the current users indicated that their business game usage level has increased or remained the same over the past five years and only 8.5% of the current users anticipate any usage level reductions in the future.

As would be expected, simulation users rated business games as a more effective teaching method than did nonusers. Using a one (low effectiveness) to ten (high effectiveness) scale, the results from the business instructor sample are shown in Table 4–5.

TABLE 4–5
Mean Rating of Teaching Method Effectiveness

	Simulation Users	Nonusers	Overall Sample
Cases	6.2	7.8	7.4
Business Games	7.1	5.8	6.1
Lectures	6.8	7.7	7.5
Textbooks	5.2	5.5	5.4

As would be expected, simulation games are ranked very high by current users. However, the surprisingly low rating of business games among nonusers is certainly an issue that business game developers, publishers, and organizations (such as ABSEL) should be addressing.

BUSINESS FIRM USAGE

The major advantage of business games, providing decision-making experience without risk, would seem to make them very desirable for use by business firms in management training programs. In fact, much of the early development of business games was by business firms for management training purposes. The first published survey of marketing games, for example, listed 29 marketing games (McRaith and Goeldner, 1962), of which twenty had been developed by business firms for their own use and only nine by academicians for university teaching purposes.

Many references to business firm users of simulation exercises can be found in business publications. An examination of the business press from the early to mid-1960's identifies the following major companies as developers and users of business games: General Electric, IBM, Westinghouse, Imperial Oil (Canada), Caterpillar Tractor, Pillsbury, AT&T, RCA, Procter & Gamble, Boeing, Joseph Magnin, May Department Stores, Sun Oil, Humble Oil, Remington Rand, and Kroger (Cohen and Rhenman, 1961; McRaith and Goeldner, 1962; Watson, 1981; Cook, 1981 and Faria and Schumacher, 1984). Furthermore, many of these companies were using more than one game. The Boeing Co., for example, by the mid-1960's was using three simulation games. *Operation Feedback* was played by employees in line for beginning management positions; *Operation Suburbia* was played by middle managers; and *Operation Interlock* was played by top management when taking retraining or refresher programs.

A review of the most recent business press, especially journals devoted to management training (e.g., *Training, Training and Development* and *Human*

Resource Management) would identify many business firms currently using simulation games. For example, many of the firms identified earlier as 1960's users are still using simulation games in their training programs. AT&T, for example, puts over 500 management trainees per year through the *Strategic Management Game* at its Aurora, Colorado training facilities (Gordon, 1985). Some recent converts to simulation game usage include Burger King, Air Canada, Union Carbide, Consolidated Edison of New York, Clairol, the Bank of America, American Airlines, Keebler, Monsanto, Union Pacific, Holiday Inns, Phillip Morris, and Sony.

While selected references to simulation usage in industry can be found in the business press along with many examples of using firms, no source has ever provided an estimate of overall usage of business games in industry.

Survey of Training Managers

A mailing list of corporate training and development managers was obtained from Alvin B. Zeller, Inc., a company specializing in the sale of mailing lists. This listing contained the names and addresses of 8,027 managers known to have training and development responsibilities within their companies. From this list, a sample of 500 was compiled. Each training and development manager was sent a personalized cover letter and questionnaire. Twenty-eight mailings were returned as undeliverable while 223 completed questionnaires were received for a response rate of 47.2% of the effective mailings.

Each training manager was asked if their company used any form of simulation game or exercise in its training programs. To make sure that there was no confusion, simulation games were described on the questionnaire and training programs were indicated to include both initial programs for new employees as well as ongoing programs for experienced managers. Of the 223 responding training managers, 122 (54.7%) indicated that their companies currently use simulation games or exercises in their training programs. Projecting the 54.7% usage rate to all 8,027 firms with training and development managers results in an estimate of 4,391 business firms currently using simulation games.

Simulation games are used in both initial and ongoing training programs and the game participants range from management trainees through to top corporate executives. The simulation games are included as part of training programs which also include training tools such as cases, lectures, group discussions, films, readings, and various written exercises. While some companies have developed their own simulation games, most are using games developed by outside training consultants/organizations.

The majority of simulation exercises being used in management training programs are board games, in-basket, and role-playing exercises. Only 28 of the 122 user companies (22.9%) indicated that they are using computerized simulation games. As such, the type of simulation exercise being used in industry is generally different from that in use in business school classes.

The percent of training program time devoted to simulation exercises ranged from 5% to 60% and averaged 29.5%. When asked about future usage of simulation games, 17.6% of the current users plan to expand usage, 73.2% plan to continue at current levels, while 9.2% anticipate reduced usage.

Of the 101 companies that are not currently using simulation exercises, 23 (22.8%) had used a simulation exercise in the past. In addition, another 17 training and development managers (16.8 percent) indicated that they have considered the use of simulation exercises and may incorporate them into their company's training programs in the future.

Survey of Management Consulting Companies

There are a number of companies that supply simulation exercises to the business community for their management training programs. Examples of these supplying companies would be the Center for Creative Leadership, supplier of a well known and frequently used game called *Looking Glass* and the Strategic Management Group, supplier of another well known game entitled the *Strategic Management Game*. The simulation games supplied by companies such as these range from relatively simple board games that can be played in several hours to very sophisticated computer-based games.

From an examination of the management training journals and discussions with training and development managers, 33 companies supplying simulation exercises to the business community were identified. Letters with return postcards were sent to the Vice-President of Marketing, Director of Marketing, or Director of Sales for each of these companies. Where the name of this individual was known, the letters were personalized. Twenty-three usable replies, for a response rate of 69.7%, have been received.

Each of the return postcards asked for a response to only two questions: (1) How many businesses does your company supply with simulation materials, and (2) What percent of all companies, large enough to have full-time training and development managers, do you feel use simulation exercises in their management training programs?

With regard to the first question, the 23 responding companies supply a total of 4,093 business firms with simulation exercises. This represents an average of 178 clients per simulation supplier. If it is assumed that the non-responding companies are similar to those who did respond, the 33 known simulation supplying companies would have a total of 5,872 clients.

In response to the second question, the range in the estimates of business firms with training and development managers that use simulation exercises was from a low of 20 percent to a high of 80%. The average for the 23 respondents was 46.4%.

DISCUSSION

The survey results reported here would indicate that business game usage is quite extensive and, if not still growing, has certainly not been declining in recent years. The survey of heads of business programs indicated that business games are in use in approximately 86.1% of all four year degree granting schools in the U.S. Projecting this percentage to all 2,013 four year schools results in an estimate of 1,733 schools in which business games are currently in use.

In terms of usage trends in business schools, the 1975 Roberts and Strauss study reported that 94.5% of surveyed AACSB schools were using business games. The AACSB subsample in the present survey showed a 95.1% usage level. This result both validates the current survey findings and indicates that business game usage has certainly not declined in business faculties.

Further results from the present survey would indicate that business games are being used in approximately 3,813 courses across all using schools, with usage being highest in the business policy and marketing areas. The estimate of schools and courses in which business games are being used seems quite reasonable in relation to findings reported by Biggs (1979) and updated by Faria (1987).

The survey of business school instructors indicated that 16.9 percent of those responding are currently simulation game users. Projecting this percentage to the 50,607 business instructors at all four year degree granting schools would imply that there are 8,553 current business game users. This number would indicate that there are approximately 2.2 business instructors using simulation games for each course in which business games are being used.

The survey of training and development managers found that 54.7% of those responding indicated that their companies use simulation exercises as part of their initial or ongoing training programs, or both. Projecting this percentage to all firms known to have training and development managers, results in an estimate of 4,391 business firms that use business games. Approximately 22.9% of these companies, or 1,006 businesses, use computerized business games similar to those used in university classes. The remainder use a wide variety of board, in-basket, role-playing, and related games.

The survey of companies that supply simulation exercises to industry showed that 23 responding companies supply a total of 4,093 business clients with simulation exercises for an average of 178 clients per supplying company. Projecting this average number of clients to all 33 known simulation supplying companies results in an estimate of 5,872 business firm users, a number very much in line with the estimate from the survey of training and development managers, especially when considering that several supplying companies likely have the same clients.

When asked to estimate the number of business firms with training programs that use simulation games, the marketing directors of the simulation supplying firms provided an average estimate of 46.4 percent. This estimate is very much in line with the 54.7 percent usage level found in the survey of training and development managers. The similarity of these results adds much credibility to the findings from both surveys.

The prime objective of the research reported in this chapter has been to estimate the total number of business game users in business schools and in industry. These findings are summarized in Table 4–6. Where possible, the results from the current study have been compared to earlier studies as a check against any very unusual results. None have been found. As such, the summary data in Table 4–6 should be highly reliable.

TABLE 4–6
A Summary of Business Game Usage Based on the Findings from the Current Survey

	Number
Business Games Available	Approximately 228
Four Year Schools Using Business Games	1,733
Courses in Which Business Games are Used	3,813
Business Instructors Using Business Games	8,553
Business Firms Using Business Games	4,391–5,872

CONCLUSIONS

The research reported here represents a first major attempt to estimate the total number of simulation users. The final estimates developed are based on over 1,700 mail questionnaires supplemented by telephone contacts and a thorough literature review. The findings show that there is a large, and seemingly growing, number of business school instructors and business firm users of simulation games.

While business game usage is very high, there are certainly additional opportunities for growth. Over 40,000 business instructors do not currently use business games. Approximately half of all business firms with training and development managers do not use simulation exercises in their training programs.

Among business school instructors, usage of simulation games is particularly light outside of the policy and marketing areas. Of concern with regard to expanded usage among business instructors is the generally low rating of business games as an effective teaching tool among the nonusers.

This opinion of business games will have to be changed if usage is to be significantly expanded.

Potential for expanded usage of simulation games by business firms also exists. In particular, only 12.5% of all business firms with training and development managers use computerized business games. This represents a large market still to be tapped. As such, while current business game usage is widespread, considerable potential for further growth still exists.

CHAPTER 5

A REVIEW OF
BUSINESS GAMES

J. Bernard Keys
William D. Biggs

The purpose of this chapter is to describe and evaluate a number of currently available computerized business games. In selecting the games to be reviewed, we used many criteria. First, the game had to be designed for use in an upper level integrative course such as business policy or a functional area course in marketing, finance, production/operations management, or personnel/human resources administration. Second, the game had to be readily available from a well-known publisher. Third, the cost of the game software and student manuals could not be prohibitive for educational institutions. In most instances the game programs described in this article are available for a nominal fee or free of charge to adopters, and the student manuals which are purchased by the students through the bookstore cost less than $20 each. Fourth, games identified as having a large number of users were given priority. Fifth, only games which had instructor's manuals available were included.

We also elected to exclude certain types of simulations. The first simulations excluded were those that were noncomputerized. These games were excluded because they do not have the level of complexity associated with the computerized games. In addition, they typically do not provide for integration. The second type of simulation excluded is that which Faria (1980) refers to as concept games. A concept game "focuses on only one aspect of each functional area" (Faria, 1980: 177). Examples of concept games are *The Sales Management Game* (Boone, Kurtz, and Braden, 1982), which focuses only on the sales aspect of marketing, and *PORT-STRAT: A Portfolio Strategy Simulation* (Gitman, Robana, and Biggs, 1980), which

Parts of this chapter are taken from J. Bernard Keys, "Total Enterprise Games," *Simulation & Games*, Vol. 18, No. 2, 225–241, and from William D. Biggs, "Functional Business Games," *Simulation & Games,* Vol. 18, No. 2, 242–267. Copyright 1987 by *Simulation & Games*. Reprinted by permission of Sage Publications, Inc.

deals with stock market investment decisions rather than business finance oriented decisions. The third type of simulation excluded is that which is oriented to specific problem solving tools such as linear programming or queing theory applications but which makes no attempt to integrate. The publication, *Computer Models in Operations Management: A Computer Augmented System* (Harris and Maggard, 1977), for example, provides models that deal with twelve production/operations oriented problems; however, these models are used to solve specific problems which are not related to one another. Thus, the student does not experience the possibility that optimization in terms of one model may lead to a less than optimum solution for another. The fourth type of game excluded is that which emphasizes a particular business function but which deals with an industry with unique characteristics. For example, the game *Airways: A Service Marketing Game* (Fisk and Fisk, 1986), which deals with marketing aspects of the airline industry, has been excluded. Relatedly, we focused on manufacturing oriented games and excluded service industry oriented games such as *Airline: A Strategic Management Simulation* (Smith and Golden 1987). The fifth type of game excluded is that which deals with business functions which are less commonly covered in business schools. For example, we will not discuss *Transportation Management: The Cunning Simulation* (Low, 1985), which deals only with the logistics function. Finally, we excluded games which could be classified as total enterprise games but which are basically designed to be used in courses such as introduction to business or business for non-business majors. These games generally have fairly limited and simplistic coverage and integration of the various functional areas as well as the environment within which the decisions are made. An example of such a game is *The World of Business Game* (Wilson and Hickman, 1982).

With this understanding of our selection criteria, we will now turn to a discussion of the games reviewed. We first discuss total enterprise games. Next, we discuss functional area games. Finally, we evaluate the games in light of a learning model. The chapter combines, modifies, and updates earlier articles by Biggs (1987) and Keys (1987).

TOTAL ENTERPRISE BUSINESS GAMES

A total enterprise game is one which includes decisions in most of the main functions of business: marketing, production, finance, and personnel. Such games require integration of the various functional areas. In addition, total enterprise games incorporate environmental factors, such as general economic conditions and interest rates as important components of the learning experience.

Total enterprise games first appeared in the late 1950's with the introduction of a game by the American Management Association. In the next few years a number of games specifically designed for collegiate education were introduced. Among the earliest of these games were *Management Decision Simulation* (Vance 1960); *Executive Action Simulation* (Herron, 1960); and *INTOP (International Operations Simulation)* (Thorelli and Graves, 1964).

In this section of the chapter we will describe, compare, contrast, and evaluate a sample of 10 total enterprise computerized business games. The games reviewed and the abbreviations used for them are: *The Executive Game* (Henshaw and Jackson, 1984)—*The Ex. Game; Manager: A Simulation* (Smith, 1984)—*A Mgr. Sim.; Microtronics* (Keys and Wells, 1987)—*Microtronics; Business Policy Game* (Cotter and Fritzsche, 1986)—*BPG; MANSYM IV: A Dynamic Management Simulation with Decision Support System* (Schellenberger and Masters, 1986)—*MANSYM; The Business Management Laboratory* (Jensen and Cherrington, 1984)—*BML; The Business Strategy and Policy Game* (Eldredge and Bates, 1980)—*BSPG; STRAT-PLAN* (Hinton and Smith, 1985)—*STRAT-PLAN; The Multinational Management Game* (Edge, Keys, and Remus, 1985)—*MNG;* and *Tempomatic IV: A Management Simulation* (Scott and Strickland, 1984)—*TEMPOMATIC IV.*[1]

The Economy and Industry Simulated

All total enterprise games include some method of depicting the economy and industry within which competing teams will operate. Most games build the economy around a set of indices of economic activity and include seasonal fluctuations, cyclical downturns and upturns, and growth trends built on quarterly decisions. One game reviewed, *STRAT-PLAN,* utilizes years rather than quarters as decision periods, which allows teams to think more in terms of "strategic" long-term horizons rather than "tactical" or short run decisions. Such a game structure is typical of the new games being developed for in-house training at many large corporations and in several of the graduate schools of management. A similar game is under construction at Georgia Southern's Center for Advancement of Business Simulation and Experiential Learning (CABSEL).

Some of the less complex games include some surprisingly sophisticated economic variables. For example, *The Ex. Game* has an inflation variable, usually found only in consulting and training games. *Tempomatic IV* calls for the use of the *Business Week Index* to tie the game to fluctuations in the

---

[1] There is also a micro-computer version of this simulation called *Micromatic: A Management Simulation* (Scott and Strickland, 1985).

real world economy. Most games allow administrators to have control over the economic indices; therefore, such an innovation can be used with most games. *MNG* utilizes an economic index with leads and lags for three of the nations including the United States, West Germany, and Japan, based on the history of the interrelationship of these economies. As in most games, the actual base index is controlled by the administrator. All games reviewed provide some type of economic forecast for the teams, but the number of quarters or years projected varies from game to game. *A Mgr. Sim.* provides forecasts six quarters into the future, whereas *STRAT-PLAN,* based on a yearly decision round, provides forecasts by market one year into the future. Some games, such as *Tempomatic IV,* actually give a forecast by market area in terms of total unit sales potential. The sales potential base in *Tempomatic IV* is modified by the *Business Week Index,* as noted earlier.

Marketing Variables

Product. The marketing variables of the various games reviewed are outlined in Table 5-1. One of the most distinguishing factors to be considered in the choice of a game is the type of product which the game portrays. Many of the games use a generic product description, defining the product only in terms of price range or customer served. The rationale for such a description is provided for the Gidget in *Tempomatic IV*: "This vagueness is intentional and precludes the participant's basing his decision on the known actions of any real company" (Scott and Strickland, 1984:1). Other games describe the product by industry or standard product classifications. For example, *MNG* uses a general product description: Product A consists of a branded consumer good sold to retailers, while Product B consists of an unfinished good sold directly to industrial customers. Defining specific products such as stainless steel flatware or cookware, as does *BML*, greatly enriches the marketing area and the potential for supplemental library and industry research. However, there is some danger that in the latter case students will simply try to mimic the more successful firms without relying on their own analyses. *MANSYM IV* incorporates a very versatile real product line description, allowing product parameters to be changed by the game administrator to simulate the small kitchen appliance, textiles, wood, and the food products industries.

Most games incorporate some means of increasing product quality or differentiating the product on a competitive basis. One of the more innovative approaches is that of *BPG*. Research and Development (R & D) expenditures can improve the product through simulated feature improvement, but they can also make available new models that the firm can introduce with a discretionary decision. Each model has a number attached to it, and once introduced, must replace the older model. Marketing studies

TABLE 5–1
Marketing Variables

Variables	1 The Ex. Game	2 A Mgr. Sim.	3 MICRO-TRONICS	4 BPG	5 MANSYM	6 BML	7 BSPG	8 STRAT-PLAN	9 MNG	10 TEMPO-MATIC IV
Forecasting	x	x	x	x	x	x	x	By Mkt. x By Nat.	By Nation x	By Area x
Products										
Research and Development	x	x	x	By Product 2	By Product	x	x	By Mkt. Product	By Nation	x
Number of Products	1	1	1	1	2	2	1	2	2	2
Product Description Generic (G)	G	Auto Radio	Micro-Computer	G	Kitchen Applian.	Flat-ware Cook Ware	Cons. Ref. Ind. Ref.	Variable Para-meters	G	G
Price	x	x	x	By Area	By Prod.	By Prod. By Area	By Mkt.	By Prod. By Mkt.	By Prod. By Nation	x
Place										
Distribution Centers					–			By Mkt.	Variable Nation	
Regional Offices										
Marketing Areas	1	1	1	4	1	2	3	3	3	3
International								x	3x	
Transfer of Product							By Mkt. By Prod.		By Nation	
Promotion	x	x			x					
Salesmen:			x	x				x	x	
Number			x	By Area		By Area	By Mkt.	By Mkt.	By Nation	x
Trained						x	x		x	x
Salaries			x		x		x			x
Commission			x	x	x	By Prod.	x	x	x	
Advertising:			x	By Area		x By Area By Prod.		x By Prod. By Area	x By Nation	
Local										x
National										x
Marketing Research										
Purchase of Mktg. Information		x			2				x	9 items
Social Responsibility										
Incidents	x									

are available stating the likelihood of a new model's sales exceeding that of the old. Each new model also has a different labor and material cost associated with it. *BML* uses a similar but less complex approach by simply allowing teams to invest funds with the hope of a "distinctive product improvement" at certain levels of accumulated expenditures on R & D activity.

Price. The price variable described in *MNG* is typical for total enterprise games. The game incorporates price-elasticity, meaning that with other factors constant, more revenue will be generated by lowering price in the elastic range and by raising price in the inelastic range. In this particular game the market for the industrial product is much more price elastic than that of the consumer product, as is true in real life. Most of the games reviewed incorporate prices in the $10–$100 range, probably because they have chosen as their products small consumer goods with which participants are most familiar.

Place. The relatively simple games such as *Microtronics, A Mgr. Sim.,* and *The Ex. Game,* do not define specific market areas for their products. Other games define markets generically in terms of price, product, quality, or area sales potential. *STRAT-PLAN* allows the administrator to establish up to three geographical market areas, two of which may be international markets. The *MNG* offers less flexibility, but a similar scenario, requiring that all teams operate out of a U.S. headquarters, but with full divisions operating in West Germany and Japan. Both games have different growth rates for each divisional market and both incorporate currency exchange rates from real-world reports.

Production

Plant Capacity. As shown in Table 5–2 all the games reviewed, except *Microtronics*, allow participants to expand plant capacity, either by building additional plants or locating new plants, often in other market areas or nations.

Capacity expansion usually requires a one quarter lag before the new capacity becomes available. *Microtronics* allows production increases by hiring additional employees and by scheduling overtime, but because of the game's emphasis on behavioral factors and its relatively small size, does not allow the scale of plant to change. BML has one of the more elaborate production functions, including two stages of production with possible plant capacity expansion in either of the two stages for two different market areas.

TABLE 5–2
Production Variables

Variables	1 The Ex. Game	2 A Mgr. Sim.	3 MICRO-TRONICS	4 BPG	5 MANSYM	6 BML	7 BSPG	8 STRAT-PLAN	9 MNG	10 TEMPO-MATIC IV
Plant Capacity										
Changes		x		x	x	x	x	x By Product x By Area	x	x
Multiple Plant				x By Area		x By Area By Stage			x By Nation	x By Area
Production Scheduling	x	x	x	By Area	x	By Stage	x	x	By Nation	By Area
Overtime			x	x	x	x			x	x
Multiple Shifts			x	x						
Stages					2	2				
Subcontracting						x				
Inventory transfers						x		x	x	x
Materials Purchase	x					x Current x Futures	x			By Area
Materials Choice					2	2	x			3
Production Workers										By Crew
Hired/Discharged			x				x			x
Scheduled			x				x			By Area
Training							x			x
Hourly Wage			x				x			x
Laid-off							x			x
Overtime Pay										x
Fringe Benefits			x						x	
Profit Sharing					x	x				
Operations Research										
Engineering				x		x		x	x	
Quality Control								x		
Cost			x			x		x		
Pollution Control										
Automation or Cost Saving Equipment					x					
Maintenance	x				2 kinds	2 stages				
Warehousing										
Allocation Finished Product				x			By Mkt.			x
Inventory Costs										
Accounting Choice					x	x				
Behavioral Incidents			x							
Executive Compensation				x		x				

Neither *MANSYM IV* nor *BML* allows capacity to be sold or reduced once it has been purchased. This is realistic since few companies can find a ready market for their plants in the short term. However, since most real-world firms can eventually find ways to dispose of unwanted plant, often recouping some capital, some game authors prefer to offer plant capacity as a reversible decision. *MANSYM IV* allows the investment in new labor saving equipment, also requiring a one quarter lag for use, but requiring payment in the quarter scheduled. *BML* allows the subcontracting of work to noncompetitive fabricators.

Production Scheduling. Simpler games allow production scheduling up to the plant's capacity level, and all except one (*A Mgr. Sim.*) of those reviewed include an overtime option. Moderately complex and very complex games include scheduling by multiple products on the same line, and often by production stages. These games include production functions that make the use of quantitative decision techniques, such as linear programming, feasible. Production that can be scheduled each quarter is usually limited by the capacity function described earlier. However, most games allow overtime or second shift operations. Some of the more complex games allow production to be contracted out, whereas others allow transfer of finished product from area to area (*Microtronics, BPG,* and *BML*) or nation to nation (*STRAT-PLAN* and *MNG*).

Materials Purchase. In *A Mgr. Sim., Microtronics, BPG, STRAT-PLAN,* and *MNG,* materials are automatically ordered when production is scheduled. Other games, some simple and some complex, include materials ordered as a major decision variable. The rationale of one of the more complex games, *STRAT-PLAN,* is expressed by the following quote:

> *STRAT-PLAN* emphasizes long-range issues. It provides opportunities to expand facilities, reduce production costs, abandon markets, etc. Because of this outlook, some issues like inventories, seasonal demand variations, or shipping delays have been played down, while others that are normally lost in the day-to-day process of running a business take on new vitality (Hinton and Smith, 1985, p. 61).

Production Workers. Issues of employee behavior have been omitted from most total enterprise games. In *Tempomatic IV* the work force is composed of three person crews of semiskilled workers and each worker is paid $2,500 per quarter plus overtime. Workers can be laid off, but automatically return in a future quarter, unless permanently discharged. There is a normal turnover rate requiring some continuous hiring and some loss of workers due to probabilistic turnover. The presence of simulated employees and crews has allowed users of *Tempomatic IV* to engage in very realistic role plays over labor contract negotiations.

PSPG includes a chapter on personnel and calls for personnel plans for salespersons and hourly workers. More unique still, by utilizing training programs or profit sharing, productivity in units per person-hour and raw materials requirements per unit can be improved. *Microtronics* includes a labor force that can be hired and terminated and whose pay can be raised and lowered. Success with the hourly employees is measured by a productivity index, and a turnover and absenteeism index. For each decision round, participants must respond to a series of behavioral incidents and each incident includes a proposal with corresponding costs and payoffs. With careful human resource management, productivity per employee can be increased and turnover can be reduced.

Research, Development and Engineering. All the games reviewed included some type of R & D variable. The R & D function for *The Ex. Game, Microtronics* and *MNG* are multifunctional and capable of lowering product costs and increasing market share. *STRAT-PLAN* includes R & D effects on product costs and quality as well as a technical investment. *BML* utilizes an engineering process study to improve plant efficiency, R & D for new product development, and quality control for improved product quality. *MANSYM IV* and *BPG* prefer to emphasize R & D on the consumer side; the former with product enhancement studies that can make a one time change in the functional features of the product, the latter by allowing the release of new products at periodic intervals of R & D investments.

In some games a certain level of maintenance is required to maintain full production capacity (*BML*); in others, maintenance expenditures tend to lower labor and materials costs (*The Ex. Game*). *BML* requires different expenditures on maintenance by production stage, and *BPG* requires maintenance expenditures for each production line. *The Ex. Game* teaches an important principle by experience, "If you permit the factory to deteriorate, it may be difficult to get its operations back into good shape" (Henshaw and Jackson, 1984: p. 17).

Other Production Variables. An interesting array of "other" features can be found in certain games. Equipment replacement costs are required to maintain production lines in *BPG; BML* allows the choice of either LIFO or FIFO in treating inventory costs as well as a standard cost system, and a weighted cost method. *MANSYM IV* allows a possible one time investment in new cost-saving equipment.

Finance

The less complex games tend to simplify their finance areas as can be seen in Table 5-3. *The Ex. Game* automatically provides loans at above normal interest rates if the firm's cash falls below zero. This special type of loan, or disaster loan, as it is called in the *BSPG* game is a variable common among the games reviewed. The other two simpler games reviewed, *Microtronics* and *A Mgr. Sim.,* allow participants to borrow funds and sell or purchase stock (variables that are present in all the other games reviewed). *BML* includes finance options of factoring, the delay of accounts payable, emergency loans, short term loans, term loans, private placements with venture capital firms, bonds, and common stock.

Both *STRAT-PLAN* and *MNG* allow the transfer of cash from market to market. In *STRAT-PLAN,* expenditures will be aborted if cash is not available in a market to cover expenditures. *MNG* uses the special loan variable to cover potential cash outages, but charges an above normal rate for this coverage. Both *STRAT-PLAN* and *MNG* operate with international markets and therefore include international currencies.

Investments and Savings. Opportunities for investments and savings accounts are uncommon among the less complex games reviewed. *BSPG*

TABLE 5-3
Financial Variables

Variables	1 The Ex. Game	2 A Mgr. Sim.	3 MICRO-TRONICS	4 BPG	5 MANSYM	6 BML	7 BSPG	8 STRAT-PLAN	9 MNG	10 TEMP-MATIC IV
Taxes	x	x	x	x	x	x	x	x	x	x
Finance								By Division	By Nation	
Short-Term Loans				x	x	x	x	x		x
Accounts Payable						x		x		
Accounts Receivable			x	x	x	x	x		x	x
Emergency Loans	x		x			x		x	x	
Factoring						x				
Long-Term Loans		x	x		x	x			x	
Venture Capital						x				
Transfer of Cash										
Among Divisions								x	x	
International Currency								x	x	
Bonds										
Issued/Sold				x		x	x			x
Negotiations						x				
Stock	x	x	x	x	x	x	x	x	U.S.	x
Purchased Sale		x	x	x		x	x	x	x	x
Dividend Payout	x	x	x	x		x	x	x	x	x
Investment				x	x	x				
Choices				CDs		4				
Officer Salary Plans				x						

allows deposits and withdrawals from an interest paying savings account. *Tempomatic IV* allows short-term investments and withdrawals at an interest rate pre-set by the game administrator. The *BPG* is creative in allowing three-month time certificates of deposit, whereas *MANSYM IV* allows firms to invest by a type of negative loan. *BML* includes an opportunity for teams to invest in any one of four short-term portfolios, each of which includes different degrees of risk which serve as collateral in the event of a cash shortage.

FUNCTIONAL BUSINESS GAMES

A functional business game is one which focuses on one of the major business functions of marketing, production and operations, personnel and human resources, or accounting and finance. While decisions in each of the areas may be required, the focus is on only one area and there are many decisions which must be integrated within that functional area. Functional business games typically do not attempt to introduce as many environmental conditions to as great an extent as do total enterprise business games.

Computerized functional business games made their first appearance during the 1960's in the areas of finance, marketing, and production. Among the earliest of these games were *FINANSIM: A Financial Management Simulation* (Greenlaw and Frey, 1967); *Marketing in Action: A Decision Game*, (Day and Ness, 1962); and *PROSIM: A Production Management Simulation* (Greenlaw and Hottenstein, 1969). In this section of this chapter we will describe, compare, contrast, and evaluate ten functional computerized business games. The games reviewed and the abbreviations used for them are: *Introduction to Managerial Accounting* (Goosen, 1973)—*MANACC;*[2] *Financial Management Decision Game* (Brooks, 1982)—*FINGAME; FINANSIM; A Financial Management Simulation* (Greenlaw, Frey, and Vernon, 1979)—*FINANSIM; MARKSIM: A Marketing Decision Simulation* (Greenlaw and Kniffin, 1964)—*MARKSIM;*[3] *MARKETER: A Simulation* (Smith, 1985)—*MARKETER; COMPETE: A Dynamic Marketing Simulation* (Faria, Nulsen, and Roussos, 1984)—*COMPETE; Marketing in Action: A Decision Game* (Ness and Day, 1984)—*MIA; The Human Resources Simulation* (Schreier, Smith and

---

[2] At the time of the writing of this article, *MANACC* was being extensively rewritten and a microcomputer version was being developed.

[3] After this chapter was originally written, *MARKSIM* was discontinued (Paul S. Greenlaw personal correspondence).

Donalinger, n.d.)—*HRS; PROSIM: A Production Management Simulation* (Greenshaw and Hottenstein, 1969)—*PROSIM;*[4] *DECIDE-P/OM: An Integrative Computer Simulation for Production/Operations Management* (Pray, Strang, Gold, and Burlingame, 1984)—*DECIDE-P/OM.*

Accounting and Finance Games

We found only one game that was oriented to the accounting function and only two that were designed for the finance area. Information concerning these simulations can be found in Table 5–4.

In some ways the accounting game, *MANACC,* could be classified as a total enterprise game since, as Table 5–4 indicates, it involves numerous marketing, production, human resources, and accounting decisions; however, since the focus is on accounting decisions, output, and analysis, we elected to classify it as an accounting game. We have not identified the specific decision areas for this game in Table 5–5 because they are so numerous, although we have indicated the total number of decisions for each business area.

In the marketing area of *MANACC,* participants must set price and allocate advertising dollars and salespersons among four territories in which the product, defined as a home appliance, is sold. Production decisions involve determining how many units to produce, adding equipment, allocating workers, ordering raw materials, selecting a raw material supplier, replacing equipment, scheduling a second shift or overtime for three departments, and providing for additional sales volume. Salary and commission rates must be established for salespersons, and wage rates must be designated for production workers. The accounting and finance decisions involve setting credit terms, payment of accounts and notes payable, retirement of bonds, attaining bank loans, issuing bonds and stock, payment of dividends, and factoring accounts receivable.

In process terms, the game contains both stochastic and lagged events, and it is noncompetitive. Although a product (a home appliance) is specified, there is no attempt to replicate that industry. Rather, the game is really a non-industry game with a product type specified. The instructor may modify the game by changing parameter values, demand figures, and history values. The output consists of detailed balance sheets and income statements, a cost of goods manufactured statement, and a fixed manufacturing overhead statement. There is no separate summary output for the administrator.

---

[4] *PROSIM* is currently being revised with both mainframe and PC versions.

TABLE 5–4
Accounting-Finance Games

Characteristics	MANACC	FINANSIM	FINGAME
Competitive	No	No	No
Industry	Yes	No	No
Individual or Team	Team	Team	Team
Team Size	3–4	3–5	No
			Suggestion
Computer	Mainframe	Mainframe	Mainframe
Complexity			
Language	Fortran	Fortran	Fortran
# of Decisions	40	14	19
# of Products	1	1	1
# of Sales Areas	4	1	1
# of Production Processes	3	1	1
Time Period	Year	Year	Quarter
Decision Areas			
Accounting Finance	[11]	[13]	[15]
Plant Capacity Purchased		1	1
Machine Capacity Purchased		1	1
Capital Budgeting Projects		3	2
Short Investment (Buy or Sell)		1	1
Riskiness of Short-term Investment		0	1
Sales Discount on Receivables		0	1
Short-term Loans (1–5 years)		3	3
Long-term Loans (Debentures)			
(Issue and Retire)		2	1
Preferred Stock		0	1
Common Stock Issue		1	1
Common Stock Price for New			
Issue		0	1
Dividends		1	1
Marketing	[9]	[0]	[2]
Price of Product		0	1
Purchase Demand & Price			
Forecasts		0	1
Production Operations	[15]	[1]	[1]
Units to be Produced		1	1
Personnel Human Resources	[4]	[0]	[1]
Strike Settlement		0	1

Bracketed numbers are the total decisions in the particular area.

The two finance games reviewed are very similar. As can be seen from Table 5–4, the decision areas are virtually identical, although *FINGAME* involves a few more decisions as well as decisions that fall into the marketing, production/operations, and personnel/human resources areas. Robana (1980) compares an earlier edition of *FINGAME* (Brooks, 1975) to the current edition of *FINANSIM* and concludes that *FINGAME* is the more sophisticated of the two. Robana (1980) notes the similarity of the two games, however, by pointing out that in both games the decisions and their consequences force the student to consider both working capital and long-term financial issues, such as cash flow, financial ratios, capital budgeting, dividend policy, and so on. He further points out that for both the emphasis is on the integration of the decisions to achieve efficient resource allocation and an optimum financial structure. Robana (1980) provides additional information concerning *FINGAME* and *FINANSIM* and recommends improvements to both games. Brooks (1978) also provides some useful background information concerning financial games.

In terms of process, both games have lagged and stochastic effects and both are noncompetitive and nonindustry specific. Each game permits the instructor to modify the game by changing parameter values, demand figures, and historical data. A major operational difference is that *FINGAME* provides for five different versions ranging from the instructor submitting all decisions to full student control with a new starting point. The intermediate versions permit the instructor to control specific decisions, reducing the number of decisions for which the student is responsible. Although this feature is not built into *FINANSIM,* it would appear that the instructor could achieve the same effect by telling students they were not permitted to make certain decisions. The instructor would then enter a common decision for each team.

The output for both games consists of an income statement, balance sheet, and a statement of supplemental information. Neither game generates separate summary output for the administrator.

Marketing Games

We found more marketing games than games from all other functional areas combined. We have elected to describe only four of them; three because they met all our criteria and the fourth (*MARKETER*) because it is the only one that was designed specifically for the microcomputer. The reader who would like information concerning other marketing games is referred to Faria (1980). The Faria (1980) article also provides additional information concerning the three older simulations that will be described. Information concerning the four marketing simulations is presented in Table 5–5.

The four marketing games differ significantly in their complexity as measured by the number of decisions made each period, with *MARKSIM* and *MARKETER* being relatively simple and *MIA* and *COMPETE* being relatively complex. In terms of the number of decisions, *MARKSIM*

TABLE 5–5
Marketing Games

Characteristics	MARKSIM	MARKETER	COMPETE	MIA
Competitive	Yes	Yes	Yes	Yes
Industry	Yes	Yes	Yes	Yes
Individual or Team	Team	Individual or Team	Team	Individual or Team
Team Size	3–5	2–3	3–4	3–5
Computer	Mainframe	Micro-computer	Mainframe & Microcomputer	Mainframe & Microcomputer
Complexity				
Language	Fortran	Basic	Fortran & Basic	Fortran & Basic
# of Decisions	12	20	101	53
# of Products	1	2	3	3
# of Sales Areas	1	1	1	1
# of Production Processes	3	1	1	1
Time Period	Quarter	Quarter	Quarter	Month or Quarter
Marketing	[10]	[13]	[85]	[48]
Product	1	1	6	9
Price	1	2	9	3
Place	1	2	9	3
Promotion	2	4	36	10
Marketing Research	5	4	25	26
Accounting/Finance	[1]	[0]	[0]	[0]
Debt Payment	1			
Personnel/Human Resources	[0]	[4]	[13]	[2]
Salespersons Hire/Fire		2	12	2
Bonuses		2	1	2
Production/Operation	[1]	[2]	[3]	[3]
Units to be produced/ordered	1	2	0	3
Production efficiency	0	0	3	0
Other		[1]		
Incidents		1		

appears to be simpler than *MARKETER*. However, since there are two
products in *MARKETER,* seven decisions are duplicate decisions rather
than being of a different type. For example, there are two price decisions,

two advertising decisions, and so on, which means the number of unique decisions could actually be less than in *MARKSIM,* if *MARKETER* was run with only one product.

In identifying the market decision areas we have elected to use the "four P's" of marketing (products, place, promotion, and price) along with the area of marketing research as our basis for grouping decisions. In terms of product decisions, *MARKSIM* and *MARKETER* are clearly simpler than *MIA* and *COMPETE.* In *MARKSIM* the only product-type decision is that of research and development, which basically influences product quality. *COMPETE* also focuses on quality control as the primary product decision. In *MIA,* on the other hand, players must select three different product characteristics for each of the three products.

The simulations handle price decisions by specifying a price for each product in a given area. Thus *MARKSIM* involves one price decision since only a single product is sold in one geographic area, whereas *COMPETE* has nine price decisions since three products are sold in three geographic areas.

The place decisions are handled differently in the four simulations. *MIA* sells its products in a single geographical area and does not specify the type of outlets eliminating place decisions. *MARKSIM* handles place decisions by requiring players to make shipments to distribution centers. *MARKETER* requires dollars to be spent on distribution improvements, which serves to reduce channel conflicts. *COMPETE* introduces place decisions through shipments to three geographic areas.

The range of complexity in the promotion area is quite high for the four simulations. In *MARKSIM* promotion consists of advertising allowances for retailers. In *MARKETER* advertising and sales promotion, such as point of purchase display, are possible. In *MIA,* advertising and sales force decisions are involved. *COMPETE* involves advertising, sales force, and promotion decisions and the complexity is much greater than in *MIA.* For example, players can allocate dollars between broadcast and print media. In addition, they can specify characteristics of the message's content. In the sales force area, *COMPETE* permits the players to allocate the sales force's time among the three products and provides for compensation on a commission basis.

All the marketing games permit players to purchase various types of information about their competitors and market conditions. As can be seen from Table 5-5, *MARKSIM* and *MARKETER* present the fewest options, whereas *MIA* and *COMPETE* provide extensive opportunities to learn about the marketing environment. *MARKETER* adds one additional decision element warranting special mention. In each decision period the players are presented with an incident with up to ten alternative solutions. For example, in one incident the Federal Communications Commission (FCC) informs the firm that its product is marginal with respect to certain FCC standards. The firm must decide whether to fix the problem, engage in testing, ignore the warning until legal action is taken, or appoint a study committee. The selected alternative is entered as part of the decision and affects the team's results with the better alternative producing positive results and the poorer alternative producing negative results. *COMPETE* has a similar feature; however, the incidents are only presented in the instructor's manual so the instructor can ignore them if he so desires.

All four marketing games have lagged and stochastic effects. Except for *MARKSIM,* all specify an industry and a specific product. Given the fact that the marketing function is the one that interacts with the external environment to the greatest extent, it is not surprising that the marketing games are all competitive, whereas the games in the other functional areas are all noncompetitive in nature. Likewise, since the product and industry characteristics are so important to price, place, and promotion decisions, it is not surprising that the marketing games tend to specify a product. All the marketing games permit the administrator to change parameter values, demand figures, and historical data.

The output for the four simulations is quite similar. All provide an income statement, although *COMPETE* provides the most information since regional income statements are presented. All four simulations provide balance sheet information, although *MARKETER* only presents asset information and the *MARKSIM* balance sheet is greatly abbreviated. Finally, all games provide marketing research information for the players. *MARKETER* also provides an inventory analysis and feedback on the incidents. While *COMPETE, MIA,* and *MARKETER* provide summary information, only *MARKETER* provides scoring for the administrator.

Personnel and Human Resources Games

We found only one published computerized personnel and human resources game; however, its availability was limited and an improved version has not yet been published. In order to be able to include a computerized personnel and human resources game, we elected to suspend our publication criteria.

The *HRS* game involves 37 decisions. We have elected to group the game's decisions using the categories of acquisition of human resources, development of human resources, rewarding of human resources, and maintenance of human resources (Greenlaw and Biggs, 1979). In acquiring human resources (20 decisions), the players must hire and/or promote five different categories of workers. In addition, they must deal with affirmative action issues with respect to females and minorities. Finally, they must decide whether to computerize and maintain a personnel records system that can facilitate the acquisition of human resources.

In the development of human resources (six decisions), the players must decide whether to provide training programs for both new hires and promoted workers and whether to install and maintain orientation and performance appraisal programs. In rewarding human resources (five decisions), the players must set wage rates for each of the five worker categories. Finally, in the maintenance of human resources (four decisions), the players must decide whether to conduct an employee attitude survey and the type of safety program to be scheduled.

In addition, in *HRS,* decisions must be made concerning establishing and maintaining grievance procedures and a quality control program relating to grievance and turnover. Thus the simulation forces the student to make budget decisions in each of the major personnel/human resources subfunctions. Like *MARKETER*, this simulation provides critical incident decisions. In addition, participants may be presented with the opportunity to budget special programs. The simulation has lagged and stochastic events. For example, a person moving to the next level in the organization's hierarchy is presented in probabilistic terms. The game is non-industry specific and noncompetitive, and the administrator may change parameter values and historical data. Since there is no product involved, there are no product demand figures. There are, however, values for the supply and demand of labor.

The output from this game includes information on the number of persons in each position, with the number of females and minorities identified to enable decision-making to deal with affirmative action and equal employment opportunity issues. The number of expected vacancies for the next period by job classification is also provided. Other information includes costs of the accident rate, grievances, productivity, quality level, morale, turnover, and wage rates. Finally, financial information is presented that identifies the total personnel department cost and the amount of the annual budget spent to date.

Production/Operations Games

We found two games designed for the production/operations function that met our criteria, *PROSIM* and *DECIDE-P/OM.* Information concerning these two simulations can be found in Table 5-6.

As can be seen, *DECIDE-P/OM* requires more decisions than does *PROSIM.* Both games have a fairly high degree of complexity because they involve multiple products being processed through two stages of production. We believe, however, that *DECIDE-P/OM* is the most sophisticated of the two games on at least two dimensions. First, *DECIDE-P/OM* requires more quality control decisions. The student must establish a quality control program involving input (sample size and acceptance quality) and output

TABLE 5–6
Production/Operations Games

Characteristics	PROSIM	DECIDE/POM
Competitive	No	No
Industry	No	No
Individual or Team	Team	Team
Team Size	3–5	3–6
Computer	Mainframe	Mainframe
Complexity		
Language	Fortran	Fortran
# of Decisions	36	49
# of Products	3	2
# of Sales Areas	1	1
# of Production Processes	1	1
Time Period	Day	Undefined
DECISION AREAS		
Production/Operations	[28]	[40]
Raw Materials	2	3
Production Stages/Lines	2	2
Machine/Centers in Stages	4	5
Levels of Labor in Stages	0	2
Regular and Overtime Labor	0	2
Quality Control	1	8
Maintenance	1	5
Marketing	[0]	[3]
Price	0	2
Demand Data	0	1
Accounting/Finance	[0]	[5]
Capital Investment	0	5
Personnel/Human Resources	[8]	[1]
Training	8	1

Bracketed numbers are the total decisions in the particular area. The bracketed number for production/operations, however, is greater than the sum of the parts due to interactive effects.

(number of samples, sample size, and upper and lower control limits) decisions, whereas *PROSIM* merely requires the student to specify a dollar amount that basically influences the percentage of product rejected. Second, *DECIDE-P/OM* permits the student to apply material requirement planning (MRP), whereas *PROSIM* does not. Although *DECIDE-P/OM* requires more maintenance decisions, the level of sophistication compared to *PROSIM* is no greater because they represent more of the same decisions rather than decisions of increased difficulty. Thus in *DECIDE-P/OM* the decision-maker must decide on the maintenance decision for each production center, therefore five maintenance decisions must be made.

Both games have lagged and stochastic effects and are noncompetitive and nonindustry specific. Both games also permit the instructor to modify the game by changing parameter values, demand figures, and historical data.

The outputs from *DECIDE-P/OM* and *PROSIM* are quite different. In fact, the output for *PROSIM* is quite different from all the games reviewed since it does not provide an income statement or a balance sheet. Rather *PROSIM's* output consists of cost, production line, inventory, and demand information. The lack of an income statement is consistent with the basic objective *PROSIM* attempts to accomplish, cost minimization. Accordingly, the output is appropriate feedback for the decisions being made. *DECIDE-P/OM,* on the other hand, provides the student with a great deal of output. In addition to an income statement and balance sheet, the student receives a cash flow statement, materials management report, a machine utilization and productivity report, a labor availability and training report, an input quality control report, and a report that provides forecasts of economic indices, prices of related goods, and marketing indices, as well as an interfirm management effectiveness report. The last report presents a rank for the firm on six criteria (profitability, acceptance sampling plan, quality control program, materials requirement planning, forecasting/stockout analysis, and nonproductive labor) as well as an overall performance rank that is a composite of the previously mentioned items. *DECIDE-P/OM* also generates an administrator's summary report for each period of play.

A LEARNING MODEL AND COMPARATIVE EVALUATION

The basic reason for selecting and using a computerized business game is to facilitate learning. Our focus in this section will be on the business games described in this article in the context of a learning model suggested by Keys (1977). The definition of learning follows that of Piaget (1973), suggesting that learning is "that ability of the student to organize reality." Most games have followed such an implied model for learning by providing three phases:

1. Experience: This phase of learning is provided by game play, decision inputs, and team interaction.
2. Content: This phase includes dissemination of ideas, principles, or concepts regarding business practices and principles.
3. Feedback: This phase includes feedback in the form of financial statements, comparative team standings, and participant and team critiques by the professor or game administrator.

The effective learning environment is created when a proper balance is achieved among these three factors. "Balance" here denotes balance in terms of the particular participant group being taught. A group of MBA students in their final course presumably would be acquainted with many business principles necessary to provide content in a moderately complex game. For college seniors, some review of business concepts is usually necessary, either within the game or by supplementary readings. For a group of freshman in an introduction to business class, most experiences should be preceded by content in a well written manual or by helpful planning sheets or decision support packages. The reader who is interested in studies dealing with learning in business games is referred to the reviews by Keys (1976), Greenlaw and Wyman (1973), and Wolfe (1986).

Comparative Evaluation: Experience

The game experience afforded by each total enterprise game reviewed can be best understood by noting some representative characteristics. Some games tend to be more marketing oriented (*BPG* and *STRAT-PLAN*) whereas others emphasize production or finance. Some games focus on behavioral experiences (*A Mgr. Sim., Microtronics,* and *Tempomatic IV*) while others emphasize analytical work (*MANSYM IV* and *BML*). Some games are more short run or tactical in nature (*The Ex. Game, A Mgr. Sim.,* and *Microtronics*); others are more long run or strategy oriented (*STRAT-PLAN* and *MNG*). Others tend to strike a balance between tactical and strategic decisions (*BPG, MANSYM IV, BML, BSPG* and *Tempomatic IV*). *The Ex. Game, A Mgr. Sim.,* and *Microtronics* are less complex and were designed primarily for lower level college courses, or very short management development programs of one, two, or three days in length.

Global evaluations of the game characteristics and decision inputs available in each of the functional games are presented in Tables 5-4, 5-5, and 5-6 for accounting-finance, marketing, and production and operations games, respectively, and in the verbal description of the one personnel and human resources game. Table 5-7 summarizes the decisions for each game.

Using the total number of decisions as a measure of overall game complexity, we would classify *FINANSIM* and *MARKSIM* as simple games (less than 15 decisions); *FINGAME* and *MARKETER* as moderately complex games (15 to 30 decisions); and *MANACC, MIA, COMPETE, PROSIM, DECIDE-P/OM,* and *HRG* as complex games (more than 30 decisions). A few notes of caution are in order, however. First, when Keys (1980) developed this classification, he was dealing with total enterprise rather than functional business games; therefore different category boundaries might be justified for functional games. Second, it may make sense to compare games within functional areas rather than across the functional

TABLE 5-7
Approximate Number of Possible Decisions Inputs per Decision Period

Game Type and Game	Accounting Finance	Marketing	Personnel Human Resources	Production Operations	Other	Total
Accounting/Finance						
Managerial Accounting	11	9	4	15	0	39
FINANSIM	13	0	0	1	0	14
FINGAME	15	2	1	1	0	19
Marketing						
MARKSIM	1	10	0	1	0	12
MARKETER	0	13	4	2	1	20
Marketing in Action	0	48	2	3	0	53
COMPETE	0	85	13	3	0	101
Personnel/Human Resources						
Human Resources	0	0	35	0	2	37
Production/Operations						
PROSIM	0	0	8	28	0	36
DECIDE-P OM	5	3	1	40	0	49

areas. Third, as noted in the discussion of the various games, some of the decisions represent more of the same rather than a difference in kind. Thus making two price decisions is not as rich an experience as making a price and a distribution decision, since the interactive effect must be dealt with in the latter case. Accordingly, games that involve only a few decisions in a number of different functional areas may be more complex than those games which include a number of similar or duplicated decisions. Fourth, the marketing games, being competitive games, have a type of complexity that does not exist in the other functional games described. Fifth, the reader should keep in mind that a game's complexity can frequently be lowered by holding some decisions back. For example, in *MARKETER* the participants could be restricted to one product. Complexity could then be increased later as the game progressed by opening up the decisions available to the participants.

Another dimension of complexity is the activities the administrator chooses to add to the game. For example, in a marketing game an administrator could require that participants present a marketing plan.

Comparative Evaluation: Content

Traditionally, total enterprise games have left the content provision largely in the hands of the instructor. Readings can be assigned, lecture provided, but the game manual itself assumes little responsibility for teaching content.

From this review of the ten total enterprise games, it appears that authors are including more content within games. For example, the latest edition of *The Ex. Game* includes a chapter on planning not found in earlier editions; *MNG* weaves numerous international business concepts among the game instructions and almost every section of its decision information, such as advertising or sales, includes a section on international trends. The marketing section of the *BPG* proliferates with examples from industry. When illustrating the short product life cycle of products and the development of replacement products, an illustration is used of Quaker States' innovative screw-on top for oil cans. The other games reviewed do not offer as much content within student manuals as these, but some provide a heavier emphasis on other types of assistance. *MANSYM IV* tends to treat variables more analytically than historically and gives numerous illustrations of how to compute and analyze strategies.

As can be seen from Table 5-8, functional business games differ considerably in the amount of content provided in the student manual. The content amount was assessed by dividing those pages identified as content pages by the total number of pages less the blank forms included in the manual. Using this approach, three of the games (*MARKSIM, FINANSIM,* and *PROSIM*) devoted more than 60% of the student manual to content, whereas all of the other games devoted less than 25% of the student manual to content. The issue of how much information (that is, content) is needed to play a business game successfully has been dealt with to some degree by Biggs and Greenlaw (1976); while the issue of game complexity is addressed by Butler, Pray and Strang (1979), Raia (1966), and Wolfe (1978).

TABLE 5–8
Approximate Number of Pages Devoted to Game Rules and Content

Games	Total Pages	Rule Pages	Content Pages	Content Forms	Overall Content
Managerial Accounting	208	47	Low	High	Low
FINANSIM	232	42	High	Low	High
FINGAME	170	72	Low	Middle	Low
MARKETER	170[a]	35	Low	Middle	Low
MARKSIM	195	50	High	Low	High
Marketing in Action	180	61	Low	Low	Low
COMPETE	166	59	Low	Low	Low
Human Resources	120[b]	35	Low	Middle	Low
PROSIM	256	24	High	Middle	High
DECIDE-P OM	198	115	Low	Low	Low

a. All of the manuals are 8″ by 11″ except for Marketer, which is 7″ by 9″.
b. Prepublication manuscript.

Comparative Evaluation: Feedback

Much of the learning process in simulation games comes through reflection by participants as they compare their conceptual models of business activities with the results of their experiences in the simulation games. Competition and activity in a simulation game are so stimulating, however, that reflection seldom occurs unless it is guided or required by either the game or the administrator. All games reviewed provide feedback of a computerized income statement and balance sheet. In addition, several of the games require structured experiences such as a break-even analysis or an organizational chart, that force reflection and learning (see for example, *A Mgr. Sim.*).

One of the major weaknesses of total enterprise games has been the overemphasis on decision inputs and game complexity at the expense of supportive content and feedback. In other words, the time span for game play is often too short to complete the learning cycle. For this reason simpler games like *A Mgr. Sim.*, with very few decision inputs, can be quite useful in short sessions or when heavily supported by other materials.

Most of the games reviewed include some kind of planning sheets or package to structure the planning of teams. It is difficult to classify these packages as solely experience, content, or feedback because the better packages include some of all three dimensions. For convenience they will be discussed under the heading feedback, since planning for game decisions tends to cause students to learn from experience by structuring their experiences. Most total enterprise planning packages include planning sheets on sales forecasting, production scheduling, pro forma income statements, and cash flow analysis.

One of the greatest innovations of recent game editions is the micro decision support packages now available for total enterprise games (*Microtronics, STRAT-PLAN,* and *Tempomatic IV* [Table 5-1]). Other games reviewed may have decision support packages under development, but information for such is not presently available. *STRAT-PLAN* requires participants to utilize *Lotus 1-2-3* and therefore requires the purchase of the Lotus package (see *STRAT-PLAN,* Table 5-1). *Microtronics* includes a decision support package known as *The Electronic Worksheets* (*EWS*) that follows the same series of hand-scored sheets noted above, but also includes a series of financial ratios. In all of the three games noted as including decision support packages, students input their projected forecast numbers, their choice of marketing decisions, production inventory to be maintained, and their history variables from the previous round of play. Their support package then either produces hard copy, if a printer is available, or projects all their completed planning sheets on the computer screen. Participants can try "what if" analysis by completing any number of marketing, production and finance options and printing out the concluding results. When participants have devised a range of options that produces the best results, they submit these to the instructor as their decisions. In the packages noted above, the instructor can accept the planning packages and load student decisions directly from it without retyping any data.

If an instructor prefers that students engage in the experience of completing written planning sheets, these can be assigned for several rounds, after which the decision support package can be distributed and employed.

The quantitative type of feedback provided in each functional game was presented earlier. All the functional games described provide adequate quantitative feedback. The game administrator could, however, elect to supplement feedback to the participants. On the other hand, the administrator could withhold some of the computer output, provide certain key values, and have the participant do the calculations necessary to generate the computer printouts. The tradeoffs in these two approaches lie between time savings and greater student involvement. By providing more of the information to participants, they may be able to handle more data and undertake more sets of decisions. Involvement and perhaps learning, however, may be reduced.

To aid game administrators in providing feedback to participants and to facilitate grading, some of the games provide a grading subroutine. Biggs (1978), discussing two approaches frequently taken in such subroutines, advocates that qualitative as well as quantitative measures be used. Others discussing grading performance in business games are Butler and Parasuraman (1975), Hand and Sims (1975), and Sims and Hand (1975).

In addition to the computer printout information, many of the forms mentioned in the previous section are in fact designed to provide feedback. In many instances these forms provide quantitative feedback (for example, pro forma statements, machine utilization, and so on); however, in some instances the feedback is qualitative (for instance, peer evaluation forms, administrator planning forms, evaluation forms, and so forth). Most of the games reviewed tend to neglect qualitative feedback.

SUMMARY

Games have improved greatly in educational value, simulated realism, and administrative simplicity since the late 1950's when games were first utilized in business schools. The ten total enterprise games reviewed in this article provide a wide spectrum of complexity from the very simple 11-decision game of *A Mgr. Sim.* to the very complex *BML* game, which has available over 60 different team decisions per round of play. First, the total enterprise games include more business knowledge and examples within student manuals than did the earlier versions. This signifies a healthy trend away from the notion that instructors merely needed to provide teams with a competitive experience, thereby allowing them to remove themselves entirely from the game experience without supplying further guidance. Second, there is a general trend toward incorporating more of the "softer" functions of business in total enterprise games, facilitated largely by an improved simulation of employees in the work force and the corresponding decisions which such simulation elicits.

This chapter presented background information about functional business games, described a number of games in each functional area, and related these games to a learning model. It is apparent that there is not a great number of these games available in some functional areas. In three of the four functional areas reviewed, however, the game user is provided a few good choices.

Many of the games reviewed have been converted from mainframe to microcomputer scoring to free instructors of dependency on data processing while conducting a class. This conversion has also made games easier to modify and has potentially placed more control of starting positions and game variable strength in the hands of instructors utilizing games. Many of the games allow students to input decisions on floppy disks.

So that no data input is required of the game administrator, the authors of the more complex games are developing decision support packages that allow students to conduct "what if" analyses and print out planning sheets for such areas as sales forecasting, pro forma income statements, cash budgeting, and ratio analyses. This development offers the hope of greatly increasing learning from games by reducing the amount of raw mechanical number processing required of students and to allow them to focus on obtaining significant results from alternative inputs. Further, this development can shorten the decision cycle time required for students to progress along the learning curve in a complex game.

The simpler PC-scored games are becoming very user friendly, often driven entirely by menus that allow them to be used in short training programs and at different sites, scored by portable PC's. The combination of the increased available range of simulation complexity, decision support package availability, menu-driven PC scoring and general microcomputer familiarity in our society has caused a significant new surge of interest in the use of business games, both in collegiate and in industrial training.

CHAPTER 6

GUIDELINES
FOR ADMINISTERING
BUSINESS GAMES

David J. Fritzsche
Richard V. Cotter

Prior to incorporating a business game into a course, the instructor is advised to determine the educational purpose the game is to serve. One should have one or more important objectives for the course which the simulation is uniquely suited to fulfill (Sanchez, 1980). These may include the integration of current or previously learned material, providing students with experience in decision-making under uncertainty, etc. The role of the game in the course should be carefully planned prior to the beginning of the academic period (Low, 1980). The investment of time in the planning process before classes begin will make the gaming experience more enjoyable and rewarding for both the students and the instructor (Greene, 1981). This chapter will provide a comprehensive guide to the factors which should be considered in the planning process. We begin with the selection of the game to use.

SELECTING A GAME

The potential business game user has a relatively large and growing number of games from which to choose. The reader is referred to earlier chapters in this book which discuss the usage and availability of business games. in addition, the reader may wish to contact CABSEL (see chapter 1) to gain additional information concerning one or more games or concerning games which have been developed since this book was published.

TYPES OF GAMES

The selection of a game will depend upon the material being taught, the level of instruction desired, the type of computer equipment available, and the administrator's teaching style. Business games can be divided into general management games developed for policy/strategy or for introduction to management courses, and functional games which focus upon a specific business discipline such as finance or marketing. Games are currently available in each of the functional areas of business and some are also available for a particular subfunction such as bank management.

LEVEL OF INSTRUCTION

The level of a game is dependent upon several factors. First, there is the number of actual decision variables which must be addressed each decision period. A simple count may be deceiving in that a number of games feature variables which are not normally used together, such as taking out a loan and investing in CDs during the same period. A team may also be unable to build a new plant in more than one area at a time. Other games require students to utilize each of the variables in the game each decision period. Of course, variables not used for a decision period may still have to be considered by the team in arriving at a decision. As a general rule, the complexity of a game increases as the number of variables increases.

Second, some games utilize decision variables which are more complex than others. For example, advertising may be implemented by arriving at a dollar expenditure in one game while a second game requires students to select media and message content in addition to dollar expenditures. The administrator must determine whether a specific simulation contains the variables which are critical to the course content and are at a suitable level of complexity.

As we have seen, the complexity of a simulation is dependent upon both the number and complexity of the variables utilized. The optimum level of complexity provides a balance between realism and playability. Realism tends to increase as the complexity of the game increases, due to the fact that the business world is a complex place. However, as a simulation becomes more complex, it becomes increasingly difficult to play. Thus less complex games are generally recommended for lower level courses with the more complex games being suitable for advanced courses. The optimal level of complexity for a simulation to possess is open to question. Certainly games that are too simple do not keep the student's attention and thus lose educational value (Wolfe, 1978). On the other hand, games that are too complex may overwhelm the student and thus also lose educational value.

In addition to the number and complexity of the decision variables, realism is influenced by the specific set of variables included as well as the manner in which the variables relate both in the player's manual and in the computer model. (One's evaluation will usually be based upon the written description in the player's manual thus trusting the computer model to provide students with results which are perceived to be as stated.) All games are abstractions from reality and, as such, include a subset of the actual variables found in the business environment. Realism is enhanced when the level of complexity is relatively similar for all of the related groups of variables in a simulation. For example, in a general business game, the complexity of the finance, marketing, and production variables should be similar. In a marketing game, the variables of the marketing mix should be nearly equal in their level of complexity, while those involving production and finance would, appropriately, be less complex.

COMPUTER REQUIREMENTS

The computer hardware and software requirements of a game are also important factors to consider in game selection. A simulation may run on a mainframe and/or on a microcomputer. It is extremely important to determine whether a game being considered will run on the equipment available to the administrator. This information can be obtained from the publisher or from the author(s) of the game.

The installation of a game on a mainframe computer will take significantly longer than the installation of the same game (if available) on a microcomputer. Administrators planning to use a mainframe should allow at least a month for installation prior to actual game use. That should allow sufficient time to adapt the game to the local operating conditions of the mainframe computer. [See Fritzsche (1975) for a description of some potential pitfalls.] It will also allow time for testing the simulation to make sure that it runs correctly, as well as to enable the administrator to become familiar with the game.

As stated above, game installation on a microcomputer is usually much quicker than on a mainframe. Normally a week's lead time is sufficient. However, the administrator must make sure that the simulation is designed to run on the specific microcomputer that is to be used. Many business games designed to run on IBM microcomputers will run on IBM compatible microcomputers. However, occasionally a game will run on an IBM but not on a specific IBM compatible. In addition, there are certain peripherals (printers, cards, etc.) which may cause installation problems for some games. It is wise to allow sufficient time to solve incompatibility problems if they arise.

Many of the latest simulations, particularly the general management games, are beginning to incorporate decision support software (DSS). DSS most often takes the form of templates for spreadsheet programs. The DSS may assist student teams in making higher quality decisions as well as providing familiarity with computers and the type of software which students will be using on the job (Fritzsche, Rodich, and Cotter, 1987). DSS also adds realism to the simulation experience. If DSS is available for a game, the administrator should check to make sure that it runs on the available computer hardware. In most cases, a commercial program such as *Lotus 1-2-3* must also be available to run the DSS.

INTRODUCING THE GAME

Students normally view a simulation as a challenging, enjoyable way to learn. To reinforce the educational purpose of a business game, learning objectives should be developed and shared with students. The learning objectives also provide a basis for student evaluation of the course at its completion. Objectives may focus upon the benefits of integrating functional skills with the game as well as upon the experience gained in developing and implementing plans. From the viewpoint of the instructor, a simulation may provide a highly motivating environment in which the student has a good time while learning and applying the knowledge and skill that are the subject matter of the course.

GAME ENVIRONMENT

A major hurdle in using a business game is the startup cost associated with introducing the game—mostly an investment in time. The cost for both student and administrator is relatively high the first time through due to the need to learn the rules of the game (simulated environment). It takes a period of time to learn the operating rules in any organization and a simulated firm is no exception. Subsequent use of the game requires much less preparation on the part of the administrator. However, each time the simulation is played, starting conditions in the form of parameter settings may need to be generated. Many games now contain programs which guide the administrator through parameter setting routines in an easy and efficient manner. Older games typically required the administrator to modify parameter settings using some type of program editor.

For students, it is always the first time through the game. Thus "startup shock" will be encountered during the first few decisions until the students become familiar with the simulated environment and rules. Most games include a player's manual which should be read by all students prior to a discussion of the game. The manual normally sets the simulation stage by discussing the history of the simulated firm, the gaming environment, the specific rules of the game, and the detailed instructions required to enter game decisions. While manuals usually provide more details than can be assimilated in one reading, the initial reading provides a general overview of the game.

Reading the manual can be encouraged by administering a short, announced quiz shortly after the time the manual is to be read. This can be followed by a discussion of the simulation and its rules in order to provide students with a solid foundation upon which to base game decisions. A thorough understanding of the manual generally requires several readings as well as numerous references during the early portion of the game. One technique used to gain the depth of understanding required to play the game prior to the first decision is to have the student teams assign management positions to their team members and make the individual team members responsible for the material dealing with their positions. This technique breaks the task down into manageable portions and thus provides a volume of material which students can more easily assimilate. The team members can become more familiar with other portions of the manual as play progresses.

While the discussion of the game may begin with an overview, the administrator is advised to move rather quickly to the details of the game in order to clear up any cobwebs which arise from reading the manual. Details which are frequently misunderstood, overlooked, or tend to cause trouble can be emphasized in order to minimize errors in early play. Specific rules which tend to cause trouble become readily apparent after the administrator gains experience in using the game. Overhead transparencies of the decision forms can be used to walk the teams through a decision and thus minimize errors due to incorrect decision entries.

The heavy initial workload, general uncertainty regarding how to participate effectively, and uncertainty or apprehension about possible unsatisfactory or negative outcomes for playing the simulation may contribute to a phenomenon that has been called "startup anxiety" (Smith, 1988). While some anxiety or stress may be beneficial (Benson and Allen, 1980), an excessive amount may be detrimental to the learning experience. An approach that has been effective is to work to build a "corporate culture" in the classroom—a culture that puts students at ease and gives pleasant anticipation of the simulation experience.

As an example of this approach, a case study concentrating on building a favorable corporate culture as a medium for implementation of a company's strategic plan is used just before introduction of a general management simulation in the business policy and strategy course. The case, "Wal-Mart Stores, Inc." (in Thompson and Strickland, 1987) portrays Sam Walton as the driving force behind Wal-Mart's corporate culture. In the case, Sam Walton often participates as a "cheerleader" at Saturday morning staff meetings. On the day for introduction of the simulation (the next period after using the Wal-Mart case), the instructor walks into the classroom twirling a baton and leads the class in a rousing cheer—"Give me a B! Give me a P! Give me a G!" (for the *Business Policy Game* by Cotter and Fritzsche, 1986). The class responds favorably and is immediately more at ease with an exercise that some had been apprehensive about. The cheer is repeated on several subsequent days and the instructor attempts to build a feeling of esprit de corps in the classroom throughout the semester.

Smith (1988) has suggested two other ways to reduce startup anxiety. One was to regularly use the simulation scenario and incidents in the classroom as illustrations of various management topics. This has the effect of building familiarity with the simulation while discussing other topics and thus reduces anxiety. The second method is to use a simulation based on a case study which the class has previously discussed. Alternately, the class may be asked, prior to the introduction of the simulation, to undertake research regarding the industry being portrayed by the simulation. These activities, prior to introduction of the simulation, tend to help build familiarity through vocabulary building and knowledge of the industry.

Prior to making actual decisions, each simulated firm may be required to develop an operating plan. The plan generally consists of a set of objectives coupled with strategies designed to realize the objectives. Students may also be required to include a mission statement and pro forma operating statements if these are deemed important by the administrator. The detail and nature of the plan are dependent upon the objectives of the course, the type of game used, the level of the students, and the preferences of the game administrator. Certainly the plan would be more complex for a business policy and strategy course than for an introduction to business course.

The business policy and strategy course instructor, for example, may wish to carefully integrate the basic concepts of the course with playing the simulation. This would give participants practice in formulating and implementing a comprehensive strategic plan. To do this, students would perhaps formulate a mission statement for their simulated company, develop appropriate performance objectives, formulate overall strategy and functional area support strategies designed to enable the firm to reach those objectives, and, finally, to lay out an implementation plan, including pro forma statements reflecting what they expect to accomplish over the course of play of the simulation.

The administrator must realize that the plan developed by each team is based upon the team's view of the environment and how the environment is perceived to respond to the actions of the simulated firm. It is highly unlikely that a firm will actually meet its stated objectives. However, setting objectives and developing strategies gives direction to the budding firm even if that direction must be changed as play continues.

TEAM ORGANIZATION

Most business games are played by teams composed of three to six students. Teams need to be organized prior to the development of the operating plan. Teams may be self-selected or the administrator may wish to assign members to teams (See Badgett, 1980 and Wilson, 1974). An advantage of administrator assigned teams is that firms can be balanced by major and/or by student abilities. A higher level of competition may result if teams are balanced rather than ending up with several very strong teams and several weak ones. If the administrator decides to assign team members, information may be obtained by passing out cards to the students and asking them to provide the appropriate information.

There are also several arguments favoring the use of self-selected teams. When students select their own teams, they can organize around common schedules and thus should have more time to work together on team business. Self-selection may, but does not necessarily, eliminate the problem of working on a team with uncooperative, poorly performing, or unconcerned students. If teams are to be self-selected, a sign up sheet can be posted containing blank, ruled spaces corresponding to the number of students allowed on each team. Students can then be notified that they must sign up by a certain date. Students who have not joined a team by that date can be arbitrarily assigned to teams.

Another successful scheme for team selection involves appointment of the "president" for each simulated company, with each of the presidents then choosing or "hiring" the other members of the management team (sometimes with each student submitting a personal data sheet and applying for one or more team positions).

There are several factors to consider when determining the number of students to place on a team. First, most games are designed to allow the running of multiple game sections (industries, regions, or worlds) which do not compete across sections. Thus if a group of students is too large for a single game, multiple sections of the game can be played concurrently. Normally a section of a game can handle a range of teams, usually from three to five or six. The problem then becomes one of determining the number of sections to run and the number of teams to assign to each section in order to accommodate the existing students.

Second, unless the game is very complicated, an ideal number of students per team appears to be from three to five (See Gentry, 1980; Remus and Jenner, 1979; Wolfe and Chacko, 1982; and Wolfe and Chacko, 1983). This also depends to some extent upon the number of explicit roles required in a simulated firm. Larger teams make it easy for a team member to slack off. Smaller teams, especially when the size reaches two, tend to result in an individual work load that is too heavy. Concern should also be given to the drop rate when assigning teams. It is good practice to size teams so that they can still function effectively if one of their members drops out of the competition. After a team has organized and begun to work on a decision, it is difficult to shift a student to another team to make up for a shortage resulting from a student dropping out. It becomes even more difficult after several decisions have been made and the team is functioning smoothly. If a shift must be made, it is better to transfer a student member of a team from another game section, thus preventing insider information from benefiting the student's new team.

DECISION ENTRY

Because business games are computer based, student team decisions must be entered into a computer prior to the simulation being run. Team decisions may be entered into the computer in a number of ways. The two most commonly used are centralized decision entry, where the administrator directly enters the decisions of each team using a decision entry program, and direct decision entry, where individual teams enter their own decision using a decision entry program. In either case, the decisions are stored on disk, floppy or hard, until the simulation is run.

By using centralized data entry, the administrator maintains control over the time the decisions are entered and over the accuracy of the data entered. Centralized data entry requires student teams to turn in a written copy of their decision form which is used to enter the decision. The form also serves as a reference when team members question an entry. Centralized entry may be required when equipment is not available for students to allow direct data entry.

Direct data entry has several significant advantages (Fritzsche, 1979). When teams are required to enter their own decisions, the responsibility of entering accurate data rests with each team (where it belongs). A good decision entry program will contain error checking routines that will catch many incorrect entries during the data entry process.

Direct entry allows students to enter data from any location where compatible computer equipment is available. If a mainframe or a micro-computer network (with modem access) is utilized, this means any location where a communication connection can be made with the host computer. Thus decisions might be entered from a dorm, home, or work if terminals (computer terminals or microcomputers with modems) are available to connect with the host computer. This is especially useful for part-time students in that decisions can be entered from a remote location thus saving time and travel costs.

If decisions are entered directly upon the team's personal floppy disk, only a compatible microcomputer is required. In this case, provisions must be made to get the disk to the game administrator prior to the simulation run. Direct data entry unlinks the simulation processing from the class meeting schedule. One or more decisions may be run between classes without physical contact between student and instructor being required. Direct entry also provides students with additional computer experience, and it relieves the administrator of the mechanical task of entering data. Thus more time is available for the creative aspects of simulation administration.

DISTRIBUTION OF GAME OUTPUT

There are two methods of distributing the game operating results produced by the computer. The output can be distributed by the administrator to each of the teams. This may be accomplished by handing the output back in class or by providing a pickup point where student teams may collect their output after a run. In either case, the output (operating results) is distributed in printed form. This method may be used even if direct decision entry is utilized.

Alternatively, the output may be stored on disk and printed upon demand by the student teams (Fritzsche, 1979). The printout may be obtained by instructing the computer to send the output to a central printer or by printing the output on a hardcopy terminal linked to the computer through direct wire or a modem. The printout may also be accessed using a microcomputer connected to a modem and a printer. If the output is stored on floppy disk, it may be printed using any compatible microcomputer and printer. As receiving the printout is not dependent upon the class schedule, it may be obtained at any location where the above equipment is available. Thus part-time students may both enter decisions and obtain printed output without going to a central location (unless floppy disks need to be exchanged). This provides a significant advantage when more than one decision period is run between class meetings.

The choice of how decisions are entered and results retrieved may depend upon the business game being used. Some games provide for only centralized decision entry and/or retrieving of results. However, many such simulations have been modified by users to provide direct operations. To learn whether such user modifications are available, the game administrator should contact the game author(s) or the game publisher.

FIRST PERIOD RUN

The time for the first period's run should be set shortly after the simulation is introduced and the teams have had a chance to develop at least a first draft of their operating plans. If centralized decision entry is used, a time must be set for the decision entry forms to be received by the game administrator. If decentralized decision entry is used, a time is set by which all of the student teams must have entered their decisions into the computer or on floppy disk. Following that time, the administrator (or the administrator's assistant) will run the simulation.

A time and place should also be specified for returning the results if printed output is to be distributed. If the game results are stored on disk and available upon demand, a time must be set when the teams can expect to obtain the current period's run.

The game can normally be run from a terminal or a microcomputer in a computer center. However, it is much more convenient and more secure to run the game from a terminal or microcomputer located in the administrator's office or home. A microcomputer (containing a modem if a mainframe game is used) is generally the most versatile device for simulation administration.

Some game administrators use the first run of the game as a practice run. They then re-run the first period after the teams have obtained the experience of making a decision and seeing the results. (See Barton, 1977 for a more complex suggestion.) This procedure would tend to be more beneficial for games which do not contain operating history. Some games will provide up to two or more years of operating history. Others simply begin with a scenario and no previous operating information. The choice of whether to use a trial run will depend upon the students' capabilities and the administrator's preference. One disadvantage of a trial run, however, is the potential negative attitude of teams who do very well on the trial run but very poorly on the first actual run.

CONTINUING THE COMPETITION

Decision Timing

Prior to running the first period of the game, a schedule should be developed for subsequent period processing. In a standard classroom setting, game periods are usually run once a week for several weeks and then run twice a week after students have become familiar with the simulation. The timing of the first decision as well as the beginning of multiple decisions per week will depend upon the number of periods of simulated play desired. Some games require a specific number of periods to be played in order for variables with long lead times to be meaningful.

It is good practice to run the game at the same time of day each period. This reduces the risk that either the student teams or the administrator will forget the running of the simulation. If centralized decision entry is used, student teams should turn in their decisions to the administrator by the specified time. If direct entry is used, teams will be responsible for entering their decisions prior to the time that the simulation is run.

The time set aside by the administrator to run the game may be significantly longer than the actual time required to run the simulation. This provides a cushion in the event that a problem occurs when the game is run.

One of the authors generally sets aside a 12-hour period prior to which the team decisions must be entered and after which the teams may print their output. The time set aside is usually from 8 P.M. until 8 A.M. During much of that time the computer is not available to the teams unless decisions are entered from off campus using a modem as the campus computer facilities close by 11 P.M. However, it provides a window in which the game can be run without hampering one's personal schedule. Of course, in this case the game is run from the author's residence using a microcomputer and a modem.

To illustrate that there is no one "correct" way, the other author plans to process the simulation immediately after the time set for student entry of decisions (usually following the end of the class period). At this time the students' interest is at a peak, and a high proportion of the students are standing by to receive the reports as soon as the game has been run. They are like sports addicts waiting to get the score on the big game of the year, and it is not uncommon to hear whoops of joy or moans of anguish while they watch their reports print out at the terminal.

While running the game over an entire quarter or semester is probably the most common schedule of game play in the academic setting, there are a number of other alternatives to consider. For example, the simulation experience may be concentrated during the last several weeks of a course or it may be condensed into a weekend or two of play. This latter method is generally used in executive development programs. The former method is used by one of the authors. The first half of the semester in the business policy and strategy course consists of lectures, class discussion, and case analysis with the simulation and related activities concentrated in the last half. Simulation processing occurs three times a week, even though class may only meet once or twice a week. Class meetings involve many small-group sessions for planning, development of comprehensive strategic plans, simulated board meetings, reports to stockholders, and critiques on game play and strategic planning. These activities are undertaken in order to reinforce the learning experience. Whatever method is used, the student teams must understand the gaming schedule so that they can plan their time commitments accordingly.

Stimulating Activities

During the course of the simulation experience, the game administrator may wish to emphasize certain business principles and constructs through the use of cases or experiential exercises. Either cases or exercises are starting to be packaged with some games. Experiential exercises can also be developed by the administrator to highlight specific issues which are deemed to be important.

Exercises generally have the advantage in that they can be tailored to specific aspects of the simulation. The game can be played a specific number of periods or until a certain situation occurs, and then an exercise can be introduced to emphasize a point or to address relevant new material. Pauses may be built into the simulation schedule for exercises, or the exercises may be utilized during the time between period runs. The exercise will typically require the teams to make a decision regarding the problem posed in the exercise. Each team may then be asked to present its decision and support the decision from the perspective of its simulated firm. After the presentations, the class may debate the strengths and weaknesses of the various team positions. Cases can be used in a somewhat similar manner.

After the game has been run for a number of periods and the decisions are starting to become somewhat routine, the initial enthusiasm may begin to wane. One way to sustain interest as well as to provide experience in crisis management is to inject a surprise into the game. This generally takes the form of some type of threat introduced into the simulated environment.

The surprise may be a strike by production workers or suppliers, a fire in the firm's plant, the announcement of a foreign competitor entering the market, or an increase in government regulation which affects the firm's cost structure, etc. Some games include suggested surprises which may be introduced. However, it is not difficult to create stimulating events for those that do not. A little imagination can provide a great many opportunities. Some surprises do not have to actually be implemented in the computer program. For example, a fire may be simulated by simply zeroing out specific entries in the team's decision file. A strike may be threatened by a labor union but may never materialize. However, if a settlement is reached, the administrator may wish to increase labor costs which can usually be easily accomplished by a change in the parameter file.

Another activity that stimulates interest and permits integration of specific course content is to ask students to prepare a written "annual report." This may be done for every simulated year or only a couple of times during the simulation. The report should emphasize the activities and/or analyses that are related to course content. Achievement or non-achievement of objectives, for example, could be highlighted with the perceived reasons why they were or were not achieved. Written reports may be supplemented or replaced with oral presentations to the "stockholders" (the other class members) or to the "board of directors" (the instructor and/or other faculty members, perhaps).

Decision Support Software

Decision support software is starting to be packaged with business games. The software usually takes the form of templates and other aids which can be used with specific spreadsheets or modeling languages which must also be available. Thus the support is only partially available with the game. One of the principal advantages of the software is that it enables student teams to use the same type of tools that are being used in the business world (Fritzsche, Rodich and Cotter, 1987). Thus students will be better prepared when they enter the job market. The possession of decision support software skills can be a competitive advantage for students searching for their first job. A second advantage is that use of the software usually enables the teams to obtain a greater depth of understanding of the business game and of the tools which are used to solve business problems.

Students can develop their own decision support software with all of the above advantages, plus that of hands-on experience of organizing and implementing their own spreadsheet models. This learning experience gives students greater skill and confidence with decision analysis than could be obtained by using preset templates prepared by someone else. After using DSS templates for analyses of several case studies, one of the authors requires students playing a general management simulation to use a spreadsheet program to develop pro forma statements and statistical models to support their forecasting and planning activities. Part of the simulation teams' business plans consists of a five-year projection of their sales, income statements, and balance sheets.

Students obtain varying levels of knowledge and skill from playing a business game which appear to be directly related to the amount of effort which they are willing to put into the game. The use of decision support software tends to enhance their knowledge acquisition for two reasons. First, they can develop a more thorough understanding of the simulation with the same level of effort by using the software. Second, the software often serves as a motivating factor which stimulates students to put additional effort into the simulation and thus further deepen their knowledge.

ENDING THE SIMULATION

Terminating the business game requires several steps. These generally include the running of the final period of the simulation, the development of analytical reports by the simulated firms, the oral presentation of the reports to a simulated stockholder's meeting, and a general debriefing discussion with the student teams.

Terminating the Computer Simulation

The administrator has two alternative methods of specifying the number of periods a game will run. One approach is to notify the student teams that they have made their last decision after the final period of the game has been run. This post announced approach will tend to eliminate end play, the unrealistic decisions which some teams make at the end of a simulation in an attempt (sometimes desperate) to try to improve their final position. If eliminating end play is to be effective, the simulation must be terminated some time prior to the last period that could be run, given the available time in the course.

End play is suspected when teams make decisions which represent a significant deviation from their past decision-making behavior and which would be unreasonable if the simulation were to continue for additional periods. For example, teams may drastically change price in order to make a huge profit, to grab a large share of the market, or to damage a competitor. They may cut advertising to the bone or fire salespeople. The objective is to improve the team's position in the last period, often to make up for relatively poor performance during the course of the game. The results of radical variable changes are hard to predict. Such decisions often end up hurting the initiating team and may distort the final period's results to the extent that innocent firms are also harmed. End play also tends to influence negatively the attitudes of students participating in the simulation experience.

The second approach to terminating the simulation is to announce the final period of the game in advance. The announcement can be accompanied with a warning that teams who engage in end play will be penalized. However, it is sometimes difficult to determine whether end play has occurred if teams are forewarned and engage in end play in an intelligent manner. The benefit of prior notification is that team members may be able to arrange their schedules more easily to accommodate the ending requirements of the game. They also know what to expect with no surprises.

Evaluation

When the simulation is completed, the administrator must evaluate the quality of play of each of the teams and provide feedback to the individual student teams. Criteria used in the evaluation process may be quantitative and/or qualitative. Regardless of the specific criteria selected, the criteria should be specified prior to the beginning of play so that the teams may direct their effort accordingly.

If quantitative criteria are utilized, the evaluation may be based upon a single criterion such as return on investment. Alternatively, the evaluation may be based upon multiple criteria dealing with the firm's operating efficiency, sales levels, profitability and financial capability. Some games include scoring algorithms which can be used to evaluate team performance (Biggs, 1978). The better algorithms allow the administrator to assign weights to the individual criterion which are used in arriving at a team's score.

The administrator may want to include some qualitative standards in the evaluation process as the quantitative criteria measure only team performance in the simulation. Students often learn as much from mistakes as from successes, and they may be more likely to remember their mistakes. However, mistakes often result in negative team performance and thus will not show up positively in the quantitative criteria. Qualitative criteria can assess the learning that takes place from both successes and failures.

Some qualitative factors which the administrator may want to consider include organizational effectiveness, the planning process, analytical methods used in decision making, and justification for decisions. Input for evaluation purposes may include a business plan focusing upon objectives and strategies, short written reports assigned during the simulation exercise and a final report at the end of the simulation. The final report may include an analysis of the firm's activities during the simulation with emphasis upon the relationship of the firm to its competitors. Each team may also evaluate how well it met its stated objectives. The important point here is for the students to understand why the objectives were not met (given their lack of experience with the simulation, this is to be expected). One may also require the teams to specify how they would modify their strategies if they were to continue playing the game after it has been terminated.

Team Presentations

In addition to the written analysis, each team may be required to hold a simulated stockholders' meeting during which time the team would provide a synopsis of its final report. The oral reports provide each team with insight into what its competitors were attempting to do during the simulation. Following each report, competing teams could serve as stockholders and question the management team. The additional questions may clarify situations which a team did not quite understand. Thus the oral reports tend to deepen the knowledge gained from the simulation. However, reports do take class time which may be in short supply.

Debriefing

After all of the simulation activities are finished, the administrator should spend some time debriefing the student teams. The debriefing may be done by meeting with each team individually or it may be done in a group setting. The group setting has several advantages. First, it is a more efficient use of the administrator's time. More importantly however, team members often learn from comments which pertain to another team's management experience. If the debriefing is held as a true discussion, the entire group format is likely to generate more discussion and student insight than the individual team format.

While there are a number of methods of debriefing, the following is one which has worked successfully in the past. During the course of the simulation, a diary is kept by the administrator of the results of each period of game play. The diary contains the administrator's perceptions of significant events by period. At the end of the simulation activity, these notes form the basis of the administrator's input to the debriefing session.

During the debriefing session, special emphasis is placed upon situations which occurred during game play that had a significant effect upon the game outcome but which the students failed to detect in their analyses. In addition, the teams' experiences during the simulation usually demonstrate specific teaching points which the administrator may wish to highlight. Finally, there are likely to be other experiences which occurred during the simulation that the administrator believes to be important and thus worthy of discussion.

The debriefing session also provides the last opportunity for students to raise questions regarding aspects of the business game experience which they may not understand. However, student questions regarding the "correct" strategy or the right decision should not be answered directly, as in most simulations "correctness" depends upon the current parameters of the simulation model interacting with the actions of the competitors.

The authors have found business gaming to be an effective and interesting pedagogical tool both for students and for administrators. We hope that our chapter coupled with others in this volume will spark the reader with the enthusiasm which we and other members of ABSEL have for business games. We extend an invitation for you to come to the next ABSEL meeting and learn more about using simulations to educate current and future business managers.

PART 3

GAME DEVELOPMENT

This section is intended for game designers as opposed to game users. Designing and programming games is an extremely time-consuming task, and a number of problems are commonly encountered. Chapter seven by Richard D. Teach discusses design issues from both a structural perspective and from their participants' perspectives. Issues such as missing participants (firms) are dealt with from a structural view rather than from an administrative view. Chapter eight by Steven C. Gold and Thomas F. Pray reviews the central role that demand functions play in large-scale simulation games and various approaches to model the demand function. It presents a robust demand function that overcomes some of the problems encountered previously.

Chapter 7: Designing Business Simulations, by Richard D. Teach

Chapter 8: Modeling Demand in Computerized Business Simulations, by Steven C. Gold and Thomas F. Pray

CHAPTER 7

DESIGNING BUSINESS SIMULATIONS

Richard D. Teach

Managers spend large amounts of their time evaluating business risks and making decisions which, hopefully, reduce these risks to the firm. The faculty in business schools are charged with training students to recognize, evaluate, and balance risks against rates of return in probabilistic terms. The same task of teaching individuals to recognize, evaluate, and balance risks is undertaken at countless business-run seminars and training sessions. Business school faculty and corporate training personnel have a variety of tools to use in accomplishing this teaching and training task, each having specific advantages in teaching skills needed in management (Teach and Govahi, 1988). The traditional lecture method has been used as has the case method. However, business games and their less formal cousins, the experiential exercises, are becoming more common in the teaching and training environments (as noted in Chapters 3, 4 and 11 of this volume), especially since microcomputer models have become available.

In the case method, one reads a scenario (usually real), defines the problem, determines a set of feasible alternatives, evaluates these alternatives in some objective manner, and selects the one that best meets the desired goals as interpreted from the case materials. The setting remains static in that new information is not available after the end of the case. In a simulation, one experiences the problems of a firm as reported in, and interpreted from, the financial and operating statements provided at the end of each round. Then one attempts to solve as many of the problems as possible in a highly dynamic situation (the situation changes with each iteration of the game) and lives with the solutions for as long as the simulation continues. In a sense, "a simulation is like a kiss, interesting to read about but much more interesting to participate in. And those that do, tend to repeat the experience" (Coote, 1987).

There are a lot of old axioms that claim that "experience is the best teacher." But, the school of hard knocks has very expensive tuition. The concept behind the use of business games for instructional purposes is that one may obtain a surrogate for experience through competing in simulations. If this is true, then the design of these simulations is critical because errors in design could lead to gaming experiences that are contrary to real world experiences and learning. This is not to say that simulations must duplicate the real world or be life-like. It means that the lessons learned from participating in simulations should reflect reality. In some firms, the belief that the ability to manage in a simulated environment is taken as a measure of an employee's ability to manage a real firm (Patton, 1987).

While the computer has not been a requirement of all competitive business simulations, its availability has provided an opportunity to incorporate a great deal of realistic complexity in these games while keeping the tasks of the administrators to a minimum (Cohen and Rhenman, 1961). Many games are mathematically simple enough that hand-held calculators can be used to determine the results of a round of play. On the other hand, while errors may occur in keying the required input for a computer, these are few when compared to the keying errors occurring when the results of games are computed with calculators, and error-trapping routines can be programmed to stop most of the input errors. The major advantage of using the computer for business simulations is not the requirements of massive calculations, but in producing the results quickly, without mathematical error, and in pre-formatted reports.

The Designer's Dilemma

Simulations and their users put designers in a quandary. Instructors want the simulation to teach or demonstrate a particular economic phenomenon, to be easy to use, and be unobtrusive to their course. Participants need some face validity and want the experience to be worth the effort and a great learning experience, as well as an enjoyable one. In a study that researched educational and video games, Malone (1981) found that the three most critical factors that must be included in a good simulation are: 1) challenge, 2) fantasy, and 3) curiosity. Conventional wisdom supports feedback and conversational dialog as the critical factors (Anderson, 1980). Malone's research showed that explicit goals that produce challenges were far more important than feedback. Fantasy has its advantages in instructional environments (Anderson, 1983).

The totality of a business setting is usually much too complex to be included in any simulation. But what should be included and what excluded? What lessons are to be learned and what knowledge is to be gained by the participants? What preparation must be undertaken by the game administrator before running the simulation? What should be the prerequisite knowledge or experiences of the participants? All of these questions must be answered by the designer prior to the construction of a useful business simulation.

CONCEPTS

Business simulations have many facets. They combine at least three concepts: simulation, games, and contests. Figure 7-1 is a simple Venn diagram showing the three types of activities which are included in the design of business simulations or games.

Simulations

According to The Second College edition of *The American Heritage Dictionary*, a simulation is "an imitation". However, in academia, the word simulation has taken on a much narrower (but frequently fragmented) meaning. In engineering and in the field of management science, simulation has been defined as, ". . . the process of designing a computerized model of a system (or process) and conducting experiments with this model for the purpose of

FIGURE 7-1
Activities Included in the Design of Business Simulations

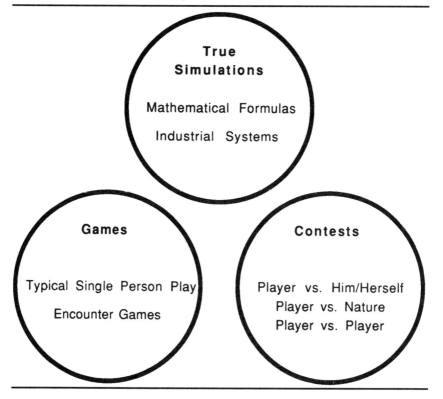

understanding the behavior of the system or of evaluating various strategies for the operation of the system" (Shannon, 1975). In this particular definition, note the linking of simulation to model building and the computer.

At the center of simulation is the concept of a system. When the term system is used in the context of a simulation, it means "the collection of objects with a well-defined set of interactions among them" (Graybeal and Pooch, 1980). In a business simulation or game, the objects are all the variables, both endogenous and exogenous, that affect the performance of any of the firms or the industry as a whole. The set of interactions are all the interrelationships or equations that determine the values of all the variables.

Games

According to the same dictionary used above, a game is defined as "a way of amusing oneself; diversion." It is also defined as "a competitive activity governed by specific rules." Let us remove the element of competition from the definition of games. What is important is that a game is an activity in which the players agree to a set of rules or conditions which govern their allowable actions in order to create a desired outcome (Suits, 1967). There is nothing said about winning. Outcomes such as laughter, fun, creativity, or embarrassment may be the goal. The rules of play are not necessarily efficient. Certainly the object of bowling is not only knocking down pins. If that were the case, one would connect two balls with a stick and roll both balls down the alley together.

Contests

A contest is defined as "a struggle for superiority or victory over rivals." The very essence of a contest is competition. The competition may be between individuals, between teams of individuals, between an individual or team and nature, and even sometimes between an individual and themselves (Shirts, 1975). If the difference between a contest and a game is identified, it is the fact that there are agreed upon rules to govern games, while pure competition defines a contest. There may be laws to govern business competition, but there are no agreed upon rules between businesses that compete. As in the film, *Butch Cassidy and the Sundance Kid,* "There are no rules in a knife fight".

Overlap of These Concepts

Figure 7-2 is a Venn Diagram showing the possible interrelationships and overlapping parts of the three concepts needed for the development of business games. The area of interest is the conjunction of all three parts.

FIGURE 7–2
A Venn Diagram of Simulations, Games, and Contests

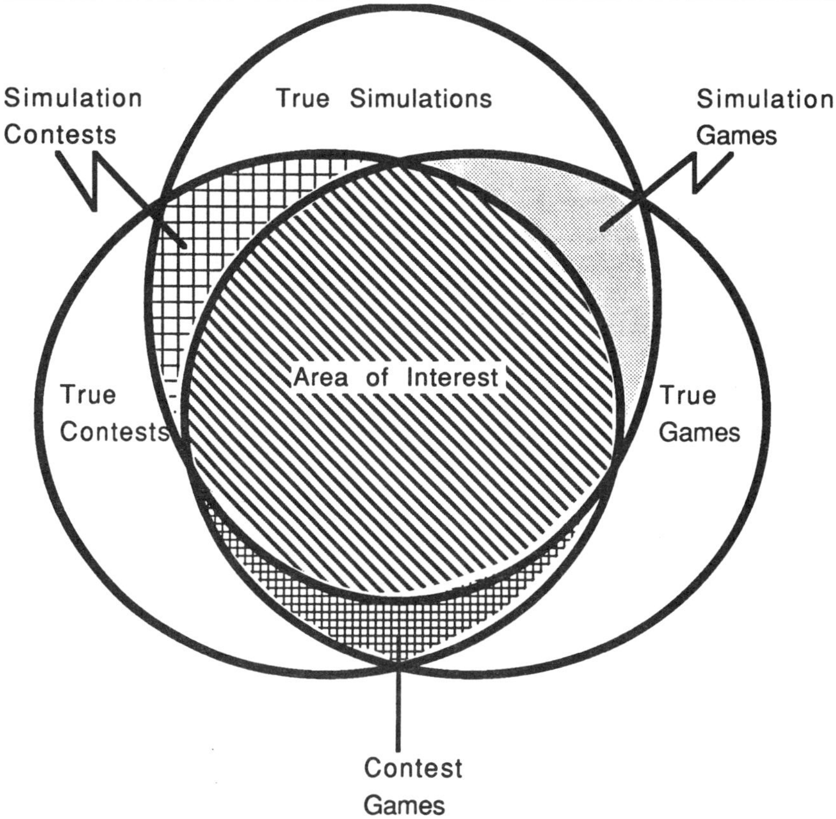

Simulation
Contests

True Simulations

Simulation
Games

True
Contests

Area of Interest

True
Games

Contest
Games

ELEMENTS OF A BUSINESS GAME

There are at least four elements found in all business simulations or games
(Armstrong and Hobson, 1969).

The Scenario

The scenario is a description of the industry that is being simulated and the
firms within the simulation. The scenario contains references to the
variables which affect the play of the game. These variables may be both
those external to the firm (seasonal and economic trends) and internal to the
firm (the decision variables themselves). Sometimes, the scenario describes
the degree of competitive interaction. Thus, the scenario is a story which

describes the economy in which the industry operates and the effect of the economy on the competing firms. In addition, it explains the potential for growth, the expected inflation rate, and what exogenous variables affect the economy (a seasonal index and/or an underlying trend). It also should explain how the endogenous variables and decision variables affect the economy: if the industry as a whole expands, does it affect the state of the simulated economy? These fundamentals must be understood to some degree by all the participants if they are to make intelligent decisions and not just input SWAGS (Scientific Wild Ass Guesses) as decisions.

There is debate on how much information to provide the participants. Insufficient information results in too much guesswork while too much information tends to overwhelm participants and results in either "analysis paralysis" or a team which gives up and guesses. Part of the answer to "How much information to provide?" is provided by the expected level of sophistication of the participants and the roles the designer expects the participants to play.

A game intended for college freshman in an introduction to business course would likely be designed with a small set of decision variables and may be an independent-across-firms simulation (that is, one in which each company is actually a monopolist). The competition between teams is based upon how well each team does against a specific environment. The results are typically reported via simple accounting statements. The analysis expected of the students might be simple cash flow calculations to determine if borrowing were necessary, estimating the price elasticities to determine the optimal price under equilibrium conditions, and simple demand forecasting to estimate manufacturing levels.

If the simulation were to be used in a senior industrial engineering class, the game would be thoroughly detailed, providing audit trails down to the machine level. Down times, amounts of scrap, maintenance costs, and operations expenses per machine would be tracked. In-process inventories at each transfer stage and product failure rates would be monitored. Decision variables would include alterations to product flows from machine to machine, as well as scheduled maintenance. It may even provide for the replacement or the removal of specific machine tools.

If the participants were expected to be mid-level executives, the interactions designed into the game might be very complex and even vague. The nature of the expected analysis of this group would likely be less statistical in nature but require more intuition than the analysis expected of college student groups.

Roles

Should participants play the role of directors of a multinational corporation, establishing policy but not reviewing operations? Should participants play a lesser role, that of operations managers, establishing sales quotas, advertising budgets, and maintenance schedules? Or, should participants manage the day-to-day activities of hiring and firing, maintaining individual machines, and managing a sales force by determining the time allocations of each brand or product in the line? Each role requires a simulation with differing amounts of detail. Designing simulations that provide aggregated data, as in monthly or quarterly financial statements with no audit trail for top managers, are much less complex than ones in which a budding marketing researcher might track the purchase histories of sample households for a specific consumer packaged-goods industry.

An Accounting System

The accounting system records each team's decisions and reports the results of the round of play in the simulation. Usually this accounting system reports the results in a set of income statements, balance sheets, and various operating reports along with some economic and competitive intelligence. The accounting systems in business simulations are considered to be aggregations of the financial and physical transactions occurring over the time period of one or more iterations of the game. However, no log is kept at the individual transaction level. Thus, invoices may not be tracked, individual bottlenecks in the production process cannot be detected, nor can the performance of specific members of the distribution channel be checked. This lack of specific information and knowledge is usually dismissed because most business games are at the "strategic" rather than the "tactical" level. However, there is no reason that more detailed records could not be included in games. With the advent of microcomputers with fast processors and large memories, transaction level information could be produced.

Algorithms

Algorithms are the operating procedures or equations which take the decisions (endogenous variables) and the simulated economic conditions (exogenous variables) as input, combine these with the historical facts on file, and calculate the outcomes or results. These procedures take into consideration the history of the past decisions by each of the firms, determine the results, and update the history file of each firm. Games with strong roles but weak scenarios and weak accounting systems are called role playing exercises. A game with a strong scenario is very similar to a case study, and games with a strong accounting procedure are called simulations (Feldt and Goodman, 1976).

PLAYER INTERACTIONS IN BUSINESS SIMULATIONS

One of the notions that is essential to a business simulation used in a classroom setting is the concurrent and active involvement of the participants. The development of interacting groups as a means of problem solving on the part of participants is a side benefit of business gaming. Groups outperform individuals working alone. Groups or teams seem to generate a number of approaches, while single individuals tend to "get into ruts". In addition, team members seem to comprehend both larger scale problems and their solutions better than do single individuals (Burton, 1987). While these interactions are intuitively felt to be an important component of business gaming, the substance of these interactions is hard to characterize. There are at least four types of interactions taking place when a business simulation is being run. These are: 1) within teams, 2) between teams, 3) between the teams and the administrator, and 4) between each team and the structure of the game (Bryant and Corless, 1986). While there are some differences of opinion about the importance of these interactions on the part of European and American simulation users, both agree that these interactions are central to all games. American business simulation users seem to "evaluate teams based on bottom line performance at the end of the simulation and determine a winner." Europeans are less concerned about "winning" and are more concerned about the "experience" (Teach, 1987a). These differences in educational culture lead to the design of very different games.

Within-Team Interactions

The contention that the dynamics of the business environment requires the involvement of others in the decision-making process lends credence to the importance of within-team interactions. In numerous situations, teams with strong group dynamics or interactions have been found to be superior to teams made up of individuals acting alone (Taylor, Berry, and Block, 1958). Simulations can be designed to encourage or discourage within-team interactions. If the output statements are simple and consolidated, it encourages strong central leadership which may result in one person running the team. If the output is complex and requires substantial additional computer manipulation, it may make the computer jock the corporate leader. If the simulation has multiple products, and the output is designed to answer product questions which reflect product-oriented decisions, the game encourages a brand-management type of interaction.

The design of the simulation output frequently determines the organizational structure and its ensuing interaction. Simulations with strong financial statements encourage those with finance or accounting backgrounds to be leaders. Games which provide detail about the manufacturing process encourage students from operations. Similar statements can be made for any other management area in which students tend to concentrate their studies. This is not to say simulations must avoid this kind of bias. But, designers and faculty, whether using simulations in the classroom or as training devices in the field, need to recognize the implication of the design upon the within-team interactions.

Between-Team Interactions

Between-team interactions differ depending upon the use of independent or dependent-across-firm simulations and the methods used to evaluate the team members and their performance. In dependent-across-firm simulations, the competition limits the interactions. Players see their corporate strategies as highly secret and as the foundation of the firm's profits. These secrets may carry over into the type of computer analysis they use or even to the types of marketing research they purchase. In these simulations, predator pricing and an attempt to drive one or more competitive firms out of business may occur. It may also be true that cooperation or outright collusion might take place. If the simulation is highly elastic in its marketing function at the firm level, but highly inelastic at the industry level, collusion is profitable.

While the simulation design affects between-team interactions, the methods of measuring performance dominate these interactions.

Interactions Between Teams and the Game Administrator

Simulations can be designed to require a large amount of support by the game administrator or the course instructor. Designs can include a provision to supply a format for news releases and bulletins to be published to all teams or, in some cases, for special messages to be sent to selected teams. Some interaction is desired but care must be taken not to overburden the game administrator.

Interaction Between a Team and the Game

Most of the interactions that take place between the team members and the simulation itself are limited to two aspects: 1) the software interface and 2) the underlying assumptions of the simulation. The software interface is the easiest to solve. Most current business simulations have used input and output devices only as means to obtain a team's decision and to display the outcomes. Little thought has been put into the design of this interface to encourage the participant or to lessen the impact of errors. There are two primary methods of decision entry. Originally, all decisions were written on a paper form, and then keyed by an assistant. Some games still use this format. As computers moved away from card formats to file formats, programs were written to replace the paper forms and to capture the decisions electronically. This is the primary method of decision entry used with desk-top or microcomputers, although many mainframe simulations have also developed input routines to record the decisions in files. In spite of this change, little thought has been given to the design of the software used to record the decisions.

The Software Interface

For simulations that provide software for decision entry, the design is important. All too many of these programs are afterthoughts. Usually written in BASIC, these programs are frequently a sequence of questions with the answers being keyed at the prompts. If an error is made and recognized, the entire sequence must be rerun. Some programs are designed to re-display the answers and give the participants one more opportunity to check their decisions before saving the data files to be used in the simulation. Some care needs to be given to the design and layout of the screen. It is not difficult to provide full-screen editors as front ends to these decision entry programs. These screens can provide the last period's decisions and ask the participant to make only the changes that are necessary. The displays could show both the names of the firms and the players, and mandatory decisions could have blinking boxes until the decisions are entered. There are many improvements that should be made to these input programs. The input programs of most business simulations remind this author of the early microcomputer programs. There have been a lot of improvements in capabilities since BASIC became a common language for microcomputer owners and the introduction of the original IBM–PC with 16K of memory, a character-oriented monitor, and a tape recorder port. Color, large amounts of memory, and fourth generation languages have increased the capabilities for improving the user interface of business simulations.

The interface between the participant and the game could be designed to enhance the learning experience. Intelligent prompts could be designed to ask questions when a decision is entered. For example, if the prices were increased, the program could ask if the team had considered the price elasticity of the product. When manufacturing levels were entered, the program could check the ending inventory levels. If they were high and the quantity to be manufactured was large, the program could provide a warning. If the students were aware of this fact, or if they were making plans for a large increase in sales, they could ignore the warning. If, however, the entry was a mistake or an oversight, a correction could be made prior to the decision, ruining what otherwise could have been good strategy but for a keying error. Making the interface smart would stimulate the level of competition and not detract from it. Intelligent interfaces could be designed to stop what are called "dumb ass mistakes," ones that can almost destroy the espirt de corps of a team. This type of error is not infrequent in running simulations. Some simulation authors and faculty claim the students should just be more careful, but that does not stop the errors.

Another type of interface could encourage students to develop a set of decision rules. One of the principles of management is management by exception; that is, making decisions in a way that allows one to spend the most effort on the hard or important decisions and very little time or effort on the routine decisions. An entry routine that contained participant defined decision rules, made suggestions based upon these decision rules, and then allowed these suggested decisions to be modified, would guide students along a path that reinforced decision-making skills. The program must have the capability for the participants to update their decision rules whenever the participants discover a better rule.

The Game Structure Interface

This interface causes substantial problems and is frequently misunderstood by both the game administrator and even the participants themselves. The problems occur when the structure or nature of the competition or the objectives of the simulation are not clearly understood by the players. If the players think there is a high degree of inter-firm competition and, in fact, the simulation is an independent-across-firms one, then lessons that the game or the instructor expect to teach will not be learned and the simulation will fail to do its job. Under these conditions, the competitively-oriented students will not perform nearly as well as less competitive students, but neither they nor their instructors may ever know why. This poor performance will not be due to bad decisions, or poor analysis, or laziness, but, instead, due to a misunderstanding of the simulation itself. The amount of time allocated to simulations is usually too short for the teams to discover the competitive structure on their own. It must be conveyed carefully and completely.

The Interaction Between the Simulation and the Course Instructor

The interaction between the simulation and the instructor determines, to a large part, the evaluation system which the instructor utilizes to appraise the performance of each participant. In the instructor's summary, the information provided to the game administrator after each run by essentially all business simulations makes direct profit comparisons easy. Because of the easy availability and the face validity of profit as an evaluation measure, most instructors use short-term or period-to-period profits as an evaluation tool. The vast majority of information provided by existing simulations is either firm profit or a derivative of firm profit. These include return on investment, return on assets, return on equity, return on sales, and earnings per share. Other values frequently reported and used as evaluation tools are sales or its by-products, including actual sales, market share, and inventory turns.

It is possible to program a report generator for the game administrator that calculated an optimum set of decisions for any one firm, given the decisions of all other firms, and report the degree of optimality attained. Single variable optimality would be very easy, but global optimality may be more difficult, depending upon the number of variables and the number of possibilities along the continuum of each variable. However, only a finite number of possibilities exists for each firm and the global optimum could be found. Such a report could be provided for each firm in the simulation. Individual firm evaluations then could be based on how far the firm's decisions were from the optimum set of decisions. This is only a short-term optimality, and would not be effective in measuring multi-period strategies, but would be greatly superior to profit comparisons.

Another reporting evaluation method would have each team forecast a set of expected outcomes resulting from the decisions. The program would report the errors in forecasting to the evaluator. This again would be easy to write into almost all existing simulations and the results could be reported in a way that direct comparisons could be made. The added input should not be difficult for most participants, as one would expect that the participants have already considered the impacts of their decisions upon the possible outcomes.

STOCHASTIC AND DETERMINISTIC MODELS

Some games are designed with stochastic elements. Certain events, such as strikes or breakdowns, take place on a probabilistic, rather than a deterministic, basis. To clarify, let me give an example. If the wage levels in a plant are below the average in the industry, the probability or likelihood of a strike at the end of the next operating period is 25%. If, however, the wages are below the average but a higher-than-average increase is given, even if the after-increase wage is below average, the probability of a strike in the next operating period is only 10%. Since events take place in probability, it is impossible to make direct comparisons across teams. What may happen after one set of decisions would not necessarily be the same if the identical circumstances were to occur again. While this may be realistic in actual firms, evaluating participants by direct comparisons under these circumstances is akin to grading based upon the toss of a fair coin, something most evaluators are loath to do. Between-team comparisons should be made only when the outcomes are determined by the decisions of each team and by the interactions of the decisions of one team with the other participating teams.

While not particularly realistic, most business simulations do not have major events triggered by stochastic processes. The guidelines provided to the players usually state explicit rules. Using the above example of a labor strike: If a firm's labor rates fall 25% below the industry, a strike will take place at the end of the current decision period unless an above average wage increase is given. This type of constraint removes the uncertainty of such an event. If a team wants to avoid a strike, it knows exactly the decision that must be made. Under the exact same circumstances, the same outcomes would occur. With the uncertainty removed, valid comparisons can be made.

If the game designer expects or intends that direct comparisons of outcomes will be used as evaluations, then stochastic events need to be avoided. If the goal is to provide a more true-to-life simulation and if direct comparisons of outcomes are not used as evaluation criteria for the participants, then stochastic events may be included in the game design.

SPECIFYING INITIAL DESIGN PARAMETERS

Many of the concepts discussed in this section were suggested by Duke (1974).

Defining the Problem

Before a business simulation is designed, there are a series of questions that must be answered, for instance, "Who is to be the client or user?" The game designed for use in an introduction to business course would be expected to be much less complex than one designed for a graduate level business policy course. The degree of face validity would need to be different as well as the complexity of the decision making.

The purpose of the simulation must be defined. Is the game to be used in an educational institution? Is it to be designed: 1) to convey the basic principles of business, 2) to be an instrument to provide dynamic and unique data for other computer programs, 3) to teach strategic planning to graduate students, or 4) is it to be designed to establish dialog between players and to promote creativity? If the simulation is to have more than a single purpose, then each purpose needs to be defined explicitly and its priority determined.

The subject matter which the simulation is to address must be well defined. Is its subject matter to reflect the total enterprise or just one or more functional areas? If the game is to be a functional game, how many decisions outside the particular functional area need to be addressed? This author has used many functional simulations in the field of marketing. Frequently, the lack of non-marketing decisions has reduced the face validity to a level that the participants no longer respond in the desired manner. For instance, the inability to remove excess cash in a marketing game sometimes provides the players with the excuse of not paying attention to the marginal rates of return. They have the cash, so why not spend it?

The intended audience, both the players and the administrators, must be considered. Will the players have similar educational prerequisites, backgrounds, and abilities? What levels of computer literacy are expected from the players and/or the administrators?

It is necessary for the designer to understand the context in which the game is to be considered for use. Will the game be the central focus or used only as a supplement to a course? Will the context be an academic or industrial training one? Over how many plays or periods will the simulation be run? The number of iterations possible in a ten-week quarter may be much less than during a sixteen-week semester, even if the number of class meetings are similar. Will the same players have repeated exposures to the game in multiple classes or training programs, or will the players see it only once?

The resource constraints on the part of the simulation developer need to be understood. Many textbook authors complain that the expected time needed to complete their work was grossly underestimated. In software development, the problem is worse. Both the financial and time commitments for proper business simulation development, programming, and testing can be very great. In writing a textbook, the cost of abandonment is measured as wasted time. In a business simulation, thousands of dollars of out-of-pocket expenses may be involved, in addition to the wasted time.

The communication medium of a business simulation is the game itself, or in the words of Marshall McLuhan, ". . The Medium is the Message." As such, we must expect all users to have some affinity for computers.

BUSINESS SIMULATIONS FROM A STUDENT PERSPECTIVE

In cases where they have been asked, students support the use of simulations as a teaching tool. It helps them understand the dynamics of business situations and motivates them in their course work (Ritchken and Getts, 1985).

Face validity is very important for most student players. If the simulation reports realistic "facts" and reacts to decisions in ways that the players think represent the real-world counterpart of the game, then most of them are willing to give the time and effort required to complete the assignments as they were intended (McLaughlin and Bryant, 1986). If non-realistic parameters are defined, such as when the salvage value of plant and equipment is greater than the replacement costs for the same capacity of plant and equipment, the players may take the playing of the simulation with less zeal than the administrator desires (Bornstein, Heapy, Milam, and Teach, 1987).

Bornstein et al. (1987) also cited issues of judging or determining "winners" as a concern of students. Was the determination of performance entirely within the context of the simulation or were factors not included in the simulation used as a basis for rating a team's performance? This issue can be critical when performance on the insinuated winning factors and the outside factors are in conflict. One should note that the students' perspectives may conflict with either the administrator's and/or the simulation designer's.

Widgets vs. Industry Specific Games

The majority of business games have been written to simulate general competitive situations. They do not purport to model a specific industry but frequently provide an industry-specific scenario to assist the decision-making. Some provide a scenario that describes a particular industry, such as the *Marketing in Action* game (Ness and Day, 1987), which represents the soft drink industry. Others suggest parameter changes to represent a variety of industries as does the *Business Management Laboratory* (Jensen and Cherrington, 1984). Others state, "the computer program reflects the workings of an imaginary consumer goods industry, and . . . is not intended to reflect the specifics of any particular real-life industry" (Henshaw and Jackson, 1978). Some of the games refer to products in a generic sense such as, "Product A is sold in a completed state with your brand on it. . . ., Product B is an industrial good bought directly from your plant on the basis of price and quality . . ." (Keys and Leftwich, 1985). The best of these non-industry specific simulations provide a very general economic condition of an oligopoly; i.e., the price elasticity is greater at the firm level than at the industry level. However, even here, a large number of business simulations do not conform to this general economic constraint (see Gold and Pray, 1983). The intent of these games is to conform to theoretically derived models of general industrial economic structure (Porter, 1980).

An alternative approach to developing theoretic economic models is to observe marketplace activity and develop a model that reproduces the observed output whenever the input agrees with or matches the industry observed input. This has been referred to as a "black-box" method (Golden,

1988). In these black-box models, an input-output interface is developed that emulates the desired relationships in the industry that is being simulated. It must be realized that one cannot generalize these simulations from the specific industry modeled to other industries or to other periods of time in which the economic relationships may have changed. The PIMS (Profit Impact in Marketing Strategies) data base held by the Marketing Science Institute may be used to observe the desired relationships within an industry. Lubatkin and Pitts (1983) concluded from a study of the PIMS data that industry specific models are better able to model performance than generalized economic models. Generalized economic models were seen as applicable only to the industry leaders.

Generalized economic models look and behave in very predictable ways. They tend to allow unlimited freedom in firm behavior and individual decisions. Unconstrained decision-making may make the model act quite differently than any actually observed outcomes. Thus the realism, or assumed realism on the part of the players, may be destroyed by the behavior of a single participant. Industry specific simulations, while harder to control, are generally accepted by students and provide more satisfaction with the play of the simulation. In university environments, one is to teach general lessons from industry specific models, not lessons directly associated with a single industry. In corporate environments, industry specific models are used because the lessons to be learned are specific, not general, in nature.

BUSINESS SIMULATIONS FROM A FACULTY PERSPECTIVE

In some colleges, business simulations are used at the freshman or sophomore level as an introduction to business. Here, the objective might be to provide students with opportunities to:

1. Gain an appreciation of the profit motive and competition in the free enterprise system,
2. Acquire a basic understanding of the major functional activities,
3. Gain an awareness of themselves in the areas of interest, attitude, and the attitude associated with success in ownership, management, labor and sales roles in manufacturing enterprises,
4. Acquire practical experience associated with career roles exercised in these enterprises, and
5. Gain a positive mental attitude, which is essential for a happy, successful career in life (Selvidge, 1987).

This is a tall order for any business game.

Situations may exist where a firm is sponsoring or subsidizing a set of runs of a business simulation and it is desirable to represent the sponsoring firm in the simulation. This may be especially true if a firm is using the simulation for its own executive training. It is possible to enrich the simulated environment by designing a simulation that allows for multiple markets and products outside of its normal operating mode. One such game is *Imaginit* (Barton, 1984) and its extension *Multiple Imaginit* (Barton, 1987).

Frequently, instructors use business simulations and introduce analytical techniques for the participants to use to help solve problems that come up during the game. For example, forecasting techniques are very useful skills to have or learn while participating in a simulation (Chiesel, 1987). Skills, such as fluency in the use of *Lotus 1-2-3*, can be taught explicitly as a separate tool used in conjunction with a simulation exercise or implicitly by "allowing" the participants to use the approaches as they play the game (see Anderson and Lawton, 1986; Dolich, 1984; and Sherrell, Russ, and Burns, 1986). The use of out-of-game software may be used in the analysis of the output of a business simulation for pricing (Rubin, 1987) or Materials Requirements Planning (Schroeder and Gentry, 1987). These computer skills have proven to be very practical ones to have when the participants are interviewing for a new job.

For some users of simulation, the degree of realism is very important. Curran and Hornaday (1987) stated, "Top management or functionally integrated simulation games are often used within a business policy/strategic management course to provide students with some semblance of what is entailed in running a 'real world' corporation." But critics point out that simulations based upon quarterly, or even monthly, decision periods are much too unrealistic and simplistic. Simulations tend to have fixed, rather than continuously changing, environments (Chiesel, 1986). Many simulations rely upon a constant cost structure, providing subtle but erroneous assumptions regarding the behavior of costs in actual firms (Teach, 1986).

Designing Business Simulations for Research Purposes

It is anticipated that future uses of business simulations will include a wide range of research topics, especially if the game designs can be more "open" (Patz, 1987). Games are considered open when the algorithms that determine the outcomes emerge as a result of the decisions and do not constrain the decisions. Because of this changing nature of the game itself, the administrator becomes a participant and not just an observer or referee.

Designing Games for Ease of Use

The ease of use is a primary concern to instructors. Games have oftentimes been added to a course which already consumes all the time students expect to spend on it. Thus, the amount of time an instructor needs to prepare the students properly before beginning a business simulation is often a hindrance to the adoption of a game. Administrative and/or logistical problems have been cited as reasons that as many as 25% of business faculty either dropped, or did not use, simulations as a part of their pedagogy (Keeffe and Cozan, 1985).

BUSINESS SIMULATIONS FROM A DESIGNER'S PERSPECTIVE

It has been claimed that designers ". . . all have a common objective of making their model as realistic as possible at a chosen level of sophistication" (Decker, LaBarre and Adler, 1987). This author disagrees. One must understand the purpose of the game, and if a high degree of realism is called for in successfully carrying out this purpose, then realism is desired. But sometimes realism may get in the way of teaching the desired lesson, and the cost of realism is not worth its benefit. As in business, the design of business simulations is a series of trade-offs. One employs his or her resources at the margin. It is how well the simulation meets its stated purposes, not its apparent realism, that is important.

Algorithms

There have been numerous articles in ABSEL Proceedings and in *Simulation and Games* which detail the algorithms used in business games which model a manufacturing environment.

Single Product Algorithms
The widely cited, single-product, industry-demand generator is an econometric model which has variable elasticities for the independent variables (Gold and Pray, 1983). This type of algorithm is discussed in detail in the next chapter. The same authors go on to show how the same general model, used with different parameters, can handle the allocation of industry demand among the competitors in the simulation.

An exponential logarithmic function with an upper bound has been suggested to represent independent variables which show declining or increasing returns to scale (Decker, LeBarre, and Adler, 1987). A rather ingenious method to calculate bivariate relationships is to graph the desired functional relationship and to interpolate from the graph for game builders who are not familiar with complex functional shapes has been detailed (Goosen, 1986).

Market Segmented, Differentiated Product Demand Algorithms
The vast majority of dependent-across-firms business simulations allocate demand by assuming that the products are perfect, or near perfect,

substitutes for one another (Pray and Gold, 1981). Industry demand is a function of average prices (either harmonic or arithmetic means), total advertising expenditures, and the combined number of individuals in the sales force. Firm demand is a function of relative price, relative advertising, and relative sales force. The degree of competition depends on the differences in elasticities between the total market demand and the firm level of demand. Some games include a quality variable, but in the form of a marketing variable rather than a product attribute. Some games allow for products to have physical or attribute differences. But only a few business simulations provide environments with different market segments, each with product demands that are dependent upon product attributes. *Markstrat* (Larreche and Gatignon, 1977), which models the consumer package goods industry, was the first such simulation known to this author. *Markstrat* contains five unique market segments and one can vary the products across six physical characteristics. *Industrat,* the same general simulation as *Markstrat,* represents an industrial marketplace (Larreche and Weinstein, 1988). Both of these simulations are very sophisticated and require substantial marketing experience prior to participating in the game. A simulation released in 1988 (Ayal and Zif) has product differentiation, but no true segmentation. The same holds for *Marketing in Action* (Ness and Day, 1985).

In order to produce interactions between product attributes and market segments and have these effects interact with the economic variables of price, advertising, etc., new approaches to demand algorithms are needed. The details of *Markstrat* or *Industrat* have not been published, to the knowledge of this author. Teach (1984) described a simplistic approach to simultaneously including product attributes and market segments in a set of demand equations, but has not published any new material on the subject.

The Use of Software External to the Simulation

There is substantial interest on the part of game designers to have participants use what is best described as decision support software as a tool in analyzing the output of a business simulation (see Fritzsche, Rodich, and Cotter, 1987). These tools generally include spreadsheet programs (*Lotus1-2-3* or others), data base managers (*dBase 3* or *Reflex: The Analyst*), or statistical packages (SPSS, mainframe or microcomputer version, *StatView,* or *Systat*). Newer proposals include the use of modeling languages such as Interactive Financial Planning System (IFPS). One business simulation, *The Business Management Laboratory* (Jensen and Cherrington, 1984), has had a decision support system built into it. This DSS package, entitled *System Laboratory for Information Management (SLIM),* is quite extensive (Courtney and Jensen, 1981). The integration of Decision Support Systems

(DDS) into business simulation software should be considered in the simulation design. This insures that the file structures can be imported into the required or suggested programs with little cause for errors. Of course, many participants simply re-type the data into the external programs, but there are always errors in keying.

GOOD AND BAD ASPECTS OF GAME DESIGN

Confucius had a comment that may describe the learning that takes place when one participates in a business simulation. He said, "If I hear, I forget. If I see, I remember. If I do, I understand." This has strong implications to the design of a business simulation. Simulations are powerful conveyers of lessons and it behooves the designers to "get it right." While there are legitimate differences in theories, many simulation writers have included poor or incorrect economic principles in their game. Lambert and Lambert (1988) discussed an all too common problem in many games, the response to advertising function. Many authors have included portions of the advertising-demand relations to be inverted. That is, demand is decreasing and advertising is increasing under ceteris paribus conditions. While this has neither theoretical nor empirical support, it is based upon a convenient equation.

Another general assumption in most business simulations designed by people in the United States is the assumption that the labor costs in manufacturing are entirely variable. The labor component of the product is usually constant (per unit) over large ranges of scheduled production. (This is almost never true of games designed by Europeans.) The most insidious form of this distortion is that most simulations allow total freedom in scheduling production. As a result, the participants soon learn to use frequent changes in production levels as a substitute for effective planning and forecasting. They can, in effect, cover up their errors and let the labor force pay for their mistakes.

In some simulations, certain variables take on very unrealistic power that players can neither detect nor do research to ascertain. In one popular marketing simulation, the R&D function is so important in the opening few rounds that small differences in these early budgets dominate the outcomes many periods later. Participants pass this secret around to their friends who take the course later. This reinforces the idea that it takes only a few tricks to run a company. Finding important information from illegal sources or in serendipitous ways appears to be better than spending money on research. This is not the lesson most want to reinforce.

In a leading international simulation, where each firm has facilities in up to three different countries, the participants are led to the conclusion that they can exploit the workers of one country simply because of a company loyalty factor built into the game for Japan. Players are sometimes told "to consider this factor," thus encouraging the Ugly American syndrome. If such "cultural awareness" is important, then the designers must incorporate it into the simulation.

MEASURING THE RESULTS

A study of ten business simulations used in business policy/strategic management courses showed that there is not a common method for measuring team performance (Pray and Gold, 1987). The ten games had different performance measures, and only two had the single criterion of overall profit. This lack of commonality may be the reason that there has been very little correlation between the results in the business simulations used in the classrooms and the performance of simulation participants studied on the job after graduation. Another reason may be that the indicators of performance provided by the game designers are the wrong ones. It may be that some intermediate measures are better indicators of performance than the ones commonly provided. Teach (1989) demonstrated that the forecasting ability of the management team was a forerunner to performance. The ability to forecast does measure one's ability to manage a simulated business because, without accurate forecasts, one does not know nor anticipate the conditions in future periods. This knowledge is a prerequisite to either strategy or tactics.

Many students become excited, and some obsessed, with business simulations. In fact, a simulation user must be somewhat careful or the students will devote so much time to the game that his or her other classes may suffer. However, there are some students who refuse to participate if they can drop the course or who become a non-functioning member of the team playing the simulation. Motivation levels are usually obvious, but what the students learned and how effective the simulations are in teaching the desired concepts are much less apparent.

In a study of recent graduates from many colleges and universities, Teach and Govahi (1988) found that simulations convey different skills to young managers than do other teaching methodologies. This study did not investigate the issue of effectiveness. After an extensive study of the teaching effectiveness of business simulations, Wolfe (1985) noted ". . it is still not known how realistic a game must be to be an effective learning experience."

SOME CONCEPTS FOR FUTURE THINKING

Currently, games are designed around an accounting cycle. Either monthly, quarterly, or annual decision periods are defined for a specific game and this single reporting and accounting cycle is used for all the decisions in the game. Why? This author speculates that this phenomenon was started when the original business games were built and has rarely been challenged. As mentioned before, business simulations had their start in the late '50s and in the early '60s. Computers which needed to do all the accounting were batch-processing machines. Thus, one needed to tie the decision periods to the accounting cycle, and all decisions had to be made on the same cycle. However, the vast majority of actual business decisions are not tied to, nor even associated with, the accounting cycle. The Chiesl chapter (chapter 9) in this volume introduces a solution to this problem.

Another challenge for simulation designers is to provide environments where all firms do not start out as identical firms, with the explicit, or even implicit, goals of maximizing profits in the short run. The assumption that all firms are equal in assets, product lines, and market power is not only an unrealistic one, but stifles both the design of the game and player's decisions (Teach, 1987b). Actual firms manufacture products that may or may not compete with all the other firms considered to be competitors.

Rarely, if ever, is there a perfect match among products within competing firms. What must be measured is the performance on a set of goals as defined by the participants in a simulation and not defined by the game designer. If the design of business simulations can be developed to a point in which variations in asset structure, market power, and competitive advantage across differing product lines are incorporated, then multidimensional measures of success must follow. Pray and Gold (1987) introduced an interesting concept on measuring, weighing, and combining different goals to produce a single performance measure. Their paper went on to claim:

> The evaluation criterion presented in this paper offers a number of advantages over the approaches currently utilized in existing business simulations. Firms are allowed to begin the simulation with different financial and operating characteristics. Given these different starting characteristics, firms select their own objectives and set different goals from each objective. Furthermore, the relative importance of each objective is specified by each firm through a 'weighting' factor. The simulation algorithm then evaluates: (1) the extent to which each firm achieves its goals, (2) the relative difficulty of the goals set by each firm, and (3) the comparative performance of each firm in relation to the competition. These measures of comparative performance do not provide a strict ranking but do segregate firms into different groups based on difficulty indices (Pray and Gold, 1987).

Separating Decision Periods from Reporting Cycles

While business simulation designers and writers like to comment on how realistic their games are, the truth is that very few simulations are even close to reality. The main reason for this lack of realism is the shackling of the decision-making to the reporting or accounting cycle. How realistic is it to have simulated clock stop, to have perfect financial and operations statements be made available, and to have all the marketing research that was requested, regardless of its difficulty, be made available at the end of the last day of the period? Another ridiculous situation is that every firm receives their data at the same time and no further competition takes place until all participants make either new decisions or have repeated old ones, again all at the same moment in time. Then, and only then, does the competition begin and run, without interruption, until the end of the next accounting cycle.

Transaction Based Simulations

If one quizzes a simulation participant who has not had previous business experience about an invoice, it becomes apparent that few have any comprehension of the importance of such a document, or even its very existence. Another important concept, typically called the 80-20 rule, is rarely known. Why do 20 percent of the customers or accounts supply 80 percent of the profits? Which 20 percent of the customers are the most profitable? A famous quote states, "I know one half of my advertising dollars are wasted, but I just don't know which half." This statement has no relevance to current business simulation players. Business simulation players never develop the concept that company sales are the result of many individual transactions, and that manufacturing is a complex, but controllable process. Today's powerful desktop computers and the availability of easy-to-use database software make transaction-based simulations a real possibility. Languages such as Simscript or GPSS have been used for years in industrial engineering to simulate processes which have queues associated with them. However, these languages have not been used to model competitive behavior, which is at the heart of business gaming.

Fuhs (1988) noticed similarities between database structures and business simulation and developed a method of diagramming the relationships in simulation games. All that remains is to design and code an event-driven business simulation. Again, this logic is consistent with the direction suggested by Chiesl in chapter 9.

Incorporating Behavioral and Cultural Variables

If a business simulation that emphasizes cultural aspects is to be designed, a new game paradigm needs to be established. This new game design must allow cultural differences to be readily noted and identified, and then the effects of the cultural differences upon the operations of the simulated industry operations to be made known directly or through out-of-class research. In addition, if the game is to be used in the undergraduate classroom, it must be easy to comprehend by the students and simple to administer by the faculty member (Teach, 1988). In order to be manageable, the set of different cultures must be limited. A simulation could be constructed where each firm operated under a different culture. Cultural issues could include simple things like sharing or restricting information, stressing the importance of continued employment in the labor markets, or of accounting rule differences. Under this new design, comparison of outcomes between firms would be counter-productive. Personnel would be transferred between teams or companies. This transfer between teams is comparable to executive transfers between a firm's divisions. It is also comparable to a situation in which an executive is hired by a competitor.

If the goals of an inter-cultural simulation are the recognition and a better understanding of cultural effects, then the evaluation of the participants needs to be linked to that understanding. This is not to exclude firm performance from the evaluation but to include more than short-term profit performance.

SUMMARY

Good design is a necessary but not sufficient condition of a business simulation. Unless the designer considers the ramifications of the various design issues, those who use the games may not accomplish their desired goals. In addition, a potentially more troublesome issue is that the participants learn the wrong lessons. They may learn counter-productive behaviors, measurement tools, and analytical methods. Designers must consider the goals of the simulation, the expected skill level of the participants, the techniques that are to be used to evaluate the players, and the tools the users are expected to apply when running the simulations. Using the wrong simulations in the wrong situations can be disastrous. This author proposes that, as with dangerous toys, designers put their conditions and built-in assumptions, including valid evaluation procedures, on the outside of the box, where all potential adopters can find them.

CHAPTER 8

MODELING DEMAND IN COMPUTERIZED BUSINESS SIMULATIONS

Steven C. Gold
Thomas F. Pray

ABSTRACT

The modeling of demand plays a critical role in the proper functioning of business simulations. Although the properties described by modern demand theory are well known, the task of incorporating these relationships in a computerized simulation and obtaining stable and consistent results under a multitude of scenarios is not straightforward. To facilitate the design, development, and use of computerized business simulations, the internal algorithms used to model demand in a competitive market are scrutinized.

The chapter begins by highlighting the properties of modern demand theory that are most important to modeling demand functions. These properties include: variable price elasticities, increasing and decreasing returns, inflection points, and interdependencies between demand variables. The types of functions utilized by simulation designers to obtain the desired demand properties are reviewed. The functional forms are divided into three major categories: linear, nonlinear, and log-linear. The characteristics of these functions are discussed and the strengths and weaknesses identified. Taking account of these concerns, a robust demand system, composed of ten equations, is presented. The recommended demand system is shown to be stable and possess the following elements: both industry and firm level demand functions with variable elasticities, the use of a harmonic mean, exponential smoothing to incorporate intertemporal considerations, and a current period stockout reallocation scheme with statistical checks on faulty decision inputs.

The chapter concludes with three numerical examples demonstrating the use and flexibility of the system. The examples illustrate how the parameters of the system can be derived by specifying the desired elasticities and inflection points, and how the system handles excessive stockouts. The examples focus on price, promotion, and R & D expenditures, but can be easily generalized to include any number of demand factors.

INTRODUCTION

At the 1981 ABSEL conference a paper presented by Kenneth G. Goosen emphasized the need to expand the research concerning the internal design or modeling of computerized business simulations. He noted that the current and past papers presented at ABSEL do *not* provide enough information to help designers develop simulations in an efficient and effective manner and concluded:

> The designing and developing of simulations . . . appears to be primarily an art form, a creative skill based on intuitive feel rather than acquired knowledge.

Up until that point in time very little information on the design of a simulation was shared. Of particular importance in the design of a simulation is the modeling of the demand system. Many demand-oriented questions were being raised, but either left unanswered or answered through trial and error by the designer. Some typical questions would include: How does one mathematically specify a market demand curve? How are the non-price factors modeled in a business simulation? Do the simulation functions have the properties described by modern demand theory? What are the advantages and disadvantages of alternative modeling approaches?

In addition to the designer's concern for such questions, users of existing games often want to modify the simulation to eliminate conventional wisdom that often occurs after several semesters of play. Sometimes this may be easily accomplished through the use of parameter records and variable parameters. Often, however, the modifications require alterations to the program itself. An understanding of the modeling process and functions can help to answer the user-based questions such as: Why was there such instability in price in this simulation? Why did all the firms spend so much on advertising and/or research and development? What can the administrator do to discourage or eliminate decisions that are unrealistic and meant to "beat the game?"

Business and management simulations, in particular, are modeled to represent the "real world" firm and market environment. Participants are supposed to gain insight into the workings of the "real world" by participating in the simulation. As a result, it is necessary for the functions and algorithms contained within the simulation to be at least consistent with economic, managerial, and financial relationships found in the business world. Although these underlying principles and theories explaining the "real world" phenomenon are well-known, the task of precisely modeling and quantifying these relationships in a simulation is not straightforward. Understanding the pros and cons of different functional forms can vastly facilitate the modeling process and ensure realistic simulation results. A proper appreciation by designers and users of the different modeling approaches can also prevent games from yielding unrealistic results (i.e. blowing up!).

In this chapter, we review, summarize, and update a series of market-level and firm-level demand-oriented modeling articles and papers that we have presented at ABSEL and/or published in SAGA.

PURPOSE

The purpose of the chapter is to:

(1) Review the theory of demand, focusing on both price and non-price factors and their elasticities and inflection points.

(2) Summarize the three major functional forms (e.g. linear, nonlinear, and multiplicative) which have been used by computerized business simulation designers to model demand. Illustrative examples are given, noting both strengths and weaknesses of the algorithms.

(3) Examine the Gold and Pray (1984) robust demand system which is a system of equations that embodies a number of key theoretical properties and practical issues including: (i) a multiplicative (power) industry demand function that incorporates the principle of interdependent marginal impacts, where the marginal return depends on the level of other variables such as price and R&D; (ii) variable elasticities for one or more of the independent variables; (iii) increasing and diminishing returns to any variable and at any desired inflection point; (iv) minimizing or eliminating the impact of irrational or faulty demand-oriented decision inputs on total market demand determination; (v) exponential smoothing to recognize intertemporal movements in the decision variables; (vi) an intrinsic stockout adjustment routine which reallocates, in the same decision period, excessive stockouts to other firms in the industry; (vii) a multiplicative variable elasticity firm-level demand equation which is used to allocate total market sales to each firm.

(4) Detail the equations (derived from the robust demand system) which are needed to derive the parameters of the system. The parameters are based on the designer's apriori specifications relating to the inflection point, and the market and firm-level price and non-price elasticities.

(5) Demonstrate how the demand system works with three different examples: (i) determining the parameters of the system given a range of elasticities and then simulating the function, (ii) determining the parameters of the system given a specified point of inflection on advertising, and, (iii) checking for and reallocating firm-level excessive demand with the intrinsic stockout routine.

DEMAND THEORY

For a business simulation to be realistic, it is necessary for the demand function to be consistent with economic theory. In this section the properties of modern demand theory will be reviewed.

Demand is a function of price, as well as a number of non-price factors which include: marketing (i.e., advertising and promotion), product quality (i.e., research and development), prices of related goods (i.e., substitute and complementary goods), consumer income, other factors (i.e., expectations, demographics, etc.). Mathematically, demand is specified as follows:

$$Q = f (P, M, R, P_s, P_c, Y, O)$$

where: Q = quantity of goods demanded
P = price of the good
M = marketing expenditures
R = research and development expenditures
P_s = price of the substitute good
P_c = price of the complement good
Y = income of the consumer
O = other important factors

Law of Demand

The Law of Demand states that quantity demanded is inversely related to the price of the good. As price increases, the quantity demanded decreases; or conversely, as price decreases, quantity demanded increases. In this case, the partial derivative of quantity demanded with respect to price is less than zero:

$$dQ/dP < 0$$

It is important to emphasize that this relationship assumes other demand factors are held constant, that is, there is no change in marketing, R&D, or other variables.

Price Elasticity of Demand

The sensitivity of quantity demanded to changes in price is measured by the price elasticity of demand. The price elasticity of demand is defined as the percent change in quantity demanded due to a percent change in price. The formula for price elasticity (E_p) is given as:

$$E_p = (dQ/dP) (P/Q)$$

The price elasticity of demand is negative since $dQ/dP < 0$. As a result a percent increase in price will cause the quantity demanded to decrease by a certain percentage based on the value of the elasticity. The value of the price elasticity depends on whether the demand for the good is inelastic, elastic, or unit elastic, that is:

$$-1 < E_p < 0 \quad \text{(inelastic demand)}$$

$$E_p = -1 \quad \text{(unit elastic demand)}$$

$$E_p < -1 \quad \text{(elastic demand)}$$

Generally, demand is characterized by variable price elasticity. At relatively low price levels, demand is price inelastic; but at relatively high price levels demand becomes price elastic. This characteristic even holds for linear demand functions since dQ/dP is constant and, as price rises, the ratio P/Q increases.

Marketing, R&D, and Demand

There is a positive relationship between marketing (or R&D) and quantity demanded. As expenditures on marketing (or R&D) rise, the quantity demanded increases (assuming other factors, like product price, are held constant). Mathematically, the partial derivatives are greater than zero:

$$dQ/dM > 0$$
$$dQ/dR > 0$$

Furthermore, demand is characterized by increasing, constant, and decreasing returns to marketing and R&D. At low levels of marketing, increasing returns can be expected. Increasing returns to marketing means the quantity demanded will increase at an increasing rate with increases in marketing expenditures. But there is a point of diminishing returns. After this point, demand will increase at a decreasing rate with increases in marketing. This property requires the following second order conditions:

$$d^2Q/dM^2 > 0 \; ; \; d^2Q/dR^2 > 0 \quad \text{(increasing returns)}$$

$$d^2Q/dM^2 = 0 \; ; \; d^2Q/dR^2 = 0 \quad \text{(constant returns)}$$

$$d^2Q/dM^2 < 0 \; ; \; d^2Q/dR^2 < 0 \quad \text{(decreasing returns)}$$

The general relationship between marketing and demand is illustrated graphically in figure 8-1. The relationship also holds for R&D.

At low levels of marketing, between 0 and M_e, demand is characterized by increasing returns, i.e., the slope of the function (dQ/dM) rises with increases in marketing. The point of diminishing returns occurs at expenditure level M_e (point E). This is commonly referred to as the "inflection point" of the function. After point E, additional expenditures on marketing will realize decreasing returns, i.e., quantity demanded will increase but at a decreasing rate, and the slope of the function (dQ/dM) declines.

FIGURE 8–1.
Increasing and Decreasing Returns to Marketing

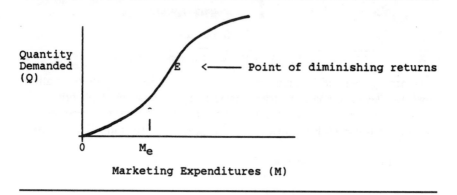

Quantity Demanded (Q)

E <——— Point of diminishing returns

0   M_e

Marketing Expenditures (M)

REVIEW OF SIMULATION DEMAND MODELING

This section addresses the issue of how demand functions are modeled in contemporary business simulations. Papers by Pray and Gold (1982) and Gold and Pray (1984) examined the underlying functional forms and properties embodied in ten business simulations. Their selection was based on three criteria: (1) the utilization of a demand function; (2) the inclusion of price and non-price factors; and (3) the availability of a source listing of the computer software program. It was shown that three types of functional forms were commonly utilized: linear, nonlinear, and log-linear. Representative examples of each of these functional forms are given below and the advantages and disadvantages are summarized.

Linear Demand Function

A representative linear function may be expressed as follows:

$$Q = a - bP + cM + eR$$

This form constrains the marginal impacts of each independent variable to be constant and independent of the values for marketing or research and development. The marginal impact of price (P) is always "$-b$" and the marginal impact of marketing (M) is always "c". Although this permits variable price elasticity, it does not allow increasing or diminishing returns to either marketing or research and development (R) variables. Furthermore, price elasticity may vary rapidly with changes in price and is very sensitive to the value selected for "b".

Nonlinear Demand Function

Nonlinear demand functions have a wide range of functional forms. The properties of these functions vary significantly depending on the precise nature of the selected form. To illustrate this form, a popular, widely used, contemporary simulation has been selected:

$$Q = (a + bCP + cM + eR) / P^f$$

where: C = percent commission on sales (a decision variable
that is specified by the participant or student user)

The marginal impact on demand with respect to changes in price is:

$$dQ/dP = -f(a + bCP + cM + eR) P^{(f-1)} + bC/P^f$$

In this case the marginal impact of price (dQ/dP) could be either negative or positive, and will vary significantly, up or down, depending on the values of the independent variables. Sensitivity analysis has shown this function to be unstable, and the results to be inconsistent with modern demand theory, unless input constraints are imposed on the decision variables specified by the simulation user and the parameter values (a,b,c,e,f) are very carefully selected. Simulations with nonlinear demand functions were found to be the most unreliable and unpredictable.

Log-Linear Demand Function

The log-linear form was the most common and may be expressed as follows:

$$Q = a P^{-b} M^c R^e$$

The marginal impacts of price (P), marketing (M), and research and development (R) vary with the levels of the respective independent variables. The marginal impact of any one variable depends on the levels of the other independent variables. To illustrate, the marginal impact of marketing is:

$$dQ/dM = caP^{-b} M^{c-1} R^e$$

However, this form constrains the marginal impact (dQ/dM) to always decrease or, alternatively, to always increase with increases in marketing, depending on the value of the term "c − 1." If "c − 1" is between zero and 1, then demand will always be characterized by diminishing returns to marketing over all levels. If "c − 1" is greater than 1.0, then the demand function will always have increasing returns to marketing. Therefore, the modeling of an inflection point is not possible with this functional form.

Furthermore, the multiplicative demand function constrains all the elasticities to be constant and independent of the values of the independent variables; a rather restrictive condition associated with this form.

Finally, the function becomes unstable for low values of the decision variables. As price approaches zero, demand approaches infinity. As marketing or research and development approach zero, the demand approaches zero. Even with a relatively low market price, demand will be zero if there are no expenditures on R&D.

A ROBUST SYSTEM FOR MODELING DEMAND

The system recommended for modeling demand is composed of five critical components: (1) a harmonic mean should be used to calculate the average market price; (2) exponential smoothing on all demand variables to capture intertemporal effects; (3) a generalized multiplicative market demand function that allows for variable elasticities; (4) a multiplicative firm-level demand function that has variable firm-level elasticities and is constrained by total market demand; and (5) a stockout routine which checks for, and if needed, reallocates excessive firm-level demand. The suggested system is presented in full in Table 8-1, and consists of ten equations. Each of the the five components are detailed below.

TABLE 8-1
A Suggested System for Modeling Demand

HARMONIC MEAN FOR AVERAGE PRICE

(1) $\quad P = n / \sum_{i=1}^{n} (1/p_i)$

EXPONENTIAL SMOOTHING ON VARIABLES

(2) $\quad P = aP_n + (1-a)P_o$; where $0 < a < 1$

(3) $\quad M = bM_n + (1-b)M_o$; where $0 < b < 1$

(4) $\quad R = cR_n + (1-c)R_o$; where $0 < c < 1$

MARKET DEMAND

(5) $\quad Q = g_1 P^{-(g_2 + g_3 P)} M^{+(g_4 - g_5 M)} R^{+(g_6 - g_7 R)}$

FIRM DEMAND

(6) $\quad w_i = k_o(p_i + k_1)^{-(k_2 + k_3 p_i)} (m_i + k_4)^{+(k_5 + k_6 m_i)} (r_i + k_7)^{+(k_8 + k_9 r_i)}$

(7) $\quad s_i = w_i / \sum_{i=1}^{n} w_i$

(8) $\quad q_i = s_i Q$

STOCKOUT ROUTINE

(9) $\quad S_{max} = f_i + \sqrt[3]{f_i(1. - f_i)/n}$

(10) $\quad STOUT_i = q_i - C * AVAIL$

The Harmonic Mean for Average Price

The harmonic mean computes the average market price by weighting low prices relatively more than higher prices. This property is desirable because, in accordance with economic theory, low-priced products (firms) generate higher quantities demanded than high-priced firms. The formula used to calculate the harmonic mean is:

$$P = n/\sum_{i=1}^{n} (1/p_i) \qquad [1]$$

> where: n = the number of firms in the industry
> p_i = the price charged by firm i
> P = the average price for the industry

A simple example will illustrate the effect of using the harmonic mean. Suppose that the market consists of a duopoly situation with firm #1 charging $10 and firm #2 charging $20. The $15 conventional mean, implicitly assigning equal weights, would overstate the "true" average price because the lower price actually would induce more sales than the higher price. The harmonic mean calculation yields an average price of $13.33, which would more closely reflect the actual weighted average for market price.

Exponential Smoothing on Variables

The demand for the product depends not only on the current values of the independent demand variables, but also on their historical values. For instance, both current and past expenditures on advertising impact sales potential of a firm. Exponential smoothing is a convenient technique allowing simulation designers to specify the role and importance of history on current demand. The conventional formulas are presented below with an example:

Exponential Smoothing Equations

$$P = aP_n + (1-a)P_o \quad ; \text{ where } 0 < a < 1 \qquad [2]$$

$$M = bM_n + (1-b)M_o \ ; \text{ where } 0 < b < 1 \qquad [3]$$

$$R = cR_n + (1-c)R_o \quad ; \text{ where } 0 < c < 1 \qquad [4]$$

> where: P = exponentially smoothed harmonic price
> M = exponentially smoothed marketing expenditures
> R = exponentially smoothed research and development

An "o" subscript indicates a period-old smoothed value, and an "n" subscript indicates the most current mean value.

The values "a", "b", and "c" (exponentially smoothed coefficients) determine the impact of the historical data on the current demand. Larger values for these coefficients are equivalent to a smaller number of terms in a moving average. For instance if "a" is .5, this will have about the same effect as a moving average with four terms in it. A value of .05 is roughly equivalent to a 39-period moving average. Both theory and evidence indicate that large values of "a" and "b" would be desirable, whereas a smaller value would be appropriate for variables such as research and development.

Market Demand

A three variable market demand function which allows for both multiplicative demand properties and variable elasticities is specified below. While equation 5 contains only three independent demand variables (price, promotion and R&D), the model can be easily generalized to the n-variable case.

$$Q = g_1 P^{-(g_2 + g_3 P)} M^{+(g_4 - g_5 M)} R^{+(g_6 - g_7 R)}$$ [5]

where: P = average price in the industry
M = average marketing expenditure in the industry
R = average R&D expenditure in the industry
g_i = parameters for $i = 1,7$
Q = total industry demand

The values assigned to the parameters $(g_1, g_2 \ldots g_7)$ depend on the designer's specification concerning the elasticities associated with the demand. The determination of the values of the seven parameters is discussed in detail in a forthcoming section of the chapter.

Firm Demand

There are three basic components of the firm demand function: the weighting function, the market share equation, and the quantity equation.

The Weighting Function
The weighting function is a variable elasticity multiplicative function similar to the market demand function previously specified. It determines the magnitude of the value that is used to calculate the market share of the firm as a function of the total market demand. The weighting function suggested is as follows:

$$w_i = k_0 (p_i + k_1)^{-(k_2 + k_3 p_i)} (m_i + k_4)^{+(k_5 + k_6 m_i)} (r_i + k_7)^{+(k_8 + k_9 r_i)}$$ [6]

where: w_i = weight of firm i
p_i = exponentially smoothed price of firm i
m_i = exponentially smoothed marketing expenditures of firm i
r_i = exponentially smoothed R&D expenditures of firm i
k_i = constants or parameters for $i = 0,9$

The values assigned to the parameters $(k_2,k_3,k_5,k_6,k_8,k_9)$ depend on the designer's specification concerning firm-level elasticities. The specification of the values are related to, and follow directly from, the determination of the seven parameters $(g_1,g_2...g_7)$ detailed in the market demand equation. The purpose of k_1,k_4 and k_7 is to prevent the weight from equalling zero. (This could only occur, however, if a firm enters a zero decision value and the corresponding exponential smoothing coefficient was 1.) k_o is a scaling factor and may be arbitrarily assigned a value to ensure that the firm weights are not too large or too small for computation accuracy.

The Share Equation
The share equation is the weight of the firm (i.e., equation 6) divided by the sum of the weights for all firms in the market. The share equation is as follows:

$$s_i = w_i / \sum_{i=1}^{n} w_i \qquad [7]$$

The Quantity Equation
The quantity demanded of firm i (q_i) is equal to the market share of firm i (s_i) multiplied by the total market demand (Q) from equation 5. The firm demand equation is as follows:

$$q_i = s_i Q \qquad [8]$$

The benefit of this approach it that it restricts the sum of the individual firm demands to the market demand determined by equation 5. However, a problem may occur with this approach. If a firm behaves in an irrational fashion (e.g., "too small" a price and/or "too large" a marketing expenditure), it may receive a large weight (w_i,) and thus an inordinate amount of the industry demand. If the firm is unable to supply the goods demanded, then the distribution of industry sales would be distorted. To prevent such a problem, a stockout (unsatisfied demand) routine is required.

The Stockout Routine

The stockout routine only comes into play if the distribution of industry sales is distorted, and it then redistributes excessive demand to the other firms in the industry via forces of supply and demand.

Two criteria must be satisfied before a stockout condition is declared: (1) the firm's share, based on equation 7, is "too large" for the market structure and the number of firms (the "too large" is defined by equation 9); (2) the firm cannot satisfy the demand which is checked in equation 10. If both criteria are met, then stockouts are redistributed to the competing firms.

In reference to the first criteria, the maximum firm share in a given market is determined by using a statistical quality control approach, the p-chart. The essence of the check is based on the firm's share being within three standard deviations of the expected share. Equation 9 demonstrates the upper limit.

$$s_{max} = f_i + \sqrt[3]{f_i(1. - f_i)/n} \qquad [9]$$

If the firm's share is greater than s_{max}, this indicates that the firm's share may be excessive, but a check is needed to see if the firm has a production level sufficient to meet the demand. This is accomplished by comparing the firm's demand potential (q_i) with the total goods available. Equation 10 performs the check.

$$STOUT_i = q_i - C * AVAIL_i$$

where: $AVAIL_i$ is total goods available for sale by firm i
 i = firm number
 C = a positive constant
 $STOUT_i$ is the stockout for firm i

To allow for a reasonable amount of error in forecasting sales or meeting production requirements, "C" should be set at a value greater than one, possibly at a value between two or three. If the share is beyond s_{max}, and $STOUT_i$ is greater than zero, then the routine reallocates the excessive demand to the other firms in the industry by normalizing equation 7, after removing the distorting firm's influence. A recommended approach to the normalization process is described in the example section of the chapter.

DERIVING THE PARAMETER VALUES OF THE DEMAND SYSTEM

Two alternative approaches may be utilized to derive the parameters of the demand system described above. One approach requires you to specify the desired elasticities of each independent variable at two different levels; the second approach requires you to specify the desired elasticity of each independent variable at the inflection point.

Specifying Elasticities Over a Range

The elasticity formulas for the demand system are:

Price Elasticities

$$E_p = g_2 + g_3 P(1 + \ln P) \qquad \text{Market Level} \qquad [11]$$

$$E_{p_i} = k_2 + k_3(p_i + k_1)(1 + \ln(p_i + k_1)) \qquad \text{Firm Level} \qquad [12]$$

Marketing Elasticities

$$E_M = g_4 - g_5 M(1 + \ln M) \qquad \text{Market Level} \qquad [13]$$

$$E_{m_i} = k_5 - k_6(m_i + k_4)(1 + \ln(m_i + k_4)) \qquad \text{Firm Level} \qquad [14]$$

Research & Development Elasticities

$$E_R = g_6 - g_7 R(1 + \ln R) \qquad \text{Market Level} \qquad [15]$$

$$E_{r_i} = k_8 - k_9(r_i + k_7)(1 + \ln(r_i + k_7)) \qquad \text{Firm Level} \qquad [16]$$

where: ln denotes the natural logarithm

Given the elasticity formulas, it is possible to solve for the parameters of the system (all g and k) by using the following three-step procedure:

1. Select a starting (or low) value for each demand variable and the corresponding elasticity value you desire.

2. Select a second (relatively high) value for each demand variable and the corresponding elasticity value you desire.

3. Substitute the selected values into the elasticity formulas.

This will give you two equations for each independent variable and two unknown parameter values. For example, in the market price (P) elasticity formula (equation 11), the two unknowns are g_2 and g_3, and the two equations for this formula come from the two selected data points for E_p and P. Consequently, the simultaneous equations may be solved to obtain the values of the unknown parameters.

ILLUSTRATIVE EXAMPLES

Three different examples are presented to show how the demand system can be used in modeling demand in a computerized business simulation. The first example illustrates how the market-level demand parameters can be established by specifying two elasticities. After the parameters are estimated, numerical values for demand are generated from the demand equation. The second illustration deals with estimating the parameters for the demand equation based on apriori specification of the point of inflection on a marketing demand variable. Values are then simulated from the demand function. The third illustration details how the stockout routine works, demonstrating the two checks and the normalization process.

Deriving Parameters by Specifying Two Elasticities

It is assumed, for ease of illustration, that the demand function consists of only two independent variables, price (P) and marketing (M). The desired elasticities and the associated values for price and marketing, are specified by the designer to be:

Price ($/unit)	Price Elasticity	Marketing ($)	Marketing Elasticity
$10.00	0.50	$ 50,000	3.00
$20.00	1.00	$150,000	1.00

Substituting the values for price and price elasticity into the market level price elasticity formula (equation 11), the following two equations are obtained:

$$0.50 = g_2 + 33.026g_3 ; \qquad [17]$$

where: E_p = 0.5 and 33.026 = 10(1 + ln10)

$$1.00 = g_2 + 79.915g_3 ; \qquad [18]$$

where: E_p = 1.0 and 79.915 = 20(1 + ln20)

Solving equations (17) and (18) simultaneously yields the parameter values:

$$g_2 = 0.15$$

$$g_3 = 0.01$$

Repeating this procedure and substituting the values for the marketing expenditures and elasticities into the market level elasticity formula (equation 13) gives the following two equations:

$$3.0 = g_4 - 590990g_5 \qquad [19]$$

where: E_m = 3.0 and 590990 = 50000(1 + ln50000)

$$1.0 = g_4 - 1937760g_5 \qquad [20]$$

where: E_m = 1.0 and 1937760 = 150000(1 + ln150000)

Solving equations (19) and (20) simultaneously, the parameter values are:

$$g_4 = 3.88$$

$$g_5 = 0.0000015$$

Consequently, the illustrative market demand function in this example is:

$$Q = g_1 P^{-(0.01 + 0.15P)} M^{(3.88 - 0.0000015M)} \quad [21]$$

The parameter g_1 is a scaling factor and may be arbitrarily assigned a value. It does not affect the elasticities. It simply determines the magnitude of demand at the starting point. For this example, the value of g_1 was set at 2.34×10^{-12}.

Simulating the Market Demand Function

The market demand function derived in the above example will be simulated to illustrate the impact of price and marketing expenditures on quantity demanded. More specifically, the simulation considers two cases: (1) the impact of variations in price on quantity demanded, holding marketing expenditures fixed at a starting value of $50,000; and (2) the impact of variations in marketing expenditures on quantity demanded, holding the price fixed at the starting value of $10.00. The results of the simulation are reported in Tables 8–2 and 8–3.

In Table 8–2, the price elasticity can be seen to increase slowly with increases in the market price. The price elasticity is initially inelastic with a value of 0.5 (in absolute terms) at a starting price of $10.00. It increases to a unitary elastic value when price reaches $20.00, as specified apriori.

TABLE 8–2
Impact of Price on Market Demand When Marketing Expenditures Are Fixed at $50,000

Price	Quantity Demanded	Price Elasticity
10.00	997,228	0.50
12.00	906,603	0.57
14.00	824,933	0.66
16.00	750,791	0.75
18.00	703,249	0.85
20.00	621,492	1.00
22.00	564,065	1.05
24.00	513,468	1.15
26.00	466,291	1.26
28.00	423,172	1.36
30.00	283,788	1.47

The marketing elasticity of demand in Table 8–3 decreases relatively quickly with increases in marketing expenditures. As specified earlier by the designer of the simulation, marketing expenditures are highly elastic at the starting point of $50,000 and decrease to unity at the expenditure level of $150,000.

It is useful to note that the advertising elasticity in this example turns negative at an expenditure level of $210,000. In this case, increases in marketing expenditures, after a point, can actually hurt market demand because of "oversaturation." This situation does not have to occur and can be altered if different elasticities are specified by the designer.

TABLE 8–3
Impact of Marketing Expenditures on Demand When Price Is Fixed at $10.00

Marketing Expenditures	Quantity Demanded	Marketing Elasticity
50,000	997,228	3.00
70,000	2,567,199	2.60
90,000	4,708,172	2.20
110,000	7,046,763	1.80
130,000	9,206,539	1.40
150,000	10,910,114	1.00
170,000	12,011,372	0.55
190,000	12,483,417	0.13
210,000	12,385,871	−0.30
230,000	11,828,334	−0.72
250,000	10,939,432	−1.16

Deriving Parameters by Specifying the Inflection Point

The inflection point represents the point at which the function will change from increasing returns to decreasing returns. As an example, let us assume that the designer wants to specify the inflection for marketing (M) to occur at an expenditure level of $100,000 and have a marketing elasticity of 2.0.

At the inflection point, the relationship between the elasticity and the level of marketing (or any selected independent variable in the demand function) is:

$$e^2 = g_4 + g_5 M \qquad [22]$$

For a derivation of equation (22), refer to the paper by Gold and Pray (1984).

Substituting the value for marketing expenditures of $100,000 and marketing elasticity of 2.0 into equations (13) and (22) yield:

$$2.0 = g_4 - g_5 \, 100000(1 + \ln 100000) \qquad [23]$$

$$4.0 = g_4 + g_5 \, 100000 \qquad [24]$$

Solving equations (23) and (24) simultaneously, the parameter values are:

$$g_4 = 3.65256$$

$$g_5 = 1.48007 \times 10^{-6}$$

The relationship between marketing and demand based on the parameter values above is illustrated in Table 8-4. As described in the previous example, a scaling factor for the parameter g_1 was arbitrarily selected to obtain the desired magnitude for demand. It does not affect the elasticities or marginal impacts of the independent variables.

Referring to Table 8-4, it can be seen that demand increases at an increasing rate up to expenditure levels of $100,000 for marketing. The marginal impact of marketing increased from 150 units of demand per dollar spent on marketing to a maximum of 182 units of demand per dollar spent on marketing. After marketing expenditures of $100,000, the marginal impact declines and demand increases at a decreasing rate, indicating diminishing returns.

The inflection point occurs, therefore, at the point specified initially by the simulation designer. Note that the shape of this function corresponds to Figure 8-1

TABLE 8-4
The Marginal Impact of Marketing Expenditures

Marketing Expenditures ($)	Quantity Demanded (Units)	Marginal Marketing Impact (Unit/$)
60,000	3,201,854	XXX
70,000	4,701,894	150
80,000	6,405,536	170
90,000	8,184,052	178
100,000	10,000,000	182
110,000	11,789,374	179
120,000	13,401,302	161
130,000	14,903,767	149

Redistribution of Excessive Demand

A simplified demand illustration is presented in this section to illustrate how the demand system can identify "outlier" decisions and if needed, adjust the demand distribution so that the market is not distorted.

For simplicity, the example assumes that there are only four firms in the market and that the system of equations that were developed to determine the total industry demand and firm share are both driven by price. Other non-price predictive variables and intertemporal smoothing methods have been excluded for illustrative purposes.

The market demand curve, a reduced form of equation 5, is as follows:

$$Q = n^* \ 5000 \ P^{-2} \qquad [25]$$

where: P equals the average market price
n = the number of firms (four in the example)
5000 = scaling factor

A weighting function, a reduced form of equation 6, was used:

$$w_i = 1000(p_i)^{-3} \qquad [26]$$

where: p_i = firm i's price

The share and quantity formulas are directly from equations 7 and 8 of the full demand system.

$$s_i = w_i / \sum_i^n w_i$$

$$q_i = s_i \ Q$$

Equation 11 uses a scaling factor of 5000 so that each firm will have a demand of 50 units at a price of $10. The industry price elasticity is constant at -2.

Outlier Identification and Removal

For simplicity of calculations it is assumed that each of the four firms were planning on setting the same price of $10. Equation 11 would then set the total market demand at 200 units and the weight and share equations would have evenly distributed 50 to each firm. If, however, one of these firms had entered a price of $1, either by accident or with the intent to disrupt the entire market, then the average price in the market would have fallen from $10 to $7.76. This, in turn, would induce the total industry demand to increase to 332, or a 66% increase. Such a sharp increase in the total demand potential induced by one firm "cutting" its price is difficult to justify and rationalize. Some designers have eliminated this particular problem by removing the "outlier" price from the industry average. The question that arises, however, is, "when is a decision an outlier?"

One method to identify outliers is to calculate the standard deviation along with the average price. If any of the prices fall above or below three standard deviations of the average, they should be removed from the average calculation. Such a check would eliminate outliers and prevent industry demand level from being distorted. A potential problem still exists, however, and this deals with allocating the demand via the share equation.

Excessive Stockouts

Since the firm-level price elasticity in this model is relatively high (i.e. 3), this $1 price will distort the distribution within the industry. The calculations presented in Table 8–5 illustrate this problem.

TABLE 8–5
Share and Firm-Level Demand Distortion

Firm (#)	p_i ($/unit)	w_i	s_i	q_i (units)
1	10	1	.001	.19
2	10	1	.001	.19
3	10	1	.001	.19
4	1	1000	.997	199.43
sum	31	1003	1.000	200

P = $10 (after removing the $1 "outlier")
Q = 200 based on equation 25

Even with the removal of the outlier decision, the market will be distorted by permitting total flexibility in pricing. If it is assumed that each firm had the same number of items for sale (from production and finished goods inventory), say 50 units, then firm # 4 would have stocked out by 150 units and the other firms would have had no sales whatsoever! Thus firm # 4 has distorted the entire market with its $1 price per unit.

Identification of Excessive Stockouts

In this illustration it is clear that firm # 4 had excessive demand potential, but what are the general conditions for excessive stockouts and market distribution distortion?

From our experience, we have found the following two-step procedure to work well in identifying: (i) when stockouts are excessive, and (ii) when the market distribution is or will be distorted. As noted earlier, the procedure involves ascertaining whether the share (s_i) is out of line statistically, and then determining if the "flagged" firm will incur a significant quantity of lost sales. For our example, the steps are detailed below:

STEP 1—The Share Check

From equation 9, s_{max} is calculated to see if the firm's share is suspect in terms of its magnitude.

$$s_{max} = f_i + \sqrt[3]{f_i(1. - f_i)/n}$$

For the example with four firms, the share check would be as follows:

$$s_{max} = .25 + \sqrt[3]{\frac{.25(.75)}{4}} = .61$$

$$\text{where: } f_i = 1/4 \text{ or } .25$$
$$n = 4$$

A "flag" should go up as a warning signal since firm # 4 had a share of .997 (based on equation 7) which exceeds .61. Statistically, it is highly unlikely that firm # 4 would have a share beyond three standard deviations from the expected share for a four firm market. However, an additional check is needed because it is possible for a firm, through effective planning, to capture a large share of the market and satisfy the demand from production and inventory.

STEP 2—The Supply Check

From equation 10, $STOUT_i$ is checked for the "flagged" firm to see if it has the capacity (i.e., inventory and production level) to satisfy the demand. If a firm has a positive value for STOUT, then it is flagged again on the second check.

$$STOUT_4 = q_4 - C * AVAIL_4 \qquad [10]$$

where: $AVAIL_4$ is the sum of current production and finished goods inventory for firm # 4

C is a constant normally between 2 and 3.

Table 8-6 presents the calculation for the example and notes that firm #4 has "flagged" on both checks.

TABLE 8-6
Identification of Excessive Stockouts

Firm #	s_i	FLAG 1	q_i (units)	$STOUT_i$ (units)	FLAG 2
1	.001	no	.19	−99.81	no
2	.001	no	.19	−99.81	no
3	.001	no	.19	−99.81	no
4	.997	YES	199.43	99.43	YES

Where: $s_{max} = .61$
AVAIL = 50 units for each firm
C = 2

From this point firm # 4 has been clearly identified as an outlier and its influence on the market should be eliminated. A share normalization method handles this tasks.

The Share Normalization Algorithm

This algorithm uses the shares determined by equation 7, normalizes them, and then distributes the excessive demand potential to the competing firms. Specifically, after a firm has been identified by the two checks, the excessive demand for the "flagged" firm is calculated and redistributed by normalizing the shares of the remaining firms. Table 8-7 demonstrates how firm #4 would be removed, the new normalized shares determined, and the revised demand potential calculated for the remaining three firms:

TABLE 8-7
The Share Normalization Algorithm

Firm	Old Share	New Share	Redistributed Demand	Initial Demand	Total Demand
1	.001	.333	49.81	.19	50
2	.001	.333	49.81	.19	50
3	.001	.333	49.81	.19	50

EXCESSIVE DEMAND FOR FIRM 4 = 149.43
NOTE: FIRM 4 WAS REMOVED IN THE NORMALIZATION

With this approach, the new shares are found by taking each old share and dividing it by the sum of the "non-flagged" firm shares (for our example, the sum is .002991). The excess demand (149.43 units) is then redistributed to the remaining firms and added to their original demand to determine their demand potential for the period.

The share normalization method uses the forces of supply and demand to reallocate the excess demand and does not rely on an arbitrary decision rule. In most existing business simulation models, a share equation is used to determine firm-level demand, so the algorithm is easy to incorporate. If the firm-level price elasticity is large and there are a large number of competing firms in the industry (say more than nine), it is possible for more than one firm to be considered an outlier. This approach will handle removing more than one outlier simultaneously. With a highly sensitive price elasticity and a large number of firms, it is quite likely for the redistribution to cause other firms to be "flagged." The algorithm can be used to handle sequential flags and continue to reallocate iteratively, if needed.

SUMMARY

The chapter has examined the internal modeling of demand in computerized business simulations that are both competitive and interactive in nature. It was found that three types of functional forms were commonly utilized: linear, nonlinear, and log-linear. The linear form has the desireable property of variable price elasticity but constrains the marginal impacts of the independent variables to be constant. The nonlinear functions varied widely in form and nature. Nonlinear functions were found to be the most unstable, having properties inconsistent with modern demand theory. Log-linear functions allow marginal impacts to change with the level of the independent variable but are not flexible enough to model inflection points. Elasticities are also constrained to be constant.

As an alternative, a demand system was offered and evaluated. The demand system was shown to possess a number of desirable properties: (1) The use of a harmonic mean to approximate more effectively the true market price as compared to the conventional mean calculation which overstates the average industry price; (2) Exponential smoothing to capture intertemporal effects and allow the designer to control the importance of history on current demand; (3) A multiplicative functional form which is stable and possesses variable elasticities, and increasing and diminishing returns to the independent variables; and (4) A stockout routine to prevent unrealistic market distortions from occurring by redistributing excessive and unsatisfied firm demand within the same period of simulation play.

PART 4

FUTURE TRENDS IN BUSINESS GAMING

This section looks ahead to the future of simulation gaming. Advances in technology have presented the opportunity to move away from relatively static batch simulation games toward truly dynamic games. For example, most current simulation games do not use a continuous clock, but rather involve a lock-step approach where all decisions are made by each firm simultaneously. The advances in computer networking now allow multiple students to access the game at once, and they are able to monitor the game environment simultaneously and continuously. Students can make decisions whenever they wish. Chapter 9 by Newell E. Chiesl discusses the process in general and then discusses the play of one of his games in detail. Another new approach to simulation gaming is open system simulation, discussed in chapter 10 by Alan L. Patz. Open system simulation allows the algorithms that determine the simulation outcomes to emerge as a result of decision making rather than having to be programmed in advance.

Chapter 9: Interactive Real Time Simulation by Newell E. Chiesl

Chapter 10: Open System Simulation by Alan L. Patz

CHAPTER 9

INTERACTIVE REAL TIME SIMULATION

Newell E. Chiesl

Instructors in the academic discipline of business administration have attempted for many years to bring realistic business episodes into the university classroom. One of the first successful attempts was at the Harvard Business School in 1909 when "Doc" Copeland introduced what is now the most widely used method to teach business courses, the Case Method (McNair, 1954.) Computer simulation and gaming is considered to have been the next major advance in bringing realism into the classroom. This method has many known advantages, but business games have often frustrated the game administrator with their high administrative requirements (Fritzsche, 1978).

The next advance at bringing realism into the classroom to business students follows a technological advance in computer ability. The advent of the interactive terminal enabled the instructor to offer students a dynamic simulation without a fixed time period or a specific number of required decisions. An interactive gaming technique which satisfies this freer format is Interactive Real Time Simulation (Chiesl, 1978).

Technology in the form of computer power and information has changed the methods by which business is conducted in the United States. Since 1980 the unit sales of advanced personal computers, work station minicomputers, and superminicomputers have experienced phenomenal growth (Infocorp, 1985). Coupled with this is the growth of software. In 1981 personal computer software sales were approximately half a billion dollars and by 1989 sales are projected to be 10 billion dollars (Field, 1985). Another type of tool providing business persons with information is the database, of which there are already 2400 in existence with new ones being created every month. According to Daniel Seligman (1985), "Lockhead, Mead, Dow Jones, *Reader's Digest,* H & R Block and the SEC are among those trying to change the world by pushing on-line databases."

The popular literature frequently discusses the increasing use of desktop micros, computer terminals, computerized telephone modems, on-line databases, and user-friendly software (for example, see Harris 1985). Managers no longer have to wait for quarterly reports, monthly reports, or weekly reports. Today there is instant accessibility to market data on the manager's desk via the desktop terminal or microcomputer.

The volatile business environment has always fostered changes in the teaching community, but, for one reason or another, schools of business have, this time, lagged behind. What is needed is for school of business classes to catch up with the hardware and software changes of the previous decade. Specifically, this chapter is an alternative for current computer simulations that are time fixed format games. These are games that have decisions based on a predetermined decision interval, for instance, quarterly or monthly reports. Marketing simulations are not realistic when decisions can only be implemented once a month and market data can only be retrieved or outputted once a month. This does not represent the workings of today's dynamic business world. Students should be subjected to the same rigors that they will experience after graduation. This means data input and output continuously when students want it, *not* when game designers allow the students to input and output at some arbitrary discrete time format.

The interactive real time simulation is the outgrowth of five instructional techniques: gaming, modeling, computer simulation, the Monte Carlo technique, and the case method. **Games** relate to conditions of business conflict over time. The participants are competitors who make use of logical thinking in order to arrive at the best possible strategy for beating their competitors (Thierauf and Grosse, 1970). A **model** is a representation of something else, as for example, the model aircraft flown in a wind tunnel is a representation of the actual flight of an 'object system', aircraft (Barton, 1970). A **computer simulation** is a simulation of a model of some situation in which the elements of the situation are represented by arithmetic and logical processes that can be executed on a computer to predict the dynamic properties of the situation (Emshoff and Sisson, 1970). The **Monte Carlo Technique** uses a random number procedure to create values for the probabilistic components of a simulation model (Anderson and Sweeney, 1976). The **case method** is a method by which students develop their problem solving and decision-making faculties in an atmosphere apart from that of the business world (Leenders and Erskine, 1973).

The Interactive Real Time Simulation is the computerizing of a case on a computer terminal containing multiple problems and a changing environment. The problem and the environment are both programmed in advance and scheduled to occur at predetermined times throughout the game. Participants of the simulation receive the written portion of the case one week in advance of the computer interaction. This will enable participants to conduct research and gather information pertaining to the case. The simulation is an interactive technique in two respects. The first way is by allowing participants to input variables, such as the marketing variables of pricing, distribution, promotion, and product quality decisions. The computer terminal interacts by instantly displaying to participants the results (outputs) of their decisions and also by providing them with new and continuous market research information not available in the written case. The players receive their new information, such as an unexpected change in the product life cycle. The participants, therefore, are interacting with the simulation by sending and receiving information via the computer terminal.

The second way the players interact with the simulation is by interacting with other participants. That is to say, the decisions made by players one through nine have an influence on the results of player number ten.

The interactive real time simulation offers a more realistic environment than standard business simulations because students are able at any time in the simulation to change their input variables without waiting until the next fixed time period. This is possible for the student because of the real time capabilities of the interactive terminal. To students, it appears that their requests are instantaneously answered. In reality, however, the main computer has probably also answered a dozen or more requests from other interactive terminal users. The decision modification time frame for the interactive simulation is very flexible, allowing students to change decision variables whenever they wish, for example, at 1.7 weeks, 3.2 weeks, or even .2 week intervals in simulation time. This simulation time could relate directly to the wall clock time of 1.7 minutes, 3.2 minutes and .2 minutes. Unlike most business games, the real time interactive simulation does not require a specific set amount of decisions be input each time period. Thus, students can change one, some, all, or no (the let-it-ride-strategy) variable(s) whenever they choose. Some of the headaches and frustrations for the game administrator caused by incorrectly typed student inputs are also eliminated, since students are able to correct instantly any input data incorrectly entered.

The interactive real time simulation is played on computer terminals in direct competition with each other. Each team simulates the object system (a microbusiness environment) using basically the same computer program. The only differences in the ten separate programs are the file names where each individual team modifies and stores its own unique decision variables. Each team program also automatically calls a file which stores the sales figures, the profit amounts, and the cumulative statistics. Each of these files has a secret password which calls the data files from storage. The players do not know and cannot obtain the scrambled nonsense names (passwords) of their own data files nor of their competitors' data files. In other words, the players of the simulation are only allowed to execute a system file which has in it the compiled program.

DISCRETE SYSTEMS

A discrete system is one in which the stated variable(s) change only at a discrete set of points in time (Banks and Carson, 1984). While few systems can really be classified as strictly discrete or strictly continuous, since one type of change predominates for most systems, it will usually be possible to classify a system as being discrete or continuous (Law and Kelton, 1982).

Figure 9-1 illustrates the probability distribution of a discrete event's value. Basically, an event with a value of five has a 15% chance of occurring, an event of value eight has a 30% chance of occurring, an event of value seven has a 5% chance of occurring, and so forth. If the strength of the event is for instance a five, this could represent the following hypothetical situations: (1) five customers walking into a store, (2) 500 units of a product being purchased, (3) five people seeing and remembering an advertisement, (4) a 5% share of market, (5) a five dollar price for a competitor's product, (6) five products being shipped on time, (7) five new government regulations being enacted by the United States Congress, (8) five more Japanese competitors entering the market place, or (9) a five million dollar profit. These have been examples of discrete-type logic developed for mathematical models and computer simulations.

FIGURE 9-1
Discrete Frequency Distribution

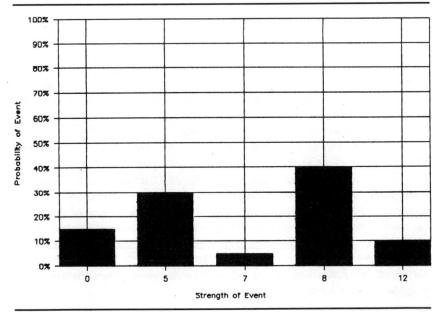

A discrete modeling technique can be used to simulate a product life cycle. The notion that products have a life cycle is an important marketing concept. Simply stated, products have a life span from birth to death. The different states in the Product Life Cycle (PLC) are seen in the traditional sales curve illustrated in Figure 9-2, which is adopted from Wasson (1974). In each stage of the PLC there are different marketing strategies to be implemented. In other words, the marketing manager adjusts the product's promotional mix, price, product quality, and distribution to the needs of the market place. A product's life cycle was selected for the following reasons:

FIGURE 9-2
Product Life Cycle

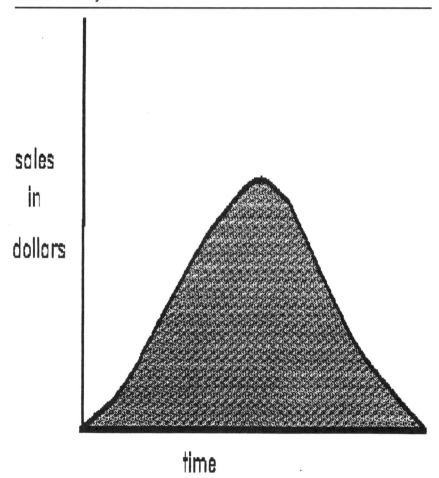

(1) the nature of demand flowing through time, (2) during a product's life, managers (and students) constantly require market data, (3) the data should be available quickly or instantaneously, and (4) managers will then need to modify their decision variables to adjust to changing market requirements.

Figure 9-3 presents how many business games have simulated the product life cycle. Upon comparing Figure 9-2 with Figure 9-3, it is readily visualized that discrete simulation games do not accurately represent the continuous business system being modeled. The reasoning for this is the aforementioned characteristics of most business games, the fixed time format. The example presented in Figure 9-3 is for a product life cycle of approximately two years. The business game simulating this product has nine decision inputs. Although fixed format games do well in simulating some parts of the discrete business system, they do not accurately represent continuous state systems, such as a product life cycle.

Upon further examination of Figure 9-3, it is noted that students can only obtain information at exactly week 12, week 24, week 36 and so forth. Students may also only modify their decision variables at week 12, week 24, week 36 and so forth. Is this a realistic marketing simulation designed to represent the real business world pedagogically? No.

FIGURE 9-3
Discrete Simulation of a Product Life Cycle

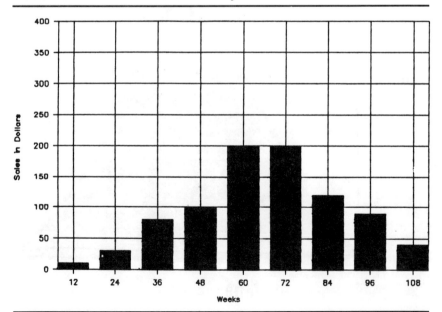

CONTINUOUS SIMULATION

Continuous simulation is the name given to the use of a digital computer to solve models with continuously changing states (Bratley, Fox, and Schrage, 1983). Most of the continuous simulation literature is concerned with full wave rectifiers (during 1974) and radio active decay (Oro-Smith and Stephenson, 1975) or models that flow through time. These are the usual applications of continuous simulation, but continuous simulation can also be applied to business games.

This section will present two continuous modeling techniques which can be incorporated into marketing simulation games. They are continuous compressed time and continuous extended time simulation games.

Both of the modeling techniques are interactive in nature. The games are played interactively on computer terminals, continuously. That means from simulation time period zero to week 100, the game is constantly being played simultaneously by all of its participants without a break in the action. In real time this could represent one hour, two hours, or three hours. This interactive type simulation is accomplished by a computer capable of accessing files through I/O devices and communicating the results (market data, market variables and market demand) to each student participating in the marketing game on computer terminals.

Figure 9–4 illustrates how a product's life cycle can be simulated by continuous techniques. When examining Figure 9–4, it is seen that students are able to obtain information and modify decisions at any time during the simulation, for instance at simulation time period A, B, and C. This corresponds to week 5, 7.1 and 9.3 respectively.

Referring again to Figure 9–4, it is seen that for the continuous compressed time simulation example, the game could be played interactively on computer terminals for two hours. In the extended time simulation example, the game is played interactively for twenty-five days.

In the extended time simulation technique, students are able to access the terminals whenever they want during the twenty-five day period. Students participating in the simulation can modify variables and retrieve market data for any simulated week during its corresponding real time.

The twenty-five day continuous extended time simulation is played in the following manner. Students play the game simultaneously and all start at the exact time. Students access the simulation game once a day, many times a day, or not at all. The participants decide. The participant can access the terminal five times or 250 times during the twenty-five day period. The computer does keep track of the time intervals between each access and then calculates a corresponding rate of demand. Through the use of a time system procedural file program, the continuous extended time simulation will periodically update participant files for competitive market data each day.

FIGURE 9–4
Continuous Simulation

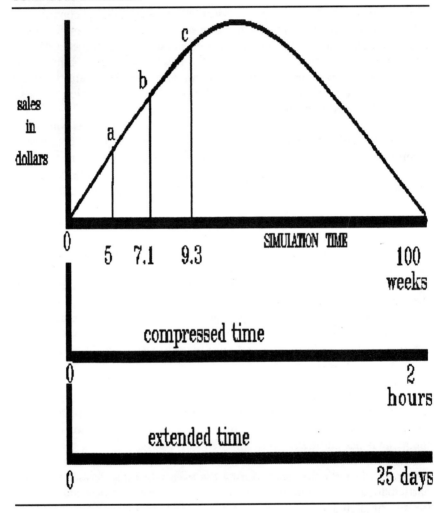

The variables that are affected the most by a rate or continuous function are promotion, distribution, and demand determination. Everything is calculated by a rate through time, a one week rate. When students input $200 for promotion, it is at a rate of $200 per week. When 2.17 weeks expire, then ($200 × 2.17) $434 is spent on promotion. How has demand been affected? If a $200 amount increases demand by an absolute amount of 50 units, then (50 units × 2.17) 108.5 units in addition are demanded. When a $200 increase results in a 10% increase in demand, then the original demand (say 600 units × 10% × 2.17) equals 130.2 units of promotional effect. Initial demand per week is determined by the interaction of the variables: promotion, product quality, amount of inventory, price, and competition. The initial demand is then multiplied by the amount of weeks since the last profit and loss statement. For example, a P & L was taken by the simulation game playing students at the 27th week. They then take another P & L at the 37th week. Ten weeks of compressed simulation time have elapsed. If their demand equals 30 units per week, total demand is calculated, (30 units × 10 weeks = 300 units demanded). This would be the calculation for a straight line product, probably in the maturity stage of the product life cycle. This is a straight line since the product is not experiencing any long-term percentage increases or decreases.

A second example is for a product experiencing a growth rate of a 5% increase per week. The calculation becomes (30 units × 10 weeks × $[(1.05)^T]$) = 488.67 units, where T = the elapsed time or 10 weeks and (1.050^T) becomes approximately 1.63.

INTERACTIVE REAL TIME SIMULATION

Interactive real time simulation is the simulation of an object system by participants who are interacting with both the computer and other participants in a real time environment. To be realistic, the participants input decisions and receive their outputs in a continuous system state.

There have been many articles on the requirements of hardware and software in real time systems (Glass, 1983; Liebowitz and Carson, 1985; Rothstein, 1970). There have been interactive articles on business systems, such as production (Falster, 1987), finance (Chase and Sepchri, 1986) and management (Johnson and Loucks, 1980). There have also been ABSEL interactive papers (Hummel, 1985; Wynne, Klosky and Snyder, 1979; Zinkham and Taylor, 1983). However, none of the literature concerns itself with the double interactive and real time interactive nature of continuous simulation.

The purpose of this section will be to illustrate: 1) the nature of real time interactive simulation, 2) the file access and modification procedure, and 3) the technical aspects of the programming. Throughout this section reference will be made to a computer simulation developed by the author entitled, *Tommie Company: An Interactive Marketing Game* (Chiesl, 1978). The purpose of the game is to illustrate, by means of computer simulation, the marketing implications of five products moving through their life cycles. The simulation can be played by two to ten teams on interactive terminals.

The computer hardware required to play the simulation is a mainframe (the one the class is using is a half Megabyte type, but 100K would be adequate), interactive terminals, and an on-line file storage system. The simulation, *Tommie Company,* could also be adapted to a micro computer network. The NOVELL network with its SNET hardware could support a practical limit of 24 simulation users. The XENIX system is also capable of support with its basic configuration of ten terminal type machines combined with a super minicomputer as the host system.

The Nature of the Simulation

An interactive business simulation offers the student a more realistic environment than the fixed-time format business game. This characteristic, referred to as verisimilitude, means that the participants experience a business environment that has the appearance of being true and real. This salient characteristic enables interactive real time simulation to be very rewarding while possibly making the fixed-format games obsolete by comparison.

Participants are able to select the length of time their decisions are simulated. The method is implemented by allowing the appropriate wall clock time (that corresponds to the compressed simulation time) to expire and then request profit and loss statistics. The method is real time dependent and relies on wall clock time being elapsed. Because of the interactive nature of the simulation technique, it is imperative that all participants initiate the simulation at as close to the same time as possible. A couple of minutes of variance is acceptable. However, when the variance is too large, it is possible that one participant will be experiencing a negative exogenuous phenomenon (i.e., demand decline) in the scenario which will adversely affect the choice of inputs, while another participant at the same moment in time is experiencing a pleasant decision making environment. Since the collective action of the group's decisions have a negative, positive, or neutral influence on each participant, it is necessary to rely on the elapsed wall time to govern the compressed simulation time for every participant.

An example will illustrate this reliance on wall clock time. In a business oriented interactive game, it is necessary to have all participants at the same time experiencing the affects of such uncontrollable factors as inflation, business cycles, introduction of a substitute product, government intervention in pricing, or a change in consumer preference. The importance of the wall clock reliance is readily seen if participants number one through nine adjust their decision price variable to the $130–$140 range, in reaction to scenario event N in the simulation, while player number ten, at the same time, markets the product at $180, while experiencing event T in the scenario. The price variance would, of course, significantly lower the demand for participant number ten's product.

File Manipulation

Figure 9–5 is a very simplistic diagram of the events through time. For ease of illustration, two participants will be diagrammed. Diagramming more than two participants would not significantly increase the illustrative effect, but would exponentially increase the difficulty of the diagram's construction. Interactive simulation techniques are able to accommodate any number of participants and data files. The only limitations are the number of terminals, amount of file storage available, and, of course, the tenacity of the programmer. Participant number one starts a marketing game by simulating the initial values of the variable given at time period A. At time period H a modification is made in the decision variables. A modification or change is made in one of the decision variables by calling up the appropriate data file. The participant of the interactive gaming technique needs no programming knowledge; the program does all the details. The data file is accessed indirectly. Indirect access means that the program receives a copy of the data file; the actual data file remains in file storage. Indirect access files can be read by many users at the same time since the original always remains in file storage and is not removed. Direct access files can only be read by one user at a time. Any changes made in the data file are made directly in file storage. This is unlike indirect access, where it is possible to change, modify, or purge a scratch copy of the data file without modifying the original file. When the modification of the scratch copy is complete, a separate program request is made (called) to the system to replace the original direct data file with the newly modified file. It is important to understand the indirect nature of the call routine. Without this feature a truly interactive and real time simulation technique would not be possible.

Referring again to Figure 9–5, participant number one continues until a read request is called at time period L. The read request is a preliminary call made before an output generation. It serves the function of gathering the collective data by reading all of the participants' data files and then summarizing the results in the form of averages. As was noted earlier, the collective decisions of the group have a positive, negative, or neutral effect on each participant.

Through the use of the above example, it has been seen that participants are able to select any amount of time they wish their decision to be in effect. Therefore, participant number one receives a profit and loss statement for time periods A–M, and M–T. Participant number two also receives profit and loss statements, but this team has their decisions in effect for different time periods, A–J and J–Z. This feature of allowing participants to change decision inputs at any time truly results in the participants playing a very realistic computer game.

Figure 9-5
File Access and Modification Diagram

(For Two Participants, One File Per Participant)

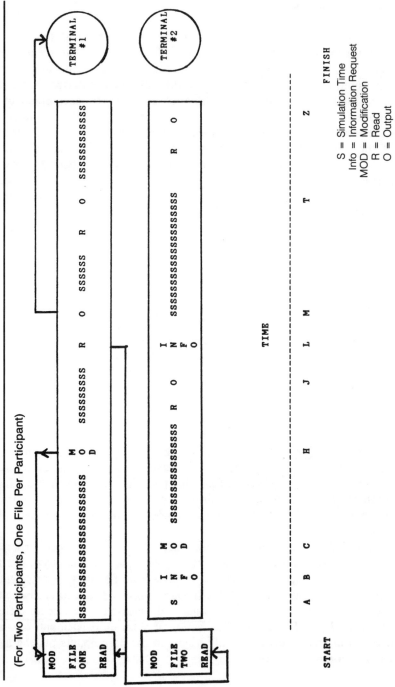

These averages, although not seen by participant #1, are used in the mathematical subroutine which calculates the results (output) of the simulated time. The output, in time period M, is then routed to the I/O terminal, from which participant number one views the output of simulated time A–M.

Participant number two, in Figure 9–5, starts the interactive simulation in a different, but more analytic manner. A request is made for information in time period B. The program responds by reading the indirectly accessed files of the other participants.

Summary statistics are then made available to participant number two. After analysis, it is determined in time period C to modify participant number two's decision inputs. Time continues until the simulated outputs of time A–J are routed to the terminal.

Performance for the two participants is then evaluated by the game administrator. Usually for a marketing game, profit and market share are the criteria.

Figure 9–6 illustrates important aspects of real time interactive simulation, file reads and data modifications. (Figure 9–6 diagrams only two players and five individual files. There could be ten players and ten files). Number one is able to read all the files with his/her most current information. Number one can only modify his/her own file. Once number one modifies his/her file, this information immediately changes all the industry averages for the competition. Similiarly player number two has the same capabilities, except for only modifying file 2.

Programming Example

Figure 9–7 presents the flowchart of the program. Participants select one of the modules. The flowchart also illustrates the internally kept clock. When 7200 seconds have elapsed, the simulation is terminated. The environmental factors are changed quarterly throughout the game. If participants require the environmental information, they input a two and receive long-run market research.

The flowchart illustrates an internal loop which returns the participant to the Input A module after selecting one of the modules. These modules are called subroutine commands in the computer program with the return in the main program. Once returned in the main program, several time variables are updated: absolute time, relative time, and time elapsed since last profit and loss statement. After the updates, the program moves to the input A module and the cycle repeats itself.

Current information is exactly that, up to the latest millisecond. Without indirect file access, a participant would only obtain the same information stored in the file as it appeared at the compiling stage of the program. The

FIGURE 9-6
Two Player File Modification Example

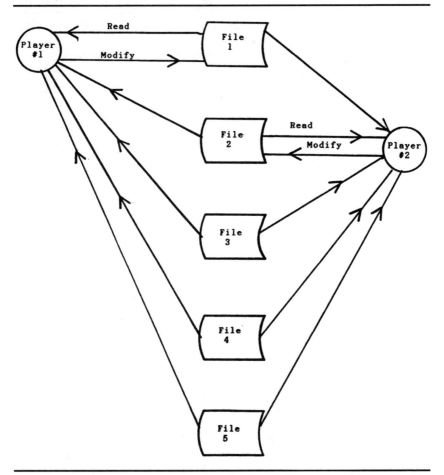

information would never change if this were the case, and no matter how many times a participant made information requests, the information result would be identical. Fortunately, this is not the case and current information is available.

Now how does this happen? The initial step is for the business game designer to determine the desired learning objectives, formulate the associated mathematical realationships, and write the computer program. Inside the program will be a call routine to store the decision variables in a file, called Player number one. The next step is to run the program and determine if all the quantitative routines in the program perform as intended. After this

FIGURE 9–7
Interactive Real-Time Simulation

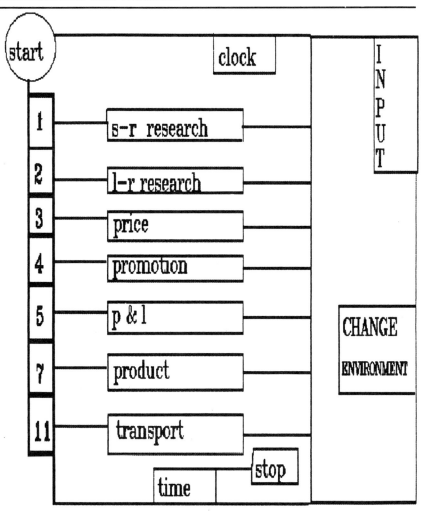

step, the same program is duplicated until ten identical programs are obtained, assuming the game administrator wants ten competitors in the market place. (Each competitor could actually be a group of one to five students.)

The final step is to go into each program and edit the file names to match the designated player's number. For instance, participant number five runs program 5 with the file name player number five. When player number five modifies a decision variable, the amount in file 5 will immediately change.

Notice that the program asks the participant which module they wish to select. If information is requested, the program calls and reads files 1–4 and 6–10. This procedure reads the current contents in those files and then takes averages of the competitors decision variables. Therefore, participants number one through ten are in constant communication with each other by leaving messages in a "drop-box" type of arrangement. In computer talk, this feature is named indirect access for data files and call subroutines inside the program.

Participant number five might request to change the amount of dollars spent on advertising per week, variable name ADV#5. Program 5 calls and gets file name file 5 (which stores decision variables), asks for the new amount and modifies file 5 by writing in the new amount. Immediately, the other participants number one through four and six through ten are able to obtain this new amount, which would change industry averages.

Participant number five requests a profit and loss statement, to determine the effect of advertising. The program starts by calling SUBROUTINE AVERAGES that calculates the average amount spent by competitors on advertising. The variable AESTU calculates part of the advertising's effectiveness. The functional form for advertising effectiveness is shown in Figure 9–8.

The time-flexibility feature is directly related to clock time. Every time a P&L statement is requested, the program determines the time internally. It is a simple procedure to then subtract one time from another. The result is the elapsed time from one P&L request to another. If, for example, the results are obtained at 6.54 minutes, the compressed simulation time, for simplicity sake, could be 6.54 weeks, months, or years. Participants are informed of this feature *before* the game starts.

SUMMARY

The simulation of the Product Life Cycle concept on interactive terminals offers business students the opportunity to experiment with marketing variables during the different stages of a product's life cycle. These experiments offer instant feedback that can be either positive or negative to students. The computer simulation of the Product Life Cycle concept, therefore, has offered to students a valuable experiential learning exercise.

The basic instructional benefits to be derived from the utilization of group interaction and interactive simulation are:

1. The interactive simulation has the ability to compress a long time frame of events into a more usable short time frame. For example, the events

FIGURE 9–8
Advertising Effectiveness

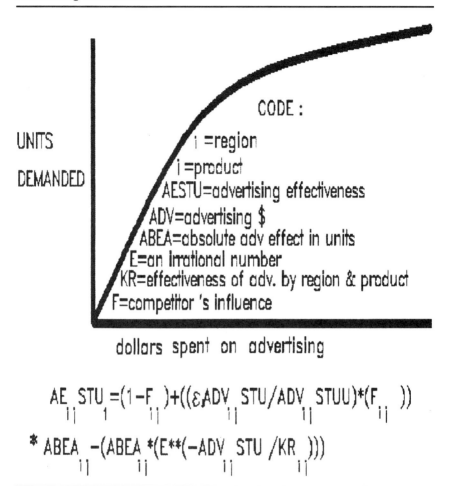

UNITS

DEMANDED

CODE :

i =region

j =product

AESTU=advertising effectiveness

ADV=advertising $

ABEA=absolute adv effect in units

E=an irrational number

KR=effectiveness of adv. by region & product

F=competitor 's influence

dollars spent on advertising

$$AE_{ij}STU_{1} = (1-F_{ij})+((\varepsilon ADV_{ij}STU/ADV_{ij}STUU)*(F_{ij}))$$

$$* ABEA_{ij} - (ABEA_{ij}*(E**(-ADV_{ij}STU/KR_{ij})))$$

occurring in a product's life during a three-year time span can be compressed into a three-hour time period.

2. The players of the interactive simulation receive instant feedback from their inputs. This enables players to review instantly their decision-making performance and to obtain information which will influence future decision-making.

3. A sense of realism, verisimilitude, is given to players of the interactive game. Students are often exposed to too many theoretical instructional approaches in a curriculum. The interactive game offers students something that has the appearance of being real.

4. Players interact with other competing teams. This competition motivates players to make optimum decisions since actions taken by one player will positively or negatively affect the results of the other opponents.

5. There is no actual disturbance of the real world business system being studied. Decisions are only simulated without regard to possible consequences to the real system. This feature allows players to learn by experimenting with one variable in the system and then to examine the affect that the manipulation has on the other interrelated variables in the system.

6. The interactive game is a group process. The pooling of resources, the establishment of communication channels, the development of leadership roles, and the appreciation of the term "synergistic effort" emerge as benefits to be derived from the interaction of members in a group. Unfortunately, members will also experience some negative features of group interaction. Some dysfunctional elements of group interaction are the self-serving intentions of group members, the "let someone else do it" attitude, and, of course, the pitfalls of using the committee approach to decision-making. Nonetheless there is an overall benefit in using the group format. The fact is that committees are a pervasive force in our society which students must learn to cope with before eventually being subjected to their subjugation.

Technological advances in computer hardware have made the use of desktop computing almost universal throughout the business world. Today's managers have instant access to market information. Because of this, there has been a change in the speed of the decision input/output process. However, the pedagogical computer simulations utilized by most schools of business have not changed with the advent of the new informational technology.

This chapter has been developed to familiarize more people with the nature and methodology of interactive real time simulations. A related purpose has been to illustrate the dynamic and very realistic nature of time-flexible games as compared to the fixed format games. It is hoped that future simulation designers will adopt this interactive technique in their computer modeling of systems.

CHAPTER 10

OPEN SYSTEM SIMULATION

Alan L. Patz

Most business policy simulations have a pedagogical intent (Thorelli and Graves, 1964). They are concerned with enhancing the degree to which students understand the flow, interrelatedness, and long range character of general management decisions (Frazer, 1978). Moreover, most simulation research focuses on a determination of the conditions necessary to integrate more fully simulation exercises and traditional coursework (Klein, 1984). Most important, most simulations are closed systems. The algorithms that determine participant results remain the same throughout a given run or execution of the simulation (Patz, 1987).

Of course, there is nothing fundamentally wrong with closed system simulations. They have been invaluable in accomplishing several business policy course purposes from both faculty and student points of view (Gordon and Howell, 1959; Patz, 1988a). Furthermore, as closed system simulation sophistication grows, so does the standing of this technique as one of the key bulwarks of the business policy field (Patz, 1988b).

Nevertheless, there are important reasons for looking beyond closed systems. Pedagogy is one, and research is the other. The purpose of this chapter, in short, is to explain why. Said in another way, the basic idea of this chapter is to argue for *open system simulation* research. This is an approach that does not rely upon fixed algorithms, and its applications are not limited to the business policy course.

The main cost of this gain in power will be an increase in simulation complexity that is several orders of magnitude beyond current models. As shown in Figure 10-1, even the most basic systems will require a multitasking environment running several programs simultaneously.

At the heart of open system simulations or, more generally, *artificial environments* is a control program that monitors data base operations, tracks all the usual accounting functions, maintains the simulation files, and, most important, directs the open system market model. As currently conceived, these market models will have an artificial intelligence (AI) base that generates market dynamics and eliminates the need for fixed or predetermined market algorithms.

FIGURE 10–1
A Generic Open Systems Design

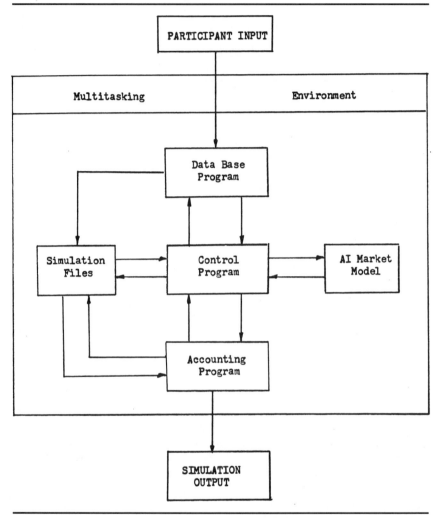

Notice also that participant interactions with an open system are through a data base, allowing complex *decision rule* inputs rather than simple statements of prices, quantities, and production capacities. In other words, such a simulation may run continuously with participants entering new decision rules at their discretion or as indicated by current market conditions. Likewise, the output may be continuous generating, for example, the specific simulation's version of a daily *Wall Street Journal.* Overall, this means that simulations may assume the day-to-day character of ongoing businesses while encouraging the development of long range strategies.

These and other basic open system interpretations are discussed in more detail later in the chapter. For now, simply note that an emphasis on simulations stresses the pedagogical use of open systems. The more general emphasis on artificial environments (AE), using more elaborate AI models, stresses the equally important research possibilities of such systems. In fact, when open systems are finally made available, they are a way to challenge and improve our assumptions in the behavioral, economic, and policy sciences (Mitroff and Emshoff, 1979).

ASSUMPTIONS AND CLOSED SYSTEM EXPERIENTIAL LEARNING

There are three reasons for taking this open system point of view. First, regarding the day-to-day integration problems with simulations and other coursework, it is assumed that simulation technologies will have a far greater effect on what happens in classrooms than pedagogical sciences will have on simulations. This perhaps nonintuitive notion, that technology drives science more than science drives technology, is a well-known result of technological innovation research (Sahal, 1981). In other words, simulations and related computer technologies will assume an ever increasing importance in the classroom. The handwriting is already on the wall, but any further development of this topic is an issue for another discussion.

Second, closed system policy simulations provide students with an opportunity to deal with the fundamental interrelatedness of several business functions, but they do so in a fashion that is unique to the algorithms contained in the specific game. Policy simulations are "wired," and there is little opportunity for participants to act upon rather than just react to the preset macroeconomic and commodity demand functions. While it is true that the participants' collective decisions can counteract basic trend and demand conditions, their effects still lie within limits set by the established algorithms. Unlike real general managers, they do not create a competitive environment within a basically open system.

Third, closed system simulations do not provide a realistic data base for use in participant decision-making. Various well-developed codes (Keys and Leftwich, 1985; Scott and Strickland, 1985) generate a wealth of administrator and participant information. However, they ignore such crucial issues as possible new entries into the simulated industry, trade in markets other than those initially defined by the rules of the game, and *specific* administrator interventions.

New entries and new markets are almost always limited in closed system simulations. The number of markets is a "given," and the number of firms is an administrator defined parameter. Likewise, the administrator is highly constrained regarding such issues as regional taxes, shipping charges, cash transfer or exchange rates, and team-by-team negotiations on any of these issues, including mergers and participation in different markets.

The opportunity for an administrator to participate as an informed, education-oriented competitor does exist simply by defining the number of teams to be $(N + 1)$ where N = the number of student teams. But, decisions made by the administrator have to be based on the assumption that team $(N + 1)$ is a going concern. Any other criterion will usually distort overall competitive results. In short, when a simulation's algorithms are fixed in advance, there simply is little room for maneuvering. Equally important, there is little room for research.

EXPERIENTIAL BACKGROUND

This disposition, of course, reflects something other than casual observation. It relies upon more than ten years of actual classroom experience with policy simulations. The games used range from an early microcomputer model (Nordstrom, 1972) to one of the most complex mainframe applications (Thorelli and Graves, 1964). In addition, the students involved range from undergraduate business majors to MBA's and practicing executives from the United States, Western Europe, Japan, and Southeast Asia. A list of the simulations employed is shown in Table 10-1.

This experience has been opportunistic because the search for appropriate packages has been limited to the ones made available by colleagues and publishers. No systematic evaluation of alternative total enterprise games was attempted. Furthermore, the approach was nonstructured because the implementation and evaluation procedures used for each simulation, with few exceptions, were the ones provided by the authors.

On the other hand, the student evaluations were generally positive with executives expressing the highest degree of satisfaction and undergraduates being the least satisfied. In other words, the degree to which students accepted the various simulations as a learning experience appeared to show a positive correlation with age.

All of these disclaimers, however, are irrelevant as far as the argument in this chapter is concerned. The key point is that in almost all cases, students learned how to "game-the-game." In general, the sequence of events followed this pattern:

1. All students experienced confusion over the rules of the simulation and how to execute a set of decisions.
2. Good students resolved the confusion, built cash flow models, and began to understand the simulation prescribed interrelatedness rules among marketing, production, finance, and overall economic functions.

TABLE 10–1
Simulation Experience Base

Simulation	Authors	Period of Use	Student Type
COGITATE	Temple, Barker & Sloane	1986–	Executive
International Operations Sim'n.	Hans B. Thorelli & Robert L. Graves	1983–1987	MBA Executive
Manager	Jerald R. Smith	1985–	Undergrad
MICROMATIC	Timothy W. Scott & Alonzo J. Strickland III	1986–	MBA
PLANETS II	U. S. Army Logistics Management Center	1982–1983	MBA
TASK	Alan J. Rowe	1980–	Undergrad
The Executive Simulation	Bernard Keys & Howard Leftwich	1985–	Undergrad
The Multinational Management Game	Alfred G. Edge, Bernard Keys & William E. Remus	1981–	Undergrad Executive
Top Managment Decision Game Executive	Joseph Nordstrom	1979–	Undergrad
USC Management Strategy Sim'n.	Paul A. Gruendemann	1972–1986	MBA

3. Average students witnessed the success of good ones, copied their procedures, and became more competitive.
4. Most students now "knew-the-rules" and played accordingly.
5. Poor students complained.
6. Minor changes in team standings occurred as students honed their gaming techniques.
7. Overall, there was no obvious correlation (based upon experience, not data) between the above references to good, average, and poor policy simulation performance and performance on case analyses, industry analyses, and specific company analyses.

Actually, more work needs to be done on this last point since some of the relevant data have been collected during the past few years. But, this is also a subject for another discussion. The key issue is that the first six findings are consistent over the ten-year period, three types of students, and different cultures. In fact, they are remarkably consistent, including a reasonable degree of satisfaction over all students even though the older ones express more interest.

EXPERIENTIAL INFERENCES

Assuming that these experiences are common among experienced simulation users, four important conclusions follow:

1. A relatively common technology, closed system simulations, produces common results in the long run. Students learn how to game-the-game.
2. Further empirical investigations aimed at arbitrary measures of student learning seem destined to repeat the same conclusions. They will reveal that this simulation or that one produces superior or inferior learning on one set of concepts or another.
3. It would appear that student interest in general management would be a more important target for closed system empirical research (Patz, 1988a). The question is: How can simulations be used to generate and nurture interest in general management as a career objective?
4. Other simulation technologies, for example, open systems, need to be developed if the full potential of simulations is to be exploited.

One part of the problem, especially in regard to the first two of these conclusions, is related to the process of closed system simulation design. That is, most simulations are developed because someone has an idea how to program:

1. An accounting sequence from the purchase of raw materials to the sale of finished goods.
2. An interesting demand function that goes beyond prices and advertising to include such factors as R&D, product differentiation, marketing efforts, and various leads and lags in these factors.
3. A special topic such as PERT or product life cycles.

Once programmed, including the basic 90% of the code concerned with accounting for each participant or team's position, the simulation is tested on a sample population, debugged, and retested. Finally, a user's manual is written to convey the necessary operating details to the uninitiated.

Herein lies the problem. The user's manual was not written first (Andersen, 1986). What people are supposed to do when participating in the simulation, playing the game, is decided after the fact of simulation design, not before.

Said in another way, the real purpose of the simulation is decided after software design problems have been solved. Typically, computer coding drives simulation purposes rather than the reverse. Thus, it is a small wonder that short-term research results lead to equivocal conclusions on simulation usefulness. Simulation purposes, for the most part, are decided by coding convenience rather than pedagogical, conceptual, or theoretical relevance.

In short, open system simulations need to proceed in the reverse order of closed system ones. That is, they need to begin with the user's manual, a statement of what is desired.

OPEN SYSTEM PRELIMINARIES

What is desired, of course, are basic statements of what needs to happen in an open system simulation. In particular, for policy simulations, answers are needed for the following questions:

1. What kinds of decision-making behaviors need to occur, and how will they be recorded in a fashion suitable for computer processing?
2. What kind of data base needs to be provided to participants prior to the decision-making sessions?
3. Can flexible computer routines be written that allow decision process modeling in a matter of minutes rather than days?
4. If the preceding problems can be solved, how can the models applicable to several participants or teams be made interactive?
5. Similar to closed systems, what sort of external constraints are required?

These are difficult questions, and answers will not be found easily. On the other hand, state-of-the-art simulation (Lee, 1987; Pritsker, 1986) and computer science (Hayes-Roth, 1985; Nii, 1986a, 1986b) developments suggest that reasonable answers are within possible-bounds. Equally if not more exciting, these developments open new research and theory avenues.

A RESEARCH PREVIEW

Assuming for the moment that these "possible-bounds" are realistic, allowing for the development of open systems, research and theoretical interests may assume roles at least as important as pedagogical interests. The reason is simple. Open system simulations, by definition, do not depend upon preprogrammed algorithms. Rather, *they generate environments* that emerge over time as a result of participant behaviors. In other words, behavior can be observed under dynamic rather than relatively stable environmental influences. Furthermore, in dynamic environments, the administrator may become one of the participants instead of acting as a referee over participant actions.

Considered in one fashion, this means that the heart of an open system simulation is a program or "driver" that generates the algorithms governing a particular run of the simulation. Then, based upon the results of the run, another algorithm set is generated. Associated with the driver is a data base generator that provides an environmental description for use by the participants. And third, another program combines the current algorithms with the data base and produces the results for the participants. This basic paradigm is shown in Figure 10–2.

Considered in a second fashion, an open system is a cross between many of the current activities in experiential laboratories and closed system simulations. Much of what happens in an experiential laboratory is for learning by observation purposes. Group and interpersonal phenomena such as decision-making, role differentiation, and communication can be observed firsthand as a practical test of fundamental motivation and perception theories. Moreover, basic changes, especially in group structures and processes, can be observed as they emerge over time.

On the other hand, policy simulation decisions are usually done in a rather "secret" environment. Participants have to infer from published data what the behavior of competitors means, and they are making their inferences with a *static* set of algorithms. Their basic environment, unlike the power-affect-status structures in group behavior, does not emerge over time.

What is needed is a reasonable combination of the two. The payoff from such an amalgamation is the development of entirely new research methods and research areas that can be investigated in the simulation mode. Games will always be important as pedagogical tools, as they have been for centuries. But they have an equally, if not more important, role in research.

In fact, the list of research possibilities in dynamic, computer generated environments is endless, limited only by imagination (Emshoff and Sisson, 1970). For example, open system simulations can be used to study:

1. Market structure and dynamics in an unconstrained rather than algorithmically circumscribed environment.
2. Decision-making that leads to the creation of markets.
3. Collaborative or collective as well as competitive strategies.
4. Leadership tactics in a laboratory (classroom or experiential learning center) that approximates actual business conditions.
5. Group structure and dynamics as competitive conditions change.
6. Decision-making in environments where competition is conspicuously absent, such as large scale projects, again using the classroom or experiential learning center as a laboratory.
7. Resource allocation decisions in competitive environments that are threatened with new entrants, a feature absent from most simulations.
8. True product development and market introduction tactics beyond a known set of predetermined simulation alternatives.
9. Service industry rather than product industry phenomena.

One way to summarize this potential is shown in Table 10–2. The two key dimensions in this table are the simulation environment and the phenomena

FIGURE 10–2
A Basic Open System Design

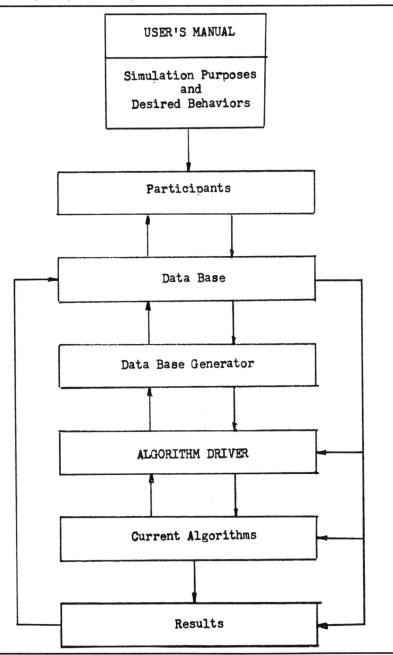

under consideration. Pairing them, or considering the various combinations, suggests a large number of research possibilities for open system simulations. For example, very little is known about decision-making patterns in planned environments such as those common to large scale projects (Patz, 1986). A similar statement can be made regarding decision-making in collaborative environments such as those found in joint ventures. New entry threats in competitive environments have already been mentioned.

Moving towards more behavioral issues, leadership styles and group dynamics are obvious phenomena for open systems study. Much of the current literature in these areas depends upon highly constrained laboratory studies or public phenomena that are difficult to measure. An open system simulation would have the advantages of both approaches and minimize the disadvantages. In short, a simulation that allows behavior to emerge has the features of ordinary social behavior, but it does so along various prescribed dimensions similar to a laboratory experiment. Thus, the measurement of social phenomena is possible without overly constraining it.

Other phenomena of interest would include technological (product and process) innovation and high technology (Patz 1981). The research issues in this case would include resource allocation patterns and risk taking behavior in different kinds of open system environments.

As already mentioned, the list is endless. At a minimum, the three types of environments shown in Table 10–2 are only a beginning, as are the areas suggested for study. Once open system simulations are available, something like Table 10–2 can be expanded at will.

TABLE 10–2
Some Examples of Simulation Based Research Projects

	Open System Environments		
Phenomena	*Planned*	*Collaborative*	*Competitive*
Decision- Making Patterns	Large Scale Projects	Joint Venture Management	New Entry Threats
Leadership/ Management Styles	Bureaucratic	Political	Strategic
Group Structure/ Dynamics	Power/Affect/Status Structures Social Roles and Social Systems Exchange/Reward Patterns		
Technological Innovation/ High Technology	Resource Allocation Patterns Risk Taking Behavior Success/Failure Patterns		

Some Research Caveats

Of course, some basic design efforts will be necessary to develop open system simulations. Just like the suggested issues than can be researched with them, they comprise an entire set of research issues. Nevertheless, some design issues are clear and they will be presented in the next section. For now, however, and at the risk of oversimplification, a few distinctions need to be made regarding open systems and other research endeavors such as artificial intelligence (AI), expert systems (ES), and decision support systems (DSS). The basic question is: Are open systems comparable to AI, ES, and DSS? Moreover, the basic answer is: No!

No doubt, it would be comforting to draw from other research endeavors such as AI, ES, and DSS. But, the problem is that none of them meet the necessary criteria even though each may benefit from open system simulation designs.

AI, for example, is an attempt to design computer hardware and software that learns from experience (Winston, 1984). Such learning may mimic human behavior, be superior to it, be altogether different from it, or be some combination of these alternatives. Any one of these results is desirable. The idea is to create machines that act intelligently, machines with programs that reprogram themselves based upon experience.

Open system simulations, however, are qualitatively different. Here the idea is to use fundamental AI techniques (Tanimoto, 1987), create environments that can be recorded in a computer, and study people's behavior in the artificial environments (AE's) created by the system. Presumably, any intelligent system could participate in such a game, but AI is a very long way from duplicating even the most primitive human characteristics. A focus on artificial environments is much more practical for now.

Even more remote, ES does not attempt to approach the basic creativity problem. Like much so-called business policy research (Hambrick, 1983), it only tries to duplicate decisions. The basic paradigm has three steps, however complicated the intervening machinations: (1) program an expert's decision rules until a computer reaches the same decisions as the expert did in the past, (2) test the decision rules on new data, and (3) recycle until the program and the expert reach the same decisions on further new data. There is not much environmental creativity in the process.

Most remote, DSS is not intended to create an environment. Its key and very useful purpose is to help a decision-maker model an environment. Such models help in the solution of accounts receivable, inventory, cost of capital, and similar decisions, but they only reflect an environment. At best, they help in resource allocation decisions (Humphreys and Berkeley, 1986); at worst, they are super spreadsheets for a dull afternoon's entertainment (Keen, 1986).

SOME BASIC OPEN SYSTEM DESIGN CONSIDERATIONS

With these distinctions in mind, and referring again to the open system policy simulation questions noted at the beginning of the preceding section, answers can be suggested regarding open system designs. To repeat, the key questions are concerned with the decision-making behaviors, data base needs, computer routines, participant interactions, and external constraints characteristic of open systems.

Looking first at desired decision-making behaviors, or writing the user's manual first (refer to the top of Figure 10–2), it is clear that the traditional participant specifications of prices, production quantities, plant capacities, several marketing stipulations, and financial arrangements need to be enhanced. Various textbook models work in this fashion, but the workaday world does not (Quinn, Mintzberg and James, 1988). Sets of rules are much more important in competitive, decision-making circumstances (Cyert and March, 1963).

For example, prices are not specified precisely. Instead, limits are provided to salespeople governing what the prices will be under different buyer and competitor circumstances. Large industrial orders command lower wholesale prices, and minimum retail prices are "suggested" by almost everyone in the value added continuum. More generally, prices are simply negotiated. In the "long run," they may conform to demand and supply curve models. However, in more well-defined time intervals, decision rules are a mainstay of business conduct (Simon, 1957).

Similarly, decision rules are the basic "inputs" by participants in an open system simulation. Moreover, just as decision rules enhance the concept of decision specifications, the concept of decision inputs to a simulation needs some enhancement. This notion, shown in Figure 10–2 as the interaction between the data base itself and the results that update it, will be elaborated shortly. For now, in order to be more concrete regarding decision rules, two examples may be as follows:

1. Lower price by 10% if the firm's price exceeds the market average by more than 15% for two consecutive weeks.
2. Expand capacity by 10,000 units when demand reaches 85% of existing capacity as long as the forecasted growth in GNP exceeds 4%.

DATA BASE CONFIGURATIONS

Decision rules, such as the two just noted, become simulation inputs only in the sense that they become part of the simulation's data base. In other words, participants are always working within and on the open system's data base. Working within the data base means that they are supplying the types of rules just noted (Widmeyer, 1987). Working on the data base means that they are analyzing the information made available to them, including their decision rule results (Gruendemann, 1987).

In this sense, a policy simulation becomes a continuous rather than a discrete process. Decisions rules may be entered at any time as part of the data base, and competitive results continue to occur whether or not any decision rule changes have been made. In fact, it is possible to design a standard closed system policy simulation using these concepts. All that is required is shown in Figure 10-2, omitting the algorithm driver and data base generator. Once again, the current algorithms would remain "wired," but decision rules and a data base would be used rather than decision specifications and discrete inputs.

Practical applications of continuous closed or open system simulations will require the posting of results on a routine basis, just like the finance section of a daily newspaper. Such continuous monitoring, however, is not a problem. Similar to current closed system policy simulations, all that has to be decided is the schedule for producing and displaying results.

COMPUTER ROUTINES

The algorithm driver and data base generator, of course, change a closed system to an open one. They modify the data base and algorithms that produce simulation results. What does this imply?

Any answer to this question probably will have several parts, and each multipartite answer can begin from many different orientations. Even an incomplete enumeration of the alternatives, along with a discussion of the associated advantages and disadvantages, is an entire topic by itself. Therefore, only one view will be elaborated here, the one that begins with a focus on the data base generator and its associated data base. In this regard, four key points are of interest—access, security, data base contents, and interactions.

First, simulation participants have access only to the data base, not the generator that produces it. Second, this requires two kinds of security, one on the generator and the other on the data base. Similar to standard simulations, only portions of the entire data base can be accessed by a given participant. These areas would include the information generated by a participant for processing by the data base generator, information that has been "purchased," and information that it made available routinely by the simulation as it proceeds. Obviously, assess to the generator itself would permit "data-snooping" and access to the proprietary information of other participants.

Third, the data base would include several different kinds of information, all managed by the data base generator. As already suggested, this would include each participant's current decision rules, current and historical simulation results, market and competitive data, and the usual income statement, cash flow, and balance sheet summaries. Except for the rules and more or less continuous operations with the data base by each participant, this content is similar to most of the well-developed games now available.

However, open system data bases need to include the continuous versions of discrete decision-making tools available in closed systems. These are the spreadsheet planning models (Keys and Leftwich, 1985; Scott and Strickland, 1985) that are available as adjuncts to the normal decision inputs of participants. What would make these models continuous is the capability to translate planning model results directly into decision rules within the data base. Equally important, however, forecasting, scheduling, and other analytical models need to be part of the data base accessible by participants in order to estimate the inputs for the planning models. In other words, a complete data base provides the capability to work through analytical models to planning models, decision rules, and the observation of results as well as other market and competitive information.

Fourth, the data base generator interacts with the algorithm driver as well as the data base. The key purpose in the relationship with the driver, in addition to the transmittal of competitive environmental information, is to transmit the current and historical sets of participants' decision rules. The environmental information and the rules, using the computer scientist's concept of a blackboard (Nii, 1986a, 1986b), constitute the algorithm driver's basis.

THE ALGORITHM DRIVER

This basis is shown schematically in Figure 10-3 (Gasser, 1987). The accumulated sets of participants' decision rules are indicated as P1 through PN, and they surround the competitive environmental information, which is the basic blackboard. Another very key set of rules, indicated by the letter D in Figure 10-3, is the actual algorithm driver.

The driver in turn has several options in deciding the current algorithms (refer again to Figure 10-2). For example, it could select participant decision rules in an opportunistic fashion. That is, a single question would be asked: Given the blackboard's current status, which set of participant rules, if applied first, would lead to the "best" outcome? In other words, each participant's rules would be applied to the data and a ceteria paribus outcome determined by holding all other decision rules constant at their previous status. The gain for each participant would be determined in the usual fashion combining measures of growth, profitability, and cash flow.

FIGURE 10-3
A Blackboard: An Algorithm Driver's Basis

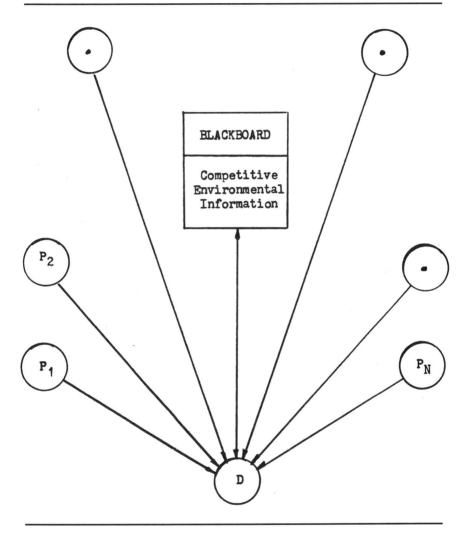

Whatever set of participant rules provided the maximum gain would be applied first and change the blackboard. The same procedure would then be applied to all remaining participants until all decision rule sets operated on a current, updated blackboard and results determined. (Note that this procedure alone opens the system.) Each set of rules is applied to updated data because the blackboard changes after each application.

This is analogous to actual markets. Each competitor is subject to the opportunistic choices of rivals, and—contrary to most economic theories—no two participants ever work with the same set of data. In fact, those who make it their business to chronicle such events (Scherer, 1980) emphasize these points. Nevertheless, there are several other alternatives for an algorithm driver.

Decision rules can be combined by testing for and eliminating logical inconsistencies (Enderton, 1972). Then, market results would depend upon a shared or mutual understanding of competitive dynamics. Once again, this view is consistent with other theoretical positions (March and Simon, 1957).

Or, as a third alternative, each participant's inputs on a given dimension, such as price, could be considered as one variable in a linear constraint in N-dimensional space, where N = the number of participants. Thus, if there are five participants, the five prices form a constraint in a hyperspace of five dimensions. The five production quantities form another, as do all other decision rule dimensions.

Then, in linear programming terminology (Gass, 1975), all of these constraints form an N-dimensional convex polyhedron within which each participant's decision rules are represented. By mapping the polyhedron onto other $(N + 1)$, $(N + 2)$, . . . dimensions, results such as market share, growth, profitability, and cash flow can be determined.

The point is that all of these options and several others can be made available to an algorithm driver, can be selected by the driver in any kind of sequence, or can be applied according to a logic that a simulation administrator desires to demonstrate. This last point, according to a logic that a simulation administrator desires to demonstrate, is what permits open systems to be research tools. The investigator is no longer bound by the artificial constraints in laboratory settings and "natural" experiments. What is desired can be produced by programming the algorithm driver.

PARTICIPANT INTERACTIONS AND EXTERNAL CONSTRAINTS

All of these driver alternatives, as well as several others, open policy simulation systems. None of them depend upon fixed algorithms, and all of the possibilities suggested in the preceding paragraphs have some basis in theory and empirical research. Equally important, it is clear that participant interactions have been defined in a different fashion. They depend upon interactions with, examinations of, and modifications to a data base. They are not limited to a weekly specification of numbers on a decision sheet, whether or not it is computerized.

Likewise, participation includes the well-known game administrator as a participant, algorithm driver executive, or both. There is no practical limit to what can be defined as an algorithm driver once the concept is simply noted and put into practice. It is nothing more than operating on the same set of data in fashions, that while different, are mutually consistent.

However, there are some external constraints that must be kept in mind. First, extreme variations in driver alternatives, while interesting, may not serve many pedagogical purposes. Research interests are different, but only a few lessons may be learned within the confines of a semester. Second, any open system design must begin with a statement of purposes. This was noted earlier in the imperative to design the user's manual first. The point is that any open system, like any other system, will not satisfy all demands simultaneously. If anything at all has been learned from the designing of computer systems, it is that all of them are limited. Like theories, they have restricted application ranges.

For example, it helps to learn basic algebra before contemplating elementary calculus. Similarly, closed system simulations may be a good first step before open system ones. If nothing else, the comparison allows a distinction between basic closed textbook models and more realistic views of the competitive environment. A simple example of this last caveat is the difference between undergraduate and MBA education purposes in business policy. Closed systems are probably more than adequate for the former and open systems most appropriate for the latter.

Once again, however, research is a different issue altogether. Among the many purposes for investigating open systems as the basis for business-related investigations is that the appropriate environments cannot be devised in any other fashion. There just is no simple way to change competitive conditions, organizational arrangements, and control systems easily and in a sufficiently short period of time to observe behavioral changes. One of the great shortcomings of organizational research is that these shortcomings are usually insurmountable. In open system simulations, however, change is a matter of convenience. Culture can be defined rather than accepted.

CONCLUSIONS

This route to open system designs, through data base and blackboard technologies, is only one way to operationalize them. There are and will be others. For example, simpler open systems appear to be possible with simulation languages (Pritsker, 1986). Similar to the algorithm driver in Figure 10–1, interactive routines can be used to generate a new set of market behavior rules for each simulation execution. Such rules of course, would be based upon the participants' past and current decision rules.

Another way to think about open systems is in terms of "pure" algorithm drivers. This is a program that does not have to rely upon data base generators or participant decision rules. It generates dynamic market structures by varying algorithms and their parameters over time. Of course, a more realistic design would include participant behavior as an important determinant of market dynamics.

However the open system concept is operationalized, the important point is that they can be discussed in terms of current and developing technologies and realistic design efforts can begin. There is no reason to think of some distant future instead of the near term. Furthermore, open systems are a good example of where the often sought but seldom realized interdisciplinary research goal can be attained. For once, policy theorists have some common ground with decision and computer scientists.

Policy, however, is not the only business field that can benefit from the design and use of open systems. The focus in this paper is on policy simulations, but the same arguments apply to most other areas of business research and practice as well as several areas of engineering and science. Open systems apply anywhere the phenomena of interest can be described as emergent. That is, the various states of the subject chosen for study cannot be predicted over time given knowledge of initial states or conditions.

In fact, it is probably fair to say that the prediction of subsequent states given a knowledge of initial ones is not the main research focus in open ststems. Again, using the modifier emergent, interest is on the possibilities or alternative future states as some phenomenon, e.g., a policy simulation, develops over time. If prediction is a concurrent result of open system analyses, this is simply another research benefit. Nevertheless, the main focus is on behavioral possibilities rather than behavioral bounds or limits.

Research project examples that fit easily into the emergent phenomena category have already been listed in Table 10-2. Even for these few it is difficult to imagine any long term interest in closed system analyses. Consider for a moment the first topic listed in that table, decision-making patterns in large scale projects. Any sort of complex behavior such as this can be constrained to a routine, closed pattern given access to sufficient resources. This sort of finding does not help much with complex project management problems.

But, by simulating such an environment in an open system, where behavior can emerge and vary over time, insights into actual decision-making patterns can be achieved. First, a simulation allows the research to be done rapidly; and second, the participants can "behave" in an environment that develops over time rather than one constrained by artificialities dictated by the linear assumptions in experimental design models. In short, open systems will make pedagogy and research equal partners in the study and design of policy and several other kinds of simulations.

PART 5

EXPERIENTIAL EXERCISES

This section changes the focus from simulation gaming to experiential exercises. Chapter 11 by R. Bruce McAfee provides a review of exercises available in the various functional areas. In order to provide a vivid glimpse of the variety of exercises, the author discusses some specific exercises (including a game show format for test preview purposes and the training of students to participate in Assessment Centers) which he has developed. Chapter 12 by James W. Schreier covers the steps involved in administering an experiential exercise successfully. The preparation stage is stressed, including the exercise selection process. Also, emphasis is placed on the debriefing stage, especially since the author's experience is that many firms do not want to give this stage sufficient time. Chapter 13 by Alvin C. Burns discusses the "live case," a term applied to an extensive student project usually conducted in conjunction with a business client. Variations include small business cases, in which students evaluate the operations and policies of the firm and then recommend possible changes; market research survey projects; and student-developed promotional campaigns for clients. The chapter will discuss problems encountered in administering the various activities. Chapter 14 by Hugh M. Cannon and Theodore C. Alex provides a framework for structuring the "live case." Given the ambiguity associated with the live case approach, students often need structure. The chapter discusses a theory-based approach which not only provides the needed structure but also provides explicit criteria for the basis of the student's grade. Chapter 15 by Lee A. Graf and Calvin E. Kellogg discusses a categorization scheme for experiential exercises, which is needed in order to systematize the cataloging of the rapidly expanding number of experiential exercises being developed. Trends in the development of experiential exercises are discussed, especially computerization.

CHAPTER 11

EXPERIENTIAL LEARNING EXERCISES: SOURCES AND SPECIFIC EXAMPLES

R. Bruce McAfee

Experiential learning exercises span a wide variety of pedagogies or formats. As Gentry has observed in chapter 2, prior ABSEL proceedings include the following formats: assessment centers, forums, group discussions, panel meetings, live cases, writing experiences, student-written textbooks, computer-assisted instruction, *COMPUSTAT* tape usage, communication workshops, Delphi forecasting, time management sessions, game show formats, learning cooperatives, internship programs, job search preparation, on-the-job training, field trips, and cases.

The purpose of this chapter is twofold: (1) to describe sources for obtaining some of these experiential learning exercises for those instructors who wish to use additional exercises in their classes; and (2) to describe some specific examples of exercises, thereby providing the reader with an understanding of the wide range of exercises which exist and, hopefully, ideas for creating new ones.

SOURCES OF EXERCISES

One of the most frustrating aspects of using experiential learning exercises is finding those which focus on the objectives or topics one wishes to cover. Unfortunately, there is no one source which catalogs all of the available exercises. Thus, instructors have no choice but to hunt through various books and journals until they find what they want. But where should one begin?

One good starting point is to review past ABSEL proceedings. Goosen (1986) states that 1974–1985 proceedings contain 233 experiential learning exercises. These cover most of the major functional areas in business and provide an incredibly diverse range of formats. In a separate publication available from him, Goosen has also categorized all of the exercises appearing in the 1974–1981 ABSEL proceedings.

In addition to reviewing past ABSEL proceedings, instructors can usually find experiential learning exercises by looking through books and journals in various functional areas. Undoubtedly, more exercises have been developed for personnel and organizational behavior topics than for any other one. While many personnel books contain a few exercises, supplementary books in human resource administration contain a much greater variety and number of exercises. Among the major ones are those by Beatty and Schneier (1981); Kelley and Whatley (1987); Kuzmits (1986); Nkomo, Fottler, and McAfee (1988); Simonetti (1988); Stevens (1986); and Wheeler, Wallace, Crandall, and Fay (1982). Personnel related exercises are also frequently presented at the Eastern Academy of Management Meetings and appear in its proceedings.

Like human resources administration, organizational behavior instructors have many sources of exercises available to them. University Associates publishes an "Annual Series on Human Resource Development" which contains a variety of exercises. They have also published a ten volume *Handbook of Structured Experiences for Human Relations Training*, a *Structured Experience Kit*, an *Applied Skills Series*, and *The Encyclopedia of Icebreakers: Structured Activities that Warm-up, Motivate, Challenge, Acquaint, and Energize.*

While many of the major principles of OB textbooks contain a few exercises, several supplementary books are also available. Hai (1986) has written a book devoted exclusively to cases and exercises (experiences). At least five books combine readings and exercises: Davis and Newstrom (1985); Gibson and Hodgetts (1985); Lau and Jelinek (1984); Lewicki, Bowen, Hall and Hall (1988); and Ritchie and Thompson (1988). One book (Dawson, 1985) blends text materials with exercises. *The Organizational Behavior Teaching Journal* also contains articles which discuss exercises, and exercises are presented at the Eastern Academy of Management Meetings and appear in its proceedings.

While many experiential learning exercises are available in personnel and organizational behavior, relatively few are available in the other functional areas of business.

In marketing, Kinnear and Taylor (1982) and Sciglimpaglia (1983) present exercises in marketing research. Other books which contain marketing exercises include Moody (1987), Peterson, Stanton and Whatley (1978), and Talarzyk (1987). Several case books are available in finance and operations management, but the author is unaware of any exercise books still in print.

SPECIFIC EXAMPLES OF EXERCISES

As the previous section suggested, experiential learning exercises span a wide variety of functional areas and formats. Indeed, the variety of exercises available and the creativity involved in developing them is amazing. In this section, some specific examples of exercises will be presented. These materials have been drawn primarily from past ABSEL proceedings and have been divided into six categories: specific company/job role plays, decision-making exercises, debate exercises, critique/evaluation exercises, game show format exercises, and assessment centers as experiential learning devices. No attempt has been made here to describe an example of each and every type of experiential learning exercise pedagogy. Rather, the purpose of this section is to present examples of some of the formats being used, including some of the more unusual ones. Hopefully, these examples will serve as a catalyst and starting point for faculty members who wish to create their own exercises.

Specific Company/Job Role Plays

One of the most common exercise formats could be labeled the "specific company/job role plays." These exercises ask students to assume they work for a fictitious firm and hold a specific job such as personnel manager, vice president of production, or sales manager. Students are then given tasks to perform and decisions to make which are similar to ones people in these positions would encounter. While many of these exercises are designed to build specific functional skills (e.g., write a job description, develop a discipline policy, prepare a performance appraisal), others focus on developing more general abilities such as decision-making and interpersonal relation skills.

To illustrate, Jolly and Fairhurst (1986) designed an exercise to teach retailing students international buying skills. The objectives of the exercise are to (1) sensitize students to foreign buying customs, (2) familiarize students with import buying, and (3) develop decision-making skills relative to international buying. At the start of the exercise, all students are assigned to either a buying team or a manufacturing team. Each buying team consists of three members: a divisional merchandise manager, a buyer, and an assistant buyer. These team members are assigned to one of four scenarios: (1) a department store seeking to purchase oriental carpets in India, (2) a mass merchandiser wishing to purchase sweaters in the Phillipines, (3) a speciality chain store seeking to purchase men's oxford shirts in Japan, and (4) a discount store wanting to purchase children's wear in Hong Kong. After conducting research regarding the economic, political, and cultural climate of their foreign country as well as other research, the teams negotiate with the foreign manufacturing teams to achieve predetermined buying goals.

Panitz (1986) has developed an exercise which addresses the topics of organizational structure and goal attainment. It is designed to expose students to the problems and challenges of meeting organizational goals by restructuring the operating portions of an academic institution. This exercise presents students with a comprehensive description of a fictitious university

(Midwestern State University), and students are asked to play the role of the academic vice president. Students are told that the university is faced with a need to reduce its budget and that they must restructure the university to obtain maximum cost savings. However, this restructuring must be accomplished within the constraints outlined by the board of regents.

While most exercises in this category are built around fictitious firms, some evolve around actual companies and actual problems. Nordstrom and Sherwood (1984), for example, had students develop a marketing plan for the Buick Division of General Motors. Students were told that they were to assume the role of Buick's marketing department and were asked to sign up to serve on committees. A representative from Buick and a local Buick dealer came to class to discuss the need for a marketing plan for two models, the Century and the Skyhawk. Ultimately, the students wrote up a final report and presented it orally to company representatives. One interesting variation of role playing (Stacy, 1988) was designed to examine the issue of employee rights in the workplace and to serve as a catalyst for discussing underlying ethical issues, ways of resolving conflicts, and changing employment mores. In conducting the exercise, selected members are asked to role play deviant student behaviors unknown to the rest of the class while the instructor enacts the abusive authoritarian character. Although numerous variations of this exercise have been conducted, a typical format is the following:

> "The instructor may meet the class on time or a little late. The instructor briefly begins the lecture and then interrupts it to deal with the student eating in class. The instructor asks the student to leave the class until the sandwich is finished. The instructor resumes the lecture only to be interrupted by a student coming very late to class. The instructor comments on the student's lateness and threatens to do something about it.
>
> "Resuming the lecture, the instructor's attention is diverted by someone horsing around. The disruption should be intrusive but not explosive, leaving a little room for doubt. The instructor asks the student to be quiet after noting that the learning environment is being disrupted. The noise continues to bubble up and the instructor finally ejects the student.
>
> "The incidents increase and culminate in the professor tossing a student out merely for disagreeing with the instructor. The instructor allows a student to offer opinions and insights contrary to the professor. The student wants to continue the discussion, but the professor finds it intolerable. The incident escalates to the point that the instructor tosses the student out with some dramatic gesture" (p. 129–130).

After the actors have played out their roles, the instructor recalls the role players and informs the class of the true nature of the experiment. A debriefing period follows focusing on any potential bad feelings toward the instructor or actors, on helping students understand their own behavior, and on employee (student) rights.

Decision-Making Exercises

Closely related to the previous category of exercises are those which require individuals or groups to make one or more decisions. These exercises differ from those in the previous category in that students do not role play. They simply make decisions or, in some cases, perform a task.

To illustrate, Gomolka and Mackin (1984) have developed an exercise which is designed to assess factors in decision-making, including risk analysis, self-confidence, self-evaluation, perception, and previous experience. At the start of the exercise, previously submitted cases are returned to the students. Then, without warning, students are told they have to make a choice between keeping the grades which they have received or giving up the grades and meeting with a group of other class members. As Gomolka and Mackin state:

> "This group, called a familiar group, will be reassigned one of the three cases just returned. However, the same grade will be assigned to all members of the group, and the grade for this one case will be a maximum of 80% of the maximum grade which could have been received on an individual basis. Thus, under this option, a maximum of 12 points may be received and substituted for the original grade received on an individual basis. This option may be utilized only if three or more of the members from the familiar group choose to give up their individual grades to work with the group.
>
> "If less than three members from a familiar group choose to rework the case in the group, a stranger group, composed of members from other familiar groups in the same circumstance, is formed. This stranger group, working on a reassignment of one of the cases, will receive a common grade which may be a maximum of 120% of the maximum score originally possible. Thus, a stranger group could receive a maximum of 18 points.
>
> "Dependent upon the outcomes of Step two, familiar and/or stranger groups are formed as necessary. These groups are given 20 minutes to come up with a group decision on the reassigned case, usually Case 1, and to hand their solution in on an answer sheet. Those individuals who decide to stay with their original individual grade are gathered together by the instructor and taken to another room, where the solutions to the assigned cases are discussed," (p. 128).

At the conclusion of the exercise, the results are discussed in terms of the factors causing a student to keep the original grade vs. choosing to join a group, small group dynamics, risk assessment, the average grade gain or loss for those joining a group, and the number of "correct" and "incorrect" decisions.

Dickinson (1986) has also used this exercise format as the basis for teaching and examining the Bayesian decision-making model. More specifically, the objectives of the exercise were to (1) identify the components of the normative decision-making situation and to consider their interrelationships, (2) compare the exercise scenario with real world decision-making situations, and (3) monitor the degree of Bayes—like behavior exhibited by the students. In his exercise:

> "Two hypothetical populations are defined, one consisting of 70% (X) cards and 30% (0) cards and the other consisting of 70% (0) cards and 30% (X) cards. Students are given samples of 50 (punched computer) cards drawn at random from one of the two populations, each card being punched with either an X or an O. As well, students are told the prior probability that the sample deck was drawn from either of the populations. Each student is given nine decks of 50 cards with the prior probability of a deck's origin being the X population varying from .1 to .9. At each of the nine trials, each student decides how many (of the 50 available) sample cards he/she wishes to purchase, records the number (on a tally sheet printed by the generation program), selects that number of cards, records the nature of each card (X or O), and decides as to the card deck's origin" (p. 178–179).

Mills (1988) has used a variation of this format to teach students the nature and importance of six different thinking styles: facts and figures, emotions and feelings, logical-negative, speculative-positive, creative and lateral, and control of thinking. This exercise begins by asking six volunteers to each wear a different brightly colored hat and to read a notecard on which examples of their assigned thinking styles are written. Then the handout "Six Thinking Hats," based on a book by the same name (deBono, 1985), is distributed to class members and described in detail. A case or problem requiring a decision is then introduced and class members, divided into six groups, think through the problem in their assigned thinking style only. New groups are assembled made up of persons from each of the six thinking style groups. The case or problem is then discussed by the new group for 15 to 20 minutes, followed by a general discussion in which students volunteer their personal learnings from the exercise. As a variation to the exercise, a six-member group can present the exercise to the class as a semester project.

Debate Exercise

Exercises can also take the form of having students debate various topics. Nkomo (see Nkomo, Fottler, and McAfee, 1988) has used this technique to help students understand both sides of controversial personnel/human resource management issues and to help them understand the policy implications of these issues. Each debate involves two teams, affirmative and negative. Prior to the debate itself, each team of three or four conducts research on a topic and prepares a written paper (8–10 pages) analyzing both sides of the topic. Among the topics are: (1) Resolved: That drug testing in the workplace makes good sense and does not infringe on employee rights, and (2) Resolved: That employers should be legally required to give employees pre-notification of plant closings or relocations. The debate itself is held in class and the two sides alternate in presenting their arguments as follows:

First Affirmative 6 minutes

First Negative 6 minutes

Second Affirmative 6 minutes

Second Negative 6 minutes

Rebuttals:

Negative 5 minutes

Affirmative 5 minutes

Audience Cross-Examination 10 minutes

After the debate, the class evaluates and discusses the presentation using an evaluation form.

While debates often follow traditional formats, a "four-way modified debate" has been used to develop student decision-making and oral presentation skills (McAfee, 1979). This approach begins by asking every student to answer in writing one specific question which appears at the end of a case and to bring his or her assignment to class. As each student enters the classroom, the instructor quickly reads his or her answer and assigns him or her to a debating team consisting of students who answered the question in a similar manner. Each team consists of no more than five students. If more than five students hold the same opinion on a case, the excess students are assigned to a team of judges. By following this procedure, four debating teams are established, as are one or more teams of judges (depending on class size).

After all the debating teams have been formed, the teams are told that a four-way debate is going to be held. They are asked to go out into the hall or to adjacent rooms to prepare to present and defend their opinion. The judges are told that their role in the debate is to "search for the truth." They are to listen to all four different sides presented during the debate and then, after the debate is over, to tell the class what they believe is the "correct" solution to the case.

At the start of the debate, all debaters are required to stand up in front and/or along the side of the classroom. All debaters are told that the debate will consist of two short rounds with a recess in between. The purpose of round one is for each team to learn the position of the other debating teams on the case. Hence, each team is asked to explain their position on the case, as comprehensively as possible, to both the judges and the other three debating teams.

As soon as round one is complete, the debating teams are told to prepare criticisms of each of the other three teams for round two, and are given ten minutes to prepare for it. During this period the judges are told to discuss what they have just heard and to begin to determine the "correct" solution to the case.

In round two, each debating team criticizes the position of each of the other teams. Unlike a traditional debate, teams are not allowed to rebut the criticisms made by the others. They must simply listen to them. This is done primarily to meet time constraints (50 minute class) but also to ensure that the debate doesn't degenerate into a shouting match, which can occur when so many debaters are present. Round two, and the debate, ends when Team Four has finished criticizing the position of the other three teams.

After the debate has ended, the judges are told to discuss the case among themselves and to arrive at a consensus, if possible. After their deliberations are complete (usually 5–10 minutes), the judging team or teams stand up and explain to the debaters their decision. A short debriefing period then follows.

Critique/Evaluation Exercise

Some exercises can be categorized as critique or evaluation exercises. In these, students are told that an organization or manager has taken one or more actions and are required to critique, usually in small groups, these actions. The student evaluations often serve as the basis for class discussion. Kuzmits (1986), for example, has developed a number of personnel-related exercises which follow this format.

In one of his exercises entitled "Ads that Work," students learn to recognize the characteristics of well-written recruitment ads and gain experience in critiquing actual ads printed in newspapers and journals. They are shown nine different newspaper advertisements and are asked to critique and then rank each using an evaluation grid which is provided. Eleven criteria appear on the grid including distinctive headlines, effective graphics, effective typeface, and avoids stereotyping. In Part II (optional) of the exercise, students are asked to clip examples of advertisements which they consider to be effective or ineffective and to write a paragraph explaining why they feel the ads fall into these categories. Part III (optional) of the exercise requires that students develop an advertisement and select the media for a hypothetical (or real) job vacancy provided by the instructor. Students are to base their media selection on research they have conducted concerning the readership habits of potential job candidates.

Kelley and Whatley (1987) use this format in their "Application Blank" exercise which is designed to teach students to identify the lawfulness/ unlawfulness of items on an application blank. In this exercise, students break into groups of four or five and evaluate an application blank which contains both legal and illegal questions. Students are given a "Pre-Employment Inquiry Guide," compiled from an EEOC Compliance Manual, to assist in their analysis. Students are also asked to discuss within their group the major job-related predictors that can be found on an application blank and their corresponding work behaviors. Finally, each group prepares an application blank that both meets legal requirements and is practically useful.

Game Show Format Exercises

All of us are familiar with the game show format as seen on television. "Jeopardy," "The Dating Game," and "Wheel of Fortune" have all captured our attention at one time or another. Interestingly, this format can and has served as the basis for experiential learning exercises.

Ireland and Hoover (1979) use this format with reference to Townsends' book, *Up the Organization*. They require students to suggest managerial responses to situations described by the game show host (other students). More specifically, students are asked to identify the managerial responses which they believe Townsend would initiate and, secondly, to give the managerial actions they feel are appropriate in terms of the cognitive and affective learning experiences they have examined up to this point in the course.

Ireland and Hoover contend that the game show format "is an excellent example of the benefits of whole-person learning. The total learning experience of each participant is highlighted by affective involvement (the thrill of competing, the desire to win, the 'owning of one's selected response,' etc.), as well as the actual game behavior (competing, persuasively communicating, dissonance reduction during debriefing, etc.). Most importantly, all of these 'process' benefits of experiential learning are not obtained at the expense of cognitive learning. In fact, just the opposite occurs." [p. 65].

McAfee (1981) has also used this format in an exercise called "The Test Preview Game." The purpose of the exercise is (1) to familiarize students with the type (question format, level of question difficulty, etc.) of questions which will be asked on the first test, (2) to reinforce specific information (cognitive or process) covered in class, and (3) to integrate information covered during the course both in class or in the text.

During the class session prior to the exercise, the class is given a general briefing on the game including a list of the game rules. Students are told that all game questions will be taken from class notes and specific chapters in the text. Two volunteers are asked to serve as emcees, and the remaining students are then divided into contestant groups consisting of three members each.

Each team is told to select one student who serves as a spokesperson for the group and one who is responsible for rolling a die.

At the start of the game, a giant snake-like figure which serves as a game board has been drawn on the black board. It contains a start circle and 100 spaces or adjoining squares. The instructor then introduces the "stars of the show"—the two student emcees who in turn describe the "valuable" prizes to be awarded to the game winners—candy bars, potato chips, and Pepsi. They also review the game rules with the participants briefly. They are:

1. The game consists of two rounds: a 20-minute regulation round and a 10-minute double point round.

2. Each contestant team rolls a die prior to the question presentation to determine the point value of the question. During the second round all point values double.

3. After being asked a question (multiple choice, true-false, short answer essay), each contestant team has 15 seconds to either answer the question or pass it to the next team. If the group chooses to answer, and answers correctly, it moves its marker forward the number of spaces designated by the die. It it answers incorrectly, it is penalized by moving back the number of spaces designated by the die. If the group chooses to pass the question, the receiving group then has 15 seconds to either answer the question or pass it on to the next contestant team. If no group chooses to answer a given question, the emcee answers it and asks a new question.

4. The team which has advanced its marker the furthest on the game board is the winner.

At the end of the game the emcees announce the winners of the game to the class and present them with the "valuable" prizes. The game is then debriefed by the instructor.

Assessment Centers As Experiential Learning Devices

An assessment center is a place in which one group of participants (assessors) systematically evaluates another group of participants (assessees) on a selected group of dimensions. These evaluations are ultimately fed back to the assessees. Normally, participants are evaluated on eight to twelve dimensions, the most frequent of which are: leadership, persuasiveness, perception, flexibility, decisiveness, organization and planning skills, problem solving skills, and oral and written communication skills. While many different dimensions can be assessed, organizations typically choose those which best fit their particular needs and requirements.

While assessment centers are widely used in industry for evaluating the promotion potential of employees, they can and have been used on college campuses as an experiential learning device. To illustrate, McAfee and Hawryluk (1986) established an assessment center and built an experimental course around it. The specific goals of the course were: (1) to provide information to students regarding their strengths and weaknesses on nine critical leadership/management skills, (2) to improve students' observation and evaluation skills and their ability to feed information and evaluations back to others, (3) to improve students' ability to evaluate themselves and accept constructive criticism and praise from others, and (4) to familiarize students with the assessment center concept and how it is used.

Students enrolled in the class were divided into two groups of ten each, one group of assessors and one of assessees. During the first two class meetings, assessors were trained in observing and feeding back behaviorally grounded information. They were also familiarized with the specific dimensions that they were to observe, as well as the exercises to be used. Following their training, assessors observed participants' behavior in four different exercises and conducted a background interview with each. Ultimately they fed back their findings, both orally and in writing, to assessees on an individual basis.

For their part, assessees completed a series of self-assessment questionnaires during the first two class sessions. They then participated in four different exercises and were interviewed by the assessors. Finally, they received feedback on each of the nine dimensions being evaluated.

Halfway through the course, participants reversed roles, i.e., assessees became assessors and vice versa. The new assessors were trained, observed assessees, and gave feedback. Assessees completed questionnaires, participated in exercises, and received feedback. Thus, all students ultimately served both as assessors and assessees.

Each student's grade was based on (1) a written self-evaluation, (2) an oral assessment of one assessee, and (3) a written assessment of the same assessee. The self-evaluation was submitted at the end of the course, after each student had been assessed. The oral assessment of another was conducted in private with one instructor present and was recorded on tape. The written evaluation was given to the assessee at the conclusion of the oral one, and a copy was given to the instructor. Each of the three course requirements counted for one third of the student's grade.

CONCLUSION: AVENUES FOR NEW EXERCISES

The term "exercise" means different things to different people. To some, an exercise and "touchy-feely" are synonymous; participants walk around, perhaps blindfolded, touching each other, presumably to gain a better understanding of themselves and others. To others, an exercise is synonymous with a role play; some participants assume the role of a supervisor while others assume the subordinate's role. The only difference between role plays is the subject of the conversation held between participants. To still others, an exercise consists of small group discussions, the purpose of which is to make a decision. Exercises to these people differ only in terms of the nature of the decision to be made. The important point here is that most people have a relatively narrow view of what constitutes an exercise. They fail to realize the wide diversity of formats which make up the exercise domain. The major purpose of this chapter has been to make readers aware of this diversity. In so doing, a number of specific examples were discussed. Hopefully, these examples will serve to encourage greater use of exercises and serve as a catalyst or starting point for the creation of new ones.

Several major trends are developing which will provide a need for the development of new exercises. In their book, *Management Education and Development: Drift or Thrust into the 21st Century?,* Porter and McKibbin (1988) contend that schools need to increase the globalization of their curriculum. The use of exercises represents an excellent avenue for internationalizing ones courses. One simple approach might be to develop exercises which involve international students on campus. Most colleges have students attending from foreign countries and some of them could be asked to participate in exercises. In addition to teaching students some specific cognitive objective, these exercises would also teach U.S. students cultural differences and the need to be sensitive to those differences. A somewhat more elaborate approach would be to develop exercises which involve the use of audio-video cassettes. These cassettes could be exchanged between U.S. and foreign universities and shown to students as part of an exercise. For example, exercises designed to teach principles of negotiation could involve U.S. students negotiating a sales or labor agreement via tapes with students at foreign universities. Students learning the principle of group decision-making could view tapes of students at foreign universities making decisions and vice versa. The exchange of tapes need not be limited just to foreign students. Rather, executives and other workers at foreign firms could also be asked to participate in exercises via video tapes or even teleconferencing.

A second area which is in need of additional exercises is the theoretical domain. At present, most exercises focus on teaching practical information. Yet, many theoretical concepts can be taught through exercises, too. Indeed, one could argue that since students often find theoretical concepts relatively dry and boring, exercises should be used to make them come to life. Several different types of exercises could be developed. Some could demonstrate the validity of a given theory or the variables involved. Others could demonstrate the strengths and weaknesses of a theory. Still others might demonstrate how a theory was developed or has evolved. Finally, exercises could be developed to demonstrate the relevance of a given theory in terms of employee attitudes and behaviors.

A third area ripe for the development of new exercises is federal, state, and local regulations and laws. When most faculty present legal information, they do so via straight lectures. As a result, students often retain little of this information beyond the examination. Exercises of various types could be developed to teach students these regulations. For example, students could be given short summaries of actual court cases and asked to discuss them in groups and determine if a law was broken. The actual court decision could then be fed back to participants, thereby teaching them the law. In addition to developing exercises which teach the law per se, others could demonstrate the effects of regulation on employee attitudes and behaviors. Still others could demonstrate the pros and cons of various laws.

CHAPTER 12

ADMINISTRATIVE GUIDELINES FOR EXPERIENTIAL EXERCISES

James W. Schreier

Administrative issues have always been a major concern to users of experiential exercises. At the first ABSEL meeting in 1974, Ralph Day summarized the conference with a focus on implementation.

> Most of these discussions indicated that even among designers of business games emphasis is shifting from the problems of design to the problems of implementation. The following topics received considerable attention . . . (1) the need to generate and maintain student involvement, (2) the need for instructor involvement, (3) the desirability of augmenting the business game with related projects, (4) the problem of evaluation, and (5) strategies for handling increased complexity in simulation games (Day, 1974).

In one of the sessions Ralph Day referred to, Harold Wilson called administration "the key to a successful gaming experience." I found then, and even more now, his comments relevant for the successful experiential experience.

> In the final analysis, three areas hold the key for success: (1) selection of a game that will contribute to the course objectives, (2) development of an operational system that will provide efficient processing of the necessary volume of paperwork, and (3) an understanding of techniques that will encourage the participation of faculty and students (Wilson, 1974).

At the Fourth Annual Conference of ABSEL, Jim Gentry and Al Burns called for a theory of the use of games and experiential exercises. At the same conference, Jim Schreier attempted to define some of the administrative roles necessary in experiential learning. Burns and Gentry identified key variables in "game conduct" including accountability, autonomy, pace, participant involvement, and user involvement. And they defined clearly some key issues related to administration by presenting a paper on "user attributes" including motive for use, teaching philosophy, freedom of choice, and resources (Burns and Gentry, 1977). Burns and Gentry's call for "a framework for positioning past and future empirical research on games and game administration" began a continuing journey that has produced greater knowledge of administrative issues and a greater awareness that perhaps we will never know everything about the complexity of administering these powerful learning tools.

Schreier took a more narrow view by focusing on the roles played by an exercise administrator. He assembled examples from several earlier ABSEL papers and proposed a model of administrator role. Although Schreier's view was narrower than Burns and Gentry's, it attempted to lay a foundation for future clarification and research. In particular, Schreier identified eight roles that an administrator plays, to some degree, in any experiential exercise. These roles (administrator, consultant, evaluator, participant, facilitator, president, observer, and presence) were defined and examined in a number of different experiential situations. Schreier concluded:

> The administration of these materials includes the roles which the instructor takes in planning, explaining, and evaluating the experience. It is important to realize that the instructor affects the results of the experience by his or her attitudes or behaviors (Schreier, 1977).

In 1978, Schreier reported that preliminary research showed the roles existed but that an instrument to measure the roles was difficult to develop (Schreier, 1978). Unfortunately, he did not continue the pursuit of this area of administration.

The Current Perspective

From these starting points, it is better to look at what we now know about the administrative issues and blend the historical research and viewpoints into the current applications. This leads to a logical examination of administrative steps based on what happens before, during, and after an experiential exercise.

BEFORE STARTING

It is very common to say that, "If you do not know where you are going, any place you end up is fine." It's true in career and travel planning. It is certainly true in experiential learning. Selection and the pre-exercise steps of preparation are critical to success. I have told organizational clients for years that if the experiential exercise works well, my role will be perceived as very effortless. My work is 85–95% completed when the exercise begins. I am there to direct, to debrief, and to rescue the exercise if something goes awry. If the administrator does his or her work effectively, the actual exercise is easy. There are always exceptions and there are certainly some particular exercises where the administrator is involved extensively throughout. But the point is worth repeating. Preparation is the majority of the success. And, preparation includes selection, materials preparation, equipment and facility setup, timing or scheduling, and selection or preparation of participants.

Selection

Selection has been examined by a few users and publishers, but little has been done to really understand the selection process on experiential exercises. In the early days of ABSEL, experiential exercises were being developed. They were being used. But, individual faculty members were inventing and reinventing exercises that found a wide audience only through dissemination at national meetings. Then and now, increased interest in experiential learning has meant increased publication of exercises. But this creates both opportunities and problems. More people are using experiential exercises because of their availability. But authors are still creating exercises for individual classes. So, choices may now be made in a similar fashion to ten years ago: choices are being made based on what is available and being marketed. A preferable option is choices being made based on learning objectives compared to a better information base of available experiential exercises.

Information is needed on the selection process. Very few surveys have been done by academics and publishers to find out adoption rates for particular materials. These are studies conducted for controlling inventory and/or marketing research. They tell us something about what's being selected. They say very little about how and why an experiential exercise is being selected. It would not be an easy piece of research. But, it would be possible. For example, one could more formally examine the relationship between instructor course objectives and the objectives set forth with an experiential exercise. One could attempt to collect some information on the process of selection, how a professor examines options for exercises, and what exercise variables are considered.

Right now it is even difficult to catalog existing experiential exercises. Publishers often do it for their own exercises. University Associates has a simple classification system for its structured experience series (Pfeiffer, 1985). But, it is still not available in a computerized data base format. Exercises are found in a variety of texts, workbooks, and several professional sources. Many are found in conference proceedings. Often the same exercise appears in slightly different formats, or stages of development, in several different sources. I suspect even more exercises could be found on course syllabi throughout the country. Organizations like ABSEL have not even attempted to catalog simulations and experiential exercises. CABSEL's efforts are long overdue and in need of significant support. There is a definite need for a data base of information with a clearly defined classification system and some powerful search and retrieval features. This is unfortunately a necessary step before some meaningful research can be done on the exercise selection process.

Material Preparation

While material preparation is not lacking information in the way that selection does, there is still a paradox. Most published experiential exercises include detailed instructions on materials needed, step-by-step procedures, questions for discussion, and defined objectives. But, again, there is little research on how these variables might affect the outcome of the exercise.

I believe this issue is becoming more and more complicated and will become a major issue in experiential learning in the 1990's. The last few years have seen a variety of experiential exercises go from five typed pages in a conference proceedings, to typeset workbooks, to exercise kits containing professionally prepared transparencies, handouts, and special props. Experiential exercises have always been used in a variety of sectors: higher education, business and industry, and non-profit organizations. But, the last few years have seen the growing acceptance of these exercises in the professional training and development field. Large, profit-seeking organizations are developing exercises based on marketing plans. Some are simple exercises found in collections at little or no cost. Some are new, conceptually sound exercises available only from the publisher. But the newer materials are well-produced and they are expensive. How these factors relate to the exercise's use and outcomes needs to become a concern of simulation/ experiential learning research.

From the viewpoint of basic information, several key points must be made about materials preparation. I have found that preparation for experiential exercises is a key factor to the exercise's success. There are shortcuts that can be taken. Most exercises do not have to be expensive. But they do require material preparation and often this is time-consuming and carries some cost. But, it is preparation that is absolutely necessary. Most experiential exercises attempt to simulate some type of organizational environment. It may be paper, some type of prop ranging from a supply of paper and paper clips to building blocks, or it may be room set-up. But whatever is recommended for a particular exercise is normally a required step for success.

An exercise might require $10–$20 worth of props: puzzles, baskets, coins, measuring tapes, building blocks, plus handouts and transparencies. Or one of them might be a $99 exercise that is purchased in kit form. Another exercise could be a paper nightmare requiring 30–35 envelopes, each containing five to ten pieces of printed material.

The problems related to these examples concern me. As the theory and application of experiential exercises grow, it is going to be important to control for complexity and cost. And it is going to be necessary to examine the effects these variables have on the other components of the experiential learning model.

Equipment/Facility Preparation

Equipment and facility preparation are another administrative concern. Some experiential exercises require additional audio-visual or recording equipment. While most of this equipment is more available today than it was a few years ago, I suspect that there are still faculty members struggling to get easels for use in classrooms, to get video recording equipment, and to get equipment available in some rooms available for use in another room. I designed a class a few years ago that required videotaping of the class about once a week. The university's audio-visual center was very helpful—when the equipment was available. If some higher ranking faculty member or administrator needed equipment, their request superseded my advance reservation. I bought $1500 worth of equipment in order to insure taping of student performance.

Room layout is a critical element in many experiential exercises. Most exercises require more room than for a normal class. An exercise with a class of 35 requires a classroom capable of holding 70. And it often requires moveable chairs. Many faculty members have spent semesters fighting with doing exercises in inadequate room sizes or layouts.

For many years I have used an experiential exercise on organization structures and communications. The props required are simple and not very costly. There's a one page handout and four decks of cards. But, a very large room, with sufficient space for four different organization structures designed with chair placements, is necessary. At one university it was rarely possible to get a room for this particular exercise. At first I tried the regular classroom and often used the hallway. But, it did not work as well as it should have. In another college, I had to reserve a large room in another building at the beginning of each semester. This was not an impossible task, but I have often wondered how much it might have inhibited others from using the exercise.

The 1980's saw the creation of "behavioral labs" in many colleges of business. They provided excellent facilities for some experiential exercises. But, there appear to be problems. Burton surveyed the use of behavioral labs in business schools and found they were underutilized and misunderstood by both faculty and administrators (Burton, 1987). Behavioral labs are often designed to do research on student reactions to certain situations. This might be different from a situation where the lab is designed for student learning. And there are some "behavioral labs" that sit idle in new buildings because faculty are not supported, encouraged, or taught how to use them. They will quickly be reallocated to other uses. There are guidelines for the design of behavioral labs (Ward, 1979). But, there are no guidelines on their use. These need to be developed. And, the information needs to be clearly disseminated so that it is used, not filed.

Timing/Scheduling

Time estimates for experiential exercises are notoriously inaccurate. When an exercise states 45–60 minutes, you can expect to finish in 30 minutes. When the next one you try says 60–75 minutes, you will spend two more class periods discussing the issues raised. The key guideline is experimentation. The instructor looking for appropriate experiential exercises must select, experiment, select, experiment, select—until you know what works, how it works, and why it works. You may never know exactly why it works. But, you will have a good idea about the what and how. Too often, in the pressure to teach a particular course or subject, we invest our time and energy in an exercise that may not be the best. Or, it may not meet the course objectives as well as one we would have to develop. But, it works.

My point is simple. Administering experiential exercises is very hard work. To the students, it seems easy. You are up in front doing very little (it seems) and they are role playing, doing an in-basket, completing a self-assessment, or analyzing a case. But, if you are really doing very little, your experiential exercise is likely to fail. Or, it means you have done more outside of class preparation than the exercise takes in class to make sure it works.

Selection/Preparation of Participants

Several ABSEL members have examined various issues related to selection and preparation of exercise participants. Burns and Gentry (1977) have included participants in their theory. Badgett looked specifically at how teams were formed for simulations and made recommendations that are clearly applicable to certain experiential exercises.

> Balanced-selection procedures are favored when competitiveness and realism are important dimensions of the simulation exercise. Peer relations are likely to be best when teams are allowed to form informally; however, good relations are likely to develop and continue during the course of the simulation when the teams are balanced (Badgett, 1980).

Studies of participant characteristics have been too numerous to include in this examination of administrative issues. A variety of different tactics have been taken to study the motivations, values, and personal characteristics of exercise participants. As the theory of experiential learning continues to develop, there will be continued attempts to identify participant factors for the success of experiential exercises. There will always be a variety of options that an instructor needs to consider as part of the goals and learning of the exercise.

DURING THE EXERCISE

If my earlier remarks about preparation being the key are valid, the activities that need to be conducted during the exercise should be easier to discuss. But, they are still very important. Here we need to consider again the administrator role, specifically the roles during the exercise, and options which can be used during the exercise.

Administrator Roles

The roles I defined in 1977 still seem valid. But the increased complexity of exercises and the increased use of technology as part of many experiential exercises seems to call for some additional roles. While it might be possible to squeeze some new duties into the previously defined roles of administrator, consultant, evaluator, participant, facilitator, president, observer, and presence, I do not believe it clearly reflects the changes that have occurred.

Many of today's experiential exercises have become more complex, more involved, and more difficult to administer. New roles are being performed because we know more about the experiential learning process. There have been some experiential exercises recently that are impossible to conduct with one instructor. And, they more closely resemble a Broadway play than an experiential exercise of the 1970's. Experiential exercises in the future are going to need casting directors, producers, and directors. Here again the organizational training and development field may lead the way. I have done experiential exercises in the private sector with professional casts of 10 or more—for a group of 25 to 30 participants. And, organizations rarely invest the time and money necessary for that type of support unless they believe that there is a payoff.

But, there is currently very little research into the effects of these variables in the effectiveness to the technique. There is going to be a greater need for some academic/business partnerships to conduct research into the effects of these variables. Business has some interest in the research. Academe has the interest, but not the resources, to conduct these types of experiments.

Churchill presented an extremely interesting part of exercise administration in a paper on the use of "the glitch."

> A "glitch" is a faculty-imposed crisis in a game environment. Its principal applicability is in management development courses, where it serves both as an entertainment and as a way to keep participants open to learning (Churchill, 1979).

There are a variety of other administrative issues related to the conduct of a simulation game that are equally valuable for experiential exercises. But, the relationship is going to have to be examined by the authors to construct bridges to the experiential exercises. Wolfe and Box's (1987) work on team cohesion and Faria's (1986) work on game conditions may be particularly useful in clarifying these issues.

AFTER THE EXERCISE

Debriefing has always been a key component of successful exercises. The link between objectives, course materials, and the exercise seems rarely, if ever, crystal clear to the participants. In the organizational world, this is even more relevant because some management development audiences resist "games" when they're "played" with Tinkertoys, Lego blocks, or paper airplanes.

Adequate attention must be given to the debriefing. Managers must process the information from the exercise and make real-life, on-the-job applications. Students must see the possible link to their own real-life experiences and possible future career situations.

Hunsaker provided the standards of debriefing in 1979. He called for the debriefing as the major opportunity for learning.

> The main function of the facilitator during the debriefing is to insure an integration of the experiences with concepts and applications to outside situations so that appropriate generalizations can be made. It is also important that the facilitator encourages participants to exchange feedback and clarify strengths and weaknesses in their interpersonal behavior. Consequently, the facilitator should direct attention to both the content and process of the exercise with respect to both conceptual and personal learnings (Hunsaker, 1978).

Certo and Lamb (1985) conducted one of the few research studies attempting to validate the debriefing process and they called for more research into the debriefing process. Their examination of a particular exercise and the goals of the debriefing indicated that close links exist from objectives, to the exercise itself, to the debriefing.

A FINAL ISSUE

If there is a final issue related to administration, it is a clear understanding of the realities of experiential learning. It is rewarding and rigorous. It is fun and frustrating. It is exciting and exhausting. And, something will usually go wrong. Like many in the field of simulation and experiential learning, I believe Murphy's Law was created by the first author of experiential exercises. There is a guideline for this problem. It's prepare, prepare, prepare. And, then you can still expect something to go wrong. I have several experiential exercises which I've run several times a year and have done so for ten years or more. They work very smoothly now—98% of the time. But, I know for each one that, sooner or later, something will happen other than what I expect. Initially I was worried about this. Now I look at each administrative "glitch" as an opportunity to test creativity and quick thinking.

Administrative issues for experiential learning are many and complex. There is a clear need for better definitions, agreement, and research to support the ideas presented here. The knowledge of how the technique works and what it can do has grown significantly over the last five years. It will continue to grow significantly over the next ten. Many of the questions are clear. The answers, even though they will be difficult to determine, will be extremely valuable for the future development of experiential learning.

CHAPTER 13

THE USE OF LIVE CASE STUDIES IN BUSINESS EDUCATION: PROS, CONS, AND GUIDELINES

Alvin C. Burns

There are several pedagogies available to business educators. Ward and Rudelius (1987) separate the various teaching approaches into two types: "ruleg" and "egrule" learning. Ruleg approaches are those which teach general rules or principles and then provide students with examples, or students are expected to apply the rules to examples. Egrule approaches supply specific examples to students, who are then expected to discover their own rules or principles. The lecture approach typifies the ruleg approach, while simulations, games, experiential exercises, and traditional case studies all apply the egrule technique. Egrule learning is an active, involving experience, but ruleg learning is a passive, uninvolving experience. Consequently, egrule learning is claimed to be more effective because students discover the rules and, theoretically at least, internalize them faster and retain them longer.

This chapter treats a ruleg approach which is equally involving, and perhaps even more involving than discovery approaches, namely, the "live" case study approach. As can be surmised from the introductory comments, the discovery pedagogies rely on inductive reasoning. That is, students go through a number of experiences and these become the basis for generalizing a pattern or rule. The live case technique, in contrast, thrusts the student into a specific business problem where rules apply, and it is incumbent upon the student to use deductive reasoning to identify the proper rules to use and apply them to the situation. In addition to this difference, the live case approach has many aspects that warrant detailed description.

Accordingly, the objectives of this chapter are:

1. To describe the live case study approach.
2. To point out differences between live cases and traditional case studies.

3. To review the various benefits gained by using live case studies.
4. To discuss the learning situation accompanying live cases.
5. To provide examples of the use of live cases in business education.
6. To itemize several potential problem areas one should address in adopting the live case method.
7. To offer guidelines to contend with these problems.

DIFFERENCES BETWEEN TRADITIONAL CASES AND LIVE CASES

The pedagogy known as the "case study," where students are provided a written description of a company situation, has been used in business education for a great many years, but a number of criticisms have been voiced against this approach. Markulis (1985) has reviewed these objections, and he notes that traditional case studies are sterile, impersonal, outdated, open to various interpretations, subject to student and/or instructor bias, sometimes unrealistic, and discouraging of rigorous analysis. Also, Goretsky (1984) presents an informative paradigm comparing four instructional methods reproduced in Table 13-1. The comparison reveals that traditional case study methods relate to the normative world rather than the real-world. In other words, he views the traditional case study as a static pedagogy, while the live case study is a dynamic pedagogy.

TABLE 13-1
Comparative Relationships of Instructional Methods

Term Paper	Case Method	Role Playing	Live Case
Possibility of non-real world	Normative world	Realistic world	Real-world

Adapted from Goretsky (1984, p. 34)

Defined succinctly, a live case study involves students working with an organization to solve some real business problem. Markulis (1985) identifies three distinguishing features:

1. Personal participation by key decision-makers in the company during the case analysis,
2. Immediate accessibility of the company for students, and
3. The company situation or strategic decision is one that has just recently been made or is about to be made.

The key ingredient in live case studies is realism. There is a real company with real products, real competitors, real decision-makers, real employees, and a real problem. The company, decision-makers, and problem have infinitely more dimensionality than can be provided in a written case. Even more significant is the ability of students to interact in a question-and-answer format with the decision-makers (and others) over a considerable span of time. The stakes are clearly higher in that students' analyses are potentially useful to the organization, and their proposed solutions will be scrutinized by the organization principals with the organization's interests in mind. The immediate educational consequence of increased motivation on the part of students has been noted by several educators (Burns, 1978; Dommeyer, 1986; Goretsky, 1984; Hafer, 1984; Hoover, 1977; Humphreys, 1981; Markulis, 1985; and Richardson and Raveed, 1980). This increased motivation is attributed to greater learning.

BENEFITS OF THE LIVE CASE STUDY APPROACH

Numerous authors have addressed the special benefits gained from the adoption of the live case approach. They accrue to the student, the instructor, the educational institution, and the sponsor organization.

With respect to benefits for the student, Bruner (1961) has noted four outcomes of experiential learning. In particular, it: (1) aids memory by forcing the learner to develop organizational schemes, (2) results in greater immediate and delayed retention of subject matter, (3) generates a greater motivation to continue learning, and (4) encourages creativity in students. Burns (1978) has noted the objectives of the live case study with more specificity:

1. It overcomes the sterility and one-way delivery of course material.
2. It provides a direct and immediate use of skills and methods learned and affords tangible reasons for learning the material.
3. The presence of a third party (i.e., the outside sponsor) supplies intrinsic motivation to learn and apply learning.
4. Actual field experience acquaints students with practical problems and solutions.
5. By staying with a project from start to completion, students gain an appreciation for the flow of activities and contingent events involved.

In addition to these advantages, adopters of live cases have noted some residual benefits. Humphreys (1981), for instance, claims that students develop more interest in supplementary materials. Markulis (1985) points out that students are exposed to professional conduct through their interactions with and presentations to real-world decision-makers. Goretsky (1984) makes note of the practical experience's value to a student's résumé, and Richardson and Raveed (1980) observe that some students are subsequently employed by the sponsoring organizations upon their graduation.

Important benefits are gained by the instructor who uses live case studies. Dommeyer (1986) identifies four. First, the instructor is more stimulated and personally rewarded by observing students involved in live case studies. Second, the instructor is educated of real-world situations. Third, a grading burden reduction may result through the use of teams and the requirement for a single, final report from each team. Finally, fewer individual "incompletes" occur under the live case approach. Other benefits have been cited by de los Santos and Jensen (1985). They point out that client-sponsored projects afford the instructor with a treasure of examples of course principles. In addition, the instructor may entertain the possibility of future consulting projects with live case sponsors who need assistance beyond the capabilities or constraints of student-teams. Alternatively, the client contacts may become important data collection sources for academic research undertaken by the instructor.

De los Santos and Jensen (1985) also note the institutional benefits of live cases, which can be turned into public relations vehicles suitable for news media stories, or constitute a part of word-of-mouth publicity in the business community. The sponsor contacts cultivated with live case projects may also provide avenues for solicitation of contributions to the department, college, or university in the future. McCain and Lincoln (1982) add the institutional gains of a favorable public image, satisfied alumni, and funds to cover expenses.

Certainly, the most comprehensive benefits analysis has been performed by these authors (McCain and Lincoln 1982), whose "Participants' Benefits and Costs" exhibit is reproduced in Table 13–2. This figure reiterates and augments the previous descriptions of benefits for the student, the instructor, and the institution. In addition, it identifies specific benefits gained by the client-sponsor which include low-cost assistance, public image enhancement, better decision-making, gain of an outside perspective, altruism, and recruiting students to become future employees. The McCain-Lincoln presentation is, in fact, a (nonexhaustive) cost-benefits choice model framework useful in the selection process when the instructor is pondering alternative live case projects for his/her classes. This model is recommended for readers who wish to improve their decision-making regarding selection of live case sponsors.

LEARNING THROUGH LIVE CASES

The chapter's introductory comments serve as groundwork to the understanding of the learning process applicable to live case studies. Complementary to this groundwork is Bloom et. al.'s (1956) taxonomy of learning objectives, described elsewhere in this book. The taxonomy identifies sequential levels of learning objectives from the lowest level of basic

TABLE 13–2
Live Case Study Participants' Benefits and Costs

Participant	Benefits	Costs
STUDENT	1. Real-world experience 2. Self-esteem 3. Future employment contacts 4. Fulfill graduation requirements 5. Self-confidence 6. Money	1. Frustration from low skill/ability levels 2. Extraordinary time demands 3. Do not see entire picture 4. Money
CLIENT	1. Low-cost research 2. Enhance public image 3. Improved decision-making 4. Outside (objective) point of view 5. Altruism 6. Exposure to potential employees	1. Money 2. Nonmonetary funds (typing, postage, etc.) 3. Management time 4. May not get quality work
INSTRUCTOR	1. Provide meaningful education 2. Sharpen skills 3. Generation of publishable data 4. Money 5. Generation of consulting contacts 6. Develop employment contacts for students	1. Excessive time (opportunity costs) 2. Effect on personal image 3. Money (travel, phone, class, etc.) 4. Not meeting course objectives
INSTITUTION	1. Favorable image in business community 2. Provide meaningful education/satisfied alumni 3. Money funds to cover research expenses 4. Donations—monetary and nonmonetary	1. Non-monetary funds (e.g., postage, typing) 2. Effect on department college, or school image 3. Failure to provide adequate education

Adapted from McCain and Lincoln (1982, p. 48)

knowledge where the student demonstrates rote memory to the highest level, called "objective evaluation," where the student demonstrates creativity, judgment, and sophisticated analytical abilities. As noted earlier, the live case approach is a "ruleg" pedagogy; consequently, the student must have a storehouse of rules to apply to the live case situation. Thus, the learning levels of: (1) application, (2) analysis, and (3) objective synthesis are involved in the solution of a live case.

Deductive reasoning must be applied in ruleg learning. Students must comprehend the rules and decide whether or not particular rules apply to specific components of the live case problem. In addition, they must analyze the live case problem to identify the components in the first place. Finally, the solution to the problem(s) necessitates a creative blending of rules and modifications of those rules, tailored to the real-world situation. One of the interesting aspects of live cases involves the uniqueness of each live case. Unlike written cases where students are provided with a standardized stimulus, each live case constitutes a different real-world situation. Moreover, the situation may change over the duration of the live case project as students gather primary information from organization principals, competitors, or various other sources. It should be obvious that this learning environment closely tracks the career environment of students once they leave the university. In other words, the live case learning closely mirrors life-long learning where the individual must constantly select and modify rules and apply them to specific instances via deductive logic in order to cope with real-world career problems.

Unfortunately, limited empirical attention has been placed on the learning effects of live case studies versus alternative pedagogies. Further, the few published studies address attitudinal effects exclusively. Hoover (1977) compared students' satisfaction with the live case approach to their opinions of other business courses. He found that 14 of 15 satisfaction items were significantly greater for the live case approach. Dommeyer (1986) compared students' attitudes toward a live case project versus an individual proposal and found significantly more positive attitudes assigned to the project, the course, and the instructor. Finally, Hafer (1984) investigated student attitudes toward the Small Business Institute live case versus lectures as well as text cases. Students indicated that the live case performed best with respect to providing the greatest depth, offering the best chance to use what they had learned, requiring the most self-motivation, and opportunity for individualized instruction. If one accepts that increased motivation and positive attitudes stimulate greater learning, these studies offer tentative support, at least, for the claim of greater learning effects.

EXAMPLES OF THE USE OF LIVE CASES

There are a number of published examples of the use of live cases, and there are any number of other possible areas where live cases could be employed. Goretsky (1984) even goes so far as to claim that live cases can be used anywhere in business education. This section corroborates his claim.

More articles have been published concerning the use of live cases in the marketing research course than have been published for other courses. Burns (1978) describes in detail the mechanics and flow of events for a live case approach he extends across the entire semester and integrates into his course. Humphreys (1981) dwells on operational considerations such as the choice of sponsors and projects, team organization, and course integration. She also discusses the critical role played by the instructor. Richardson and Raveed (1980) reveal how they improved the quality of their marketing research live case projects by adding structure and charging clients a fee. De los Santos and Jensen (1985) outline project conduct and identify problems and benefits. Dommeyer (1986) conducted the empirical study described above, and McCain and Lincoln (1982) advocate the cost-benefits framework detailed in Table 13-2.

Other authors have noted different areas of marketing where the live case is appropriate. Goretsky (1984) describes five different live case project areas: advertising; distribution channels; industrial/governmental marketing; international marketing; and marketing information systems. Thistlethwaite and Zimmerly (1978) also describe a marketing management application area.

With respect to other business functional areas, additional published articles exist. Hoover (1977), for instance, describes his use of it in the business and society course. Markulis (1985) details its adoption in the business policy course, and Hafer (1984) notes its use in the Small Business Institute course.

As evidenced by Goretsky's (1984) claim, there is no reason to consider these examples a complete list of the application areas. Instead, it should be obvious that virtually any business functional area—accounting, finance, economics, management, hospitality management, quantitative methods, and so on—is amenable to the live case approach, since the application of business education is ultimately in some organizational context.

IMPLEMENTATION OF THE LIVE CASE APPROACH: PROBLEMS AND SUGGESTED SOLUTIONS

The McCain-Lincoln benefits and costs presentation in Table 13-2 notifies potential adopters of the live case approach that significant disadvantages accompany the important advantages. In fact, McCain and Lincoln (1982) are quick to point out that the live case method can be "painful" if not managed properly. They allude to the "suffering bastard" comment of Gentry (1979) in describing the high instructor involvement requirements of live case studies. Humphreys (1981) also observes that the major disadvantage of using the live case method rests in substantially more operational problems than with other approaches. This section will treat six major problem areas systematically and offer some guidelines to minimize them.

Sponsor/Project Recruitment and Selection

The essential prerequisite for implementation of the live case approach is a pool of sponsored projects for the term at hand. Obviously, with only a few potential projects, student teams will grow to uncomfortable sizes and the learning process will be diluted for individual students. Some suggestions concerning the stimulation of sponsor demand are to be found. De los Santos and Jensen (1985) offer some logical approaches, such as personal contacts, solicitation with small business and business development programs, continuing education programs, or even community service bulletins or testimonial letters from satisfied clients. They also note the importance of word-of-mouth publicity in the business community. Markulis (1985) suggests phone calls to previous and potential sponsors, and Humphreys (1981) broaches sending memos to other faculty members to recruit their assistance. Another sponsor-generating device used by this author is to place advertisements in the local newspaper.

Generation of sponsor prospects can be effected fairly easily according to these authors. However, there are problems apparent when one reviews the types of sponsors and their expectations. De los Santos and Jensen (1985) have itemized a variety of sponsors with which they have worked including Girl Scouts, fraternities, universities, televisions stations, airlines, concert promoters, and retail organizations. Richardson and Raveed (1980) also note a variety of sponsors and further point out that clients without previous experience with students doing live cases have widely varying expectations about the results. Markulis (1985) points out a problem with too many small companies responding and inhibiting the generalizability of learning to larger organizations. Sometimes sponsors equate the live case experiences with free consulting by the instructor (de los Santos and Jensen, 1985), or sponsors are sometimes reluctant to divulge certain sensitive information to students (Markulis, 1985; Richardson and Raveed, 1980). It is important, at the same time, to realize that students are thrust into an unusual learning situation. Markulis (1985), for instance, notes the possibility of student intimidation, while Richardson and Raveed (1980) observe a lack of student self-confidence danger in live case studies.

In short, there is a need to screen potential live case project sponsors with clear criteria (de los Santos and Jensen, 1985). Markulis (1985) volunteers four criteria which are reproduced with slight modifications as guidelines below:

1. Sponsors must guarantee willingness of key people to participate face-to-face with students.
2. There must be important changes or decisions in the organization which are appropriate for analysis under the course content.

3. There should be reasonable proximal location of the organization to the university.
4. There should be availability of company data and trade data to students.

Certainly the most well-developed listing of sponsor-project criteria is espoused by McCain and Lincoln (1982). Described by de los Santos and Jensen (1985), these criteria are presented as additional guidelines below:

1. Projects should illustrate the application of theory and practice as covered in class material.
2. Projects should be selected that can be completed in a reasonable amount of time.
3. Projects should be interesting and challenging to students in order to ensure an educational experience and not just cheap labor.
4. Sponsors must be willing to pay for the expenses incurred in conducting the project in a timely fashion.
5. Sponsors should be willing to ensure that cooperation, assistance, support, and, hence, time necessary to provide students the information they may require for the project.
6. Whenever feasible, care should be taken in assessing the need for the project and the probability that recommendations will be seriously considered by the sponsor rather than the use of the project as a charitable or business deduction.
7. When appropriate for some institutions, some additional consideration may need to be given for nonprofit, religiously affiliated, and/or charitable organizations over their counterparts or vice versa.

Project Scheduling and Timing

Virtually all educators who have used live case studies realize the need for advance planning and scheduling. Both Markulis (1985) and Richardson and Raveed (1980) mention difficulties in coordinating business sponsors' schedules and student teams' schedules for meetings. De los Santos and Jensen (1985) and Richardson and Raveed (1980) warn of the danger of students not completing the project by the end of the academic term, forcing the instructor to explain to sponsors the reason for delay, or to complete the project him/herself.

Scheduling and timing problems are inevitable, so the objective should be to minimize their occurrence. If the criteria concerning client willingness and availability to students are employed, this objective will be served somewhat. Nevertheless, most live case users agree on the necessity of drawing up a timetable of project tasks and events and ensuring that the time table is honored. Burns (1977), for instance, offers a week-by-week accounting of his schedule; de los Santos and Jensen (1985) recommend the use of PERT charting to sequence events and assign responsibilities; Humphreys (1981) notes the instructor's role in project control. Recommendations which eventuate in this problem area are listed below:

1. Identify all tasks necessary to complete the project.
2. Identify the sequencing of these tasks, possibly with flow chart assistance.
3. Determine the approximate time frames of the tasks.
4. Develop a master schedule of the tasks, giving start and completion target dates.
5. Gain agreement from the sponsor and the student team as to the schedule.
6. Assign responsibilities (instructor, sponsor, student team, and individual student) to accomplish the tasks according to schedule.
7. The instructor should compare actual to targeted dates and act as a control agent if the schedule is not being honored.

Student Organization and Evaluation

Student organization refers to the composition of student teams which work with each sponsor project. This area is somewhat problematic since the number of live cases varies per class, the size of classes is not constant, and the mix of students often must be taken into consideration. Little has been written about student team size and composition for live case studies. With respect to size, the nature of the live case project has some bearing. For instance, marketing research live case projects are reasonably uniform in that students must go through specific steps to accomplish a survey. Thus, three to five students can usually handle a simple survey with sample size of 100. However, Small Business Institute consulting teams must determine the problem(s) and address them systematically. The problem varies from client to client, and the solutions may range from setting up an accounting system to developing an inventory control system. Some problems obviously require more studentpower than do others. The downside to large teams, on the other hand, is loss of coordination. Large teams often experience difficulty meeting as a whole group, and sponsors are resistant to troops of students with which they must interact. Of course, commuter students are most afflicted with the difficulty, so student group size must also reflect the realities of student characteristics specific to each campus. It has been this author's experience that a target size of five-plus-or-minus-two rule of thumb seems to work reasonably well, especially if the onus is placed on students to form teams based on their classes and work schedules so as to maximize the opportunities of group meetings.

Composition of student groups is best effected voluntarily rather than arbitrarily or randomly. This approach complements the previous requirement that student teams can meet conveniently and frequently over the duration of the live case project. It is helpful to offer some guidelines to students who form teams voluntarily, however. In Small Business Institute or business policy live case study instances, the instructor may wish to suggest that the team have a representative from the various major functional areas of business in order to effect specialization areas for team members. Alternatively, students can be warned of the need for a mix of strengths ranging across good analytical skills, writing skills, oral communications, and so forth. Perhaps the most critical aspect of team composition is the selection of a team leader who will be an effective liaison for the team with the sponsor and the instructor.

Evaluation of individual student learning remains a difficult process with live case studies. This author and others (de los Santos and Jensen, 1985; Humphreys, 1981) have adopted a system of peer evaluation augmenting the overall team performance evaluation. While not perfect, one approach is for the instructor to determine an overall grade to the team's performance (e.g., to grade the final report) and to use confidential evaluations provided by all team members of each other team member plus self-evaluations. These evaluations are averaged for each student and used to adjust the final grade for that student. This author, for instance, has each team member evaluate each other member on a 100% scale, and the average percent rating is applied to the team's project grade. Thus, those with 100% averages receive the project grade individually, while others receive their average percentage of the project grade as the individual grade. Granted, this system is not perfect; however, if students are periodically reminded of this evaluation system, and urged to negotiate agreements with team members regarding equitable work over the duration of the live case, it is workable.

Thus, regarding student team organization and evaluation, one should:

1. Identify the amount and nature of work required for each live case project.
2. Adopt a mechanism which forms teams appropriate to the live case project tasks necessary to be performed (e.g., functional specialization, skill specializations, etc.).
3. Decide on a suggested ideal group size consistent with: (1) the amount of work to be performed and (2) the constraints of student population characteristics. A handy rule of thumb might be five-plus-or-minus-two.
4. Require student groups to identify a (strong) group leader who will be the liaison for the group with the sponsor and the instructor.
5. Adopt an evaluation system which acknowledges the possibility of uneven contributions by individual team members and adjusts the

individual student's grade based on peer evaluation of the effort contributed.
6. Periodically remind students of the peer evaluation system and their need to negotiate the live case project work load distribution based on other class requirements or other commitments.

Compensation and Reimbursement of Student Costs

A characteristic of the live case study approach unparalleled by any other pedagogy is the expenses factor. Normally, a live case requires students to incur out-of-pocket costs. Such costs might include automobile or other transportation expenses to visit the client or collect information, duplication expenses for questionnaires, long distance telephone charges, mail expenses, typing expenses, graphics or artwork costs, and copy service expenses. Alternatively, some of these expenses might be borne by the instructor's department or college. In either case, the potential exists for expenses to become a troublesome aspect of the live case study.

Few authors have discussed this aspect. de los Santos and Jensen (1985) describe how they submit a preliminary and then a final budget to the clients for approval. Richardson and Raveed (1980) indicate that they charge sponsors a flat fee. No one has pointed out the bothersome mechanics of requiring students to maintain records and retain receipts, or of actually reimbursing students once the term is over, nor of the inevitable late-paying client.

Compensation is a different matter. It is apparently generally assumed that the instructor's time and contributions are part of his/her job description as an educator, and the sponsor should not feel obligated to pay for those services. However, the use of department or university resources is another matter since operating budgets are impacted. This author has used a system where students are reimbursed for out-of-pocket expenses once they submit receipts (generally along with the final report), and the sponsor is asked to make a donation to the department in addition to expenses reimbursement to assist the department in its educational mission. Undoubtedly, a number of alternative systems exist, such as the Small Business Institute where funding is provided for with a grant, but some general guidelines such as the following should cover the majority of cases:

1. Gain written acknowledgement from sponsors that students out-of-pocket expenses will be reimbursed in a timely fashion.
2. Submit an estimated expenses budget to the client. Gain approval in the very early stages of the live case study.
3. Require students to maintain expenses records and retain expense receipts. These should be submitted along with the final report.

4. Require students to maintain internal records of which students incurred which expenses. Identify a single student who will be responsible for final disbursement of expenses to team members.
5. Require sponsors to cut reimbursement checks immediately after receiving the expenses report so students will be reimbursed before they end the term and leave campus.
6. If desired, develop an account (e.g., a university foundation account) appropriate for donations from sponsors.

Instructor Involvement

The potential of instructor self-abuse is a universally acknowledged liability of the live case study method. For instance, de los Santos and Jensen (1985) and Richardson and Raveed (1980) are in agreement with McCain and Lincoln (1982) regarding the heavy contact commitments of the live case approach. Similarly, Humphreys (1981) identifies at least three roles the instructor must play over the duration of the live case study. She points out the instructor must be a consultant to the sponsor as well as to individual student teams who come to him/her for assistance. The instructor must also be a project controller who polices the schedule of necessary events and who also serves as a quality controller for each team project. Finally, the instructor must perform student evaluations, juggling the project grade, peer evaluations, and special circumstances involved in the grading phase. Interestingly, de los Santos and Jensen (1985) mention the possibility of other faculty members perceiving the high involvement of the live case method instructor as consulting rather than as teaching.

There are no apparent "easy" avenues to suggest regarding instructor involvement. Sponsors will expect the instructor, and not a graduate assistant, to contact them initially and remain in contact over the life of the project. Student teams must be prodded and reminded of deadlines. They must also be constantly monitored as to quality of effort, and the instructor will need to forestall any procrastination tendencies concerning assembling the final report. Some guidelines to consider include:

1. Develop an understanding with sponsors that the project is a student project which will have a professional appearance but is not to be considered in the category of professional consulting: its purpose is a learning experience.
2. Decide on a reasonable number of projects per class; balance the class size with the number of projects, subject to your own time resources anticipated for that term.
3. With each project, identify specific dates as checkpoints when you will work with the student team. Make clear that you expect significant progress to be made between checkpoint dates.

4. Insofar as possible use other class members as resources. For instance, have student teams make interim report presentations in class and open their work up to constructive class criticism (Humphreys, 1981).
5. Consider the use of class time to meet with individual teams.
6. Consider the use of a graduate assistant or a graduate student on independent study as a projects expeditor who will work with specific teams to solve the simple problems, without your involvement, and release your time for the tougher problems.
7. Include a minimum of one week slack time in the final report deadline at the end of the term.

Liabilities Involved With Live Cases

Because an outside organization is involved, there are three potential liability areas which rear their ugly heads. The emphasis is placed on the word "potential," as the literature does not contain any horror stories in the knowledge of this author, but informal discussions with live case users have revealed some embarrassing instances where sponsors have misused the results, competitors of sponsors have applied pressure to see the final reports, or students have failed to deliver the findings to sponsors. With regard to the first potential liability area, it is conceivable that sponsors will be disappointed with the final results, perhaps refusing to reimburse students or even complaining to university administrators. Alternatively, liability may ensue from a sponsor who becomes overly zealous in using the project's findings. A case in point is where a company created an advertisement saying the marketing department at the local university had conducted a study and found the company's products to be the best on the market. In reality, it was a live case study team's findings. So, both negative or positive liabilities exist.

The second liability area which should concern live case study adopters is student safety. If students are travelling off-campus as part of course requirements, there exists potential liability regarding injury. Students visiting production facilities are exposed to various dangers, and it is possible that personnel from the sponsoring organization may create uncomfortable and compromising situations for students. The third area concerns student conduct. Dommeyer (1986) notes that students may commit illegal acts such as trespassing, harassment, or breach of confidentiality. To be certain, these scenarios are highly unlikely eventualities, but forewarning of them is necessary here.

Fortunately, legal issues in experiential education have been addressed by Richardson and Summey (1980). They offer strategies for avoiding unintentional contractual obligations in three areas: (1) soliciting live case clients; (2) specifying the project terms; and (3) project funding. In a nutshell, they recommend that the instructor become educated on legal implications of his/her agreements with sponsors; furthermore, that he/she be diligent in informing all parties involved of the limits of obligations.

While not definitive in the least, the following guidelines are offered. If a reader is concerned about any of these, he/she should consult the appropriate legal expert:

1. Draft a statement for the sponsor stipulating the parameters of the live case study. Some points to include are: (1) the student learning objective; (2) points of confidentiality, if any; (3) acknowledgement that the instructor, department and university are not sanctioning the team's conclusions; (4) agreements concerning expenses reimbursement; and (5) noting that implicit contractual obligations should not apply.
2. Determine the university's liability for students injured off-campus while performing course requirements. Use appropriate release forms (e.g., those often used for field trips), if recommended by the university legal personnel.
3. Determine, if appropriate, the sponsor's insurance and other legal protections for visitors who are injured on site.
4. Inform students of illegalities they may perform out of ignorance or failure to understand the consequences of their actions.
5. Make clear that sponsors are making donations, not paying compensation, to the department.
6. Review the Richardson and Summey (1980) article for insights.

CONCLUSION: LIVE CASE STUDY PEDAGOGY IS NOT FOR EVERYONE

By now it should be obvious that the live case approach has special requirements which must be met in order for it to succeed. Relative to other pedagogies, the live case approach represents less certainty, less structure, less uniformity, and less control. At the same time, it represents more ambiguity, more involvement, more liability, and more serendipitous benefits. The decision to adopt the live case approach rests, ultimately, on a personal level and must take into consideration the other obligations, pressures, and objectives which uniquely constitute an educator's goals agenda.

This chapter cannot resolve the decision for readers; however, it has sought to portray the benefits, problems, and unique features of the live case study approach in a candid manner. The several guidelines proposed will serve to minimize most of the major difficulties encountered and, hopefully, to maximize the several benefits. If you wish to join the ranks of the "suffering bastards," at least your eyes are open to some ways of reducing the suffering.

CHAPTER 14

STRUCTURING A LIVE CASE: A METHOD AND EXAMPLE FROM AN INTRODUCTORY ADVERTISING CLASS

Hugh M. Cannon
Theodore C. Alex

Instructors of college-level business administration classes face two major problems in addressing the needs of today's professional management environment. The first is that of achieving relevance or a sense of how the course material relates to real-world situations. The second is preparing students to understand and use the increasingly sophisticated management theory now available. As a rule, this is done by utilizing one of two approaches:

1. The *inductive* approach suggests that students examine real-world situations and draw inferences regarding the principles that govern them.
2. The *deductive* approach suggests that students learn principles and then deduce their logical implications for the real world.

The inductive approach is most closely associated with the Harvard case method. In explaining this method, Corey (1982) draws an analogy between case study and the experience of a natural history student who was asked by his professor to sit in front of a fish and note its key characteristics. After three days of intensive study, and no little proding by the teacher, the student had acquired not only a knowledge of the specific fish he had studied, but he had developed a meaningful framework for integrating this knowledge into a larger system of understanding.

On the surface, this story would seem to be far removed from the study of business strategy, but in fact it is very relevant, especially for the case method of teaching. Corey notes that by intensively studying a variety of different cases, students should be able to develop not only a knowledge of the specific cases they have studied, but also a framework for integrating this knowledge into a larger system of understanding.

Proponents of the deductive approach question the applicability of the fish-watching analogy because today's business students seldom have the patience of Professor Corey's fish watcher. If they do not see the pattern the professor is goading them to discover, they will tend to ignore the issue and move on. With several different classes, school activities, and often outside jobs pressing on their time, they cannot (and are generally not otherwise disposed to) spend time "discovering" things that could have been explained to them in a few simple words.

The deductive approach offers a promising alternative for addressing these problems. Teachers can highlight those principles that are most important for students to learn and then provide students with examples of how the principles can be applied in real life.

One problem with this approach is that many "theory" teachers fall short of teaching theory. For instance, the organization of popular advertising texts suggest that introductory advertising courses are taught according to a descriptive model. That is, they seek to describe various facets of advertising and explain how they operate in society. Kleppner's (1985) classic text has set the tone, focusing our attention on description of advertising decisions rather than the other aspects of the way advertising operates.

Even when the teachers teach theory, students often have trouble establishing the deductive link between theory and practice. Again using an advertising example, Aaker and Myers' (1987) advertising management text provides a good example of the problem. The text provides an excellent synopsis of current research on how underlying marketing and advertising phenomena operate, but it says very little about how students should use their knowledge to make actual managerial decisions.

The live case method (Richardson and Raveed 1980; Burns 1988) would ideally address these problems. It forces students to go beyond a descriptive knowledge of what decisions managers typically make, forcing them to make actual decisions themselves. Making these decisions should also force them to make the deductive link between theory and practice.

In practice, students often have trouble making this link. They fail to see the implications of the theory they have studied for practical management situations. As a result, many instructors have sought to add structure to the live case method (Richardson and Raveed, 1980; Frey and Keyes, 1985).

This paper describes a method for structuring the live case. It uses an example from a beginning advertising course to show how theory can be used to develop a series of planning experiences that guide student decisions through throughout the case.

THE THEORETICAL UNDERPINNINGS OF THE MODEL

The structured approach presented in this paper draws on two general managerial concepts. The first is the general notion of decision stages. Archer (1980) reviews a number of different models of managerial decision stages, suggesting his own nine-stage model. All of the models focus on the notion of stages, however, including some form of problem definition, identification of alternatives, and strategy selection. The case-structuring method described in this paper follows this basic model, leading students to systematically analyze problems, identify strategic alternatives, and select the best strategy from among available alternatives.

The second concept is the notion of a hierarchy of plans and objectives (Colley 1961; Winer 1965). Colley (1961) suggests that advertising decision-making involves a hierarchical chain of theory. At the corporate level, the theory seeks to explain how a company might achieve its corporate objective of profit. The theory suggests that this may be done by selling goods. Selling goods, then, becomes the marketing objective. Marketing theory suggests that the company might sell goods by stimulating brand preference. Thus, brand preference becomes an advertising objective. Colley's book elaborates on his basic hierarchical planning model by suggesting specific types of marketing and advertising objectives a company might pursue.

Following Colley's lead, several attempts have been made to make Colley's basic model more useful. For instance, Colley conceptualized the persuasion process in terms of a specific hiearchy of effects (Lavidge and Steiner 1961). Kotler (1984) sought to build the conceptual bridge between Colley's hierarchy and other similar models of communication effectiveness. Aaker and Myers (1987) developed an updated version of Colley's model, drawing on McGuire's information-processing model of advertising effectiveness (Lipstein and McGuire 1979).

Ray (1982) broadened the approach suggested by Aaker and Myers, identifying several different kinds of information processing hierarchies, noting the kinds of situations in which each one might be valid. Foote, Cone, & Belding Communications (Berger 1985; Ratchford 1987; Vaughn 1980, 1986) used this approach to develop an actual advertising planning model (the "FCB model") that helps identify the kind of communications strategy most likely to work in any given advertising situation.

The framework used in this paper draws heavily on the theory developed in these previous studies, extending it to form a new relatively detailed model for advertising planning. It conceptualizes advertising planning as a decision sequence, much as the one suggested by Ray (1973), except that the sequence follows a relatively rigorous hierarchy of strategy and objectives such as the one suggested by Colley (1961). Furthermore, it draws heavily on attitude theory to suggest strategic advertising alternatives, following the general approach suggested by Boyd, Ray, and Strong (1972).

What follows is a brief description of an introductory advertising course that seeks to overcome the problems we have just discussed. It uses a DAGMAR-like model to develop a series of applied advertising assignments, thus linking theory and practice. The assignments complement the more general descriptive material students may read on their own in any number of popular textbooks. Since most of these texts are both comprehensive and readable, class lectures can be devoted to the development and use of the planning model in completing class assignments.

Most advertising educators address Colley's approach in their classes, but few have fully integrated his theory-based planning model into their courses. Therefore, students find the model difficult to apply in practical advertising situations.

THE PLANNING MODEL

Table 14–1 illustrates the planning model. Following Colley's lead, the model assumes that the corporate objective is to increase profit. Theory suggests that the company might use marketing to do this by increasing margins or by increasing the quantity sold.

In the second stage, increased margins or volume become the objective. Marketing strategy makes high margins possible by creating differential advantage through market segmentation or product differentiation. It increases the quantity sold in one of three ways: (1) by bringing people into the market, (2) by increasing product usage, or (3) by winning market share.

Note that the strategy at one level provides the objective for the next. This was the key to Colley's integration of theory and practice in his model. Every strategy calls for another level of theory to implement it, where theory establishes the causal relationship between the strategic variables and the objectives they are used to achieve. Unfortunately, Colley's model stopped with advertising objectives. But advertising objectives are where the real substance of the course should begin.

As shown in Table 14–1, the model suggested in this paper continues through two more levels of theory. The distinguishing characteristic of advertising theory is that it addresses the way people think, while marketing strategy addresses the way they behave.

The advertising theory upon which the planning model is based assumes that consumers operate according to a type of psychological program. Their information-processing activities are governed by a set of instructions that is determined by the nature of the program that is operating at any given time.

TABLE 14–1
A Model for Advertising Planning

Level of Strategy	Objectives	Strategic Variable
Corporate Strategy	Increase profits	Margin Quantity sold
Marketing Strategy	Increase margins	Segmentation Differentiation
	Increase quantity sold	Market size Usage rate Market share
Advertising Strategy	Segment or differentiate	Frame of mind Evoked set Evaluative criteria Perceptions

	Increase:
	  Market size
	  Usage rate
	  Market share	

Creative Strategy	Stimulate the target: Frame of mind Evoked set Evaluative criteria Perceptions	Logical/serious Associative/serious Logical/light Associative/light

This is commonly referred to as the consumer's frame of mind. According to the model, advertising strategy has four elements:

1. *Frame of mind.* What frame of mind must an ad evoke in order to ensure that consumers process the message properly?
2. *Evoked set.* What target behavior would be desirable for consumers to consider engaging in as a result of the ad?
3. *Evaluative criteria.* What criteria should the ad encourage consumers to use as a basis for deciding whether to engage in the target behavior once it is in their evoked set?
4. *Target perceptions.* What consequences should consumers perceive as coming from the target behavior after being exposed to the ad?

These four strategic elements are very broad, thus making the planning system applicable to many different kinds of advertising. In practice, target behaviors are generally a product or brand, implicitly linked to product purchase, trial or usage. Evaluative criteria and target perceptions are the benefit preferences and perceptions we would expect to find in a standard "joint-space" positioning analysis. That is, preferences are what people want, and perceptions are what they think they are getting from a product. Thus, the only differences between the model and a conventional advertising strategy model are the ideas that can influence the way people process an ad by deciding what frame of mind we want to evoke at the outset of advertising exposure and the specificity about the kind of behavior the ad is designed to promote.

While advertising strategy addresses the mental changes proposed to stimulate through advertising, creative strategy addresses the persuasive techniques the advertising uses. Thus, creative strategy draws upon consumer behavior and persuasion theory to evoke the desired frame of mind, to bring the target behavior into the evoked set, to encourage use of the desired evaluative criteria, and to promote a belief that the target product or behavior offers the desired benefits.

The actual creative strategies tend to vary along two dimensions, as illustrated in Table 14-2. First, the persuasive style varies between logical and associative, depending on whether the advertising task is to involve consumers in a problem-solving or a problem-finding type of mental activity. Problem-solving involves considered choices aimed at solving a specific consumer problem (a "left-brain" type of activity). Problem-finding involves a process of arousal in which symbols are used to focus consumer's attention on a particular need—a woman in a bikini being admired by men to remind women of the need to be attractive, for instance.

Second, the persuasive style will vary in the seriousness of its tone, depending on how ego-involved consumers are likely to become with the advertising message.

TABLE 14-2
A Classification Scheme for Creative Strategies

	Type of Mental Activity	
Message Involvement	Problem Solving	Problem Finding
High	logical/serious	associative/serious
Low	logical/light	associative/light

The model is by no means complete. Creative strategy should provide executional objectives, and executional strategy itself might be broken down into several levels of theory regarding the way visual and verbal elements interact to form an effective ad. Furthermore, the advertising message needs to be supported with media and budgeting theory that determine how, where, when, and how frequently it will be delivered.

Notwithstanding its limitations, the planning model shown in Table 14–1 provides the core theory around which a course can be structured. The next section will discuss the actual structure of such a course.

STRUCTURING A COURSE

The course is structured around a "thread" case and seven assignments. I change the actual case each quarter to keep students from passing "solutions" from one class to the next. In this paper, I will use the Apple Macintosh computer as an illustrative case.

Assignment 1: Market Analysis

The first assignment consists of a market analysis. Students are provided with several pages of written material regarding the marketing situation. In addition, it is suggested that students visit stores, talk to salespeople, review advertisements, and otherwise prepare themselves for a marketing analysis. The analysis itself consists of short answers to the following:

1. *Usage Analysis.* Why do people use the product? How do they use it? What needs does the product serve? Do different people use the product for different reasons? If so, how are the people different? What needs are being served for each group? What potential needs might be served by the product, both physical and psychological? How important a role does the product play in people's lives?

2. *Resistance Analysis.* What obstacles do companies in this industry face? Why doesn't everyone use the product? What would it take to win over non-users of the product?

3. *Competitive Strategy Analysis.* How would you characterize the marketing strategies currently being employed by the key companies competing in the industry? How have these strategies changed over time? How appropriate do you think these strategies are (have been)?

4. *Product Analysis.* What kinds of competitive products are on the market? What are the key differences among them? What is their relative market share? How do consumers view them?

5. *Pricing Analysis.* What role does pricing play in the consumer decision process? How has pricing fit into the marketing strategies applied by different companies in the industry?

6. *Distribution Analysis.* What role does distribution (the kinds of stores or other means through which products are sold) play in the strategy used by different companies? What are the key needs of distributors?

7. *Promotion Analysis.* What is the company's key problem? What might cause the company to fail in achieving its objectives? What might cause the company to succeed beyond its objectives? What are the *key* facts of the case?

The purpose of this assignment is threefold: First, it gets students into the case. When they have finished, they usually have a fairly good grasp of the problem. Second, it teaches them some specific approaches to market analysis. Third, it forces them to grapple with the concept of competitive strategy. It sensitizes them to the concept of strategy in general, thus preparing them for the remaining assignments.

Assignment 2: Marketing Strategy Exercise

The second assignment requires students to write a formal statement of marketing strategy. The statement includes four parts:

1. *Problem/Situation.* This section consists of a brief statement indicating the major marketing problem, or challenge the company faces. It should consider the nature of the company's objectives, the product, the market, the competition, and so forth. While this portion of the statement will typically contain key background information, its formal role is to establish the company's marketing objectives.

2. *Alternatives.* This section indicates what alternative strategies the company should consider. Students should list only the three or four most plausible alternatives.

3. *Solution.* This section indicates which of the alternatives the company should select. It then explains the major steps the students propose for implementing the strategy.

4. *Rationale.* This section explains why the students selected the strategy they did. Their rationale should provide a logical reason for accepting one strategy and rejecting the others.

The marketing strategy exercise is introduced in class with a brief discussion of several different cases. The students receive sample strategy statements for each example so that they have several models against which to test their understanding of the strategy concepts. Table 14-3 provides a sample marketing strategy statement for the Macintosh computer case.

Assignment 3: Advertising Strategy Exercise

The third assignment requires students to write a formal statement of advertising strategy. The exercise follows directly from the planning model shown in Table 14-1. A week before the assignment is due, the students are provided with a marketing strategy statement (Table 14-3). They are instructed to develop several alternative advertising strategies to implement the recommended marketing strategy.

The basic components of advertising strategy have already been discussed. The strategy statement contains six elements:

1. *Advertising Objectives.* This section translates the marketing strategy into a general statement of advertising objectives. In practice, there is a gap

TABLE 14-3
Statement of Marketing Strategy for Apple Macintosh Computers

---

PROBLEM/SITUATION. IBM has assumed the role of "industry standard" in the personal computer market. In response, Apple developed the Macintosh—a computer that is more sophisticated than the IBM-PC, but so simple that anyone can learn to use it very easily. How should Apple market the Macintosh?

ALTERNATIVES:

1. Industry Standard—Replace IBM as the industry standard, building on Macintosh's superior attributes to take business away from IBM in the business-oriented market.

2. Uncomputer—Expand the computer market by appealing to people who are intimidated by conventional computers, capitalizing on Macintosh's simplicity and user friendliness (Macintosh is so simple it does not even seem to be a computer).

3. Next Generation—A combination of #1 and #2, replacing IBM-PC as the industry standard and expanding the market based on Macintosh's simplicity.

SOLUTION: Uncomputer (strategy #2)—promote Macintosh as a modern technological tool that is so simple it doesn't even seem to be a computer.

RATIONALE: The "uncomputer" concept takes the intimidating mystique out of computers, focusing on the things a computer can do for people rather than the technology by which these things are done. It makes computers truly accessible to everyone, regardless of their technological orientation.

The "industry standard" strategy (strategy #1) is not viable because the business "industry standard" is established by the attitudes of managers in the "Fortune 500" business community. IBM is too firmly entrenched in this market to be displaced.

The "next generation" strategy (strategy #3) is not viable because sophisticated business people are not generally intimidated by computers. Combining this with the fact that IBM is firmly entrenched in the sophisticated business market, strategy #3 seems to have little basis for success.

---

in the translation. While marketing strategy might be to increase market share in a given market, advertising objectives might be to increase brand preference. This is because other elements of the marketing and promotional mix are also working to implement marketing strategy. Advertising is usually given one portion of the overall marketing task.

2. *Strategy Names:* The names should represent the essence of the strategy. Students should include a brief description highlighting the strategy's key elements.

3. *Key Benefit and Positioning:* The key benefit and position represent the basis for selling the product and the way the product is to be positioned in the libraries of consumers' minds.

4. *Strategic Elements.* Each strategic element should contain two kinds of information:

• The basic focus of the strategy draws on the four components of advertising strategy discussed earlier in the paper: (1) the frame of mind the advertising is supposed to evoke; (2) the target behavior the advertising is supposed to place in consumers' evoked set; (3) the evaluative criteria; and (4) the target perceptions.
• The major advertising tasks that must be carried out in order to implement the strategy.

5. *Advantages and Disadvantages.* This section should summarize the major strengths and weaknesses of each strategy alternative.

6. *Recommendations and Rationale.* This section should indicate which strategy the students recommend and why.

Table 14-4 illustrates how these guidelines might be incorporated into an advertising strategy statement for the Macintosh computer. Note that the individual strategies might vary on any one or more of several points. Developing a full statement of several alternative strategies helps students understand the essence of the strategy they actually choose. The key elements of a strategy will usually emerge in the discussion of advantages and disadvantages.

As with the marketing strategy statement, the students are introduced to advertising strategy by discussing a number of cases providing them with sample advertising strategy statements for each.

Assignment 4: Creative Strategy Exercise

The fourth assignment requires students to write a formal statement of creative strategy. Again, the exercise follows directly from the planning model shown in Table 14-1. A week before the creative strategy assignment is due, the students are provided with an advertising strategy statement (Table 14-4). They are instructed to develop a creative strategy statement to implement the recommended advertising strategy.

In the case of popular and current products such as Macintosh, students are usually very much aware of the product's advertising. As a result, a different strategy than the company is currently using is recommended. In Table 14-4, for instance, Apple chose to use the "Anyone can use it" strategy. The students are required to implement the "new tool" strategy.

The creative strategy statement provides the major working document from which copywriters and art directors will work. Therefore, it contains more detail than would otherwise be needed for a simple creative strategy. It includes seven sections:

TABLE 14–4

Advertising Strategy Statement for Apple Macintosh Computers

		To stimulate a desire among non-computer users	
Advertising Objective		To stimulate a desire among non-computer users to use a Macintosh "uncomputer"	
Strategy Name	Strategy 1: Anyone can use it— a computer that is so easy to use, anyone can use it	Strategy 2: New tool—a new creative tool for enhancing productivity	Strategy 3: Typewriter substitute a powerful easy-to-use typewriter
Key Benefit	Focus: Simple, powerful	Focus: Powerful	Focus: Powerful, simple
Position	Task: Position Macintosh as a powerful computer that is so easy to use, anyone can use it	Task: Position Macintosh as a powerful new creative tool for enhancing productivity	Task: Position Machintosh as a powerful, easy-to-use substitute for typewriters
Strategy Element 1: Frame of Mind	Focus: Frustrated computer user Task: Evoke a frustrated computer user frame of mind	Focus: Creative achiever Task: Evoke a creative achiever frame of mind	Focus: Frustrated typewriter user Task: Evoke a frustrated typewriter user frame of mind
Strategy Element 2: Target Behavior	Focus: Macintosh Task: Stimulate people to consider buying a Macintosh	Focus: Computers, Macintosh Task: Stimulate people to consider buying Macintosh as a new, useful type of computer	Focus: Comptuers, Macintosh Task: Stimulate people to consider buying Macintosh as a typewriter-like computer
Strategy Element 3: Evaluative Criteria	Focus: Simplicity Task: Bring simplicity into salience as a criterion for evaluating computer usage	Focus: Power (possible uses) Task: Create a need for power as a criterion for evaluating computer usage	Focus: Power (features) Task: Stimulate a need for power as a criterion for evaluating the computer as a substitute for typewriter usage
Strategy Element 4: Target Perceptions	Focus: Simplicity Task: Convince people that Macintosh is a powerful computer and yet simple enough that anyone can use it	Focus: Power Task: Convince people that Macintosh is capable of increasing their creative productivity	Focus: Power, simplicity Task: Convince people that Macintosh is as simple to use as a typewriter and yet is powerful enough to justify the extra cost
Advantages and Disadvantages	Advantages: Appeals to the many people who feel they should be using a computer but who are intimidated	Advantages: Addresses the positive needs that motivate computer usage rather than the negative needs that inhibit it	Advantages: Easy to implement, it addresses issues that every typewriter user has experienced

TABLE 14–4 (continued)

	Disadvantages: Potentially alienates people who like Macintosh's features but who will not admit to being intimidated by computers	Disadvantages: Hard to convince many creative achievers that they really need a computer	Disadvantages: Hard to convince typewriter users that added features are worth the extra cost
Recommendation and Rationale	Recommendation: Strategy 2		
	Rationale: The "new tool" strategy encompasses the positive motivations that underlie both strategies 1 and 2, thus giving the strategy a much broader appeal than either of them individually. Good creative strategy can incorporate the simplicity of Macintosh as support for its advanced technology, thus heading off computer anxiety with a positive rather than a negative appeal.		

1. *Advertising Objectives.* This section provides a statement of the specific mental activities the advertising should stimulate in consumers.

2. *Target Market Description.* This provides demographics, psychographics, product usage, or other descriptive information to help copywriters visualize the kind of person to whom they are writing.

3. *Competitive Position.* This section provides an elaboration of the "positioning" portion of the advertising strategy statement. It should give the copywriter a clear idea of the category in which the product will be competing, how consumers will think about the product, to what products it will be compared, and/or what products it will replace.

4. *Promise.* This section should reflect the "key benefit" from the advertising strategy statement. As a matter of form, however, it should be stated as a promise. Verbally or non-verbally, explicitly or implicitly, advertising should promise consumers that they will receive some benefit if they do what the ad suggests.

5. *Support.* Support provides facts, figures, and/or secondary attributes or benefits to support the promise. As a rule, logical creative strategies will require considerable support while associative strategies will require little, if any.

6. *Creative Objectives and Strategy.* Creative objectives are provided by the tasks outlined in the advertising strategy statement. Thus, there will be four creative objectives. Note that the advertising must be simple, generally focusing on a single idea. Like great art, however, great advertising can communicate on several different levels at once. This section of the creative strategy statement is designed to capture the subtle nuances of the creative strategy on paper.

5. *General Notes on Strategy.* This section contains any special considerations copywriters should bear in mind when developing an actual ad. For instance, it gives the strategist an opportunity to elaborate on the different levels of communication implicit in the creative strategy. It also provides a means of explaining threads that should connect a single ad to other ads in the same campaign.

Table 14–5 illustrates how these guidelines might be incorporated into a creative strategy statement for the Macintosh computer.

TABLE 14–5
A Creative Strategy Statement for Apple Macintosh Computers

Advertising Objective	To stimulate a desire to use the Macintosh as a creative tool for enhancing personal productivity.
Competitive	Macintosh will occupy a new position as a powerful tool for enhancing productivity. People should not position it as a computer, but as an "uncomputer"–a machine so sophisticated that it speaks to creative people in their own language. In this sense, the new category will be created by positioning Macintosh against the old generation of conventional computers that require people to become technicians in order to use them.
Target Market Description	Highly educated, upscale professionals and managers; achievement-oriented people with a verbal rather than a quantitative orientation— lawyers and journalists rather than physical scientists or accountants, liberal arts graduates and Grad-Ad students rather than MBAs, managers in small to middle-sized businesses and service organizations rather than Fortune 500 companies. These would tend to be people who can benefit from the things a computer can do, but who would not generally consider themselves the kind of person who would use a computer.
Promise	Macintosh will increase your creative productivity through modern computer technology without requiring you to develop technical computer expertise.
Creative Support	• Macintosh combines highly sophisticated micro-computer technology with the simplicity of operation we expect from modern household and office equipment • People can learn the basics of using Macintosh in a matter of minutes. • Macintosh functions are set up in a desktop metaphor, providing users with such useful tools as "folders," "note pads," a "clipboard," "trash" cans, a "calculator," a "calendar," a "clock," "MacWrite" for typing, different typing "fonts," "MacPaint" for making illustrations, and so forth. All these can be picked up and used (by means of a "mouse"), just as they would on a desk. • Setting up margins, making corrections, rearranging paragraphs and pages, and performing other troublesome typing and editing functions are much simpler on the Macintosh than they are on even the most sophisticated typewriter. • Macintosh is smaller, simpler but faster with a more sophisticated microprocessor than the IBM-PC. • Macintosh comes with a shoulder-strap carrying case so that it can be carried about easily.
Creative Objectives and Strategy	Objective 1: Evoke a "creative achiever" frame of mind Strategic Element 1: Portray symbols that are associated with values of creativity and achievement

TABLE 14–5 (continued)

Objective 2: Stimulate people to consider Macintosh as a new, useful type of computer	Strategic Element 2: Show that Macintosh addresses clearly recognizable creative activities
Objective 3: Create a need for power as a criterion for computer usage	Strategic Element 3: Show how powerful computer features can help people save time and achieve a higher quality of creative work
Objective 4: Convince people that Macintosh is capable of increasing their productivity	Strategic Element 4: Document the fact that Macintosh represents a new kind of computer, offering the features portrayed in strategic element 3.

General Notes on Strategy	The strategy will communicate at three levels: (1) Strategic element 1 will be associative and value-expressive, emphasizing values of creativity and achievement motivation. (2) Strategic elements 2, 3, and 4 will be logical and instrumental, emphasizing Macintosh's basic competitive position. (3) The campaign should carry a tone of tasteful condescension toward other computers. While their efforts are laudable, their complexity is the sign of an immature industry. A truly sophisticated computer should free users of the burden of technology and free them for creative work. This is an ego-defensive appeal designed to protect people from concerns that they are being unsophisticated if they use a machine as simple as the Macintosh. Note that the campaign will feature several different executions, each featuring a different type of creative achiever.

Assignment 5: Creative Execution Assignment

The fifth assignment requires students to execute a creative strategy in two different media. This puts them to the actual test of integrating theory with practice. Strategy is an abstraction, but this assignment requires the actual layout and copywriting of an ad.

A pleasant fringe benefit of this approach is that the statement of creative strategy introduces a strong element of objectivity into the grading process. The statement of creative strategy states very specifically what the ad needs to accomplish. The grader need only evaluate how effective the ad is in accomplishing its objectives.

Assignment 6: Media Assignment

The sixth assignment is built around the simple notion of media cost efficiency. Using media exposure, cost, and exposure effectiveness data that is provided for product users (owners of personal or home computers, in our example), the assignment asks students to answer a series of questions regarding alternative media plans. They must calculate:

1. Cost per thousand exposures
2. Cost per thousand target market exposures
3. Cost per thousand effective target market exposures
4. Gross rating points
5. Target market gross rating points
6. Net rating points
7. Target market net rating points.

Assignment 7: Budget Assignment

The seventh and last assignment is built around the basic economic model of marginal return on advertising expenditure. In class, the assumptions behind different budgeting models are discussed. The assignment then gives them test market data and requires them to develop the following analyses:

1. An "optimal" budget based on marginal analysis.
2. A "percent-of-sales" budget.
3. A "task and objective" budget based on a "share-of-voice" model.
4. A payout analysis based on a budget that includes "investment spending."

SUMMARY AND CONCLUSIONS

The live case method offers considerable promise for helping instructors achieve relevance and theoretical rigor in their teaching. It achieves relevance by providing a problem in which students must make actual management decisions, much as they would in the real world. This not only builds a conceptual link between the material studied in the classroom and real-world applications, but it provides an added dimension of learning by exposing students to many of the same environmental pressures the would experience in real management positions (Sensbach and Adler 1986).

In many cases, however, the live case approach confronts students with a larger conceptual task than they are prepared to handle. Ideally, they would take the principles learned in their courses and readings and apply them through deduction to their case project. In practice, they often fail to establish the deductive link, resorting to intuition or simply wild guessing. The structured approach described in this paper narrows the gap between theory and practice, thus making theory easier to apply.

CHAPTER 15

EVOLUTION OF EXPERIENTIAL LEARNING APPROACHES AND FUTURE DEVELOPMENTS

Lee A. Graf
Calvin E. Kellogg

Experiential learning is defined as ". . . a sequence of events with one or more identified learning objectives, requiring active involvement by participants at one or more points in the sequence" (Walters and Marks, 1981, p. 1). The central tenet of experiential learning is that one learns best by doing. This chapter focuses on two major topics related to experiential learning. First, the evolution of various experiential learning techniques will be examined. Implicit in this exploration is the examination and discussion of several technological developments which may revolutionize experiential learning. Second, a method of classifying various approaches to experiential learning is suggested.

THE EVOLUTION OF EXPERIENTIAL LEARNING

Experiential learning has evolved from being an exploratory, experimental technique in the 1950's and 1960's at growth centers such as the National Training Laboratories and the Esalen Institute, to being common practice in a variety of learning settings. The active involvement of students through experiential learning is considered an effective teaching technique which improves student understanding of the topic. Learning theory literature suggests that immediate reinforcement, such as that offered by experiential learning, plays a major role in determining the quality of learning (Estes, 1972).

Experiential learning has gone through several periods of change over the past thirty or so years. At least four major periods can be identified. The evolutionary "tree of experiential learning" presented in Figure 15-1 represents those changes. The periods of branching shown on Figure 15-1 are:

FIGURE 15–1
Tree of Experiential Learning

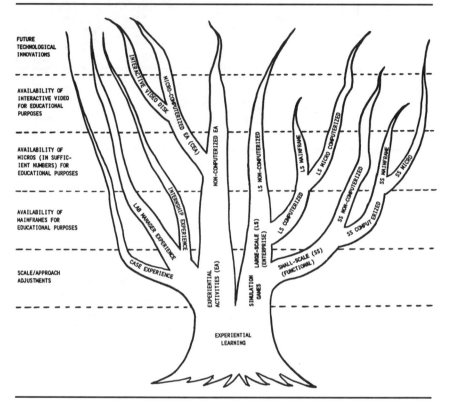

scale/approach branching, availability of mainframe computer branching, availability of microcomputer branching, and video technology branching. The latter three changes are technology driven; however, the technology only provided the impetus for the branching. The branching periods are very similar to the phases of development in simulation gaming proposed by Wolfe and Teach (1987). The scale/approach branch is similar to Phases I and II, the mainframe computer branch to Phase III, and the microcomputer branch may be likened to Phase IV in the Wolfe and Teach model.

Scale/Approach Branching

The first major branching in experiential learning occurred with the evolution of the concepts of simulation gaming and experiential exercises. Proponents of each approach began to develop activities based on the advantages of each while still clinging to the root concept of experiential learning. The definitions of simulation and experiential exercises show the clear delineation of the two concepts:

> A simulation may be defined as a sequential decision-making exercise structured around a model of a business operation in which participants assume the role of managing the simulated operation (Greenlaw, Lowell, and Rawdon, 1962, p. 5).
>
> Experiential exercises attempt to facilitate the instruction and learning of behavioral concepts by structuring relevant situations which require active student participation (Crino, 1979, p. 315). An experiential exercise is a task designed with specific circumstances to generate trainee behavior which can be observed, discussed, and evaluated against interpersonal theory (Certo, 1975).

Obviously, the original focus for simulations was on decision-making from a macro perspective, while experiential exercises focused on micro issues in a behavioral or technical area. The techniques were also different from the perspective of the concept of student "immersion" in learning. Simulation students were typically placed in a very complex, unstructured situation which required integration of many concepts. Experiential exercise participants were usually placed in a more structured, controlled situation in which they practiced more specific skills.

While very early simulations were all non-computerized, game developers' efforts took two primary directions: general management or enterprise (large scale) simulations, and functional (small scale) simulations (Stewart, 1961).[1] The large scale (LS) or enterprise simulations were hand scored. Some of these had a reduced number of variables in the formulas; some introduced chance elements in such a way that random-number tables could be used in place of numerous hand calculations; some reduced the range of choice so that answers could be read directly from a previously prepared table; and some simply shifted a substantial share of the computational burden to the game player. Conversely, small scale (SS) or functional simulations were aimed more at middle or lower levels of management and stressed a particular management function, for example, production, marketing, inventory control, finance, or other business function (Stewart, 1961).

---

[1] In addition to enterprise and functional games, Stewart (1961) identified two other game categories she called "industry games" and "bureaucracy games." However, the author argued that all industry games might equally well be classified under "enterprise" or "functional" headings. The "bureaucracy" nomenclature simply denoted games aimed at providing training in administration rather than business skills. The distinction drawn between enterprise and bureaucracy games was vague in 1961 and, in Stewart's own words, this nomenclature was objected to "quite strenuously." This work will not differentiate between enterprise and bureaucracy games, but will consider both as enterprise games.

While scale changes were being made in simulation games, various new experiential learning approaches, special off-shoots to the standard experiential activity (EA), were evolving. In addition to the commonly thought of EA, such experience-oriented activities as internship experiences (IE), lab manager experiences (LME), and case experiences (CE) were beginning to appear on the scene. Internships provide students with the opportunity to gain real-world experience in a participating firm or business organization through an approved cooperative program between a business school and a firm. An intern works for the firm on an approved project and gains college credit for the experience. A lab manager is a student enrolled in an advanced course who is asked to lead a group of introductory students through various exercises and projects in a laboratory setting. While the lab manager task may take many forms, it is usually viewed as an experientially-oriented program designed to give the student exposure to "real" authority and responsibility and to help them develop skills in such areas as communication, leadership, motivation, influence, coaching, and performance evaluation and feedback (Couch and Graf, 1981). Finally, case experiences attempt to prepare participants for management positions by providing them with general business facts and the skills necessary to deal with common managerial problems.

Mainframe Branching

The gap between simulations and experiential exercises was further widened by the second major branching period in the evolution of experiential learning. The arrival of the mainframe computer allowed for the development of very technically complex, full scale organizational simulations. General business games with their complex algorithms were "designed to give people experience in making decisions at the top executive level and in which decisions from one functional area interact with those made in other areas of the firm" (Cohen and Rhenman, 1961, p. 140). While the availability of mainframes significantly impacted upon simulation gaming, it had no noticeable impact upon experiential activities.

Microcomputer Branching

The next major change to influence experiential learning was the widespread availability of microcomputers. Almost immediately, simulation authors began to download and re-write mainframe simulations for use on microcomputers. By 1986, there were at least eleven microcomputer versions of general business simulations (Biggs, 1986).

Along with the increasing popularity of microcomputer versions of mainframe simulations came a further blurring of the distinction between experiential exercises and simulation games. While functional simulations had been available since the scale/approach adjustment phase, microcomputer branching has brought on a proliferation of small scale, functional simulations. Functional simulations are games designed to "focus specifically on problems of decision-making as seen in one particular functional area" (Cohen and Rhenman, 1961, p. 140). The term "small scale simulation" was coined by Gentry and Burns (1984) and is a further subclassification of a functional simulation. A small scale simulation focuses on a narrow range of topics or even a single topic within a functional area (see Frazer, 1985 and Dennis and Pray, 1982). As one may begin to see, many of these small scale simulations are as much, if not more, like experiential exercises than simulation games.

Some of the first computerized experiential activities (CEAs) were technically oriented. Traditionally, experiential exercises focused on behavioral issues. With the arrival of the microcomputer, educators began to realize that students could be encouraged to utilize software to get "hands-on" technically oriented experience. Suggestions for the use of decision support packages to teach concepts were provided as early as 1980 (Sugges, 1980); four years later the use of spreadsheets in experiential learning was suggested by Gentry and Burns (1984).

In addition to the appearance of technically oriented computerized experiential activities, CEAs focusing on behavioral aspects began to appear (see Friend, 1985). These computerized experiential activities attempted to capitalize on the advantages of using computers for the purpose of educating students.

Historically, faculty members were hesitant to let the computer teach (Hofstetter, 1985). The argument frequently voiced was that students should not be guinea pigs in educational experimentation. Of course, the educators only wanted to perform controlled evaluations before trusting the computer with students. This situation has changed dramatically in recent years. Today, a researcher wishing to compare a computer-based instruction system with a traditional system might be hard pressed to find a colleague willing to allow his/her students to be the control group. The colleague would be much more interested in utilizing the "experimental" computer technology.

Research summarized by Steinberg (1977), while limited, suggests that computer-controlled instruction results in faster learning with achievement equal to that with student-controlled learning. Computer-aided instruction (CAI) has been reported to be as effective as teacher conducted learning (Kulik, Kulik, and Cohen, 1980; Spuck, 1981). In fact, Kulik (1980, 1983, 1983–1984) found statistically significant differences in student achievement in favor of students who learned with the computer. These findings were consistent at all educational levels (college, secondary, and elementary). Yet, several authors have concluded that the computer is not being well used in the field of education at present (Burns and Bozman, 1981; Holzman and Glazer, 1977). Avner, et al. (1980) suggest that one of the special benefits of using a computer in the learning process is that the computer can be used to judge complex student responses necessary for determining mastery of concepts and for managing student progress based on such measures. The only identified shortcoming to computer controlled learning is an occasional decrease in student motivation.

Although there will always be isolated instances of resistance, in general, student acceptance of computers in education is positive (Jenkins and Dankert, 1981). In addition, the increased usage of computers at the elementary and high school levels during the last five years (Becker, 1987) will further reduce "terminal" anxiety on the part of college students. The overall evidence clearly supports the use of computer technology in the learning environment. This general acceptance of computers in instruction sets the stage for the next major branching phase in experiential learning. This phase is only now in its infancy.

Interactive Video Branching

Interactive video technology and authoring systems for personal computers, the most recent outgrowth on the tree of experiential learning, may contribute to an even further blurring of the distinction between experiential exercises and simulations. Videodisc technology is fast becoming one of the most exciting technological developments in recent years with respect to experiential learning. It is rapidly becoming the accepted approach for training employees in corporate America (Pepper, 1986; Walden, 1984). Videodisc technology permits interactive role playing with multiple scenarios. For example, assume the following scenario:

> A supervisor in the midst of giving an annual performance appraisal to a subordinate breaks the news that the employee's work has not been up to par all year. The employee has had no warning during the past twelve months and takes the news badly—very badly. The supervisor, now under attack, responds in kind. Later, after a bit of reflection on the incident, the supervisor wishes he'd handled it differently. A manager/employee relationship has been damaged and it's too late to do it over (Chain Store Age, 1986, p. 128).

Through the use of interactive video, supervisors can learn how to respond appropriately in just such a situation, before it actually occurs.

Interactive video is also used in many sales training programs. A sales trainee will be faced by a videotaped "customer" presenting specific reservations concerning a sale. Based on the sales trainee's reaction, other taped scenarios will be triggered. This process continues until the trainee either "loses" or closes the sale. If the trainee loses the sale, immediate feedback is provided showing how the customer's objections should have been handled.

Research indicates that people retain up to 300 percent more information when using interactive video because they are actively involved in using that information (Pepper, 1986). Pepper (1986) also reports that companies find that trainees take 25 to 50 percent less training time when using interactive video.

The following comments from a roundtable discussion for *Computer Based Training,* a magazine for computer-assisted instruction (CAI), reflect the trends for interactive video (Smith, 1987):

> I think interactive video will gradually replace computer based training just like sound movies replaced silent movies. (Bob Yeager, Intercom)
>
> The application for interactive video right now is everything from management training around human interaction to safety training, any kind of training where you have interaction between people or between people and machines. (Steve Becker, Learncom)
>
> Anytime realism becomes a major component of what you're doing, interactive video should be considered—should be the medium of choice. (David Hon, Ixion)

Smith (1987) reports that over 33,000 interactive videodisc units are in use in corporate training facilities. If the above comments are even minimally accurate, one would expect the use of interactive videodisc technology in corporate training centers and university classrooms to expand during the next decade.

From a less sophisticated standpoint, the growing availability of advanced text editing devices will increase the value of computerized experiential learning. The availability of light pens, mouses, and touch panels will facilitate student interaction with the computer. Saywer (1985) reported that students did much better using the more sophisticated entry devices compared to the traditional keyboard. In addition, a study by Gaynor (1981) found the less the delay in response time, the higher the student's level of subject mastery.

All of the above comments seem to suggest that many behavioral experiential learning activities in the future will be videodisc based, allowing student input through voice or touch panel. However, quantitatively-oriented experiential learning activities may depend on more traditional technologies which emphasize high speed interactive graphics for both textual and pictorial display (Smith, 1987).

CLASSIFICATION OF TYPES OF EXPERIENTIAL LEARNING

As previously discussed, the early, clearly recognizable distinction between simulation games and experiential exercises no longer exists. In an effort to classify accurately various forms of experiential learning, the authors have identified the characteristics of each sub-type of simulation game and experiential activity. Table 15-1 provides a summary of this classification scheme. Below are listed the characteristics that will be utilized to differentiate between the various simulation game and experiential activity formats.

Characteristics of Simulation Games and Experiential Activities

Iterations
The number of times a decision must be made for a participant to develop an understanding of the phenomena is at the heart of the concept of iterations. This measure is akin to the concept of duration as proposed by Burns and Gentry (1977). Duration is "how long the exercise lasts: number of decision phases, number of days, or weeks it takes the exercise to run" (Burns and Gentry, 1980, p. 17). However, iterations specifically focus on the number of decision phases and is not time bound as is duration.

Simulation requires a series or set of decisions (multiple iterations) to have full impact on learning, whereas, experiential exercises can have noticeable impact after only one iteration. The concept of experiential exercises being single iteration does not imply that a person cannot benefit by multiple trials on a specific experiential exercise. Such multiple "runs" would simply allow for reinforcement of skills taught by the exercise.

Chained Decisions
Chained decisions reflects the fact that the results of one set of decisions influence the decisions in future iterations. Obviously, most experiential exercises are not chained since they involve only single iterations. Simulation games, on the other hand, require participants to live with past decisions and do not allow the participants to begin anew for each trial. The fact that experiential exercises are, for the most part, non-chained does not mean that separate experientials cannot be chained together to learn specific skills. The concept of an experiential training unit was developed by Certo (1975) for just that purpose. Also, the idea that experiential exercises do not have chained decisions does not suggest that a participant in an experiential activity may not be required to make literally hundreds of decisions during a single iteration of the exercise. Non-chained simply means the results of one iteration are not the input or starting point for a second iteration.

Functional/Environmental Scope
Functional/environmental scope deals with the number of business functions and outside considerations involved (Burns and Gentry, 1980). The concept of functional/environmental scope revolves around the issue of the number of skills that must be utilized and the number of skills one is attempting to teach through the use of an experiential learning exercise.

TABLE 15–1
Characteristics of Experiential Learning Formats

Formats:	Iterations		Chained Decisions		Environmental Scope		Debriefing		Competitive Environment		Skill Focus		Computerized	
	Single	Multiple	Chained	Non-Chained	Single Topic	Multiple Topics	Content	Process	Yes	No	Technical	Inter-personal	Yes	No
Large-Scale (Enterprise) Computerized		X	X			X	Yes	No	X		Yes	No	X	
Large-Scale (Enterprise) Non-Computerized		X	X			X	Yes	Yes		X	No	Yes		X
Small-Scale (Functional) Computerized		X	X		X		Yes	No	X		Yes	No	X	
Small-Scale (Functional) Non-Computerized		X	X		X		Yes	No	X		Yes	No		X
Non-Computerized Experiential Activity	X			X	X		Yes	Yes		X	Yes	Yes		X
Computerized Experiential Activity (CEA)	X			X	X		Yes	No		X	Yes	No	X	
Lab Manager Experience	X		?			X	Yes	Yes	?		Yes	Yes		X
Case Experiences	X			X	X	X	Yes	No		X	Yes	No		X
Internship Experience	X			X	X	X	No	No		X	Yes	Yes		X

Debriefing
Debriefing focuses on a discussion of what has occurred after an experiential activity has been completed. Debriefing for simulations focuses primarily on the technical issues and understanding why functional decisions lead to the results in the simulation. Experiential debriefing is much more behaviorally oriented and, among other concerns, tends to focus on the relationships that developed.

Competitive Environment
Simulations typically take place in a competitive environment. Students, or student groups, compete against either the computer or other groups of students in all forms of simulation. Competition in an experiential exercise is very unusual unless the experiential is designed to allow the students to experience the impact of competition (see any of the conflict and/or power experiential exercises). The typical experiential exercise allows the student to learn by participating without the worry of trying to "beat" some other entity.

Skill Focus
Skill focus refers to type and range of skills being taught by a particular form of experiential learning. Traditional simulation games focus on the development of integrative, conceptual, and technical skills. Experiential exercises have tended historically to focus on the development of behavioral and/or interpersonal skills.

Computerized
The final criterion to be used to distinguish types of experiential learning revolves around the utilization of computers for the delivery of the experience. For many years simulations relied on computers, while experiential exercises did not. That distinction is no longer present; however, the use of the computer is important in subclassifying the approaches to experiential learning.

Experiential Delivery System

Now that the classification criteria have been examined, these criteria can be used to categorize experiential delivery systems. The following does just that.

Computerized Large Scale Simulations (CLSS)
The common characteristics of these games are the intensive interaction of the complex environments and the utilization of sophisticated computer programs for controlling the input and output necessary for game operation

(Chen, 1977, p. 254). Computerized large scale simulations (CLSS) have multiple iterations, a series of chained decisions, multiple topics and high levels of functional/environmental involvement, content debriefing, and no interactive feedback. The games are operated in a competitive environment and focus on technical and/or conceptual skills. Obviously, the computer plays an integral role in the CLSS. Examples of CLSS are provided in Table 15-2.

Non-Computerized Large Scale Simulations (NCLSS)
Even though non-computerized large scale simulations (NCLSS) use a total enterprise approach and require several iterations of chained decisions, there are a number of major distinctions between CLSS and NCLSS. NCLSS are non-computerized and tend to focus on behavioral issues and the development of interpersonal skills. Unlike computerized simulations which pit teams of participants against one another, NCLSS emphasize problem solving behavior, not competitive tactics. Process debriefing is an integral part of NCLSS. The goal of the approach is to hold players' managerial techniques up to scrutiny (Petre, 1984). Examples of popular NCLSS are provided in Table 15-3.

Computerized Small Scale Simulations (CSSS)
The major distinction between computerized small scale simulations (CSSS) and CLSS is that of focus. CSSS or functional simulations focus on functional issues such as marketing, human resource management, inventory control, etc. The major factors which distinguish CSSS from experien-

TABLE 15-2
Examples of Computerized Large Scale Simulations (CLSS)

Multinational Management Game	Edge, A. G., Keys, B. and Remus, W. E.
The Business Policy Game	Cotter, R. V.
The Business Management Laboratory	Jensen, R. L. and Cherrington, D. J.
The Executive Game	Henshaw, R. C. and Jackson, J. R.
The Executive Simulation	Keys, B. and Leftwich, H.
Tempomatic IV: A Management Simulation	Scott, C. R. and Strickland, A. J., III
The Business Strategy and Policy Game	Eldredge, D. L., and Bates, D. L.
Mansym IV	Schellenberger and Masters
Decide	Pray, T. and Strang
Business Policy Game	Cotter, R. V. and Fritzsche, D. J.

See Appendix A for complete sources.

TABLE 15–3
Noncomputerized Large Scale Simulations (NCLSS)

Looking Glass	Lombardo, McCall, and DeVries
Looking Glass II	Lombardo, McCall, and DeVries
The Organizational Game	Miles and Randolph
Simmons Simulator, Inc.	Simmons, et al
Financial Services Industry	Stumpf, S., et al

See Appendix A for complete sources.

tial activities are that CSSS has multiple iterations of chained decisions, whereas experiential activities are single iteration non-chained exercises. Also the focus of CSSS is on technical issues in functional areas.

The CSSS is simply a computerized simulation which focuses on a specific functional area in order to provide the student with an in-depth experience in making decisions and applying concepts in that area. The students usually compete against one another and the simulation lasts for several rounds. Debriefing is typically content focused. Examples of CSSS are provided in Table 15–4.

Non-Computerized Small Scale Simulations (NCSSS).
The non-computerized small scale simulation (NCSSS) is a functional simulation that does not depend on the computer for scoring and processing. NCSSS can focus on behavioral or functional issues. Examples of NCSSS are *Shennadoah: A Supervisory Simulation, Fischtale: A Production Simulation,* and *Business Logistics Game* (Jackson and Morgan, 1983).

TABLE 15–4
Computerized Small Scale Simulations (CSSS)

Transportation Management Simulation	Graham and Gray
Boy George	Jackson, Gentry, and Morgan
Sales Management Simulation	Day and Dalrymple
Water Quality Management Simulation	Sharda, Willett, and Chiang
CHECKSIM	Davis, Ceto, and Rabb
Inventory Simulation	Ferguson
Marketer	Smith
Inventory	Frazer

See Appendix A for complete sources.

These simulations are functional in nature, require several iterations of chained decisions, focus on content debriefing, are competitive, and are hand scored.

Non-Computerized Experiential Activities (NCEA)

Non-computerized experiential activities (NCEA) involve the traditional experiential exercise. These activities can include in-basket exercises, role playing, and hypothetical situations. As previously described, the aim of a NCEA is to provide the student with a structured process within which he/she can apply specific behavioral concepts.

The emphasis on skill building and the development of competency-based education (Hayes, 1979) in business curricula has fueled the growth of experiential learning packages to accompany "traditional" textbooks. Initially, experiential exercises were available for "principles" textbooks, particularly principles of management; however, today experiential packages exist in some form or fashion as support material for almost every business subject (e.g., accounting, communications, personnel/human resources management, economics, statistics). The interested reader might consider examining *A Handbook of Structured Experiences for Human Relations Training* edited annually by Pfeiffer and Jones for a good sampling of the variety and forms of experiential exercises in the human relations area.

The textbook marketplace is clearly a salient measure of the importance, acceptance, and place in the learning process occupied by experiential exercises. Yet, in an attempt to continue to expand the educational process, each teaching pedagogy continues to evolve. Experiential exercises, now widely accepted, are entering an exciting new phase, computerization.

Computerized Experiential Activities (CEA)

The computerized experiential activity (CEA) is a one-time or short-term activity in which a person or group of persons, utilizing interactive software, carry out some task that relates to a specific topic (Graf and Kellogg, 1986). The CEA focuses on the individual developing in specific skill areas during the session. The CEA does not involve chained decisions. That is, a decision a student makes in one session does not carry forward and influence the starting point in future sessions. Also, the application of a particular skill can be accomplished in a single iteration.

For example, a student could be presented with a scenario for which he or she were asked to choose the appropriate leadership style based on the Vroom/Yetton framework. The student's initial choice would be entered, then the computerized experiential exercise would carry the individual through the model providing the "correct" response and explanation at each node until the appropriate leadership style was determined. This process could continue, via new leadership scenarios, for as long as the student wished to practice the model. Note that this would be a single iteration and does not involve decisions that would influence the starting point for the individual's next round of practice (i.e., the next leadership scenario).

The CEA is simply an exercise. As such it is a set of activities used to engage participants directly with the content of the experience. Exercises consist of step-by-step procedures that are clearly defined and intended to provide opportunities to become familiar with and practice skills, to generate feelings and reactions, and to facilitate participant's movement through the learning experience (Walters and Marks, 1981).

To summarize, a CEA is a single iteration, non-chained, computer-based form of experiential learning. The exercise can focus on either technical or behavioral skills, is non-competitive, and debriefing focuses on content not process.

Examples of single topic computerized experiential activities are found in Table 15-5. Several packaged computerized experiential activities are provided in Table 15-6. These packages contain a series of experiential activities on various functional topics and are good examples of how computerized experiential activities can be combined to form an educational training unit. While many of the benefits to be derived from utilizing CEAs are known, numerous questions remain. Table 15-7 lists a number of the unanswered questions related to CEAs.

Lab Manager Experience (LME)

A number of reports in the *Organizational Behavior Teaching Review* and its predecessor have described programs which divide classes into smaller groups (or labs) led by student lab managers. Bradford and Le Duc (1975), Bradford and Porras (1975), Cohen (1976), and Graf and Couch (1984–1985) are examples. In both the Bradford and Le Duc and the Graf and Couch reports, student lab managers, enrolled in advanced courses, prepared and administered exercises to small groups of students in an introductory course. These advanced students or lab managers get opportunities for valuable learning experiences which differ from the usual classroom experience.

In the Graf and Couch (1984–1985) report, lab managers served in supervisory roles which were intended to help them develop managerial skills in communicating, group leadership, performance evaluation, and coaching. Both end-of-course evaluations, and survey results of graduates who had previously served as lab managers, provided strong support for the value of the lab manager experience as preparation for real-world management responsibilities (Graf and Couch, 1984–1985). Furthermore, 91 percent of respondents evaluated the lab manager responsibility, as compared to other learning opportunities, as being in the top quarter of their undergraduate learning experiences (Graf and Couch, 1984–1985).

TABLE 15-5
Examples of CEAs Appearing in ABSEL Proceedings

Year 1985

"Using the computer as a planning aid in an applied marketing course," Kagel.
Developing a media plan.

"Integrating microcomputers in the marketing curriculum through the use of marketing COMPUPROBS," Cosenza, Boone, Kurtz.
Fourteen models/techniques used in marketing management with exercises and problems.

"Microcomputer demonstration exercises for a course on creativity and problem solving," Friend.
Computer programs which involve students in the JUGS, HANOI, and CRYPTA tasks measuring creativity and cognitive characteristics.

"A reactive microcase pedagogy," Lambert and Lambert.
An interactive "microcase" taking 15-30 minutes of microcomputer time. Individual student interacts with microcase doing analysis and making decisions.

Year 1986

"How to use microcomputers in human resource management courses," Taylor.
Provides an example of an computerized experiential to determine if adverse impact has occurred in an organization.

"Assessing the effects of a computerized study guide in macroeconomic principles: a statistical analysis," Altieri and Papathanasis.
Test of the effectiveness of a computerized study guide in reinforcing macroeconomics concepts taught in the classroom.

"Using of multiple microcomputer application programs to teach fundamental business concepts and practices," Miller.
Used seven different commercially available packages to provide students with hands on experience in queuing, ratio analysis, inventory control, etc.

"A decision support system for capital funds forecasting," Shane and Bailes.
A DSS to guide and instruct business students in preparing a Capital Funds forecast.

Year 1987

"An expert systems approach for teaching marketing case analysis," Cannon and Morgan.
Presents a procedure for using an expert system development program to enhance marketing student's case analysis skills.

"Learning macroeconomic theory and policy analysis via microcomputer simulation," Edwards.
Presents a representative set of three macroeconomic models which the students solve via computer.

"Teaching about sampling in a marketing research class," Finn.
Describes an exercise which allows students to draw samples and understand the meaning of sampling distributions.

TABLE 15–5 (continued)

"An expert system for financial planners," Guin and McGregor.
Requires a student to develop an expert system which will predict the answers of an "expert" in financial planning.

"The gamesmanship of pricing: Building pricing strategy skills through spead-sheet modeling," Rubin.
Utilizes a 1-2-3 template to allow students to develop differing pricing strategies and understand pricing issues.

"Teaching MRP experientially through the use of Lotus 1-2-3," Schroeder and Gentry.
Application of an MRP problem embedded in a logistics game.

"The application of spreadsheet software technology to complex taxpayer elections," Watkins.
1-2-3 is utilized to show students the election path and decision model that provides the largest annual annuity to the plan participant.

"Oil and gas well investment analysis using the Lotus 1-2-3 decision support system," Wingender and Wurster.
Introduces the students to widely used measures of investment worth.

See Appendix A for complete sources.

While the lab manager may administer numerous exercises in labs during the experience, each exercise is unique (single iteration). Decisions are for the most part non-chained because of the real-world nature of the lab experience. Previous decisions on how to deal with a particular non-participator, for example, may in a few instances affect a lab manager's future decisions and actions. In these very few instances decisions may be chained. Furthermore, while the exercise topic is generally limited, the multiplicity of factors surrounding the exercise with which the lab manager must cope (i.e., conflict among group members, time management, motivation of non-participating members) make the experience multi-dimensional. Lab experiences can and should involve both content debriefing (i.e., debriefing an exercise topic) and process debriefing (i.e., evaluating the effectiveness

TABLE 15–6
Computerized Experiential Activity (CEA) Packages

Personal Computer Projects for Personnel and Human Resource Management	Beutell, N. and Schuler
Interactive Cases in Organizational Behavior	Moberg with Caldwell
Interactive Cases in Management	Sherman, J. D.

See Appendix A for complete sources.

of communicating an exercise topic). If the performance of groups within a manager's lab is a determinant of the lab manager's course grade, the environment can be seen as competitive. The lab manager experience is designed to improve the manager's technical skills (i.e., how to evaluate student performance) as well as interpersonal skills (i.e., how to communicate more successfully with ineffective performers). Finally, the very nature of the lab experience does not permit computerization.

Case Experience (CE)
The case approach, popularized by the Harvard Business School, is a pedagogy frequently utilized to examine completely and analyze one or a few behavioral entities, often over an extended time period. This approach to learning attempts to prepare participants for management positions by providing them with general business facts and skills necessary for dealing with common managerial problems. Cases are assumed to be representative of real business situations and their use helps students learn to apply their skills and abilities to business situations (Markulis, 1985). Although the case approach has been deemed appropriate for all business courses, the pedagogy is not without controversy. Argyris (1980) and Davies (1981) point out several potential flaws in the case method.

TABLE 15-7
Potential Research Questions Related to Computerization of Experiential Activities

---

Which topic areas are most appropriate for computerization of exercises based on student, faculty, and business perceptions?

What impact do computerized experiential activities have on managerial skill or competency development?

Do computerized experientials result in higher levels of achievement than other pedagogies in various subjects?

What impact do CEAs have on student understanding of specific topics in a course?

How does student learning style influence satisfaction with and performance on computerized experiential activities?

What is the cost/benefit ratio of CEAs versus other traditional pedagogies?

What is the general level of availability of required equipment for computerization of experiential activities in schools of business?

What class sizes are required for CEAs to be effective?

What is the appropriate method for integrating CEAs into a class?

What major perceptual barriers exist which might lead to student, faculty, or administration resistance to the utilization of CEAs?

How many CEAs currently exist and in what topic areas?

Cases are single iteration, nonchained and noninteractive. They typically focus on integrative skills and are used in a noncompetitive situation. Debriefing focuses on how and why the decisions were made, rather than the behavioral aspects of the decision process.

New approaches to case pedagogy are beginning to appear. The use of live or operating cases has been suggested by several authors (Argyris, 1980; Andrews and Noel, 1986; Bartlett and DeLong, 1982). In addition, the use of video tape for cases has been suggested (Madden, Robertson, and Brenensthuhl, 1983). Obviously, there are potential videodisc applications for the case approach if videotape applications exist. When interactive video technology is applied, cases will come in two forms, computerized and noncomputerized.

Internship Experience (IE)

One increasingly popular form of experiential learning is the internship. An especially cogent argument made in favor of internship programs is that the student, academic institution, and sponsoring organization alike derive benefit from their existence (Zigli, 1981–82). Knowles (1974) reported that cooperative education, internship, and practicum programs can be found in more than 1,000 two- and four-year colleges across the country. English (1985) indicated that one in five students in higher education was involved in an internship program during the academic year.

Why the increasing interest in student interns? Apparently both educators and business organization have begun to recognize the practical benefits that can be derived through internship programs:

> "An internship gives students a much more realistic view of the world of work. It also gives them perception, maturity and more accurate expectations when they graduate," says William Mobley, dean of the College of Business Administration at Texas A&M University (English, 1985).
>
> "Internships are our prerecruiting program," says Bob Patek, manager of recruitment and placement for Chrysler Corporation. "We use them to find the best talent before somebody else does." Adds R. J. Haynes, manager of recruitment for the Shell Oil Company, "Those who have had internships have a leg up" (English, 1985).

While there are numerous benefits to be derived by interns, participating firms, and academic institutions, internships also carry with them certain disadvantages. Zigli (1981–1982) identified the advantages and disadvantages for each of the above mentioned parties.

Student Intern
Benefits

Develop a mature sense of responsibility in the student.

Better prepare students for their chosen careers while enhancing their employment potential.

Permits students to test learned principles in real-world situations.

Usually allows students to earn academic credit.

Disadvantages

Involvement may delay graduation.

The real-world involvement may create an attitude of cynicism by the student toward theory.

The internship may be unchallenging, unrewarding, not germane, or even counterproductive for the student.

Academic Institution

Benefits

Offers an entirely new learning situation.

Provides a valuable linkage to the business community.

As an extension of the academic institution, may do much to enhance its public image.

Provides one avenue for faculty to keep abreast of current practices in their profession.

Enhances communication between students, practitioners, and faculty.

Disadvantages

Is a very unstructured experience.

Relies on an evaluation system with wide variation.

Measures of success are virtually impossible to establish.

Occupies faculty time which may detract from other academic responsibilities.

Often utilizes performance criteria established by the participating firm which may, in some instances, be academically unsound.

Participating Firm

Benefits

Provides the firm with a pool of potential employees.

Allows firm an opportunity to assess future employees more effectively.

Brings to the firm a myriad of beneficial new ideas, attitudes, and values.

Enhances contact and communication with the university, its faculty, and resources.

Provides them with a vehicle to complete special, short-run projects.

Disadvantages

Disrupts the normal work flow.

May prove more costly than other options for work completion (e.g., temporary employees).

Alters existing interpersonal work relationships.

Places additional demand on supervisor's time.

Internships are single iteration experiences with non-chained decisions. An internship could relate to a very narrow task assignment or topic, or it could involve numerous assignments or topics. For the most part, there is little content or process debriefing of the internship experience. While competition may be keen for obtaining an internship, the actual experience is non-competitive. The student's technical as well as interpersonal skills should develop through the interning experience. The experience is, of course, non-computerized.

THE FUTURE OF EXPERIENTIAL LEARNING

Based on the review of types of experiential learning and the technology which can be applied to the various forms of experiential learning, the authors suggest the following with regard to experiential learning:

1. The distinction between experiential exercises and simulations will become even more blurred due to the rapid growth of small scale simulations and computerized experiential exercises. For example, Digital Equipment Corporation has developed a computer-based experience called "Decision Point: A Living Case Study" that presents information concerning an organizational problem and provides the trainee several courses of action (McCune, 1987). Participants are given interactive feedback of how effectively they have dealt with a series of organizational problems, and the exercise also allows patterns of decision-making to be identified. The exercise uses touch screen technology, interactive video, and even sound tracks (McCune, 1987). Is this a simulation, a case, or an experiential exercise?

2. Interactive video technology will become a part of simulations, experiential exercises, cases, and lab experiences. This will occur due to decreases in the cost of interactive video technology and the availability of low cost, powerful authoring systems to develop exercises. Videodisc players and authoring systems are available for less than $10,000 and the price continues to decline (Roman, 1986).

3. Large scale simulations will begin to have embedded experientials. This will occur due to technology (interactive video) and academia's realization that no single experiential pedagogy will address all student learning needs. In fact, Kaplan (1985) recognized the potential to integrate behavioral incidents used in non-computerized experientials and simulations with computerized large scale simulations.

4. Interest in experiential learning in collegiate schools of business will increase due to the recent findings of the AACSB study focusing on outcome measures to assess programs (Porter and McKibbin, 1988). The results of this study, and the trend toward outcome assessment, suggests that students need practice and application opportunities for their behavioral skills. Short of internships, the various forms of experiential learning provide the perfect vehicles for delivering that opportunity to practice.

PART 6

THE EVALUATION OF EXPERIENTIAL LEARNING

Whenever new pedagogies are developed, one should ask relevant questions such as whether they work and how they compare in terms of student learning with existing approaches. While studies have been undertaken to evaluate the success of experiential pedagogies, the quality of the research has been somewhat uneven. The evaluation of the effectiveness of various pedagogies involves a large number of variables which pose threats to the experimental study's internal and external validities. Chapter 16 by Alvin C. Burns, James W. Gentry, and Joseph Wolfe categorizes a large number of those variables and discusses their probable impact. Chapter 17 by Joseph Wolfe reviews the literature investigating the effectiveness of simulation gaming and then suggests areas which need future research. Chapter 18 by Jerry Gosenpud reviews the literature assessing experiential instructional methods in order to (1) draw conclusions about the value of experiential learning, and (2) raise issues regarding the nature and quality of research evaluating experiential learning.

CHAPTER 16

A CORNUCOPIA OF CONSIDERATIONS IN EVALUATING THE EFFECTIVENESS OF EXPERIENTIAL PEDAGOGIES

Alvin C. Burns
James W. Gentry
Joseph Wolfe

Despite the fact that the use of experiential approaches in the classroom is often met by an enthusiastic reception from students, one must ultimately face the question of relative effectiveness. Not to be distracted by the natural excitement generated by experiential approaches, one must question as to whether these approaches actually facilitate learning. The need for such evaluation is multifold. First, there is a need to compare the efficacy of experiential pedagogies to "traditional" approaches such as one-way delivery in the forms of lectures, assigned readings, or stand-up presentations. On a different plane, there is a need to compare alternative experiential pedagogies competing to achieve the same learning end. Implicitly, we should be seeking to discover and adopt the "best" pedagogical climate for our students, for, in the absence of this concern, the educator is continually plagued with opportunity cost and efficient time use questions. Unfortunately, a paucity of solid empirical evidence exists regarding the relative effectiveness of experiential techniques.

Although an unfortunate state of affairs, the lack of research on the experiential pedagogies is reasonably explained. One school of thought on the subject is exemplified by Schreier (1981), who believes the quarry so elusive and our research tools so prone to error that pedagogists must trust their intuition and use the decision rule of "if it feels good, do it." This view, while not shared by all experiential pedagogists, parallels the sentiments of many who are convinced by personal assessments of face validity and thus moved by observations of their students' apparent enjoyment with experientials. A different view is espoused by researchers (e.g., Butler, Markulis, and Strang, 1985; Cook, 1986; Kelley and Easton, 1981; Parasuraman, 1980; Pierfy, 1977; Sugges, 1981; and Wolfe, 1976, 1981) who have noted problems with education research conducted in business programs. Two fundamental problem areas plaguing experiential pedagogy research emerge when one reviews the writings of these authors. On one hand, there are thorny conceptual problems pertaining to definitions, domain boundaries, and theoretical bases which underpin and frame pedagogical research. On the other hand, there are significant methodological difficulties such as experimental design, institutional constraints, time considerations, student population restrictions, or even ethical questions which deter all but the very naive or most steadfast pedagogical researchers.

In this chapter, we adopt the normative view that experiential learning should be tested with rigorous research. In addition, we believe personal observations constitute weak evidence best considered as hypotheses. However, we are well aware of the pitfalls awaiting this research. Our intent, therefore, is to offer a conceptual framework on which to build a research agenda designed to address the attendant methodological problems. To state our purposes more systematically, they are as follows:

1. To sensitize readers to some thorny issues involved in the evaluation of experiential pedagogies.
2. To describe the differences between internal, external, and transfer-internalization validity concerns in the evaluation of learning effects of experientials.
3. To discuss considerations encountered in the conceptualization and measurement of two criterion variables, learning and attitude.
4. To delineate variables potentially affecting the effectiveness of experiential pedagogies.
5. To indicate some ways to measure these variables; and
6. To specify some possible relationships between the variables.

A MODEL OF THE REAL-WORLD/EXPERIENTIAL WORLD RELATIONSHIP

It is useful to depict the two "worlds" addressed by experiential pedagogies. Figure 16-1 portrays this dichotomy. The Figure encompasses the complete process of designing, administering, and evaluating experiential exercises. The starting point is certain phenomena and rules believed to exist in the real-world. That is, educators must believe that order rather than chaos exists in the real-world and that specific principles, concepts, theories, or

FIGURE 16–1
The Real-World / Experiential World Paradigm

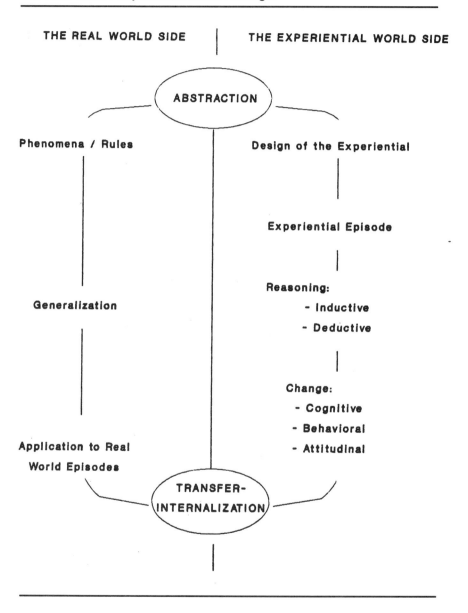

relationships should be taught to students so they can cope with the real-world. Through the process of abstraction, these rules are identified and built into an experiential exercise. Abstraction refers to the stripping away of irrelevant details and aspects and simplifying the rule such that it characterizes the operation of the experiential exercise. For instance, the phenomenon of price elasticity of demand might be translated into a simple linear regression equation, or the rule of span of control might be designed into a case study where a president reorganizes his company and creates a dozen divisions. In both cases, superfluous detail is omitted to minimize distraction away from the operation of the rule.

Because a learning experience is being designed where the student must discover the rule(s), a certain amount of superfluous noise or detail is usually added to challenge the student to discover and test the rule. Thus, in the price elasticity example, the experiential designer adds information on fixed and variable costs and the prices of substitute goods, identifies the product(s) under study, and provides socio-economic background on the consumers. In the span of control case, the designer may create personalities for the divisional heads, insert union contract negotiation deadlines, and describe the educational and career background of the president.

Ultimately, the student is run through an experiential episode, and probably though a series of such episodes to build up a set of observations. The student is urged to apply inductive and/or deductive reasoning to discover the systematic aspects of the experiential's operation. Ideally, the student applies the scientific method to his experiences with the experiential episodes: making observations; forming tentative hypotheses about the rules; experimenting with the experiential exercise to test the hypotheses; revising them based on these results; and ultimately gleaning the secret(s) hidden therein by the experiential designer. Learning occurs in the form of a change in the student. Cognitive change could occur in the form of identifying and retaining the rule(s). Behavioral change could accompany cognitive change wherein the student can articulate and apply these rules, and attitude change may occur as well in the form of emotional assignment to the learning experience.

In theory, business educators are concerned with lifelong learning effects. Thus, there is a transfer of the learning effects of experiential experiences into the real-world. Transfer refers to whether or not a priori learning facilitates or interferes with the performance of a later task (Ward and Rudelius, 1987). In our model, the student internalizes the learning experiences and applies them to real-world episodes. As pointed out in the definition of transfer, the prior learning may help the student cope with the real-world or it may fail to assist problem solving here. Over time, the success record of applying the internalized rule to real-world episodes will dictate whether or not the learned rule is generalized and becomes part of the student's personal mental set of real-world phenomena and rules. At this point, the learning loop is closed. That is, there may be a strong correspondence between the educator's taught map of real-world phenomena and rules and the student's map of the same, or there may be non-correspondence. In the latter case, the non-correspondence may be the consequence of modifications of these rules by the student over a period of experiences in the real-world, or it may result from entirely new rules discovered by the student through any of a number of learning processes out of the control of the educator.

This paradigm of the division and relationships between the real and experiential worlds affords insight into the evaluation problem facing pedagogical researchers. If we desire valid evaluations of the learning consequences of experiential exercises, there are three types of validity which must be addressed. First, there is internal validity, defined here as a change in the student in the desired direction explicitly caused by the experiential. Obviously, internal validity concerns the experiential world side of the paradigm exclusively. Stated succinctly, the research question becomes, "Did the experiential pedagogy affect learning within its own domain?"

This twofold question is clearly nontrivial. To answer the first question requires careful control of extraneous influences and changes in the student-subjects. Take a simple case as an example of the necessity for these controls. Students in a personnel management course are given bogus application forms and vitas of three applicants for a director of public relations job. Once the choice is made by each student, scenarios of the next five-year job performance of each candidate employed for that position are provided. Students are expected to learn the rule that applicant qualifications and job description specifications should be matched as closely as possible in order to make a good choice. The evaluation of learning is done with a comprehensive course examination at the end of the term. The rationale for defending the internal validity of this experiential becomes "post hoc, ergo propter hoc," or because the students went through the experiential episode and they answered correctly on the exam, the experiential is responsible for their learning the rule. However, any number of competing hypotheses can be posited because of the lack of control in this experiment. For instance, students may have already known the rule; they may have read about it in assigned reading; they may have picked it up from students who took it last term; they may have encountered it in another class; they may have been tipped off somehow in the wording of the examination question; and so forth.

The second aspect of the internal validity question is even more difficult to address without rigorous controls, for it necessitates the use of two or more groups of students, one for each competing pedagogy. Questions of group equivalence, instructional standardization, timing, and common measures of learning must be addressed in addition to those just posed. In other words, one cannot correctly attribute learning effects of experientials without acute concern for good experimental design.

Adherence to good experimental design raises the issue of external validity. Here the question posed is, "Can the results of an internally valid experiential learning effects study be generalized to other experiential world cases?" This question is especially relevant and constitutes the most damaging complaint against the vast majority of experiential research to date. Almost none can be generalized because it is bound by sample constraints, course-specificity, institution boundaries, or treatment idiosyncrasies. This situation is unfortunate in the sense that experiential researchers are constantly hampered by a lack of resources not to mention practical constraints which usually confine research to their own campuses. Research on all types of learning is implicitly weak in external validity. Regardless of these limitations, there is a clear need to address external validity as has been done in a few instances (i.e., Norris, 1986; Norris and Snyder, 1982).

Once the internal and external validity of the experiential research has been assured, the transfer-internalization validity issue must be addressed. Transfer-internalization validity pertains to the real-world side of the paradigm, and it asks the question, "Did the experiential-based learning transfer to the student's ultimate success in his/her career?" In other words, did the internalization of the rules gained though experiential episodes and generalized to the student's career situation enhance his/her ability to cope with the real-world? Very few researchers have tackled this question; an exception is Wolfe and Roberts (1986).

This form of validity also encompasses a two-part analysis. First, there is the issue of the faithfulness of the phenomena and rules communicated in the experiential to the real-world. For instance, many experiential models of real-world phenomena assume linear relationships, yet most real-world relationships are nonlinear. Thus, when a student discovers a linear price-quantity relationship in a simulated industry, it is possible that this learning will be inconsistent with the industry of his/her career. Apart from this aspect, it should be apparent that the student will adapt his/her education to the career situation, seeking to refine a personal set of rules which optimize the attainment of personal career goals. This continual refinement is theoretically endless and implicitly idiosyncratic; consequently, the rules identified by the educator may fit the industry, but they may be inconsistent with the student's career values. This state of affairs is problematic to researchers seeking to document the long-term effects of experiential learning by tracking the performance of students in the real-world and attempting to link that criterion with their involvement in experientials during their university days.

IMPLICATIONS OF THE THREE TYPES OF VALIDITY
FOR THE MEASUREMENT OF EFFECTIVENESS

Before delving into the conceptual and methodological problems of measuring learning, it is appropriate to review the alternative mechanics of measurement as they relate to internal, external, and transfer-internalization validity. Traditional measures exist in the forms of objective tests (multiple choice, true-false, definitions, sentence completion, etc.) and essay tests. Both types are applied to assess learning within the experiential world. That is, learning is measured by a student's performance on these tests, and it is assumed that whatever pedagogy or pedagogies used in the course are responsible for learning. Nontraditional measuring techniques include written analyses of textbook cases and "live" applications where students recommend a solution to a real organization's business problems. These two are equivalent in that they both present the student with a novel problem but one for which the student has gained the tools to solve over the course. The nontraditional techniques are in reality experiential episodes used to measure learning rather than used to facilitate the discovery of rules. None of these measurements, however, is useful unless the researcher has guaranteed internal validity, for as noted earlier, if a competing hypothesis about the cause of learning can be tendered, the true learning effects of an experiential are in question.

The identical measures of learning can be used to generalize findings to other experiential situations; however, the requirements of external validity enter into the picture here. Once internal validity is assured, external validity must be addressed, for the two are independent considerations. Given the great diversity of university situations, differences between functional business areas, and variations allowable in the administration of experientials, there are myriad factors which must be addressed. Consequently, an appropriate goal is to identify experiential situations which share characteristics and to gain external validity within relevant boundaries. For instance, one might measure the effectiveness of experientials used in the principles of management course taught at major state universities in accredited institutions with primarily on-campus student populations and in class sizes between 35 and 45 students. In short, experiential research is well-advised to corroborate internally valid findings with studies performed in similar situations as a first step toward external validity assessment. A gradual expansion of the boundaries, contingent on the findings in the previous step, seems an appropriate long-term research strategy regarding external validity.

The measurement of transfer-internalization validity occurs either in capstone courses or from longitudinal studies. Capstone courses typically require students to integrate learning from previous coursework to solve the problems presented in the capstone course. Generally, capstone courses provide a standardized problem set supposedly faithful to the industries into which students will enter on career tracks. Thus, they are surrogates. Further, these problems should be solvable with the application of rules learned in previous courses, and students' performances should be directly comparable. Performances should be indicative of learning in previous courses except for the confounding factor of individual differences between students such as motivation, intelligence, or resources. In reality, however, performance in capstone courses is influenced by several other factors such as group dynamics, educator review of course content, testing methods, and the experientials used in that course. Longitudinal studies, in contrast, track students in their various career paths. The differences in career situations must be addressed, however, for the reasons noted earlier. Again, transfer-internalization research encounters the most difficult problems because of lack of control of extraneous factors. Enumeration of these factors is beyond the scope of this chapter; nonetheless, research should address this issue area early in the design stages.

The central purpose of this chapter is to delineate a rather large number of variables which are critical to successful experiential research. We draw on our own previous work (Burns and Gentry, 1977, 1980; Gentry and Burns, 1981; Wolfe, 1985) as well as the work of several others (Brenensthul and Catalanello, 1976; Cohen and Rhenman, 1961; Gosenpud and Miesing, 1982; Greenblat and Duke, 1981; Greenlaw and Wyman, 1973; Parasuraman, 1978; Schellenberger, 1981; Schneier, 1977). The intent of this chapter is to organize thinking about research on experiential pedagogies, but it stops short of proposing a programmatic research agenda. The chapter's value is therefore primarily conceptual rather than methodological. Of primary concern are internal and external validity issues, for in some cases, failure to be concerned with these variables interferes with the study's internal validity. However, given the need for generalizable research findings, attention to these variables will also go far to address external validity. Good experimental design dictates that both internal and external validity be assured before the experiment is conducted.

LEARNING—THE CENTRAL CRITERION VARIABLE

Although learning can be defined easily as a change in cognition or behavior consistent with the desires of the educator, there are some troublesome considerations in this criterion. A false assumption exists connecting measures of performance and measures of learning in many studies. Intuitively, one wishes performance and learning to be equivalent; however, intuition is a poor guide here. Performance measures generally relate to indicants of success such as return on investment or profit in simulations, "correct" answers to case studies, satisfactory performance on test questions, and observed behavior consistent with proper skills acquisition. Unfortunately, all of these performance indicants can imply learning when learning has not occurred. Performance may be affected by luck, random guessing, or poor performance of other students. Learning, on the other hand, requires the successful internalization of rules, skills, or behaviors which may or may not accompany successful performance. Perhaps the best example to cite here is the case of learning which occurs as a consequence of the mistakes of the learner. In fact, "learning by doing" cannot be effected unless performance ranges from unsatisfactory to satisfactory; otherwise, there is no reason to "do" more than one time. The point is that researchers are predisposed to link positive or "good" performance with learning, but the learner can formulate rules from negative experiences just as easily as with positive ones. In short, the researcher should not fall into the trap of a monotonic coupling of performance and learning. Performance is not a surrogate for learning.

To complicate matters further, fundamental difficulties exist in the customary measurement of learning. First, there is usually no baseline to determine whether or not the learner entered the experiential with the learning already achieved from some other experience. Second, the assessment of learning is subjective in that some minimum level of performance or change in performance must be specified as the point where learning has been demonstrated. Third, most tests of learning are custom-made and are never subjected to rigorous reliability and validity assessment. For instance, performance in an experiential exercise may be unrelated to understanding of the concepts involved as has been contended by Greenlaw and Wyman (1973) and Parasuraman (1980). Finally, there is the question of whether or not the measurement instrument is properly matched to the type of learning involved. Schellenberger (1981) noted, for example, that some exercises may emphasize the learning of knowledge or the development of specific skills. Parasuraman (1981) has claimed that a goal of business simulation gaming is to teach students the process of effective decision-making. In either case, the learning measure must coincide with the objectives of the experiential episodes. Thus, the researcher must identify the type of learning involved along cognitive as well as behavioral dimensions before constructing measures of learning.

To address this last issue, we advocate the use of Bloom et. al. (1956) classification scheme which identifies six different levels of cognitive learning. This scheme is summarized in Table 16–1. The table describes each level and the appropriate assessment mechanism(s) for each. The classification/measurement scheme emphasizes the need to identify early the level of learning sought by the experiential. If, for instance, its purpose is to provide an awareness of the general topic area, methodologies aimed at the higher levels of learning may be counterproductive. On the other hand, if the objective is to improve students' abilities to apply concepts, the use of multiple choice questions from the instructor's manual is inappropriate. Of special note, the Bloom et. al. taxonomy is particularly relevant to business experiential learning assessment in our minds since it accommodates the broad range of learning facilitated by the myriad of experientials and simulations in business education. In other words, one must be extremely careful about delineating the level(s) of learning effected by an experiential and matching the assessment with it properly.

Granted, adoption of the Bloom et. al. classification scheme does not solve all the various problems in the assessment of learning noted earlier. However, it does provide a framework within which to begin systematically working on these difficulties. At the very least, its adoption permits the evaluator to match the domain of learning, delineated in the learning

TABLE 16–1
Bloom's Taxonomy of Learning Objectives

Learning Objectives	Description of the Learning	Student is Assessed by
1. Basic Knowledge	Student recalls or recognizes information.	Answers to direct questions and mutiple choice tests.
2. Comprehension	Student changes information into a different symbolic form.	Ability to act upon or process information by restating material in his/her own words.
3. Application	Student discovers relationships, generalizations and skills.	Application of knowledge to simulated problems.
4. Analysis	Student solves problems in light of conscious knowledge of the relationship between components and the principle that organizes them.	Identification of critical assumptions, alternatives and constraints in a problem situation.
5. Objective Synthesis	Student goes beyond what is known, providing new insights.	Solution of a problem that requires original, creative thinking.
6. Objective Evaluation	Student develops the ability to create standards to judge, to weigh, and to analyze.	Logical consistency and attention to detail.

objectives of the experiential, with the level of learning identified in the taxonomy and to select an assessment vehicle which is consistent with both. The scheme offers guidance in the pursuit of internal validity and provides a structure for the measurement of learning across studies helpful to external validity concerns.

ATTITUDES—A SOMETIMES SERENDIPITOUS RESULT

The Bloom et. al classification scheme is not restricted to cognitive and/or behavioral changes effected by an experiential episode. There is an important third dimension of change which invariably takes place regardless of whether or not cognition or behavior has been changed. This dimension is affect, or the emotional assignment made by the student as a result of the experience. Some researchers have incorporated attitude in their experiential pedagogy research (i.e., Faria, 1986; Fritzsche, 1977; Kelley and Whatley, 1980). Affect is either positive or negative, but rarely neutral. The foci of affect are myriad. A case in point is Burns and Sherrell (1984), who compared alternative experiential pedagogies and found differences between alternative pedagogies for the attitude dimensions of: student-teacher relations, perceived knowledge about the topic, perceived decision-making skills gained, enjoyment, and appreciation for the subject matter. In other words, attitudes may be formed or changed toward the course, the instructor, the experiential exercise, the student him- or herself, other students, the subject matter, or even toward the educational process. Conceptually, at least, there is no compelling association between cognitive change and affect nor between affect objects. That is, while learning of some skill may result from an experiential, the student may consider the experience distasteful and lose respect for the instructor. At the same time, he/she may have formed closer friendships with fellow classmates and experienced an enhanced self-image.

Except for some concern with student satisfaction with the course, experiential evaluation research has omitted affect measures. There are important reasons to be concerned with experientially-produced affect of all types. Emotional states influence one's reasoning, and most experientials assume either deductive or inductive reasoning to take place in order that students discover the rules secreted in the experiential. Thus, if an experiential generates negative attitudes, there is cause for believing that this negativism may interfere with the mental processes of participants. Similarly, positive attitudes may assist reasoning as students would be more inclined toward experimentation, risk-taking, and trial-and-error without fear of the experiential, instructor, or other students. Counterarguments may be put forth by opponents or embellishments found in previous research (i.e., Golen, Burns, and Gentry, 1984). The point remains: attitude is typically an outcome of experiential exposure, and affect may influence learning during the experiential.

On a different level, affect may influence long-term learning by facilitating or inhibiting transfer and internalization of cognitive and/or behavioral learning gained through the experiential episodes. Obviously, negative attitudes accompanying a cognition may exacerbate its internalization in that the student may refrain from applying the learned rule to real-world episodes for fear of possible negative consequences, for instance. Alternatively, positive affect may encourage these applications since the expected result has pleasant associations.

Still another area of impact by affect is student demeanor. Over time, the affective consequences of experientials may change a student's self-perception; his/her perception of other students; and his/her relationship with the instructor, course, and subject matter. Burns and Sherrell (1984) claim that affect changes may be responsible for behavior changes in students as they engage in future experientials or interact with instructors in subsequent courses.

Attitude, in our view, serves as a moderator to the learning process. Understanding the attitude-learning relationship is a logical goal given our previous points about the face validity of experientials and the need to investigate hypotheses gained by observation through rigorous experimentation.

THE FUNDAMENTAL EQUATION

The primary purpose of this paper is to enumerate those variables, other than treatment variables, which have either intervening or direct effects on learning and/or attitude consequences. Kelley and Easton (1981, pp. 139–140) have noted,

> It is tempting to conclude that there is little future in research aimed at making general statements about the efficiency of one teaching method versus another . . . More importantly, in controlling for variables other than teaching method the results are necessarily conditional. These conditions, which include the teachers involved, type of subject, educational objectives, type of students, etc., will be different for each situation in which the particular teaching method will be employed.

Various categorization schemes have been presented (Burns and Gentry, 1977; Greenlaw and Wyman, 1973; Kelley and Easton, 1981; Schnellenberger, 1981; Schneier, 1977; Wolfe, 1985) and are summarized in Table 16–2. While all of these schemes use different labels, close scrutiny reveals considerable similarity. Consequently, we will use the categorization scheme with which we are most familiar (Burns and Gentry, 1977) but will incorporate variables from other authors' frameworks to ensure completeness. Also, we hasten to point out that while these ennumerations appear complete, they are obviously not exhaustive.

From these variables, a fundamental research equation can be stated:

LEARNING modified by ATTITUDE =
f[EXPERIENTIAL USED (CONCEPTS, NATURE, CONDUCT)
determined by (STUDENT ATTRIBUTES,
EDUCATOR CONSIDERATIONS)]

This fundamental research equation points out the rather formidable task facing experiential pedagogy researchers and further emphasizes the need for systematic investigations of several types. In addition, our previous discussions on validity considerations, measurement, and the confounding influences of attitude infer the necessity for programmatic rather than ad hoc research endeavors.

The central criterion variable is learning defined as cognitive and/or behavioral change measured appropriate to the level of learning identified in the Bloom et. al. taxonomy. Equally important is the dependent variable of attitude which has been described as multidimensional, multideterminant, and independent of learning but influential to the learning process. The primary independent variable identified in this equation is the experiential exercise used. However, as related in the description of the experiential/ real-world model, a range of concepts may be included in the experiential

TABLE 16–2
Various Categorization Schemes for Independent Variables

Burns and Gentry (1977)
  Concepts Covered in the Exercise
  Conduct of the Exercise
  Nature of the Exercise
  Student Attributes
  User Attributes
	Greenlaw and Wyman (1973)
	  Administration
	  Administrator
	  Game
	  Participant

Kelley and Eaton (1981)
  Presage
  Context
  Process
	Schneier (1977)
	  Environmental
	  Group-Level
	  Individual-Level
	  Task

Schnellenberger (1981)
  Administration
  Game
  Participant
	Wolfe (1985)
	  Administration
	  Administrator
	  Game Design
	  Player and Group Characteristics

exercise, and these concepts differ in complexity, theoretical nature, number, or along other dimensions. Similarly, the nature of the experiential is an important variable largely under the control of the instructor. For instance, how many episodes, the number of decision variables involved with each episode, participant grouping, and course integration are manipulable and may be hypothesized to influence learning and/or attitude. The last independent variable is the conduct of the experiential episodes which includes accountability, autonomy, pace, and other episode-specific factors.

Originating the learning process are student attributes and administrator considerations. The former set pertains to demographic, personality, intellectual ability, and various participation characteristics of the students involved in the experiential, while the latter group addresses the philosophy, motivations, resources, choice set, and other instructor-specific factors which guide the instructor's use of the experiential for that particular learning experience.

DISCUSSION OF THE SEVERAL CONSIDERATIONS IN THE BASIC EQUATION

Each independent variable and moderator variable is multidimensional. That is, a number of different aspects can be identified, and Table 16-3 summarizes the dimensions discussed in each one. Unfortunately, some aspects are qualitative; others are quantitative; and still others may be either depending on how they are interpreted. The purpose of this section is to generate some conceptual appreciation for each variable by describing the various dimensions we have identified. Our comments are a combination of intuitive and admittedly subjective observations, and wherever possible, we attempt to describe the range of eventualities within each dimension. Consequently, this section is intended to open readers' eyes to the considerations. The subsequent section provides some tentative operationalizations.

Concepts Covered in the Experiential

Probably any business concept imaginable can be incorporated into a game or experiential exercise, but concepts can vary considerably along several dimensions. It is advantageous to identify the nature of this variability in each case.

Complexity
Business concepts can range from the simple to the very complicated. Simple concepts tend to be found in prerequisite courses and/or in the introductory materials for higher level courses. Taken singularly, simple concepts proba-

TABLE 16–3
Dimensions of the Independent Variables

Concepts Covered in the Experiential
   Complexity
   Theoretical Nature
   Functional/Environmental Scope
   Precision
   Stochasticism
   Number

Nature of the Experiential
   Duration
   Decision Variables
   Intergroup Competition versus Results Sharing
   Participant Grouping
   Course Integration
   Potential for Modification
   Degree of Realism

Experiential Conduct
   Accountability
   Autonomy
   Pace
   Participant Involvement
   Educator Involvement
   Debriefing

Student Attributes
   Ability to Learn
   Willingness to Learn
   Ability to Participate
   Willingness to Participate
   Number
   Demographic and Personality Characteristics

Educator Considerations
   Motive for Use
   Teaching Philosophy
   Familiarity with Topic
   Choice Set
   Resource Base

bly do not require elaborate learning experiences, whereas more complicated concepts are better demonstrated through "learning by doing" teaching strategies.

Theoretical Nature
Business concepts vary in their level of abstraction, ranging from those which are readily applied to those which are largely theoretical and require

much more rigorous study to comprehend and apply. Theoretical concepts tend to require an inductive approach while applied concepts are often learned by deduction. Induction implies many experiences and much evidence from which to reason, while deduction suggests the application of learned concepts.

Functional/Environmental Scope
Some concepts are often restricted to a single business decision while others cut across several business functional areas. The former usually concentrates on partial solutions with many variables held constant, but the latter must be handled more dynamically.

Precision
Some concepts are much more precisely defined than others, and their relationships with other business functions may be very explicit. Other relationships may be less intuitive, and thus require greater experiential learning effort.

Stochasticism
Business concepts may be stochastic or deterministic. Sometimes experientials are designed with deterministic models that appear to be stochastic as, for instance, the decision inputs of several firms in a simulated industry which yield seemingly random outcomes. Such experiences can confuse the game participants, enticing them to consider random that which is not. Practically any experiential which does not allow the participant to pursue cause and effect experimentation will have the same result.

Number
How many business concepts are illustrated within a single game or experiential? When one examines even simple experientials, there may emerge a considerable number of concepts which act as foundations. If students are to learn a multitude of concepts, the learning situation is substantially different from an experiential where they learn very few.

Nature of the Experiential

Just as the business concepts being illustrated in an experiential are diverse, settings vary greatly. Reflection reveals a number of dimensions to the nature of an experiential, most of which are specified below.

Duration
Experientials vary greatly in the amount of class time allocated to them. There are experientials requiring a complete semester of participation, and

those which can be executed in a matter of minutes. Generally, long duration exercises must be considerably more involved than short ones, although this condition does not always hold. Nevertheless, duration surely has ramifications for the dependent variables.

Decision Variables

Exercises may be categorized by the nature and number of decision variables necessary for meaningful participation. In general, the complexity of the game increases directly with the number of decisions required per episode. The nature of decisions can vary greatly: one experiential may only require quantitative decision variables, while another may be restricted to purely qualitative decisions.

Intergroup Competition and Results Sharing

Group versus individual learning is a salient dimension of the experiential. In situations where students participate against one another, the results of any one participant's decisions are confidential. Here learning varies by participant since not all participants experience equal success. Those with poor competitive records are often briefed of their errors when the exercise is completed. Learning for them is extraneous to participating in the experiential, for it results from a case study of the winners. Other types of exercises utilize group shared learning wherein participants compete against the game and report the results of their efforts during class discussion. In theory, learning under this situation should be more uniform across students.

Participant Grouping

Class size and the complexity of experientials dictate the composition of participant grouping. Larger, functionally diverse experientials typically necessitate team groupings and specialization by participant within the group. Inasmuch as teams are usually formed randomly, there is always the risk that a team's members may unfairly represent one end of the "curve," and that the team's performance eventuates from the combination of native abilities (or lack thereof). Wolfe (1985), for instance, suggested that the method of team selection (assigned versus self-assigned) may be a separate variable that could influence the outcomes obtained from a simulation game. Similarly, team cohesion effects have been documented by Wolfe and Box (1986, 1987) as have group size effects (Wolfe and Chacko, 1981a, 1981b). Further, Schneier (1977) listed a large number of group-level variables: size, composition (hetero/homogeniety), interpersonal attraction, atmosphere, cohesiveness, maturity, role conflict/ambiguity, coalition formation, and status differentials.

Course Integration

Each course represents a specific body of knowledge, and the researcher must appreciate the degree of overlap between the exercise and concepts being taught. Confounding this problem is the degree of integration of the exercise into class presentation. Some experientials are specifically designed to teach concepts and require very little interference, but others assume that participants have been schooled on the concepts and are ready to apply them with little instructional support from the experiential itself.

Potential for Modification

Some experientials readily lend themselves to modification. For instance, it may be possible to incorporate parameter changes which permit the experiential to range across different situations. Further, changes may be necessary to prevent "optimal strategies" from being passed on by the student grapevine.

Degree of Realism

Intuitively, the more the exercise's environment represents a real-world process, the more motivated students will be to participate. Exercises with higher face validity presumedly facilitate the motivation to learn and the transfer of academic insights into the real-world.

Experiential Conduct

Apart from the two classes of variables just discussed, experientials may be characterized by a number of attributes specific to their conduct. While most experientials have directions or advice on administration, many educators see fit to break away as they become more familiar with it and their students' capabilities.

Accountability

The amount of weight given to the experiential may determine the amount of effort put forth by the student and affect subsequent learning. Also, to the extent that the exercise involves an integrated group effort, the ability to relate individual learning or results to the exercise decisions and performance may be lessened.

Autonomy

Separate from accountability is the degree of autonomy afforded to each participant. Large teams may tend to reduce autonomy and thereby encourage mediocre performance; small teams or individual participation may tend to heighten autonomy and pinpoint responsibility.

Pace
At one extreme are experientials with lock-step procedures, where all participants are constrained to the same decision set at prespecified points in time. Pace is set by the educator. On the other hand, there are situations where participants set their own pace, manipulating decision variables in experimental fashion and deciding for themselves when learning has taken place.

Participant Involvement
The degree of participation expected of students is also a variable. Using the same experiential, for instance, one set of students may be required to perform extensive competitive analysis, sophisticated statistical procedures, and experimentation, while another set may do nothing more than discuss the experiential during a single class period.

Educator Involvement
Important differences exist with regard to the potential for educator involvement across experientials. Furthermore, the administrator's familiarity with the game will influence involvement and possibly performance (Sanders and Gosenpud, 1986). Most tend to spend more time on their own experientials than they do with those designed by others. Some experientials require or encourage much educator involvement during operation, while others require little beyond orientation.

Debriefing
As Wolfe (1985) noted, it is universally accepted that some type of post-experiential episode(s) analysis with discussion should take place to consolidate impressions and externalize experiences. The quality of debriefing will vary depending on such aspects as the nature of events occurring during the experiential, the educator's ability to elicit discussion, the size of the class, or the amount of class time available.

Student Attributes

Observations across several universities support the intuitively obvious statement that students vary across aptitudes, skills, motivations, backgrounds, and a host of other factors.

Ability to Learn
Students exhibit differences in their capacity to learn, and these differences obviously impact the learning experience. There are two aspects of this variable. First, there is the intellectual ability of the student as shaped by biology and environment. Second, there is the student's store of concepts

constituting foundational skills and knowledge. With the latter factor, prerequisites and curriculum may assure a minimum level of preparedness; nonetheless, each student constitutes a special case.

Willingness to Learn
Separate from ability is the desire to learn. Anyone who had been involved in continuing education or extension courses has confronted the student who has great desire to learn but who is hamstrung with a rusty cognitive process. Similarly, many of us have been frustrated by the bright but uninterested student.

Ability to Participate
At first glance, ability to participate may appear redundant to ability to learn, but deeper reflection reveals they are conceptually distinct. Many experientials require special time and place commitment in the forms of team meetings, computer terminals, data entry, props, and the like. Commuter students and evening students have limited ability to participate, while on-campus student populations probably do not have the same constraints.

Willingness to Participate
Motivation to be involved varies by student. Some exhibit great enthusiasm to experiment with novel situations, while others are reluctant to do so.

Number
Large classes are generally mismatched with experientials expecting individual participation over a multitude of episodes, while small classes do not fit large multifaceted business strategy simulations. Similarly, some experientials require many participants or participant-teams to compete and add dynamics to the experiential, while others pit the computer or experiential administrator against individual students or student-teams.

Demographic and Personality Characteristics
Gosenpud (1986), Greenlaw and Wyman (1973), Schneier (1977) and Schellenberger (1981) have all pointed out that factors such as sex and age or personality differences may determine experiential performance and learning.

Educator Considerations

Educators who use experientials have several characteristics that identify them uniquely and which may also influence the learning process experienced by their students.

Motive for Use

It is important to examine the motives of experientials users for adopting these pedagogies. In some instances, the motives may stem from the need to test experientials developed by the educator, while in other cases the motive may relate to compliance with what the educator perceives to be the expectations of peers. Book publishers often include experiential exercises and computer simulations as part of adoption packages; consequently, the motive for use may originate in the availability of the experiential. In short, the motives of administrators for using experientials are varied and may not always be in tune with the educational goals stipulated for students.

Teaching Philosophy

Philosophies regarding student workload, achievement standards, and educator style vary greatly. For various reasons, the amount of work expected of students is not constant across educators and sometimes not uniform across different courses taught by the same educator. Similarly, some evaluation systems reward overachieving students, while others have more modest expectations. Finally, some educators thrive on constant student contact, but others prefer to be more formal in their relationships.

Familiarity with the Topic

Educator familiarity with the topic may have important implications for the effectiveness of experientials used. For instance, the first-time educator may be less capable of integrating the experiential into the course than the educator who has taught the subject matter many times and knows all topics intimately. Similarly, greater experience with the topic area may lead to more effective administration of the experiential.

Choice Set

Ideally, each experiential is selected from several alternatives; however, there are at least two reasons why this ideal may not occur. First, few educators are totally aware of all the alternative experientials for a particular topic, especially since some of them are unpublished or published in obscure sources. Also, there probably exists a natural resistance to change, and this trait would certainly restrict the choice set over time. In either case, the set of alternatives would be constrained and the experiential selected not necessarily the best available.

Resource Base

Each educator and his/her institution is differentially endowed with resources. The resource base encompasses budget, secretarial support, student assistants, computer size and availability, and time. In theory, at least, greater resources should assist administrators in their goals of effective pedagogy implementation, while scarce resources most certainly hamper the attainment of these goals.

PRELIMINARY OPERATIONALIZATIONS OF THE SEVERAL VARIABLES

Gentry and Burns (1981) have sought to operationalize most of the several variables just described and have even gone so far as to provide a proposed questionnaire. Table 16–4 summarizes the Gentry and Burns' (1981) initial attempts to measure these variables and operationalizes those not addressed in the original paper. As presented, they are a blend of definitions and quantification attempts. The paper (Gentry and Burns, 1981) contains a questionnaire used in their research effort. Unfortunately, these two researchers found such great diversity across business faculty members in different disciplines that their empirical study was never brought to fruition. Nonetheless, the operationalizations are still useful as starting points for any research to be conducted on a more modest scale.

HYPOTHESIZED INTERRELATIONSHIPS AMONG THE VARIABLES

The principal purpose of this chapter has been to describe several variables claimed to have differential impacts on the outcomes of experiential learning. Of primary concern is the need to recognize, control, manipulate, or at the very least, measure the influence of these factors when conducting experiential learning evaluation research.

To provide some guidance for future research in this area, it is worthwhile to discuss their expected relationships; however, with over thirty different variables identified, a complete specification of all interrelationships is certainly beyond even the most ambitious modeler's abilities. Consequently, we have opted to tender some hypotheses about general relationships between the seven categories of variables.

To begin, however, it will be handy to adopt a general framework of exogenous, endogenous, and outcome (dependent) variables. As described earlier in the paper, the ultimate outcome variable is learning measured as performance and/or internalized rules or skills. However, attitudes are often seen as outcomes of experiential pedagogies moderating learning. Exogenous variables in our model are those which would be considered antecedent to and generally out of the control of the experiential educator, but nonetheless important in determining the effects of experien-

TABLE 16–4
Preliminary Operationalizations of the Variables

CONCEPTS VARIABLES

Complexity	Simplicity of the concept versus its complexity; the ease with which the concept is understood
Theoretical Nature	Degree of abstraction in the concept; pragmatic (operational) versus theoretical concepts
Functional/ Environmental Scope	Number of business functions and outside considerations involved
Precision	Imprecise (implicit) versus precise (explicit) relationship of concepts to business decisions in the exercise
Stochasticism	Degree of random variation in the concept(s) versus degree of determination in the concept(s)
Number	Number of concepts or subconcepts used or taught

NATURE VARIABLES

Duration	How long the exercise lasts, number of decision phases, number of days or weeks it takes the exercise to run
Decision Variables	Absolute number of decisions or phases over the duration
Results Sharing	Degree to which participants formally share the results of their game or exercise experience with one another
Participant Grouping	Number of participants in a group
Course Integration	Amount of time devoted to the exercise, administration and teaching-related concepts
Potential for Modification	Ability of administrator to change parameters and environments in the exercise or game
Degree of Realism	Amount of realism in the experiential

EXPERIENTIAL CONDUCT

Accountability	Ability to relate individual results/learning to exercise decisions/performance
Autonomy	Individual responsibility for performance versus group consensus decisions
Pace	Lock-step versus free-form pace; degree of control of pace by participants versus administrator
Participant Involvement	Amount of time required (per week or semester) for the average participant
Educator Involvement	Amount of time required (per week or semester) in teaching and administering the game and evaluating participants
Debriefing	Amount and type of debriefing used

TABLE 16–4 (continued)

STUDENT ATTRIBUTES	
Ability to Learn	Capacity of participants to learn due to intellectual level and situational factors
Willingness to Learn	Attitude toward learning: positive to negative
Ability to Participate	Amount of outside interests, obligations or other constraints on participant's time
Willingness to Participate	Attitude toward participating: positive to negative
Number	Number of students in the class
Demographic and Personality Characteristics	Socioeconomic status of students; Interpersonal and personality-specific factors
EDUCATOR CONSIDERATIONS	
Motive for Use	Self-serving versus student-serving motives
Teaching Philosophy	Amount of time expected of the student in the course
Familiarity with Topic	Number of years studied, taught or worked with the topic
Choice Set	Awareness of other experientials which could accomplish the same or similar ends
Resource Base	Amount and quality of resources available for running the experiential

Based on Gentry and Burns (1981)

tials. Endogeneous variables are those which are manipulable, subject to the constraints imposed by the exogeneous factors, and serve as primary determinants of the outcomes. These factors are specific to the experiential, and both direct and indirect (moderator) effects are identifiable for the endogeneous variables.

Figure 16–2 presents the seven different types of variables cast in a possible causal model and categorized as to type of variable. In this model, the antecedent variables which serve as "givens," at least in the short run in which experientials operate, are: (1) Student Attributes and (2) Educator Considerations. Thus, it is important to inventory both of these factors and to identify situations in which the experiential under scrutiny is taking place. Immediately endogeneous to these factors is the Concepts variable. That is, it seems logical to expect Educator Considerations to effect directly the Concepts selected to be taught by experiential pedagogy. Similarly, it is probable that Student Attributes will have some bearing of the selection of what Concepts will be taught experientially. The Concepts involved will

FIGURE 16–2
A Model of the Interrelationships Among the Variables

Antecedent Variables	Endogeneous (Experiential-Specific) Variables	Outcome Variables

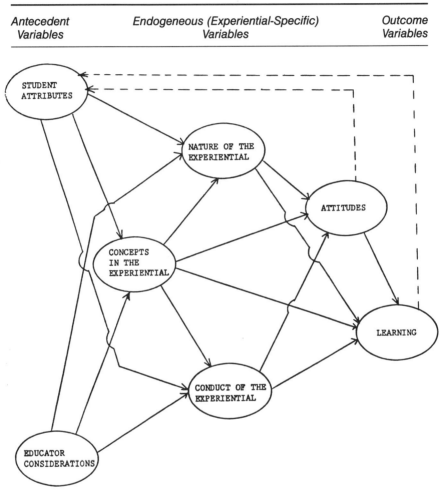

likewise have some impact on the Nature of the experiential episodes adopted as well as the specific Conduct of those episodes. Obviously, both Student and Educator Attributes will determine the Nature and Conduct of the experiential as well. The Nature and Conduct of the experiential will intervene or moderate the effects of the Concepts involved to impact on Student Attitudes, and Student Attributes will probably have some relationship to Attitudes formed as well. Finally, Learning will exhibit a relationship between Attitude, the Conduct of the experiential, the Nature of the episodes, and the central Concepts identified for Learning. Both Learning and Attitude feed back to alter Student Attributes.

Clearly, there is need for an enlightened research endeavor testing these hypothesized relationships. To reiterate our previous criticisms, the vast majority of what little empirical research exists is fragmented to the point of looking at simple relationships between a single component of one of the endogeneous variables (e.g., participant group sizes) to a single measure of learning. Also, the preponderance of research has ignored validity issues. Lastly, very little research has transcended one-shot, institution-specific boundaries. Thus, the generalizability of research findings is extremely limited.

To attack properly the issue of documenting effects of experiential pedagogies, a research agenda must be established. This paper has sought to identify critical issues we believe are facing researchers in this area as well as to provide elaboration on several factors which we consider salient in a total picture of experiential pedagogy evaluation research. There truly is a cornucopia of considerations in this area, and we urge, along with Nordstrom (1982), that researchers adopt a systematic approach to selecting specific problems rather than arbitrarily selecting isolated relationships between idiosyncratic variables. If we continue along the latter path, definitive statements about the efficacy of experiential pedagogies will never be possible.

CHAPTER 17

THE EVALUATION OF COMPUTER-BASED BUSINESS GAMES: METHODOLOGY, FINDINGS, AND FUTURE NEEDS

Joseph Wolfe

This chapter will review what is believed can be reasonably stated about the teaching efficacy of machine-based business games given the nature of the research available. Despite statements regarding its paucity or quality (i.e., Loveluck, 1983; Stone, 1982), the literature is both voluminous and useful as it contains a number of studies of utilitarian value. Unfortunately, this literature is seemingly unknown to a vast number of influential business educators and, therefore, both the gaming initiate and the general reader are given a false impression of the depth and variety of literature available as well as little appreciation of its long history. For example the widely-read and instant classic by Campbell, Dunnette, Lawler and Weick (1970) cited only one study (Raia, 1966) relating to business game effectiveness although ten additional evaluations were in the literature at the time. In another review of the business education literature thirteen years later, Loveluck (1983, p. 309) stated that business games ". . . have never been scientifically evaluated as a management teaching device so that their use really rests on the intuitive feelings of those who, experienced in using them, are convinced of their usefulness", although the sequential ten-year reviews by Greenlaw and Wyman (1973) and Wolfe (1985) were able to present sixty-one fairly rigorous studies covering the same time period.

This review will attempt to accomplish several purposes—the delineation of what is known and not known about the teaching value of business games, a review of the hazards and pitfalls accompanying pedagogical evaluations with the hope that realistic expectations and creative research designs and methods will ensue, and an understanding of those areas where both cumulative and path-breaking business gaming research can be conducted.

A REVIEW OF WHAT IS KNOWN ABOUT THE EFFICACY OF BUSINESS GAMES

Over 300 articles were considered for inclusion in this review. To be selected, the research examination had to involve a machine or computer-based simulation and had to relate game, player, or instructor attributes to learning levels (or secondarily to game performance as a proxy for learning) as specified in chapter 16. Each study also had to possess a fairly rigorous research design. This invariably meant the use of controlled and roughly equivalent study groups as well as objective performance or learning measures unless the creation of a subjective outcome was the goal of the study. Accordingly, anecdotal or testimonial reports were excluded despite the importance of the research issues they often pursued. This does not mean the studies selected for review were paragons of research virtue, however, but instead that their findings were less equivocal or refutable than those offered by studies employing weaker research designs or subjective attestations.

As a way of organizing this rather large and diverse literature and to encourage cumulative research, all relevant research has been categorized within the dictates of the variables and overall model presented in Chapter 16 by Burns, Gentry and Wolfe. Various liberties were taken at times when a greater elaboration or finer gradation within each major independent variable was considered appropriate.

Concepts Covered in the Experiential

Complexity
In the Burns, Gentry and Wolfe schema complexity dealt with the complexity of the concepts embraced by the simulation. The business gaming literature itself has instead dealt with games of differing levels of complexity and concept abstraction, although the "interactiveness" of a simulation's routines undoubtedly adds to a game's complexity, also, as well as allowing the teaching or modeling of more complex concepts. The issue of a game's complexity is inexorably intertwined with the number of discrete decisions made for each of the simulation's iterations, the number of functions and sub-functions modeled in the game, and the degree of abstraction possessed by the concepts employed. Raia (1966) found that *MANSYM* (Schellenberger, 1965) taught equally-well in either its simple or complex versions, although the complexity range allowed by the game itself was somewhat restricted. Much later Wolfe (1978) employed three different games in a study of the learning effects of more complex games. In this case complexity was defined by the number of words in the player's manual, the number of decisions required per iteration, and the size of the simulation's program.

The simplest game allowed four decisions per round, the intermediate game allowed eleven decisions, while the most complex game featured fifty-six decisions per play. The complex game produced the highest learning levels on a before/after knowledge basis, although the other two games also produced learning. Alternatively, Butler, Pray and Strang (1979a) found that learning levels did not differ by game complexity through their use of *DECIDE* (Butler, Pray and Strang, 1979b).

Simplicity of Concepts Being Taught

No direct research has been conducted on the success of simulations given the simplicity or degree of sophistication found in the concepts that are manifest in the game. In a study of the comparative teaching qualities of games versus casework in business policy courses, Wolfe and Guth (1975) found that each pedagogical technique was equally successful at imparting facts but that the *Purdue Industrial Administration Decision Simulation* (PIADS) was superior at teaching conceptual knowledge. The concepts examined were not classified as to their level of simplicity, although they had been originally designed for use in the Harvard MBA program which may indicate their level of sophistication. In a well-controlled examination Keys and Bell (1977) used the same instrument in a replication-type study to determine the mastery of principles and facts through the use of games and cases with and without the use of readings. Although the less complex *The Executive Simulation* (Keys and Leftwich, 1977) was employed, it too produced significant improvements in knowledge levels when used in combination with cases. The addition of the readings, however, did not significantly increase knowledge. Alternatively, Pearce (1979) found that case-oriented students outscored game-oriented students in three of nine fairly straight-forward content areas in essay-style strategy statements.

Theoretical Nature/Degree of Abstraction

No direct research has been conducted on how game players deal with the generally abstract nature of a simulation or how they relate to the abstract theory employed in the game's algorithms. A face validity study by Wolfe and Jackson (1989) found that game players felt the relatively concrete or mechanistic production function in *The Business Management Laboratory (BML)* was more realistic than its more abstract demand function, although admittedly it is both more difficult to model an oligopolist's demand function or to detect if it is not modelled correctly. In reality, the researchers had inserted a "glitch" or bug in one of the game's algorithms. This glitch was inserted into its relatively abstract, sophisticated, and interactive demand function. None of the study's participants were able to detect the demand function error. The presence of the unrecognized glitch, however, had no effect on the reality perceptions of the players, nor in their playing performance.

Functional/Environmental Scope
The roles or duties required of the player are related to the number of business functions or sub-functions allowed in the experiential exercise. Byrne (1979) concluded that even the relatively simple *The Executive Game* was a viable management training environment because the simulation allowed players to engage in eight of the ten managerial roles and skills which Mintzberg (1973) had found were exhibited by real-world executives. In this regard the game exhibited a type of external validity.

Nature of the Experiential

Duration
No studies have been conducted on what constitutes the ideal or optimal number of decision rounds for a successful game experience. Cangelosi and Dill (1965) found within the very complex *Carnegie Tech Management Game* that a team goes through a series of organizational learning stages— an initialization (wait and see) stage, a search (experimentation) for clues to success stage, a comprehension stage (the discovery of key relationships), and a final maintenance stage where decisions become routinized. The time-frame for these developmental stages were not cited nor were learning or performance results presented. Wolfe (1978) found in a study of the learning effects of game complexity, however, that self-assessed learning levels peaked earlier in the less complex games and that learning plateaus occurred at each simulation's year-end decision round given the games employed in the study used quarterly decision rounds. Accordingly a natural rhythm appears to be associated with business game play, and the ideal playing length of a game may be dependent upon the game's complexity as well as upon the skills of those engaged in the simulation.

Participant Grouping or Team Size
Although not a study of team size effects on group learning, Gentry (1980) found that team size had an effect on the group's output performance and the occurrence of within-team dissension. Two, three, and four-member teams played *LOGSIMX* (DeHayes and Suelflow, 1971) for 10.0% grade credit in an undergraduate business logistics course. Increased team size was accompanied by an increased probability of the team's obtaining a talented and motivated player while dissension was highest on the three member firms. The general effects of team size on game attitudes and learning curves have been investigated by Remus and Jenner (1981) and Newgren, Stair, and Kuehn (1980). Although the effects in the first study were confounded through the use of different simulations and learning environments, those who won the game clearly enjoyed the experience while those who "lost" were less enthusiastic. The Newgren et al. study compared the learning

curves generated by one versus three member teams playing *ENSIM* (Gooding, 1976) in an MBA business policy course. Single-member firms took longer to make their initial decision but they were able to complete their decisions more quickly thereafter. On the average, the solo firms took 72.4 minutes to make their mean decision set while the trios took 108.9 minutes.

The direct learning effects of team size has been studied by Wolfe and Chacko (1983). Business policy students (n = 115) were placed on either one, two, three, or four member teams within the *BML* (Jensen and Cherrington, 1977) for 55.0% grade credit based on economic performance. Profits increased by team size until the firm contained three players. Both three and four member firms increased their business policy knowledge the most while one member firms experienced the greatest number of course drops and company bankruptcies.

Two other studies have investigated team intrastructure rather than the raw numbers of players involved. Lucas (1979) placed 94 MBA students on eight member functionally and hierarchically divided teams in the very complex *NYU Management Game.* Players focused on the appropriate activities within their functional areas and they employed analyses that were correct for functional-area success. Unfortunately, learning outcomes were not measured so the amount of knowledge-gain obtained from the simulation's structure was unknown although the students exhibited behaviors indicative of correct learning.

Degree of Realism

The need for a simulation to possess at least minimal face validity has been axiomatic in business gaming. Recent attention has focussed on the algorithmic validity of various commonly-adopted simulations (Gold and Pray, 1983, 1984; Goosen, 1981; Pray and Gold, 1982, 1984; Teach, 1984). Although it has been accepted as an article of faith that a simulation should be realistic for it to be able to teach valid lessons, the need for this realism, or the degree to which realism should exist, has never been validated. In the previously cited Wolfe and Jackson (1989) study, it was found that students were unable to detect the "glitch" that had crippled the demand function of a relatively complex game. This glitch had no discernible effect on each team's assessment of the game's validity nor the team's economic performance.

Experiential Conduct

Accountability

Business games have usually been group or team learning experiences except under experimental conditions. This group aspect will probably be emphasized even more in the future as management educators have begun to realize the major role that group decision-making structures will play as a method for dealing with increasingly complex organizational environments. No study has directly studied either the relationship between individual inputs and learning nor with the accountability of an individual to the group's total learning or achievement. Philippatos and Moscato (1969a, 1969b, 1971, 1972) conducted a series of studies on the effects of information availability on playing performance, but how this information was shared within the firm was not presented. Dill and Doppelt (1963) found that a person's learning within a complex game was a function of the centrality of the individual's functional position, while Wolfe and Box (1988) found that high economic performance was not correlated to such individual factors as (1) the leader's individual contribution to the team or (2) the GPA of the team's highest academic achiever. Instead company success was related to such group factors as aptitude similarity regardless of aptitude level and efficient group decision-making sessions.

Participant Involvement
Related to participant involvement is the degree to which team members operate together and subordinate their personal interests to the interests of the group. Commonly termed "cohesion", the study of this aspect appears quite often in the more recent gaming literature. Norris and Niebuhr (1980) found that superior rates of return on equity were obtained by two to five member teams with high endgame cohesion. It was reasoned (but not quantitatively proven) that early agreement on the team's goals, interaction frequency, and intergroup competition brought about the requisite level of cohesion. Interestingly, the use of self-selection as a basis for determining team competition did not automatically create initially cohesive teams. Miesing (1982) performed a longitudinal study on large-sized firms (twelve to thirteen self-assigned members) within the *Harvard Business School Game* for twelve decision rounds. A factor analysis found the dimensions of cohesion and control were significant in a firm's success. The highest performing teams were relatively high on both dimensions, the middle performing teams emphasized one over the other, and the poorest performers were relatively low on both dimensions. Other studies have tried to engineer a team's initial cohesion in an attempt to increase the performance level of the companies so obtained. Both McKenney and Dill (1966) and Deep, Bass, and Vaughn (1967) found that teams that had been socialized through respective human relations coursework and quasi T-group experiences did not outperform randomly assigned teams. Wolfe, Bowen, and Roberts (1989), however, found that sensitivity training produced teams that were both initially cohesive and higher performing than non-trained teams. These cohesive teams possessed a greater degree of team-directedness, expressed higher levels of openness, and were more responsive to increased stress levels employed in the experiment.

Educator Involvement

The adoption of a business game is invariably accompanied by a more labor-intensive effort for both the student and the instructor. Although no studies have been made on the amount time an instructor must ideally devote to the administration, coaching, and debriefing of a business game, research has been conducted on the need for instructor guidance of the experiential learning process as well as on the ability for instructors to influence playing behavior through their counseling posture. In an early study by Dill, Hoffman, Leavitt, and O'Mara (1961), faculty advisory boards adopted one of three styles ranging from strongly active to strongly passive. The two teams that were subjected to a strongly active style with specified organizational and reporting requirements outperformed all other teams in the very complex *Carnegie Tech Management Game.* A study by Wolfe (1975a) compared the learning effects of the *Purdue Industrial Administration Decision Simulation* plus guided cases versus the simulation plus seven unguided experiential exercises in a senior level business policy course. The guided group outperformed the unguided group on a before/ after concepts examination thus making suspect the claim that experiential exercises are naturally self-motivating and self-directing (Kolb, Rubin, and McIntyre, 1974). In another study that demonstrated the need for instructor involvement, Fritzsche (1974) employed *Marketing Strategy* (Boone and Hackleman, 1975) in a junior-level games versus lectures study. Weekly, 15-minute consultations were provided the game group and class time was used for decision-making sessions and print-out pickup and delivery. Although no pre-course knowledge measures were taken, the game group outperformed its lecture counterpart on both examinations employed in the course. The Keys and Bell (1977) study already cited took great care to insure that feedback was fairly immediate, but the differential value of this feedback was not directly examined within the research design employed.

Student Attributes

Ability to Learn

Some of the very earliest research in the business gaming literature dealt with the relationship between student aptitude or achievement and game performance under the rationale that business games are valid if the better students obtain higher economic performance. Unfortunately the relationship between student aptitude/ability has often been confounded by team or group factors. Dill (1961) found no correlation between a team's average aptitude score as measured by the Aptitude Test for Graduate Schools of Business (ATGSB) and its cumulative profit. Also at the graduate level, Potter (1965) obtained slight correlations (.07 to $-.07$) between ATGSB's and a firm's rate-of-return on investment (ROI). In another study of aptitude, McKenney and Dill (1966) created MBA teams of above average, average and below average ability based on ATGSB's and undergraduate and first-term graduate school grade point averages (GPA's). As hypothesized the better teams obtained the greatest profits, while the poorer teams obtained the lowest economic performances. Another set of studies dealt more with student achievement rather than merely the potential for achievement as indicated by aptitude tests. At the undergraduate level both Vance and Gray (1967) and Gray (1972) found correlations ranging from .285 to .365 between business school GPAs and an economic performance index in four separate samples. Vance and Gray, however, found no correlation between a team's aptitude (SAT), all-college GPA's, or its all-quantitative GPA. Estes (1979) found a similar correlation ($R = .32$, $p = .0001$) between a student's overall grade point average (GPA) and profit performance in three-member *Mads-Bee* (Estes and Honess, 1973) teams. The research cited thus far has been conducted within graduate and undergraduate business policy courses. In the area of freshman economics both Cox (1974) and Marston and Lyon (1975) found that student ability may be related to the learning effects obtained from a business game experience. In the former case the very best and the very worst students (out of a total sample of 173) improved their knowledge by playing eight macroeconomic simulations. The latter study's results are more difficult to understand and interpret as three study years are reported and inconsistent results were obtained. The first study from 1970 used three member teams playing the *National Income Simulation Game* (NISG) with nonsignificant differences between the experimental and control groups when measured by the Test of Understanding in College Economics (TUCE) (Fels, 1968). The following year both the average and superior students learned more than their control counterparts while the poorest students from both groups performed in a similar fashion on TUCE. In 1972 single-member teams played *NISG* plus the *Marketplace* and *Wheat Market* games in class, although only the first game carried grade credit. No TUCE-related differences were found by student quality. As has already been noted, the results found thus far may have been confounded by group process factors. To eliminate those effects Wolfe (1978) created 90 single-member firms within a number of industries in *BML*. A positive relationship invariably existed between student grades, aptitudes, and economic performance. As examples of the significance found, a correlation of .503 existed between the firm's earnings and the student's university GPA, .351 between earnings and the Social Science ACT, and .415 between rate-of-return on equity (ROE) and the student's quantitative course GPA.

Number

No rigorous studies have been conducted on the teaching efficacy of business games in large classes versus small classes. Anecdotal evidence exists, however, that business schools may employ games for their entertainment value or potential for multi-section integration (Downey, 1982) without taking the necessary steps to insure the simulations are administered correctly (Wolfe, 1977).

Demographic and Personality Characteristics

The effects of personality characteristics on business game play have received a modest amount of research attention. An early study by Kennedy (1971) found that students with a higher degree of cognitive complexity as measured by a Paragraph Completion Test outperformed students low on this variable. Hoffmeister and DiMarco (1977) used *The Financial Management Decision Game* (Brooks, 1975) to examine six personality characteristics (achievement, order, autonomy, endurance, time competence, and locus of control) hypothetically related to playing performance. No relationships with performance were found as measured by accumulated wealth. The authors reasoned that the low 15.0% grade weight given for performance may not have motivated those players with high achievement needs or an internal locus of control. Wolfe and Chacko (1980) measured three attributes that have been related to how real-world decision-makers define their environments (cognitive structure, ambiguity tolerance, and category width) found in business policy seniors on single-member firms. Although the students described their standardized environments in conformance with their individual personality characteristics, their company's economic performance was not related to the three attributes studied.

Educator Considerations

Motives for Use

Studies have not been conducted on the motivations lying beneath the reasons instructors do or do not employ business games. Surveys have generated game adopter profiles as well as their subjective attitudes and reactions to the business game as a pedagogical method (Biggs, 1979; Couvillion, Pray and Strang, 1979; Summers and Boyd, 1982, 1983, 1984). As an example of this work, Faria and Nulsen (1978) found in an ABSEL-based sample that the game user versus nonuser was slightly younger, higher-degreed, and lower ranked. For those currently using simulations, most learned of them through their own use of them as a student closely followed by learning of them through colleagues. Over 50.0% of the respondents had been using games for six to ten years and their primary reasons for beginning their use was an attempt to give students a realistic experience and to continue the positive, enthusiastic feedback they were obtaining from their students. Their dissatisfactions with simulations were the time commitment required, computer center problems, and the difficulty of assigning accurate individual grades. The use of games by instructors may be self-serving to the extent that certain instructors felt games made the courses more interesting to themselves, made them feel they were accomplishing something, and it relieved them of having to deliver lectures.

Choice Set

No studies have been made on how an instructor chooses the particular simulations ultimately used in the classroom situation, nor how the instructor balances the choices between alternative pedagogies. During gaming's early years a large number of both man-based and machine-based games were available (Zuckerman and Horn, 1973), but this number was deceiving as many were poorly documented, nonportable, and fraught with local computer center operating problems. Today, fewer games are available but they are commonly accessible, especially in their personal computer versions (Fritzsche, 1987; Horn and Cleaves, 1980). So, in this sense the choice set is larger even though the absolute number of games is less. In his recent review of functional games, however, Biggs (1987) found it difficult to find commonly available games in the areas of accounting and production, while a wide variety of games can be found in the business policy and marketing areas (Keys, 1987).

Attitude About the Experiential

The early and almost universal observation that students enjoy playing business games has come under closer scrutiny in recent years. The Dill and Doppelt (1963) study cited earlier stated that a player's initial expressions of interest tended to persist throughout a simulation, although a reexamination of their data by Greenlaw and Wyman (1973) revealed that the correlation between pre-game and post-game interest was not significant $(R = 0.23)$ and that post-game interest was strongly related $(R = 0.86)$ to the team's performance. Attitudes about a simulation experience may also be strongly influenced by student ability or preparation for play. Eliason (1972) created teams that had either strong quantitative or qualitative backgrounds for competition in the *Interactive Decision Simulator.* The qualitative teams reported being frustrated by the experience while the quantitative teams said they were overwhelmed. The team size study by Remus and Jenner (1981) has already been cited regarding attitudes about the simulation. Their finding that winners enjoy the experience while the losers do not has been replicated in Remus (1977), Remus and Jenner (1981), and Faria (1986) as well as the earlier cited study by Estes (1979). Based on a very large sample of students $(n = 316)$ collected from twelve business policy courses over a six-year period, Kaufman (1976) found that positive attitudes about the simulation did not generate superior course grades when compared to case-taught students. Another business policy-based study by Catalanello and Brenenstuhl (1977) also found that positive attitudes were associated with business games, but also that subjective statements about the simulation's value (over comparable discussion or experiential exercise sections) were not borne out by superior performance in cognitive tests or problem solving skill. A study by Mancuso (1975) obtained similar results using a privately published game called *BROADEC* in a marketing course at Xavier University of New Orleans. Students (n = 59) divided between game versus case sections performed no differently on their examinations, although the game students were more positive about their simulation and its teaching effectiveness.

FUTURE RESEARCH NEEDS AND AREAS OF CONFLICTING RESEARCH RESULTS

Although the business gaming literature has investigated a number of areas and over 50 fairly rigorous studies have just been cited, a large number of areas have never been rigorously researched or could bear replication. Many other studies have not used learning or game performance as the criterion variable and therefore did not fit the parameters of this review. Given these qualifications, the following summarizes those areas deemed worthy of more research within the model presented by Burns, Gentry and Wolfe.

Concepts Covered in the Experiential

The game-construction areas of precision, random variation, and the number of concepts taught by the experiential exercise are candidates for further gaming research, although all are intertwined with the issue of a game's requisite complexity for optimal learning. In the creation of a simulation, the issue is usually not what to put into the simulation but rather what to leave out of the model while maintaining the necessary degrees of face validity, seductiveness, and conceptual and mechanical balance.

Nature of the Experiential

All business games are competitive games in the sense that participants either compete against each other singly or on teams within a market structure created by the computer, or they compete against the computer itself, although players or teams do not interact with each other. General business and marketing games represent the former type, while many functional games such as *Introduction to Managerial Accounting* (Goosen, 1973), *FINGAME: The Financial Management Decision Game* (Brooks,

1982) and *DECIDE-P/OM: An Integrative Computer Simulation for Production/Operations Management* (Pray, Strang, Gold and Burlingame, 1984) represent the latter. For most marketing games and the general business game, results and methods for pursuing the firm's economic interests are not shared until after the game has ended, although an instructor may coach each team as it proceeds through the simulation. Coaching is simplified somewhat within most nonmarketing functional games as each team plays against a common problem set contained in the program. It is not known whether learning is maximized when competition is conducted in either an interactive or noninteractive situation, although it has been accepted on faith that marketing and top management games must create zero-sum environments, while all other functional games can propose optimal solution sets.

Research has not been conducted on the learning effects of game/course integration, although surveys have been made on grade weights assigned, games employed, and casebooks used. These aspects are nontrivial, as a business game is rarely the only knowledge source in a course, so trade-offs between pedagogical inputs, grading weights assigned to the experience, and the integration of game concepts into other parts of the course are possible, probable, and desirable. Various business games have attempted to integrate themselves into a course's total learning package by combining a game with cases (Broom, 1969; Eldredge and Bates, 1980), readings, mini-lessons, and highlights (Edge, Keys and Remus, 1985; Henshaw and Jackson, 1984). Other administrator's manuals provide pre-game examinations of game-related materials to encourage easier entry to the gaming experience (Strickland and Scott, 1985), but the value of these examinations, text materials or other add-ons, such as the decision support packages that accompany the newer games (Affisco and Chanin, 1988; Hinton and Smith, 1985; Keys and Wells, 1987; Schellenberger and Masters, 1986; Strickland and Scott, 1985) for improving learning or play has not been determined.

Although a desirable simulation feature, the effects of game modification on learning levels has not been researched. Once installed, Biggs (1987) has observed that a game has a relatively long shelf life within an instructor's repertory, so the ability to change a game's parameters or its general environment serves to keep the game fresh. All general management games allow for some type of modifidation, if only within their level of economic activity, while functional games are less flexible in this regard. *IMAGINIT* (Barton, 1978) is especially flexible regarding the number of two-product industries that can be simulated, while *STRAT-PLAN* (Hinton and Smith, 1985) allows the administrator to simulate up to three territories, or even nations with accompanying international currency exchange consequences. The ability to modify a game is a necessary feature if one wishes to frustrate both functional and dysfunctional hall gossip, provide all players with an equal chance to succeed, and to minimize the use of old, programmed solutions to the simulation without having to install or rotate new simulations every year or so.

Experiential Conduct

Because most business games are conducted in group learning situations, the ability to hold individuals accountable for their contribution to a group product, and to reward and punish incorrect individual actions has been frustrated. Wolfe and Roberts (1985-1986), in a study that employed a wide range of grade weights for team performance, found no relationship between learning levels and grade weights, and therefore concluded that grade weights neither encourage nor discourage learning. Students expressed a sense of equity, however, between the amount of course credit given for game participation and the time they spent on the experience. Instructors have employed various methods to determine an individual's within-team performance, including secret team ballots, peer stock bonuses, and complaints to the administrator. Undoubtedly free riders exist on teams and certain players are more responsive to their company's needs than others. The use of self-selected teams may overcome this feature, but it has been found that self-selection does not result in superior playing performance and, therefore, learning may not be enhanced by this method.

In gaming's early years of mainframe-based simulations, all decisions were processed remotely in the batch mode. In a sense the field has not progressed very far from this lock-step situation, although the personal computer has facilitated administrator control, lowered a game's operating costs, and has encouraged the creation of computer-based decision support systems (Fritzsche, 1987). No commercially available simulation allows for "real-time" or self-paced play, although the learning effects of this development are enticing and almost upon us. The chapter by Newell Chiesl on real-time, continuously interactive simulation is recommened to the interested reader.

The role of feedback and the need for instructor involvement in the experiential process has been advanced and examined to some degree in the literature. The amount and type of debriefing employed has not been studied, although it is recognized that game closure is desirable and individually-obtained learning stimuli should be collected or focussed. Instructors have employed mock press conferences, stockholder's meetings, year-end reports, and term papers or diaries as methods for creating worthwhile debriefing experiences. *STRAT-PLAN* (Hinton and Smith, 1985) creates de-brief viewgraphs as part of its administrator's support package, but research has not been conducted to determine whether these efforts alter the learning levels that have already been obtained from playing the game itself.

Student Attributes

A student's willingness to learn may be related to the much-studied ability to learn area. A business game, however, creates a somewhat unique learning environment which may or may not reward the abilities or personality types that are rewarded in more traditional classroom settings. It has been found that those with low ambiguity tolerances prefer structured classes; those with high needs for achievement may not care to place a large amount of their apparent success in the hands of lower achieving classmates. These feelings could create initially negative attitudes or an unwillingness to participate, which could then persist throughout the gaming experience. Those with needs for either power or abasement may have positive feelings about a game, and these attitudes could maximize the learning of these personality types.

Related to this willingness to learn area is a student's willingness or physical ability to participate for the extended periods of time demanded by a typical simulation. Most games require a large degree of participation, either because of their complexity, which requires a high division of labor within a team, or their functional diversity, which requires the integration of diversity for organizational profits. If students are either physically, socially, or psychologically unable to participate in the gaming experience, the very basis of the implementation of experiential learning theory is threatened. Students in commuter-type school situations, or those attending school on either a day or evening part-time basis, may not be physically available for the long team meetings which usually accompany a gaming application.

Educator Considerations

All areas entailing educator considerations by Burns, Gentry and Wolfe (except knowledge of the choice set and resources available) have been subjected to survey type studies, but research has not been conducted into the effect all educator considerations have upon learning or game performance. It seems apparent that learning would be enhanced by the instructor's own enthusiasm about the game being played, whether authored by the instructor or not (Coats and Smidchens, 1966; Rosenshine, 1970; Sanders, 1985), and that the adoption of a game would be facilitated by a wealth of resources and prior exposure to games and their delivery method. Rigorous research needs to be conducted in this area, as one study found that instructor enthusiasm had little effect on examination performance (Sanders and Gosenpud, 1986) in a wide variety of business courses, while the advent of PC-based games has removed many of the historical impediments to game adoption by eliminating the baneful computer center, while simultaneously delivering the power of the mainframe to even the most deprived of institutions.

Relationship Between Game Performance and Learning

This review has considered three decades' worth of experience with business games. More recently the literature has shifted its research focus from studies that attempted to determine whether games taught anything to studies that have attempted to determine how games brought about their results. This is a healthy move in many respects as it focuses attention on the process and inputs of a gaming experience, thereby encouraging a more detailed view of the affairs of a stimulation. Unfortunately this move has also left unknown the relationship between game performance and learning. Since gaming's earliest years the literature has implicitly accepted the notion that teams that have performed well in the game have learned the most, but this basic relationship has not been investigated. Although two critical incident studies found that players traced effective performance behaviors to game success (Wolfe, 1975b, 1976), and that a pattern of internally consistent immediate success criteria are related to game profits (Hand and Sims, 1976), there is other evidence that team success may be the determination of the game's correct strategy early in the simulation. Teams that are initially better organized (Gosenpud, Miesing and Milton, 1984; Miesing, 1982) and consistently follow a strategic plan (Gosenpud and Wolfe, 1988; Wolfe and Gosenpud 1989) perform better in a game. This end result from initial action, however, does not directly measure the amount of knowledge gained from the total gaming experience, and the use of game performance as a proxy for learning overlooks those who are learning belatedly through the process of "undoing" initially incorrect actions. Basic research should be conducted in this area while simultaneously pursuing an understanding of those experiential processes and inputs that facilitate optimal learning.

Figure 17-1 summarizes the literature that has just been reviewed within the Burns, Gentry and Wolfe model. All underlined considerations have been investigated, while those not underscored have remained unresearched or have evidenced an indeterminate relationship with learning. Game performance has been inserted as an uproven proxy for learning, while attitudes are shown to have pervasive before, during, and after effects on both performance and learning.

PROBLEMS AND CONCERNS IN THE EVALUATION OF PEDAGOGICAL INNOVATIONS

The literature search for this chapter was a heartening one, as it found a number of studies that were well-conducted and meaningful attempts to understand the relationship hypothetically existing between business games and individual learning in academic settings. The search was also somewhat

FIGURE 17-1
Actual and Hypothesized Relationships Between Antecedent, Endogenous and Outcome Variables

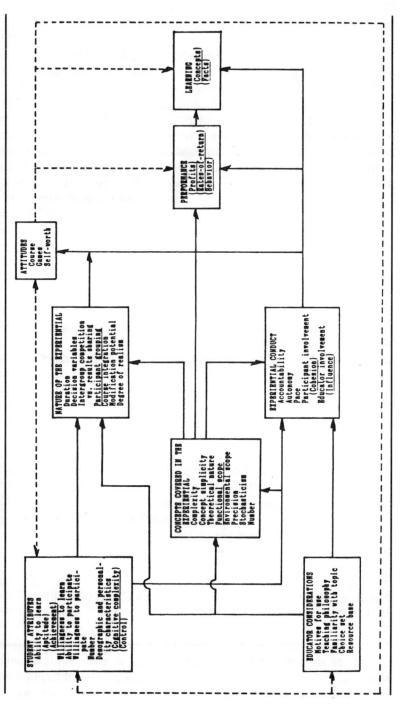

disheartening, however, as the field was strewn with casualties due to the frustrations and compromises attending real-world pedagogical research. This review can serve an affirmative purpose by pointing out the significant problems attending attempts to validate the effectiveness of teaching innovations in typical university settings, and to make recommendations for a more constructive research design phase by researchers, as well as altering the views of those who consume and evaluate pedagogical research.

Pedagogical evaluations are plagued by problems and concerns found in three areas—sufficient research designs, adequate levels of statistical significance, and ethical concerns for human subjects. Turning first to the construction of the sufficient research design, the classic experimental ideal requires the creation of at least two identical groups, one of which is exposed to the pedagogical innovation. Performance is then measured in an objective fashion at the end of (and also preferably before) the experiment, and those measurements are compared for significant statistical differences. Paraphrasing Cooke (1986, p. 112), however, these requisites are hard to obtain and are complicated by the mechanics of experimental testing.

1. Each group or course section must be identical and offered at the same time and during the same semester. All course material must be taught in the same fashion by the same instructor from the same syllabus. Every action and statement made in one section must be duplicated in the other section(s).

2. Each group must be assembled randomly to assure the existence of identical properties on all unmeasured factors that could affect the experiment's outcome. With true randomization the need for a pre-test, which could create a Hawthorne Effect, does not exist. If a pre-test is employed, all groups must have identical means and standard deviations on the pre-test. Additionally, each group should contain more than 30 subjects to allow the assumption of a normal sampling distribution.

3. All groups must be unaware of the conduct of the experiment.

4. Class time cannot be devoted to the innovation. If time is used in such a manner, a placebo must be employed in the control section(s).

5. All subjects must make every effort to score as high as possible on all tests that are administered.

6. High intercorrelations must exist between the course's subject matter, the content of the educational innovation, and the objective measurement of the innovation's effect.

7. To insure that floor or ceiling effects do not exist, the test's difficulty level must allow a wide performance range with the presence of no more than one zero score or one perfect score.

8. All tests must be administered in the same fashion and under ideal testing conditions.

Given these strict requirements, it can be seen why critics can confidently state that pedagogical research designs or the implementations of their designs are often "seriously flawed". In reality, however, certain defects are more detrimental than others, and it is only the judgmentally assessed probable damage caused by these flaws, rather than the absolute deviation(s) from the ideal, that must be considered. To wait for the perfect research situation would mean that research could never be conducted.

The next problem area in the construction of pedagogical research deals with appropriate statistical significance levels, the nature of significance, and the practical and pedagogical costs associated with Type I and Type II errors. The conservative approach to the adoption of a new technique would be to reject any innovation until it proves itself to be clearly superior to the technique currently being employed. In this regard the emphasis is on the avoidance of a Type I error—the incorrect acceptance of an innovation. It can be argued, however, that the demonstration of clear superiority of the new technique over the old, given the older method is presumedly performing at a fairly high level, would be extremely difficult to obtain at the traditional .01 or .05 level of significance. If the innovation is relatively inexpensive and it does not completely replace the previous pedagogical technique, no real harm can come from its acceptance if there is a possibility it is effective. As business games are usually used in conjunction with other more orthodox knowledge delivery techniques, we should guard more against committing a Type II error—stating that an innovation is not effective when in actuality it is effective. This error unnecessarily deprives students of a useful learning experience.

The last problem area associated with the conduct of pedagogical research relates the statistical arguments just presented to human subjects concerns within an experimental situation. The American Psychological Association has issued guidelines for the conduct of experiments involving human subjects, with the intention being the protection of such subjects from unnecessary psychological stress or physical injury. Business games do not entail physically harmful situations, athough mental stress accompanies teams as they strive for success or as they obtain disappointing outcomes. Accordingly, any pedagogical evaluation inherently presents only a limited degree of stress upon its participants. Another type of harm could emanate from manipulations required by the research design. During the experiment the control group will be deprived of the teaching innovation that may have some degree of value.

In this sense they are being sacrificed to an experimental condition over which they have no control. Should the simulation be valueless for the experimental group, they too will be victimized, for they have engaged in an exercise that has not benefited them. Whether the innovation as a result of the experimental process is determined to be successful or unsuccessful, a relatively large number of students will be deprived of an optimal education, or they will spend a misguided amount of time on a worthless exercise.

Viewed another way, however, pedagogical research must be conducted. First, pedagogical research is needed to determine the degree to which the innovation is an improvement over alternative methods. If the improvement is marginal and the costs of using the innovation are high, a decision to not implement the innovation may be in order. Conversely, if the improvement is marginal but the costs of the innovation are low, a decision to implement may be correct. Second, if the innovation is successful in one location under trial or ad hoc conditions, internal validity research must be conducted so the innovation can be implemented at other sites for the educational community's benefit. Only through validity studies appearing in competent journals can it be demonstrated that the effects of a particularly successful simulation are not uniquely bound to a school's particular institutional factors. Third, research needs to be performed to insure that the innovation, once accepted by the general academic community, is practiced in the correct manner so it does not harm individuals through misfeasance. This research would document what must be accomplished to obtain the complete benefits of the innovation.

ON THE REQUIREMENTS FOR A CUMULATIVE RESEARCH BASE IN BUSINESS GAMING

If business gaming's knowledge base is to proceed in an efficient fashion as possible, it must create a series of cumulative studies which systematically build on past studies, while venturing into areas of inquiry never before explored. Unfortunately, this review has seen that certain areas have been over-researched, many other areas have been left untouched, and much of the research is uninteresting or trivial. This has resulted in a lack of real progress in many important areas. Although certain research areas have been plowed again and again, it is more than redundancy that has inhibited progress in business gaming research. Progress would increase if the field worked harder at retaining and building upon the research base that already exists, and if the field worked harder at producing interesting, significant research.

When designing a research project, care must be taken that past knowledge is retained and built upon so that needless reinventions and faulty replications are not pursued. In recalling the literature, these recollections also must be made as objectively as possible. Although latitude exists for interpretive differences, a few examples might illustrate why cumulative research is hard to obtain under current practices. In a study of the value of the experiential approach, one pair of authors (Kelley and Whatley, 1979, p.

235) stated during their literature review that a particular research study used a "design, hypothesis formulation, and sample . . . [that did not] allow any conclusions" while Keys and Bell (1977, p. 36) said the same study ". . . used the best research design to be found in [the] experiential learning literature [and therefore] every attempt was made to replicate [the] technique" in their own study. In another widely-cited commentary, Neuhauser (1976) claimed that "business games have failed." In support of his position only three of the twelve available rigorous studies were cited. In advancing his position, Neuhauser cited only one supportive study, although eight other positive studies were in the literature. In addition to being selective regarding citations, articles were interpreted to fit the author's thesis. In Neuhauser's citation of McKenney (1963), only the negative conclusions were mentioned, while the overwhelmingly positive results were ignored. Other findings were distorted. Neuhauser (1976, p. 126) concluded the research by Hand and Sims (1975) "show[ed] no significant evidence for the claims of game practitioners", although the authors themselves (Hand and Sims, 1975, p. 708) stated their findings contributed to "confidence in the internal construct validity of the game" being employed at Indiana University. Certainly the truth lies somewhere within the extreme ranges presented in these examples, but in these cases the diversity of opinion may have created more heat than light, more dust than substance.

One additional activity should aid in creating a cumulative research base in business gaming. ABSEL has suggested that all papers submitted for conference review include every salient feature of the gaming application after the guidelines created by Nordstrom (1982). This guide, coincidentally, covers the basic areas included in the Burns, Gentry and Wolfe model. Conformance to the guide would make the gaming application's particulars understandable to all for possible replication, enlightened improvement, and accurate critiquing.

The second requirement for an advance in the field lies within the very basic nature of the research itself. To advance a field, its reseach must be interesting. Davis (1971) has proposed an intriguing idea where the theories that have had significant impact are those theories that are interesting. "Interesting" has little to do with pure truth or empirical research, but instead challenges certain assumptions held by others. If assumptions are not challenged or denied, the research question or project results will be deemed trivial or obvious and therefore uninteresting. Campbell, Daft, and Hulin (1982) recently asked 29 organizational scholars to recall the beginnings of both their most significant and insignificant research studies. Those studies that were considered significant were the result of activity and exposure (solitude and isolation was less likely to produce significant research outcomes), the convergence of several activities and interests, intuition and feelings rather than logical analyses, an attempt to explain or understand a phenomenon, and real-world based (ideas were tangible, useful, and were not elaborations of abstract, academic ideas). The insignificant research was based on expediency (it was inexpensive and easy to accomplish). Statistical technique or method took priority over theory and understanding, unmotivated by a desire for knowledge and understanding, and a lack of theory or a working-out of the complex theoretical issues involved was the result.

Unfortunately for this review, more research fell into the insignificant category than the significant. Interesting and therefore significant research could be performed in the areas of before, during, and after game attitude change (and the durability of those attitudes), as well as in assumed relationship between game performance and learning levels. Other challenges to conventional wisdom would be the field's use of self-selected teams as an automatic device for creating highly cohesive work units which would in turn learn more from the game experience. Another challenge to conventional wisdom would be investigations into the relationship existing between game realism and learning levels—at what level of reality or complexity are students able or unable to translate their somewhat existential activities into the more generalizable intellectual requirements of the course.

CONCLUSION

This review has found that educator considerations within the experiential learning situation have not been researched as they relate to either game performance or learning. Additionally it was found that game performance has been employed as a proxy for course-related knowledge gain, although the accuracy of this proxy relationship has never been investigated. In business gaming's earliest years, much attitudinal research was conducted with the belief that positive attitudes were indicative of learning. In reality it appears that attitudes about the game, the course, and student feelings of accomplishment or self-worth are related more to game performance. Not investigated has been the effect of pre-game attitudes on either the willingness to learn or to participate in the particular learning situation created by a business game. This is an important area for future research, as the experiential method requires high individual involvement if it is to be successful.

Certain Student Attributes have been related to game performance. Cognitive complexity affects how the game's environment is decribed, but an individual's view of the simulated world had no effect on performance results. The role of achievement in game success is related to team effects where high individual grade performance is positively related to firm performance; team or group interaction effects appear to moderate team performance through a participant involvement factor researched in the literature as Cohesion within the Experiential Conduct variable. Additional research in this latter variable has been conducted in the area of educator involvement, where it has been found that instructors can influence the decisions made by teams.

Only two Concepts Covered in the Experiential variable have been researched. Contradictory findings have been found regarding learning and game complexity while functional scope or roles within the game appear to be related to individual learning levels. Only a business game's team size has been studied within the Nature of the Experiential variable, although a simulation's verisimilitude has begun to receive recent theoretical attention.

Although a number of studies were reported in this review, many more could have been included had their research plan been more rigorously designed or implemented or the theoretical underpinnings of their hypotheses better conceptualized. Additionally, many interesting studies examined the business gaming process without relating the process variables to learning, which was the dependent variable in this review. Accordingly, much additional research can and must be done, and this research must be accomplished in a fashion that is more rigorous and capable of being replicated.

CHAPTER 18

EVALUATION OF EXPERIENTIAL LEARNING

Jerry Gosenpud

This chapter deals with experiential learning evaluation. Its purpose is to review the literature appropriate for assessing the effectiveness of experiential instructional methods in order to draw conclusions about the value and effectiveness of experiential learning. This paper will be in four sections. The first consists of a discussion of issues which frame the scope of this review. The second contains a discussion of problems inherent in both experiential learning and the process of evaluating it, problems which make it difficult to undertake rigorous experiential learning evaluation studies. The third consists of a review of experiential evaluation research. The fourth consists of tentative conclusions drawn from the first three sections, a further discussion of research related issues, and suggestions for further research.

SCOPE

Since the construct experiential learning is not well defined and since there are many articles potentially relevant to a discussion of experiential learning evaluation, establishing the scope of this chapter is important.

The following discussion focuses on three issues defining the limits of this article:

1. What are appropriate experiential learning assessment studies to review?
2. What type of research study is appropriate?
3. What are relevant dependent variables?

Appropriate Experiential Learning Assessment Studies

Since the purpose of this chapter is to draw conclusions about the value of experiential learning to the business school classroom, all literature relevant to accomplishment of that purpose should be included. In order to define what literature is relevant, two questions arise. The first regards the pedagogical unit of research focus. What is being evaluated or reviewed in the study? Is it a program, a teaching method, or an exercise? It should be noted that this question has been discussed earlier in this text (Gentry, 1990). This chapter will review studies of experiential exercises, courses, or programs taught either entirely or in part with the experiential method. In addition, part-time, long-term, or short-term experiential training or management development programs will be reviewed. This study will also focus on teaching methods clearly innovative and experiential in that they require the behavioral and cognitive involvement of the participant. This review will stay away from studies of full-time on-the-job training programs studies because results from these studies do not apply in business school classrooms. This article will not review studies concerned with the case method (except where the purpose of the case method is to give the learner experience in a desired case-related skill, e.g., problem-solving), or traditional active teaching methodologies, such as solving accounting problems in an accounting course.

The second scope-related question involves the context of the studies reviewed. Studies in educational environments other than business schools may be generalizable to the business school context, and some are included in this chapter. For the most part all studies in universities are transferable, as are studies of programs and exercises outside of universities, as long as they are applicable to the business school setting. Contexts outside the university include sensitivity training groups, management development programs, and high schools. In addition, findings from some laboratory experiments are generalizable to the experiential classroom, and these studies will also be reviewed.

Appropriate Types of Research Studies

Essentially three types of studies will be included. These types were chosen because these are the types of research most frequently undertaken, and because their results are useful for improving the business school classroom. These are straight evaluation studies, contingency studies, and studies focusing on features of experiential learning.

Straight Evaluation Studies
In this type, the purpose of the study is to assess effectiveness of experiential courses, exercises, programs, or methods. Researchers seek whether the experiential method produced intended results or is superior to another method given some criterion.

Contingency Studies

These studies are designed presuming that there is no one best way to teach something, that different participants may react differently to the same set of circumstances (Brenenstuhl and Catalanello, 1979), and that a given teaching method may be more or less effective depending on conditions (Gosenpud, 1982).

Assessment of Experiential Features

These are assessments or features of experiential exercises or programs, rather than assessments of the exercise or program itself. Examples of features include exercise duration or complexity of decision-making required in an exercise. Burns, Gentry, and Wolfe (1990) and Wolfe (1985) have listed potentially assessible features of the experiential method.

Relevant Dependent Variables

The dependent variable refers to the terms of evaluation or what has changed or improved as a result of experiential learning. This study will focus on all variables which scholars have presumed to be influenced by experiential learning. These include cognitive learning, behavioral change, skill development, and attitude change. Bloom's taxonomies (Bloom et al., 1956; Krathwohl, Bloom, and Masia, 1964) are appropriate means for categorizing outcomes. Attitude change includes attitudes toward the course or program.

PROBLEMS

The most obvious problem with experiential learning evaluation research is the lack of rigorously designed studies. There are relatively few studies attempting to assess experiential learning effectiveness (Brenenstuhl and Catalanello, 1979; Bunker and Cohen, 1978; Sugges, 1981) and most of the research that does exist assessing experiential learning lacks sufficient rigor (Cleggs, 1987; Wolfe 1981). Wolfe (1981) feels that maintaining rigor in experiential learning assessment is important since there is controversy surrounding experiential learning's value, and because nonrigorous evaluation research only adds to the confusion surrounding the controversy.

Wolfe (1975) also points out that many features of the ideal research design are probably impossible to implement in experiential learning. These include random selection of treatment and control groups, proper pretesting, standardized appropriate pre- and post-testing, and capturing all the sources of learning that occur in an experiential learning environment for measurement purposes. Kelley and Easton (1981) also point to the difficulty for research purposes of sufficiently controlling all the factors that impact the experiential learning situation. For these authors, these factors include teacher attitudes (toward the course, the teaching methodogy and students), student values, the teacher-student relationship, and classroom features such as class size.

Identifying and specifying outcomes of experiential learning is particularly problematic. Usually the teacher or designer of an exercise defines what is to be learned. However, the learner often learns things not intended by the designer, and often this unintended learning is more valuable because it is relevant to the learner. The problem for assessing experiential learning is that evaluation, defined by the designer, may miss the real worth of the experiential experience because what is valuable for the learner is defined by the learner and may have nothing to do with the designer's intention.

In addition, in experiential learning intended outcomes are often vague since the focus of experiential learning is usually on very complex, abstract phenomena. Let us take for example, an exercise focusing on leadership style. Leadership style is not very concrete, and it is complex in that it encompassess many behaviors. It would be difficult for an evaluator to specify a key goal for a leadership style exercise and to designate appropriate concrete measures to assess goal attainment. In such an exercise, different learners are learning different things, making thorough evaluation difficult.

Therefore, as Adelman (1986) suggests, it is important to focus on much more than how well an experiential program has accomplished its intended outcomes. The fact that specifying outcomes is difficult suggests that dependent variables should be open-ended. Instead of, or in addition to, trying to predefine what participants will have learned and how they will have changed, participants should simply be asked what they have obtained from a given experience. This suggestion runs counter to some common wisdom. Burns, Gentry, and Wolfe (1989), House (1979), and Wolfe (1976) are among the many researchers who stress the importance of keeping dependent measures concrete and specific and measuring dependent variables as precisely consistent with designer goals as possible. The above argument proposes avoiding such specification.

A more subtle problem with experiential learning evaluation research is that most studies are of the straight evaluation variety and very few are theory based. From straight evaluation studies, readers learn whether a teaching method is effective or not. From theory-based evaluation studies, readers discover other things in addition. For example, why is a given teaching method more effective, or what about it makes it effective? There are at least three reasons for the lack of theoretical bases for most experiential evaluation research. First, experiential programs and exercises are often chosen without a great deal of thorough forethought. If program choice is not based on forethought, then evaluation is unlikely to be theory based. Second, until recently experiential learning researchers were intent on proving the worth of experiential learning. This facilitated evaluative research rather then theoretical research. Third, the subfield of pedagogy evaluation has always accepted less rigor than many other subfields in a given discipline, and this has been true in business, education, and management development. One of the features of low rigor research is a lack of theoretical bases. Since low rigor is accepted, non-theory based experiential evaluation research has been acceptable for presentation and publication.

There are notable exceptions, in that some previous studies have been theory based. Basuray and Scherling (1979) and Brenenstuhl and Catalenello (1979) have done studies based on contingency theory hypotheses. Gentry and Burns (1983) have done research testing hypotheses identifying variables crucial to the success of experiential exercises. Bowen (1987), in a nonresearch article, developed a theory designating environmental features that make for greater learning in an experiential setting. Finally, Burns, Golen and Gentry (1983) undertook a study which emerged from hypotheses concerning how experiential learning differs from other learning methods.

REVIEW OF STUDIES

Straight Evaluation Studies

Table 18-1 summarizes straight evaluation studies or studies simply evaluating experiential learning. These studies either compare experiential learning with other pedagogies on some criterion variable or show changes in some criterion from before to after the implementation of an experiential pedagogy.

Table 18-1 is organized by dependent variable. Contained in it are 14 articles focusing on cognitive learning as a dependent variable, 19 using attitude change as a criterion, and 18 focusing on behavioral acquisition or change as a criterion.

Studies in Table 18-1 are identified by author(s). This table shows the kind of pedagogy assessed (either a course, part of a course, or training program) in each study, whether a control group was utilized, the control group's nature and how it was selected, the specific dependent variable (or variables), how the dependent variable was measured, whether or not there was pre-testing, and the results of the given study.

Cognitive Learning
The 14 articles in Table 18-1 utilizing cognitive learning as a criterion yield 23 comparisons of objective exam results between experiential and other kinds of teaching methodologies. The table also shows four comparisons

TABLE 18–1
Summary of Straight Evaluation Studies

I. Cognitive Learning as a Criterion Variable
A. University semester long classes

Authors	Type of Experiential Pedagogy Assessed	Control Groups and Method of Selection	Criterion	Measure of Criterion	Pretest	Results
Basuray and Scherling (1979)	Two semesters of an organizational behavior course	A lecture/discussion section of same course. Selection by student registration	1) Cognitive learning	Objective graded exam	Yes	No differences
				Nongraded objective standardized exam	Yes	No differences
			2) Cognitive complexity	Two objective standardized exams	Yes	No differences
Brenenstuhl and Catalanello (1979)	Lab section of a management course which also used lectures	Discussion and simulation labs of same course. Selection random	1) Cognitive learning	Objective graded exam	Yes	No difference between experiential and other groups
				Objective nongraded exam	Yes	No difference between experiential and other groups
			2) Problem solving skills	Case analysis	Yes	No difference between experiential and other groups
Hoover and Whitehead (1979)	Management course	Lecture/discussion section of same course. Selection by student registration	Cognitive learning	Objective graded exam	No	No differences
				Objective nongraded exam	No	No differences
Kelley (1979)	Two semesters in a personnel management course	Lecture/discussion section of same course. Selection by student registration	Cognitive learning	Objective graded exam	No	Experiential section scored higher
Wolfe (1976)	Policy course	Case/simulation section of same course. Selection random	Cognitive learning	Essay exam		Experiential section scored lower

TABLE 18-1 (continued)

B. Units or parts of University Classes

Burns and Sheffell (1952)	A course unit on site selection	Simulation, case and discussion question groups. Selection random	Cognitive learning	Objective exam on topic	No	No difference between experiential and other groups
Graf and Couch (1985)	A supervisory training program for undergraduates	Applicants for same program not yet receiving training	Cognitive learning	Objective exam on topic	No	No differences
Minor, Das and Gale (1982)	Specific units in an organizational behavior course	Case and discussion groups on same topics. Selection random	Cognitive learning	1) Objective exam on topic	No	No difference between experiential and other groups
				2) Essay exam on topic	No	No difference between experiential and other groups
				3) Objective exam four months later	No	No difference between experiential and other groups
Ross, Hughes and Hill (1981)	Field experience for pre-service teachers	Group given lectures on topics covering field experience. Selection random	Cognitive learning	1) Exam covering field experience	No	Superior scores for those with field experience
				2) Objective graded course exam	No	No differences

C. Programs for Managers

McAllister (1983)	A program teaching sensitivity towards group processes	Untrained managers were asked to assess other group experiences. Selection method not specified	Perception of learning	Questionnaire	Yes	Trained groups perceived they increased learning to a greater degree than untrained group perceived learning in other experiences
Zenger and Hargis (1982)	General supervisory training in five organization	Untrained groups in four organizational training programs. Selection method not specified	Cognitive learning	Objective exam	Yes	Trainees gained from pre- to post-test

TABLE 18–1 (continued)

D. Elementary School Programs

Di Vesta and Peverly (1984)	Active self organization of concept acquisition	Group for whom concepts were organized by teachers (passive organization)	Concept acquisition	Objective exam	No	Active organization group learned more

E. Reviews

Armstrong (1979)	Reviewed five studies of courses: 3 undergraduate courses in marketing, 2 marketing courses in a management institute	Lecture section of same courses. By student selection	Cognitive learning	Objective test	No	No differences in any of the studies
Caroll, Paine and Ivancevich (1972)	Reviewed studies assessing the case method and role playing	Lecture programmed learning and films. Selection method not specified	Cognitive learning	Unspecified	Unspecified	Case method found to be superior to lecture in one study reviewed
			Problem solving skill	Unspecified	Unspecified	Role playing found to be effective in all of studies summarized

II. Attitude Acquisition and Change as Criterion Variables

A. Attitudes towards the experience

Armstrong (1979)	Reviewed four studies of courses: 2 undergraduate courses in marketing, 2 marketing courses in a management institute	Lecture section of same courses. Selection by student selection	Attitudes towards course	Questionnaire	No	Experiential students had a more favorable attitude in all sections

TABLE 18-1 (continued)

Study	Method	Comparison	Variable	Instrument	Control	Results
Brenenstuhl and Catalanello (1978)	Lab section of a Management course which also used lectures	Discussion and simulation labs of same course. Selection random	Enjoyment of course	Questionnaire	No	1) Experiential students enjoyed course to a greater degree than discussion students 2) Simulation students said they accomplished more than experiential students
			Feelings of accomplishment	Questionnaire	No	
Burns and Sherrell (1982)	A course unit in site selection	Simulation, case and discussion question groups. Selection random	Attitudes towards courses	Questionnaire	No	No difference between experiential and other groups
			Benefits of class	Questionnaire	No	Experiential students perceived greater benefits than discussion question group
Hoover and Whitehead (1979)	Management class	Lecture/discussion section of same course. Selection by student registration	Attitudes towards course	Questionnaire	Students' attitudes towards previous classes used as a pretest	Experiential students had more favorable attitudes
Kelley (1979)	Two semesters in a personnel management course	Lecture/discussion section of same course. Selection by student registration	Attitudes towards course	Questionnaire	No	Experiential students had more favorable attitudes
McAllister (1985)	A program teaching sensitivity towards group process	Untrained managers were asked to assess other group experiences. Selection method not specified	Attitudes towards course	Questionnaire	No	Program participants said this program was superior to other group experiences

TABLE 18–1　(continued)

Study	Type of training	Control group	Variable	Measure		Results
Moskowitz, Schaps and Malvin (1982)	Training program for teachers to help students develop socio-emotionally	Untrained teachers. Selection method not specified	Attitudes towards course	Questionnaire	No	Experientically trained students had favorable attitudes towards the program
			Acquisition of skills	Questionnaire	No	Experientically trained students said they acquired more skills
			Attitudes towards goal achievement	Questionnaire	No	No differences

B. Changes in Attitudes from before and after an experiential experience

1. Sensitivity Training

Study	Type of training	Control group	Variable	Measure		Results
Baumgartel and Goldstein (1967)	Sensitivity training focused human relations course for undergraduates	None	Political values	Allport-Vernon-Lindzey study of values (1962)	Yes	No change as a result of training
			Religious values	Allport-Vernon-Lindzey study of values (1960)	Yes	Religious values decreased with training
			Need for self to be in control	Firo-B scale (Schutz 1958)	Yes	No change as a result of training
Burke and Bennis (1961)	Sensitivity training for adults	None	Self-concept ideal self-concept discrepency	Semantic differential	Yes	Discrepancy decreased with training
Gassner, Gold and Snadowsky (1964)	Sensitivity training	Untrained individuals matched as to gender and profession	Self-concept ideal self-concept discrepency	Semantic differential	Yes	Discrepency for both trained and control groups decreased significantly
Kassarjian (1965)	Sensitivity training for adults in an extension course	Adult students in an evening Business Administration class. Selection method not specified	Inner vs. outer-directedness	Riesman's scale (Riesman, Glazer and Denny 1958)	Yes	No differences in changes in criterion measure between trainees and controls

TABLE 18-1 (continued)

Miles (1965)	Sensitivity training for high school principals	Untrained principals matched to trainees	Attitudes towards leadership	Ohio State leader behavior questionnaire	Yes	No differences in changes in criterion measure between trainees and controls
			Attitudes towards group participation	Group participation scale (Pepinsgy, Siegle and Van Altra 1952)	Yes	No differences in changes in criterion measure between trainees and controls
Smith (1964)	Sensitivity training for managers	None	Need for affection and control in self and others	FIRO-B (Schutz 1958)	Yes	Compared to controls, trainees became less controlling and more affectionate and wanted more control and less affection from others with time
	Sensitivity training for students	Control group of students. Selection method not specified	Need for affection and control in self and others	FIRO-B (Schutz 1958)	Yes	Compared to controls, trainees became less controlling and more affectionate and wanted more control and less affection from others with time
2. Role Playing						
Janis and King (1954)	Role playing	Untrained. Selection method not specified	Attitudes on topic related to role play	Questionnaire	Yes	Role playing group changed opinions in direction towards their role to a greater degree than controls
Janis and Mann (1965)	Role playing on smoking habits	Untrained. Selection method not specified	Attitudes towards smoking	Questionnaire	Yes	Role playing group changed opinions on smoking to a greater degree than controls

TABLE 18–1 (continued)

	Role playing	Untrained. Selection method not specified	Attitudes on topic related to role play	Questionnaire	Yes	Role playing group changed opinions in direction towards their role to a greater degree than controls
King and Janis (1956)	Role playing	Untrained. Selection method not specified	Attitudes on topic related to role play	Questionnaire	Yes	Role playing group changed opinions in direction towards their role to a greater degree than controls

3. On-the-Job Training

Grater (1959)	Leadership training for managers	None	Self concept, ideal self-concept discrepency	Bills index of adjustments and value	Yes	Discrepancy decreased with training
Hand, Richards and Slocum Jr (1973)	Human relations training for managers	Untrained managers. Selection random	Attitudes towards leadership	Leadership opinion questionnaire (Fleishman, 1953) 90 days past training— 18 months past training—	Yes	No differences over time for trainees or controls Trained group increased significantly in attitude of consideration; for for controls no differences between pre and post test
				Supervisory behavior description questionnaire (Fleishman, 1953) 90 days past training— 18 months past training—		No differences over time for trainees or controls Both trainees and controls increased significantly in attitudes of consideration
			Need for others to be in control	FIRO-B scale (Schutz 1958)	Yes	No change as a result of training
			Need for others to be affectionate;	FIRO-B scale (Schutz 1958)	Yes	Need for others to be affectionate decreased with training

TABLE 18–1   (continued)

Study	Type	Control		Method		Results
Swierczek and Carmichael (1985)	Supervisory training	None	Attitudes towards subordinates	Likert survey	Yes	Trainees attitudes changed towards advocating greater subordinate involvement

III. Behaviorial Change and Skill Development

A. Sensitivity Training

1. Actual Studies

Study	Type	Control		Method		Results
Boyd and Ellis (1964)*	Sensitivity training for middle managers	Control group utilized. Selection method not specified	Unspecified	Open ended questions to co-workers regarding trainee changes after returning to job	No	Increased sensitivity, improved communication and interpersonal skills for trainees. Results not reported for controls
Bunker (1965)	Sensitivity training for high school principals	Each trainee nominated an untrained control	Unspecified	Open ended questions to co-workers regarding trainee changes after returning to job	No	Sensitivity increased and communication and interpersonal skills improved for twice as many trainees as controls
Underwood (1965)	Sensitivity training for supervisors	Control group of matched supervisors	Unspecified	Trainees reported on changes	No	Trainees gained in interpersonal skills
Valiquet (1964)	Sensitivity training for middle managers	Control group formed by asking trainees to nominate a control who had never been in a T-group	Unspecified	Open ended questions to coworkers regarding trainee changes after returning to job	No	Increases in role flexibility and greater tolerance of differences were reported by greater number of trainees than controls

2. Reviews

Study	Type	Control		Method		Results
Campbell and Dunnette (1968)	Reviewed five studies on the effects of sensitivity training	Control group used in one study but method not specified	Assessed T-group effectiveness in terms of trainees' vocabulary after training	Asked trainees to describe people and content analyzed answers	Yes	Increased interpersonal terms used to describe people from pre to post training

TABLE 18–1 (continued)

B. Roles Play Experiments

1. Actual studies

Study	Program	Control / Selection	Topic	Measurement	Significant	Results
Bolda and Lawshe (1962)†		None	Sensitivity	Responses to essay exams and cases	Yes	Sensitivity increased

2. Reviews

Study	Program	Control / Selection	Topic	Measurement	Significant	Results
Carroll, Paine and Ivancevich (1975)	Supervisory training programs	Not specified	Interviewing and leadership skills	Not specified	Not specified	Interviewing and leadership skills improved
Fry, Kidron and Schriesheim (1975)†		Not specified	Confidence, behavior habit change	Not specified	Not specified	Confidence increased. Behavioral habits did not change

C. Management Training

Study	Program	Control / Selection	Topic	Measurement	Significant	Results
Goldstein and Sorcher (1973)	Two training programs which combined modelling, role playing and performance feedback					
a. For nurses		Untrained nurses. Selection random	Empathy	Coworker ratings	Yes	Trained nurses became more empathetic
b. For supervisors to learn orientation, motivation, and disciplinary techniques		Untrained supervisors. Selection random	Turnover and productivity	Unit statistics	Yes	Trained supervisors had significantly lower turnover and higher productivity
Hand, Richards and Slocum Jr (1973)	On the job training program for middle managers	Control group used but composition not specified	Middle manager sensitivity, consideration and production orientation	Coworker assessment	Yes	Trainees became more considerate and sensitive
Zenger and Hargis (1982)	On the job supervisory training	Untrained control group used. Selection method not specified	Sensitivity towards subordinates	Coworker ratings	Yes	Trainees became more sensitive towards subordinates.

TABLE 18–1 (continued)

			D. Other types of training			
Gill, Berger and Cogar (1983)	Training in Micro-counselling	Trainees themselves served as controls. They were tested three times, twice before training and once after training	Counselling skill assessment	Trainer observations	Yes	Counselling skills increased as a result of training
Smith, Szabo, and Trueblood (1980)	Manipulative instruction for elementary school children	Similar students received graphic instruction. Selection random	Metric measure skill acquistion	Objective examination in skill acquistion	No	Students who received manipulative instructions performed better.

Notes: *Taken from Cambpell and Dunette (1968)
†Purpose of study was to do research and not to assses a particular experiential pedagogy

of non-objective or essay exam results. Of the 27 comparisons, 20 yielded no differences between results from experiential and other pedagogies.

Drawing conclusions from these data is not justifiable, given that the data are only based on 12 studies and two reviews. However, two points should be made. First, the majority of the data suggests that the experiential method is neither superior nor inferior to others in helping students learn cognitively. Second, a tentative hypothesis emerges from two of the studies. DiVesta and Peverly (1984) hypothesized that the active self-organization of tasks would result in a more generalized understanding of concept formation; as hypothesized, the results show superiority for the active method. Also Ross, Hughes, and Hill (1981) found superiority for student teachers in the field (over those who stayed in the classroom) in terms of knowledge covering the field experience, but not knowledge covering the whole course. Both of these studies were well designed with adequate controls and, in both, care was taken to insure that controls were taught the material that those in the more experiential groups learned actively. In both cases, the experientially-taught group showed greater cognitive learning for the material which the experiential group learned actively. These studies suggest that when tests closely examine material covered in the experiential learning situation, those taught experientially do better.

Attitudes
The 19 studies utilizing attitudes as a dependent variable are of two types. Seven of the studies assessed an experiential experience in terms of the attitudes towards the experience, and the other 12 assessed the experiential pedagogy in terms of changes in attitudes from before to after an experiential experience.

The seven studies assessing experiential learning in terms of attitudes towards the experience yielded 14 comparisons. For ten of the comparisons, students taught by the experiential method expressed significantly more positive general attitudes towards their learning experience than did those students exposed to other teaching methods. In these studies, positive general attitudes were in terms of greater course benefits, a higher quality teacher-student relationship, more satisfaction, or a greater feeling that skills were acquired.

Twelve studies assessed the experiential method in terms of changes in attitudes from before to after an experiential experience. Six of those studies assessed sensitivity training in terms of attitude change, three assessed role playing and three assessed on-the-job training programs. Regarding the impact of sensitivity training, no pattern emerges. Some studies show changes in attitudes from experiencing sensitivity training, others show no changes. And, too few studies focused on any specific attitude for conclusions to emerge.

The results regarding the impact of role playing and general on-the-job training indicate that attitudes do change as a result of these experiences. All three studies assessing the influence of role playing showed significantly more attitude change for role playing trainees from before to after training than for controls, and all three studies assessing the influence of general on-the-job training programs show significantly greater attitude change for on-the-job program trainees than for controls.

Behavioral Change/Skill Acquisition

Eighteen of the articles in Table 18-1 which assessed experiential exercises or programs feature behavioral change, skill acquisition, or skill development as an indication of effectiveness. Nine of these assessed sensitivity training, three assessed role playing, two assessed on-the-job training programs, and four assessed programs that were either multifaceted or difficult to classify.

Of the 18 studies, 17 reported positive results in that experiential methodologies helped participants either acquire skills or change behavior. This suggests that experiential learning techniques are helpful in effecting behavioral results. All nine of the studies assessing sensitivity training report significant behavioral change or skill acquisition for trainees. Two of the three role playing studies report positive results, and both multifaceted programs and both the general on-the-job managerial training programs report positive results. More than other specific behavioral dependent variables, these positive results were in terms of increased sensitivity, increased consideration, and increased interpersonal competence on the part of trainees.

It should be noted that some of the above results transferred beyond the training environment. Hand, Richards, and Slocum (1973) found training effects on the job eighteen months after training. Goldstein and Sorcher (1973) found effects in unit productivity and turnover after training. So, for this study training transferred beyond the trainee's behavior into unit-wide quantitative results. And, seven of the behavioral acquisition studies utilized coworker or supervisor observation of trainees back on the job as ways to measure effectiveness. For these studies, too, training survived the back home transfer, and training goals were realized after training concluded.

Two of the studies that dealt with behavioral acquisition were in fact experiments rather than training programs. Both utilized experimental controls, and both report favorable outcomes for experiential learning. Gill, Berger, and Cogar (1983) found that trainees learned a minicounseling technique significantly better after observing and discussing the technique than before. The trainees served as their own controls and were tested three times with training coming between times 2 and 3 and with learning scores increasing significantly more between test 2 and 3 than between 1 and 2. These results suggest that positive outcomes emerge from an "involved" instructional method. Smith, Szabo, and Trueblood (1980) found that subjects receiving manipulative instruction acquired metric measurement skills to a greater degree than subjects receiving graphic instruction. In this study, effectiveness was measured in clearly behavioral terms, and measures were carefully constructed to reflect instruction. The subjects were seven-year olds, but the results are meaningful because this is one of the few well-controlled experiments testing graphic versus manipulative instructions in producing behavioral outcomes, and in this study the experiential manipulative approach produced superior results.

In five of the studies in Table 18-1, behavior changes were assessed and significant changes found without prespecifying or hypothesizing the expected nature of the change. All five studies assessed sensitivity training, and all five authors explained that prespecifying behavioral changes would be inconsistent with the uniqueness of the sensitivity training experience.

Contingency Studies

There are many ways to skin a cat, and many ways to enhance learning. Contingency theory presumes that there is no best way to enhance learning, that some ways are better than others under some circumstances, but worse than others under other circumstances. Contingency means many things. It may mean that some learners learn better with one teaching method than with another. Or, it may mean that a given teaching method is effective for one type of learning task but not for another. The exent to which a given instructional method is effective has been hypothesized to be contingent on a number of factors including instructional goals, course content, instructor characteristics, learner characteristics, organizational support for the instructional method in question, and instructor-learner compatability. However most of the contingency studies on experiential learning have focused on only one of the above factors, learner characteristics, and these ten studies are summarized in Table 18-2. This table is nearly identical to Table 18-1, with the main difference being that Table 18-2 has a column identifying the characteristics upon which instructional method effectiveness is hypothesized to be contingent.

Of the ten studies, nine were designed to test the degree to which outcomes in experiential learning are contingent on learner capability or learner personality, and six of the nine show that learning outcomes are in fact contingent on one of these two factors. Of the six, only two had control groups and the six studies varied too much with regard to dependent and contingent variables to draw conclusions. Yet for the sake of further research, it should be pointed out that in experiential learning environments, contingency hypotheses have been supported in the majority of studies.

Two studies found that outcomes from experiential learning are contingent on characteristics other than those of the trainee, and one of those

TABLE 18–2
Summary of Contingency Studies

Author	Type of Experiential Pedagogy Assessed	Contingency Conditions	Control	Criterion	Measure	Pretest	Results
			a. Contingent on Characteristics of Individuals				
Bennis, Burke, Cutter, Harrington, and Hoffman (1957)	Sensitivity training	Personality characteristics such as dominace and need for affection	No	Self and ideal self-acceptance in groups	Role behavior inventory	No	Personality characteristics did not affect extent of self and ideal self-acceptance
Brenenstuhl and Catalanello (1979)	Management course	Learning styles (Kolb, 1974)	Discussion and simulation sections of some course. Selection random	Cognitive learning	A final exam		Convergers significantly out performed assimilators, accomodaters, and divergers in simulation and experiential sections but there were no differences across learning style in discussion sections.
				Absenteeism			Accomodaters were absent significantly less than other students in experiential sections, but there were no differences in absenteeism in discussion or simulation sections
Gill, Berger and Cogar (1983)	Training in Micro counseling	Experience in the specified counselling method	Trainees themselves served as controls. They were tested three times, twice before training and once after training	Counseling skill assessment	Trainer observations	Yes	The most naive trainees changed their counseling behavior the most while experienced trainees changed the least.

TABLE 18–2   (continued)

Study	Program	Variables	Control	Dependent variable	Measure	Control group	Results
Gosenpud (1982)	Experiential organizational behavior course	Age, amount of supervisory experience and locus of control (Rotter, 1966)	No	Self acceptance, tolerance for ambiguity	Semantic differential. Tolerance of ambiguity scale (Budner, 1962)	Yes	Youngest, those with the least supervisory experience and those with external locus of control became more self accepting and more tolerant of ambiguity
Hand, Richards and Slocum Jr (1973)	Human relations supervisory training program	Consultantive vs. autocratic managerial style	Non trained supervisors. Selection random	Concern for Human aspects in work environment	Perceptions of both superiors and subordinates	Yes	Both consultantive and autocratic supervisors showed increased concern for human aspects.
Harrison and Lubin (1965)	Sensitivity training	Person vs. task orientation	No	Learning about self expressiveness, warmth and comfort	Trainee judements	No	People oriented trainees were more expressive, warm and comfortable; task oriented trainees learned more
Kelley and Easton (1981)	Personnel course	The need for achievement, dominance and self acceptance	No	Cognitive learning early and later in the course	A cognitive exam	No	Those with high need achievement, dominance and self acceptance scores performed more poorly on a cognitive exam early in the course, but performed better on a cognitive exam later in the course.
Mathis (1958)	Sensitivity training	T-group trainability index based on openess to communication regarding affection, aggression, and intra personal conflict	No	Level of sensitivity, sophistication, and productivity	Observer ratings	No	People scoring highest on this trainability index were rated higher by observers on sensitivity, sophistication, and productivity

TABLE 18–2 (continued)

Steele (1968)*	Sensitivity training	Sensing vs. intuiting personality trait	No		Trainer ratings	No	Whether trainees were sensing or intuiting did not affect trainer ratings of value changes
				b. Contingent on Other Characteristics			
Kelley and Easton (1981)	Personnel course	Instructor reputation	A lecture section of the same course. Selection by student registration	Cognitive learning	Graded exam	No	Cognitive learning was greater with instructor with better reputation
Zenger and Hargis (1982)	On-the-job supervisory training	Extent of management support for training	No	Sensitivity towards subordinates	Coworkers assessment of behavior change	Yes	The higher the level of involvement from management, the greater the sensitivity of the trainees

Note *Taken from Campbell and Dunette (1968)

studies is worthy of mention. Zenger and Hargis (1982) reviewed five supervisory training programs, and trainees became more sensitive to employee needs with training. In addition, the evidence indicated that the degree of positive change was related to the extent of management support of training. The higher the level of involvement from upper management, the greater the change.

This is worthy of mention because it is consistent with other results from the organizational change literature. According to this literature (Kanter 1983), innovations are more likely to work when there is top management support for them. The Zenger and Hargis results suggest that the above holds for experiential training as well as other innovations.

Studies Focusing on Features of Experiential Learning

The interest in this section is on features of experiential learning that help make it more effective. It should be noted that in most of the studies discussed below, identifying features of experiential learning that help to make it more effective was not the explicit purpose of the study. However, these studies were conducted in such a way that implications regarding effective features are discernible. The features discussed in the section below include feedback, meaningfulness, exposure, and communication barriers.

From consideration of these studies, the feature of experiential learning that most clearly influences its effectiveness positively is feedback. In the studies in which role playing was found to be effective in changing behavior (Bolda and Lawshe, 1962; Goldstein and Sorcher, 1973), feedback was an integral part of training. Gentry and Burns (1983) also suggested that knowing outcomes facilitates learning, but warned that outcome feedback can be fallible as people focus on false positives rather than false negatives.

Another feature that appears to impact experiential learning is meaningfulness. Bolda and Lawshe (1962) concluded, that when training touched the trainee on an emotional level, it had more impact. DiVesta and Peverly (1984), in their experiment on conceptual transferability, found that learning was significantly greater when the concept being learned was meaningful. Finally, Ingersoll (1973) concluded from a review of role playing assessment studies that role playing situations that were more involving for the learner enhanced learning.

There is mixed evidence as to the influence of exposure on effectiveness. On one hand, Locke, Johnson, Kirgin-Ramp, Atwater, and Gerrard (1986) evaluated a delinquent education program which exposed trainees to the hardships of prison life. These authors found that the offense rate of juveniles with court appearance records who were trained in this way were no less likely to commit offenses than a control group trained by counselling. This suggests that exposure is not a key ingredient to behavior change.

On the other hand, in Ross, Hughes and Hill's study (1981) of in-service teachers, the training program included two major features, exposure to the actual field experience and discussion of that experience. Trainees did not actually teach, but they did significantly better than controls on an exam. There are two ways to interpret this result. One is to interpret training as exposure. Then the results indicate that exposure facilitates learning, a result inconsistent with results of Locke et al. The second is to interpret the field experience as a meaningful experience for trainees. Then the result supports the conclusion from Bolda and Lawshe's and DiVesta and Peverly's work that experientially-based learning is greater when the experience is meaningful.

The Burns, Golen, and Gentry (1983) study is also worthy of discussion. It is similar to the above studies in that it focused on elements of experiential learning. However, it is different in that it sought to find aspects of experiential learning that differentiated it from other learning methods rather than aspects that promote experiential learning effectiveness. The most relevant result involves communication barriers. The authors found experiential learning did not differ in inherent communication barriers from other involving pedagogies such as the simulation and cases. It, along with other involving pedagogies, did differ from the lecture, however. The lecture evoked concerns about instructor bias, failure to listen to students, and lack of feedback, whereas, the active pedagogies gave rise to concerns of student interpersonal and status difficulties and conflicting attitudes.

CONCLUSIONS

This review raises a number of issues and suggests a number of directions that experiential learning evaluation research should take. However, I have one general conclusion that permeates these suggested directions. The conclusion is that researchers should stay away from the kind of study where the experiential method is compared with others, usually in terms of some very general measure of cognitive learning, and almost always a course exam. The purpose of this kind of study is usually to prove the worth of experiential learning. This type of study is value laden, stimulates unnecessary controversy, and the knowledge gained from it is in terms of winners and losers and nothing else.

There are other reasons for avoiding this type of study. As Schreier (1981) noted, those who want to teach experientially will do so, and those who want to criticize the method will also do so, regardless of how lecture and experiential students score in course exams. As discussed below, how well students do on course exams is more closely related to their own motivation levels than to type of teaching methodology. In addition, studies undertaken so far show the experiential method to be equal to others in cognitive learning. As Bowen (1987) has pointed out, the best teaching is to employ an optimal mix of several teaching strategies, and the boundaries between experiential and other types of learning are less clear than we labelers would like to believe. Finally, many studies show that how much material is learned is contingent upon student characteristics. So, the question of which method is better evokes so much complexity that determining a better method is virtually impossible. We should try to go beyond this question.

The rest of this section will be organized around four specific issues. The first deals with experiential learning and cognitive outcomes, the second deals with measuring experiential effectiveness in terms of behavioral acquisition and change, the third focuses on outcome variables, and the fourth focuses on suggestions for future research.

Experiential Learning and Cognitive Outcomes

Does experiential learning enhance cognitive learning better than other methods? At first glance the answer is clearly no. The vast majority of studies assessing the relative effectiveness of the experiential method in terms of cognitive learning have shown no differences between it and other pedagogies. Most of these studies were undertaken in university classrooms and most used the graded final exam or a general, standardized conceptual exam as the dependent variable. In all but two of 23 comparisons there was no difference between the experiential and other methods. Therefore, it should be tentatively concluded that in university classrooms the experiential method is neither better nor worse than other teaching methods for enhancing cognitive learning attainment.

However in four studies reviewed (Burns and Sherrell, 1982; DiVesta and Peverly, 1984; Ross, Hughes, and Hill, 1981; and Smith, Szasbo, and Trueblood, 1980), all with comparison's groups, effort was taken to create a test that measured the specific concepts learned in the experiential exercise or program. In three of the four studies [DiVesta and Peverly; Ross, Hughes, and Hill; and Smith, Szasbo, and Trueblood], learning was significantly greater in the experiential group than in the comparison. This suggests that when care is taken to design a test, to be specific to the goals of the learning experience, the experiential method may be more effective.

Obviously the results of three studies are not enough on which to base a conclusion. Most likely if a course exam covers general concepts, students will learn what is necessary to do well on the test regardless of the course teaching method. This is so because, to students, knowing what is on the test is more important than the teaching method of the course. Under these circumstances the experiential method will be about as effective as others, and future research comparing the experiential method under these circumstances will probably reach foregone conclusions.

What happens when the tested material closely parallels the goals of the experiential exercise or program is less clear. Too few studies have been undertaken to know if any teaching method is superior when outcomes measured are in very close accordance with the pedagogical goals, but it is possible that some *are* superior to others and more research under these circumstances will be very beneficial.

Experiential Learning and Behavioral Acquisition and Change

Most advocates of experiential learning argue that its value is in the affective and behavioral domains (Bloom et al., 1956; Krathwohl, Bloom, and Masia, 1964). And although many were methodologically flawed, the vast majority of studies assessing experiential learning techniques have found that experience based training has helped trainees acquire new skills or change their behavior in desired directions. Studies have been reviewed showing experiential training of various types to help trainees become more inter-personally sensitive and improve communication skills.

However, almost all of the studies reviewed have taken place outside of the university classroom. Of the 18 studies reviewed assessing experiential learning in terms of behavioral acquisition and change, only one (Gill, Berger, and Cogar, 1983) used college students, and those were graduate students in counseling.

Of the studies reviewed evaluating university courses utilizing contrasting teaching methods, most assessed in cognitive terms. Some assessed in general attitudinal terms as well, covering, for example, how satisfied or motivated students were in the course. Rarely, if ever, have researchers assessed entire courses in behavioral terms, and rarely, if ever, have course designers specified attitudes or personality characteristics that should likely change with successful course completion. Finally, rarely, if ever, have researchers designed studies assessing contrasting teaching pedagogies in terms of desired behavior or personality variable change. This should not be difficult and it should be done. For example, marketing courses might be designed to help students become more sensitive to consumers' needs or more persuasive, and researchers could design studies comparing experiential and other pedagogies for attaining those goals. Or, organizational behavioral courses could cover such concepts as adapting to uncertainty and interpersonal sensitivity, and researchers could design studies comparing experiential and other teaching methods in accomplishing those aims.

Outcome Variables

In five of the sensitivity training studies reviewed, evaluation measures were open-ended in that researchers merely asked learners what they gained from their learning experience. And, in the problem section of this paper, I suggested that there were benefits to open-ended evaluations. Later in the paper, I suggested that there are advantages of carefully tying outcome measures to targeted learning goals for puposes of evaluation. Perhaps these two methods of evaluation seem contradictory. However, I believe both ways to measure outcomes are appropriate, depending on the type of learning experience assessed.

If the learning experience itself is open-ended, if that which is learned varies with the learner, and if repeated versions of the experience are variable, then merely asking participants what they have gained is appropriate. This has been a typical way to measure outcomes in a t-group (Campbell and Dunnette, 1968), and it seems to be an appropriate way to measure general experiential experiences such as a course or multifaceted training program. On the other hand, if the learning goals are clear and specific, then tying outcome measures to the learning goals is appropriate. This was done in a number of studies reviewed here. Burns and Sherrell (1982) designed experiential, discussion, case, and simulation sections to deal with marketing site selection and designed an exam to test knowledge of site selection concepts in all sections, and Ross, Hughes, and Hill (1981) designed a field experience for in-service teachers, expected them to learn certain concepts about that experience, created a control group to listen to a lecture about those same concepts, and tested both groups on concept attainment.

It should be pointed out that at least one evaluative study used both the open-ended and the variables-tied-to-learning-goals methods to measure outcomes. Swierczek and Charmichael (1985) utilized a needs assessment technique to set ten learning targets for a supervisory training program and designed measurement indices to assess training in terms of those ten targets. They also asked each participant two open-ended questions, "What did you learn in this workshop?" and "How will you apply those skills back at work?" The authors pointed out that the open-ended questions were given to help eliminate potential response biases inherent in the specific target defined indices.

Suggested Directions for Future Research.

It is clear from this review that there is much to learn and to research about the effectiveness of the experiential pedagogy. Two directions for future research were discussed earlier: 1) tying outcome measures to learning goals and 2) evaluating experiential learning on the basis of behaviorial and specified attitudinal outcomes. Researchers should pursue two other directions. First, they should attempt to assess the external validity of experiential learning. This means assessing gains from experiential programs in the external environment, the larger university and the workplace. It should be noted that some of the behavioral acquisition studies have done this as indicated earlier, but note also that none of these are university-based. There is precedent for discussing and assessing the external validity of a university teaching methodogy. Norris (1986) and Wolfe and Roberts (1986) have discussed the external validity of the computer simulation as a teaching approach, and Wolfe and Roberts (1986) have undertaken a follow up study of simulation players. In that study, these researches assessed simulation validity by obtaining correlations between simulation performance of university students and their salary and promotion levels in the workplace five years later. In similar but not identical ways, the external validity of university-based experiential instruction could be obtained. For example, one section of a supervision course could be taught experientially, another with a different pedagogy. The effectiveness of each method could be assessed in terms of quickness of promotion of its students past the initial supervisory position after graduation.

A second future direction involves undertaking theory-based research. Through our studies, we need to learn more than just whether a given teaching method is effective. We need answers to such questions as why a given teaching method is effective and under which conditions this method is better than others. Studies assessing features of experiential learning seem particularly valuable. Such studies not only help identify what it is about experiential learning that is beneficial, but they also help us to understand aspects of the instructional process that are crucial to all kinds of learning. For example, this review has found that feedback is important to the experiential learning process. It could be hypothesized that feedback is important to learning enhancement for all pedagogies and studies testing this hypothesis could be undertaken.

A great deal of space has been devoted to the inadequacies of and the difficulties in doing experiential learning assessment research. A whole section has been devoted to inherent problems. Methodological difficulties existing in many of the studies have been made apparent, and the opening subsection of this article's conclusion criticizes a major thrust of experiential evaluation research. In addition, it should be made very clear that a major rationale for undertaking experiential evaluation studies lacks foundation. This rationale is that evaluation studies are needed to prove the value of experiential learning to a suspicious wider community. This rationale is no longer credible. The facts are that most academicians, especially those in business, education, medicine, and engineering, value applied and innovative teaching methodologies. New experiential textbooks come out continuously and in many general textbooks experiential exercises or suggestions for field learning experiences accompany each chapter. There are training and development firms that create and utilize experiential programs, and many private sector training programs contain a large experiential component.

In addition to the above, there are many reasons for not even bothering to undertake experiential evaluation research. Bunker and Cohen (1978) note that evaluation is expensive, time consuming, risky, and very difficult to do right. In addition, Schreier (1981) offers one of the most powerful reasons for not doing experiential evaluation, that is that practioners do not pay attention to it.

> . . . we are all capable of intuitively evaluating what we do. This capability
> . . . is something most professional educators develop after years and years of
> course work, research attempts and practical experience. We seem to develop
> an uncanny ability to sense, if we care to, the success of our lectures,
> examinations, experiential exercises, simulations and cases.

Perhaps this is unfortunate, but most of us trust this intuitive evaluative sense to help us decide what to teach more than the results of other people's evaluative studies. Most teachers will teach experientially if they want to, teach some other way if that is their desire, and use a mixture of methodologies that makes sense to them. So I am not trying to be glib when I ask, "Why even try to evaluate experiential learning?" It is difficult to do right. We no longer have to prove the value of experiential techniques by doing evaluative research. At least some teachers will do what they want regardless of research results, and most of the research done so far is inconclusive anyway.

The question deserves a serious answer, and the answer that follows is serious. There is so much we do not know about the teaching-learning process that well-designed research on its outcome cannot help but be valuable. That goes for all teaching-learning processes and that goes for the entire teaching-learning process from goal-setting to evaluation.

Most learning experiences are designed; either a program or exercise is planned or lectures are written before they are delivered. These plans should involve the setting of learning goals, and it is important for the manager of the learning experience to set attainable learning goals and to design learning experiences that will likely help learners attain those goals. In addition, Adelman (1986) suggests a number of questions that designers should think through. One such question is whether the underlying learning experience rationale is coherent, logical, and well grounded theoretically and empirically. If it is not, there may be little justification for proceeding with the program.

Another involves the consideration of antecedent conditions. That is, does the intended learning experience design account for individual and subgroup differences relevant to intended outcomes? If possible, learning experiences should be tailored to individual needs. Also, issues regarding dependent variables should be faced. It is important to design measurement indices carefully, but researchers should also ask whether potent unintended processes transpire. If so, open-ended measures should also be used.

Research design issues also should be faced. Many of these are outlined by Campbell and Stanley (1963). In addition Miles (1965) lists the main research design strategies he used in evaluating t-groups. These included careful criterion measurement and refinement, the use of role-homogeneous populations, the location of plausible control groups, the assessment of possible test-treatment interaction, the predictive analysis of components thought to cause change on criterion measures, and the use of large numbers of measures.

The major ingredient is care. Evaluative research can help us gain a great deal of knowledge and understanding about the teaching-learning process. But, in order for all of us to gain that knowledge, researchers and teachers need to take the time and effort to design a learning experience so that learners learn from it and so that what they learn is comprehensible. They also need to take the time and effort to design the research evaluating the learning experience so that scholars and practitioners can draw valid conclusions about the effectiveness of the teaching learning process being studied.

APPENDIX A

Large Scale Computerized Simulations

Cotter, R.V. (1985), *The Business Policy Game,* Englewood Cliffs, NJ: Prentice-Hall.

Cotter, Richard and David J. Fritzche (1986), *Business Policy Game,* Englewood Cliffs, NJ: Prentice-Hall.

Edge, Alfred, Bernard Keys, and William E. Remus (1985), *The Multinational Management Game,* Plano, TX: Business Publications, Inc.

Eldridge, David L. and D. L. Bates (1984), *The Business Strategy and Policy Game,* Dubuque, IA: William C. Brown.

Henshaw, Richard C. and James R. Jackson (1984), *The Executive Game,* Homewood, IL: Richard D. Irwin.

Hinton, Roy W. and Daniel C. Smith (1985), *STRATPLAN,* Englewood Cliffs, NJ: Prentice-Hall.

Jensen, R. L. and David Cherrington (1984), *The Business Management Laboratory,* Plano, TX: Business Publications, Inc.

Keys, Bernard and Howard Leftwich (1985), *The Executive Simulation,* Dubuque, IA: Kendall/Hunt Publishing Company.

Keys, Bernard and Robert Wells (1987), *Microtronics,* New York, NY: John Wiley and Sons.

Pray, Thomas F. and Daniel R. Strang (1981), *DECIDE,* New York, NY: Random House.

Priesmeyer, H. Richard (1987), *Strategy: A Business Unit Simulation,* Cincinnati, OH: SouthWestern Publishing Company.

Schellenberger, Robert E. and Lance A. Masters (1986), *MANSYM IV: A Dynamic Management Simulation with Decision Support System,* New York, NY: John Wiley and Sons.

Scott, C. R. and A. J. Strickland, III (1984), *Tempomatic IV: A Management Simulation,* Boston, MA: Houghton Mifflin.

Scott, Timothy W. and Alonzo J. Strickland (1985), *Micromatic: A Management Simulation,* Boston, MA: Houghton Mifflin.

Smith, Gerald (1984), *Manager, A Simulation,* Boston, MA: Houghton Mifflin.

Large Scale Non-Computerized Simulations

Lombardo, Michael M., Morgan W. McCall, Jr., and David L. DeVries (1983), *Looking Glass,* Glenview, IL: Scott, Foresman and Company.

Lombardo, Michael M., Morgan W. McCall, Jr., and David L. DeVries (1987), *Looking Glass II,* Glenview, IL: Scott, Foresman and Company.

Macmillan, Ian and Thomas Ference (undated), *Simmons Simulator,* Unpublished Proprietary Game, Columbia University.

Miles, Robert H. and W. Alan Randolph (1985), *The Organization Game: A Simulation,* Glenview, IL: Scott, Foresman and Company.

Stumpf, Steven (undated), *Financial Services Industry,* Unpublished Simulation, New York University.

Small Scale Computerized Simulations

Davis, Samuel, Gary Kochenberger, Edward Reutzel, and John Tyworth (1986), "Demonstrating the Role of Simulation in Strategic Operations Planning: A Case Study in Bank Check Processing Location in Analysis," *Developments in Business Simulation and Experiential Exercises,* Vol. 13, Alvin Burns and Lane Kelly (Eds.), 166–169.

Day, Ralph L. (1986), "A Sales Management Simulation for the PC: An Integrative Tool for Sales Management Courses," *Developments in Business Simulation and Experiential Exercises,* Vol. 13, Alvin Burns and Lane Kelly (Eds.), 63–65.

Frazer, J. Ronald (1983), "BANKRUPT—A Deceptively Simple Business Strategy Game," *Developments in Business Simulation and Experiential Exercises,* Vol. 10, Lee A. Graf and David M. Currie (Eds.), 98–100.

Frazer, J. Ronald (1985), "Advantages of a Multi Game Simulation Course," *Developments in Business Simulation and Experimential Exercises,* Vol. 12, James W. Gentry and Alvin C. Burns (Eds.), 177–179.

Graham, Robert G. and Clifford F. Gray (1969), *Business Games Handbook,* Chicago, IL: American Management Association.

Jackson, George C. (1982), "SIMCOM I: A Computer Based Simulation Model for Evaluating Physical Distribution Strategies Involving Order Consolidation," *Developments in Business Simulation and Experiential Exercises,* Vol. 9, David Fritzsche and Lee Graf (Eds.), 120–123.

Jackson, George C., James W. Gentry, and Fred Morgan (1985), "A Computerized Logistics Game for Micros," *Developments in Business Simulation and Experiential Exercises,* Vol. 12, James W. Gentry and Alvin C. Burns (Eds.), 111–113.

Sharda, Ramesh, Keith Willett, and Shen An Cheng (1986), "A Water Quality Management Simulation," *Developments in Business Simulation and Experiential Exercises,* Vol. 13, Alvin Burns and Lane Kelly (Eds.), 146–151.

Smith, Jerald R. (1986), "Marketer: A Microcomputer Simulation in a High Tech Industry," *Developments in Business Simulation and Experiential Exercises,* Vol. 13, Alvin Burns and Lane Kelly (Eds.), 157–158.

Small Scale Non-Computerized Simulations

Bittel, Lester (1977), *Shenandoah Management Games for Supervisors,* New York, NY: McGraw-Hill.

Fischer, William A. and Joseph B. Mazzola (1987), *FISCHTALE Enterprises,* Glenview, IL: Scott, Foresman and Company.

Jackson, George C. and Fred Morgan (1983), "Business Logistics Game," *Proceedings,* Southwestern Marketing Association, Houston.

Keyt, John C. and Ernest R. Cadotte (1981), "CHIPS: A Marketing Channels Management Game," *Developments in Business Simulation and Experimential Exercises,* Vol. 8, William Biggs and David Fritzsche (Eds.), 242–246.

Computerized Experiential Activities (Packages)

Beutell, Nicholas and Randall S. Schuler (1986), *Personal Computer (PC) Projects for Effective Personnel Management,* St. Paul, MN: West Publishing Company.

Boudreau, John W. and George T. Milkovich (1988), *Personal Computer Exercises in Personnel/Human Resource Management,* Plano, TX: Business Publications, Inc.

Moberg, Dennis J. and David Caldwell (1988), *Interactive Cases in Organizational Behavior,* Glenview, IL: Scott, Foresman and Company.

Penley, Larry E. and Yolanda E. Penley (1988), *Human Resources Simulation: Using Lotus 1-2-3,* Cincinnati, OH: SouthWestern Publishing Company.

Sherman, J. Daniel (1988), *Interactive Cases in Management,* New York, NY: Harper & Row, Publishers, Inc.

Computerized Experiental Activities (Stand Alone)

Cannon, Hugh and Fred W. Morgan (1985), "An Expert Systems Approach for Teaching Marketing Case Analysis," *Developments in Business Simulation and Experiental Exercises,* Vol. 14, Lane Kelly and Patricia Sanders (Eds.), 31–33.

Cosenza, Robert, Louis E. Boone, and David L. Kurtz (1985), "Integrating Microcomputers in the Marketing Curriculum Through the Use of Marketing COMUPROBS," *Developments in Business Simulation and Experiental Exercises,* Vol. 12, James Gentry and Alvin C. Burns (Eds.), 54–55.

Edwards, W.F. (1987), "Learning Macroeconomic Theory and Policy Analysis Via Microcomputer Simulation," *Developments in Business Simulation and Experiental Exercises,* Vol. 14, Lane Kelly and Patricia Sanders (Eds.), 50–52.

Finn, David (1987), "Teaching About Sampling in a Marketing Research Class," *Developments in Business Simulation and Experiential Exercises,* Vol. 14, Lane Kelly and Patricia Sanders (Eds.), 57–62.

Friend, Kenneth E. (1985). "MicroComputer Demonstration Exercises for a Course on Creativity and Problem Solving," *Developments in Business Simulation and Experiential Exercises,* Vol. 12, James Gentry and Alvin C. Burns (Eds.), 135–139.

Guin, Larry and John McGregor (1987), "An Expert System for Financial Planners," *Developments in Business Simulation and Experiental Exercises,* Vol. 14, Lane Kelly and Patricia Sanders (Eds.), 80–83.

Kagel, Richard (1985), "Using the Computer as a Planning Aid in an Applied Marketing Course," *Developments in Business Simulation and Experiential Exercises,* Vol. 12, James Gentry and Alvin C. Burns (Eds.), 50–53.

Lambert, Nancy and David R. Lambert (1985), "A Reactive Microcase Pedagogy," *Development in Business Simulation and Experiential Exercises,* Vol. 12, James Gentry and Alvin C. Burns (Eds.), 172–176.

Rubin, Ronald S. (1987), "The Gamesmanship of Pricing: Building Pricing Strategy Skills Through Spreadsheet Modeling," *Developments in Business Simulation and Experiential Exercises,* Vol. 14, Lane Kelly and Patricia Sanders (Eds.), 175–178.

Schroeder, David L. and James W. Gentry (1987), "Teaching MRP Experientially Through the Use of Lotus 1-2-3," *Developments in Business Simulation and Experiential Exercises,* Vol. 14, Lane Kelly and Patricia Sanders (Eds.), 179–182.

Watkins, Larry E. (1987), "The Application of Spreadsheet Software Technology to Complex Taxpayer Elections," *Developments in Business Simulation and Experiential Exercises,* Vol. 14, Lane Kelly and Patricia Sanders (Eds.), 219–222.

Wingender, John and Jack Wurster (1987), "Oil and Gas Well Investment Analysis Using the Lotus 1-2-3 Decision Support System," *Developments in Business Simulation and Experiential Exercises,* Vol. 14, Lane Kelly and Patricia Sanders (Eds.), 245–249.

APPENDIX B

COMPUTERIZED BUSINESS SIMULATION PACKAGES

Aronson, M. B. and J. H. Gekoshi (1984), *The Strategic Management Game,* Philadelphia, PA: Strategic Management Group, Inc.

Babb, E. M. (1979), *Purdue Supermarket Chain Management Game,* Cambridge, MA: Simtek.

Barton, R. E. (1974), *The IMAGINIT Management Game,* Lubbock, TX: Active Learning.

Beutell, N. J. and R. S. Schuler (1986), *Personal Computer (PC) Projects for Effective Personnel Management,* St Paul, MN: West Publishing Company.

Boone, L. E. and E. C. Hackleman Jr. (1971), *Marketing Strategy,* Columbus, OH: Charles E. Merrill Publishing Company.

Boone, L. E., D. L. Kurtz, and J. L. Braden (1989), *The Sales Management Game,* New York, NY: McGraw-Hill Book Co.

Boudreau, J. and G. T. Milkovich (1988), *PC Exercises in Personnel/Human Resource Management,* Homewood, IL: Richard D. Irwin.

Brobst, B. and R. Bush (1982), *Marketing Simulation: Analysis for Decision Making,* New York: Harper and Row Publishers.

Brooks, L. D. (1987), *Financial Management Decision Game (FINGAME),* Homewood, IL: Richard D. Irwin, Inc.

Carrell, M. R. and J. R. Smith (1988), *Collective Bargaining Simulated,* Columbus, OH: Charles E. Merrill Publishing Company.

Chapman, R. G. (1988), *BRANDMAPS: The Competitive Marketing Strategy Game,* Englewood Cliffs, NJ: Prentice-Hall.

Cosenza, R., L. E. Boone, and D. L. Kurtz (1988), *Marketing COMPUPROBS.* Dallas, TX: Business Publications, Inc.

Cotter, R. V. and D. J. Fritzsche (1985), *Modern Business Decisions,* Englewood Cliffs, NJ: Prentice-Hall, Inc.

Cotter, R. V. and D. J. Fritzsche (1986), *The Business Policy Game,* Englewood Cliffs, NJ: Prentice-Hall.

Cretien, P. D. (1989), *Sales Pro: Sales Management Simulation,* Columbus, OH: Merrill Publishing Company.

Cretien, P. D. and D. F. Jennings (1988), *Management: A Simulation,* Columbus, OH: Merrill Publishing Company.

Darden, B. R. and W. H. Lucas (1969), *The Decision Making Game,* New York, NY: Appleton-Century-Crofts.

Day, R. L. and D. J. Dalrymple (1985), *Sales Management Simulation,* New York, NY: John Wiley & Sons.

Edge, A. G., B. Keys, and W. E. Remus (1985), *The Multinational Management Game,* Dallas TX: Business Publications, Inc.

Eldredge, D. L. (1984), *INTOBUS,* Dubuque, IA: Wm C. Brown Publishers.

Eldredge, D. L. and D. L. Bates (1984), *The Business Strategy and Policy Game,* Dubuque, IA: Wm. C. Brown Company Publishers.

Faria, A. J. and J. R. Dickinson (1987), *Lap Top: A Marketing Simulation,* Dallas, TX: Business Publications, Inc.

Faria, A. J., R. O. Nulsen, and Roussos, D. (1984), *COMPETE: A Dynamic Marketing Simulation* Dallas, TX: Business Publications, Inc.

Fisk, J. T. and R. P. Fisk (1986), *Airways: A Services Marketing Game,* New York, NY: John Wiley & Sons, Inc.

Frazer, R. (1975), *Business Decision Simulations: A Time Sharing Approach,* Reston, VA: Reston.

Frazer, R. (1977), *Introduction to Business Simulation,* Reston, VA: Reston.

Funk, J. A. and A. Smith (1985), *Chairman of the Board,* Chicago, IL: Dryden.

Galloway, J. C. Jr. and J. R. Evans (1987), *PAINTCO II: A Computerized Marketing Simulation,* New York, NY: Macmillan Publishing Co.

Gates, D. E. (1986), *Tyme Management: A Sales Territory Market Simulation,* Homewood, IL: Richard D. Irwin, Inc.

Gitman, L. J., A. Robana, and W. D. Biggs (1981), *PORTSTRAT: A Portfolio Strategy Simulation,* New York: John Wiley and Sons.

Goosen, K. (1973), *Introduction to Managerial Accounting: A Business Game,* Glenview, IL: Scott, Foresman and Company.

Greenlaw, P. S., M. W. Frey, and I. R. Vernon (1979), *FINANSIM: A Financial Management Simulation,* St. Paul, MN: West Publishing Co.

Greenlaw, P. S. and M. P. Hottenstein (1969), *PROSIM: A Production Management Simulation,* New York, NY: Harper and Row Publishers.

Greenlaw, P. S. and F. W. Kniffin (1964), *MARKSIM: A Marketing Decision Simulation,* New York, NY: Harper and Row Publishers. Out of print, 1987.

Gupta, S. K. and R. T. Hamman (1974), *Starting A Small Business: A Simulation Game,* Englewood Cliffs, NJ: Prentice-Hall Inc.

Henshaw, R. C. Jr. and J. R. Jackson (1986), *The Executive Game,* Homewood, IL: Richard D. Irwin, Inc.

Hinton, R. W. and D. C. Smith (1985), *STRATPLAN,* Englewood Cliffs, NJ: Prentice Hall, Inc.

Infoware (1984), *Bank President,* Nashville, TN: Infoware.

Jensen, R. L. (1989), *A Management Experience: A Computer Simulation,* Plano, TX: Business Publication, Inc.

Jensen, R. L. and D. J. Cherrington (1984), *The Business Management Laboratory,* Dallas, TX: Business Publications, Inc. (New Edition due out in 1989).

Johnson, G. A. and T. Hendrick (1984), *Cope: A Computer Oriented Production Exercise,* Dallas, TX: Business Publications, Inc.

Keiser, S. K. and M. Lupul (1977), *Marketing Interaction: A Decision Game,* Tulsa, OK: PPC.

Keys, B. (1988), *Microtronics,* New York, NY: John Wiley and Sons Publishers.

Keys, B. and H. Leftwich (1977), *The Executive Simulation,* Dubuque, IA: Kendall/Hunt Publishing Company.

Larreche, J. and D. Weinstein (1988), *INDUSTRAT: The Strategic Industrial Marketing Simulation,* Englewood Cliffs, NJ: Prentice-Hall.

Low, C. R. (1985), *Transportation Management: The Cunning Simulation,* New York, NY: McGraw-Hill Book Company.

Mason, C. H. and W. D. Perreault Jr. (1987), *The Marketing Game!,* Homewood, IL: Richard D. Irwin, Inc.

McFarlan, F. W., J. L. McKenney, and J. A. Seiler (1970), *The Management Game: Simulated Decision Making,* New York, NY: The Macmillan Company.

Meredith, J. (1977), *The Hospital Game,* Cincinnati, OH: Shasta Publications.

Mills, L. W. and D. B. McDowell (1985), *The Business Game,* Boston, MA: Little, Brown and Company.

Ness, T. E. (1987), *QSC Pizza Shoppe: A Computerized Business Simulation,* Chicago, IL: The Dryden Press.

Ness, T. E. and Day, R. L. (1984), *Marketing in Action: A Decision Game,* Homewood, IL: Richard D. Irwin, Inc.

Nichols, A. C. and B. Schott (1972), *SIMQ: Business Simulation Game for Decision Science Students,* Dubuque, IA: Kendall/Hunt Publishing Company.

Penderghast, T. (1988), *E.S.P.: Entrepreneureal Simulation Program,* Chicago, IL: Harcourt Brace Jovanovich, Inc.

Pettit, D. (1985), *Bu$iness Sen$e: A Decision-Making Simulation,* Reading, MA: Addison-Wesley.

Pitta, D. and M. Sewell (1988), *Competition and Strategy,* Boston, MA: Allyn & Bacon.

Priesmeyer, H. R. (1987), *Strategy: A Business Unit Simulation,* Cincinnati, OH: South-Western.

Reality Technologies (1986), *Business Simulator: An Executive Training Tool,* Philadelphia, PA: Reality Development Corp.

Reality Technologies (1988), *Business Simulator: Collegiate Edition,* Cincinnati, OH: South-Western.

Schnaars, S. P. (1985), *Microsim: A Marketing Computer Simulation Game,* Chicago, IL: Dryden.

Scott, C. R. Jr. and A. J. Strickland III (1984), *Tempomatic IV: A Management Simulation,* Boston, MA: Houghton Mifflin Company.

Scott, T. W. and A. J. Strickland III (1985), *Micromatic: A Management Simulation,* Boston, MA: Houghton Mifflin Company.

Smith, G. N. (1983), *The Briton Manufacturing Co.,* New York, NY: Harper & Row, Publishers, Inc.

Smith, J. R. (1985), *Enterprise II: A Simulation,* Boston, MA: Houghton Mifflin Company.

Smith, J. R. (1987a), *Manager: A Simulation,* Boston, MA: Houghton Mifflin Company.

Smith, J. R. (1987b), *Marketer: A Simulation,* Boston, MA: Houghton Mifflin Company.

Smith, J. R. and P. A. Golden (1987a), *Airline: A Strategic Management Simulation,* Englewood Cliffs, NJ: Prentice-Hall, Inc.

Smith, J. R. and P. A. Golden (1987b), *Entrepreneur: A Business Simulation,* Boston, MA: Houghton Mifflin Company.

Smith, J. R. and P. A. Golden (1989), *Portfolio: A Strategy Simulation,* Englewood Cliffs, NJ: Prentice-Hall, Inc.

Smith, W. Nye, E.E. Estey, and E. F. Vines (1974), *Integrated Simulation,* Cincinnati, OH: South-Western Publishing Co.

Sprenger, C., K. Werdkamp, and C. Burns (1987a), *Lite Flight: A Computerized Accounting Simulation,* Homewood, IL: Richard D. Irwin, Inc.

Sprenger, C., K. Werdkamp, and C. Burns (1987b), *KC's Deals on Wheels,* Homewood, IL: Richard D. Irwin, Inc.

Strang, D. and T. A. Pray (1981), *DECIDE,* New York, NY: Random House, Inc.

Thorelli, H. B. and R. L. Graves (1964), *International Operation Simulation,* Encino, CA: Glencoe Press.

Wilson, H. and R. Hickman (1982), *The World of Business Games,* New York, NY: John Wiley and Sons Publishers.

Zocco, D. P. (1987), *Investor,* Cincinnati, OH: South-Western Publishing Co.

BIBLIOGRAPHY

Aaker, David A. and John G. Myers (1987), *Advertising Management,* Englewood Cliffs, NJ: Prentice-Hall.

Adelman, Howard S. (1986), "Intervention Theory and Evaluating Efficacy," *Evaluation Review,* 10, 65-83.

Affisco, John F. and Michael N. Chanin (1989), "The Impact of Decision Support Systems on the Effectiveness of Small Group Decisions: An Exploratory Study," *Developments in Business Simulation and Experiential Exercises,* Vol. 16, Thomas Pray and John Wingender (eds.), 132-135.

Ahern, J. R., L. J. Bonanni, B. J. Ellis, J. C. McWhorton, T. D. Potter and D. W. Whelan (1968), *An Excerpt From a Study of Simulation Games as Training Procedures,* Washington, D.C.: Industrial College of the Armed Services.

Anderson, David R., Dennis J. Sweeney, and Thomas A. Williams (1976), *An Introduction to Management Science.* St. Paul, MN: West Publishing Co.

Andersen, Michael E. (1986), personal communication, Los Angeles: University of Southern California.

Anderson, Philip H. and Leigh Lawton (1986), "Integrating Personnel Computers into a course as a Decision Support Tool," Alvin C. Burns and Lane Kelley, (eds.), *Developments in Business Simulation and Experiential Exercises,* Vol. 13, 212-215.

Anderson, Philip H. and Leigh Lawton (1988), "A Form and Process for Non-confidential Peer Evaluations," in Pat Sanders and Tom Pray (ed.), *Developments in Business Simulation and Experiential Exercises,* Vol. 15, 121-124.

Anderson, Ronald E. (1980), "Computer Simulation Games, Exemplars," R. E. Horn and A. Cleaves (eds.), *The Guide to Simulation/Games for Education and Training,* Beverly Hills, CA: Sage Publishing, 37-46.

Anderson, Ronald E. (1983), "Innovative Microcomputer Games and Simulations," *Simulation and Games,* 14 (March), 3-9.

Andlinger, G. R. (1958), "Business Games—Play One," *Harvard Business Review,* 28 (no. 3), 115-125.

Andrews, E. S. and J. L. Noel (1986), "Adding Life to the Case Study Method," *Training and Development Journal,* 40 (no. 2), 28-29.

Archer, Earnest R. (1980), "How to Make a Business Decision: An Analysis of Theory and Practice," *Management Review,* February, 54-61.

Argyris, Chris (1980), "Some Limitations on the Case Method: Experiences in a Management Development Program," *Academy of Management Review,* 5 (no. 2), 291-298.

Armstrong, J. Scott (1979), "The Natural Learning Project," *Journal of Experiential Learning and Simulation,* 1, 5-12.

Armstrong, Robert and Margaret Hobson (1969), *Gaming/Simulation Techniques: An Introductory Exercise, Management by Objectives,* Birmingham, U.K.: Institute of Local Studies, University of Birmingham.

Armstrong, Robert H. and Margaret Hobson (1975), "Introduction to Gaming-Simulation Techniques," Cathy Greenblat and Richard D. Duke (eds.), *Gaming-Simulation,* Halsted Press, 82–91.

Assa, Isak (1982), "Management Simulation Games for Education and Research: A Comparative Study of Gaming in Socialist Countries," *Simulation and Games,* 13 (December), 379–412.

Avner, A., C. Moore, and S. Smith, (1980), "Active External Control: A Basis for Superiority of CBI," *Journal of Computer Based Instruction,* Summer, 15–18.

Ayal, Igal and Jehiel Zif (1989), *Product Manager,* Englewood Cliffs, NJ: Prentice-Hall.

Badgett, Tom F. (1980), "Forming Participant Teams in Simulation Gaming," *Experiential Learning Enters the Eighties,* Daniel C. Brenenstuhl and William D. Biggs (eds.), 107.

Banks, Jerry and John S. Carson II (1984), *Discrete Event System Simulation,* Englewood Cliffs, NJ: Prentice-Hall.

Barnett, T. (1984), "Evaluations of Simulations and Games: A Clarification," *Simulation/Games for Learning,* 14 (Fall), 37–44.

Bartlett, C. A. and D. W. DeLong (1982), "Operating Cases to Help Solve Corporate Problems," *Harvard Business Review,* 60 (No. 2), 68–70.

Bartlett, Robin L. and Timothy I. Miller (1981), "Evaluating the Federal Open Market Committee Simulation: A Complementary Teaching Technique," *Simulation & Games,* 12, 29–49.

Barton, Richard F. (1977), "Double Play for Gaming Effectiveness," *New Horizons in Simulation Games and Experiential Learning,* Carl C. Nielsen (ed.), 3–8.

Barton, Richard F. (1970), *A Primer on Simulation and Gaming,* Englewood Cliffs, NJ: Prentice-Hall.

Barton, Richard F. (1978), *The IMAGINIT Management Game,* Lubbock, TX: Active Learning.

Barton, Richard F. (1984), "A Simulation Model for Conglomerates," in Alvin C. Burns and Lane Kelley (eds.), *Developments in Business Simulation & Experiential Exercises,* Vol. 11, 189–193.

Barton, Richard F. (1987), "How to Multiply Your Management Game," in Lane Kelley and Patricia Sanders (eds.), *Developments in Business Simulation & Experiential Exercises,* Vol. 14, 6–9.

Basuray, Tom and Steven A. Scherling (1979), "Cognitive Complexity Development in Lecture vs. Experiential Organizational Behavior Classes." *Journal of Experiential Learning and Simulation,* 1, 13–28.

Baumgartel, H. and J. W. Goldstein (1967), "Need and Value Shifts in College Training Groups, *Journal of Applied Behavioral Science,* 3, 211–226.

Beatty, Richard W. and Craig Eric Schneier (1981), *Personnel Administration: An Experiential/Skill Building Approach,* (2nd ed.), Reading, MA: Addison-Wesley Publishing Co.

Becker, Henry Jay (1987), "Using Computers for Instruction," *Byte,* February, 149–162.

Bennis, W., Burke, R., Cutter, H., Harrington, H., and Hoffman, J. (1957), "A Note on Some Problems of Measurement and Prediction in a Training Group," *Group Psychotherapy,* 10, 328–341.

Benson, H. and R. Allen (1980), "How Much Stress is Too Much?" *Harvard Business Review,* September-October, 86–92.

Berger, David (1985), "The FCB Grid." *Proceedings of the Advertising Research Foundation 31st Annual Conference.*

Beutell, Nicholas and Randall S. Schuler (1986), *Personal Computer (PC) Projects for Effective Personnel Management,* St. Paul, MN: West Publishing Company.

Biggs, William D. (1978), "A Comparison of Ranking and Relational Grading Procedures in a General Management Simulation," *Simulation & Games,* 9, No. 2 (June), 185–200.

Biggs, William D. (1979), "Who is Using Computerized Business Games? A View from Publisher's Adoption Lists," in *Insights into Experiential Pedagogy,* Vol. 6, eds. Samuel C. Certo and Daniel C. Brenenstuhl, Tempe: Arizona State University, 202–206.

Biggs, William D. (1986), "Computerized Business Management Games for Tyros," *Developments in Business Simulation and Experiential Learning,* Vol. 13, Alvin C. Burns and Lane Kelley (eds.), 187–194.

Biggs, William D. (1987), "Functional Business Games," *Simulation & Games,* 18, 242–267.

Biggs, William D. and Paul S. Greenlaw (1976), "The Role of Information in a Functional Game," *Simulation & Games,* 7, 53–64.

Biggs, William D. and T. M. Slocum (1976), *Faculty Guide to Computer Programs Available in the Computer Program Library (DBUSLIB),* Alfred, NY: School of Business and Administration, Alfred University.

Biggs, William D. and T. J. Smith (1982), "Adapting Mainframe Business Simulations to Mini Computers," in David J. Fritzsche and Lee A. Graf (eds.), *Developments in Business Simulation and Experiential Exercises,* Vol. 9, 260–263.

Bittel, Lester (1977), *Shenandoah Management Games for Supervisors,* New York, NY: McGraw-Hill.

Bloom, B. S., M. D. Englehart, E. D. Furst, W. H. Hill, and D. R. Krathwohl (1956), *Taxonomy of Educational Objectives: The Classification of Educational Goals. Handbook 1: Cognitive Domain,* New York: David McKay Company, Inc.

Bolda, R. A. and C. H. Lawshe (1962), "Evaluation of Role Playing," *Personnel Administration,* 25, 40–42.

Boone, Louis E., and Edwin C. Hackleman (1975), *Marketing Strategy,* Columbus, OH: Charles E. Merrill.

Boone, L. E., D. L. Kurtz, and J. L. Braden (1982), *The Sales Management Game,* Tulsa, OK: Pennwell Books.

Bornstein, Jacques, Gary Heapy, Michelle Milam, and Richard Teach (1987), "Simulation: The Players' Perspective," in Lane Kelley and Patricia Sanders (eds.), *Developments in Business Simulation & Experiential Exercises,* Vol. 14, 13–15.

Boudreau, John W. and George T. Milkovich (1988), *Personal Computer Exercises in Personnel/Human Resource Management,* Plano, TX: Business Publications, Inc.

Bowen, Donald D. (1987), "Developing a Personal Theory of Experiential Learning: A Dispatch from the Trenches," *Simulation and Games,* 18, 192–206.

Boyd, Harper W., Jr., Michael L. Ray, and Edward C. Strong (1972), "An Attitudinal Framework for Advertising Strategy," *Journal of Marketing,* 36 (April), 22–33.

Bradford, D. L. and R. Le Duc (1975), "One Approach to the Care and Teaching of Introductory O.B.," *The Teaching of Organizational Behavior, 1* (no. 1), 18–24.

Bradford, D. L. and J. I. Porras, (1975), "Restructuring the Classroom: A Design for a 36-person T-group," *The Teaching of Organizational Behavior,* 1 (no. 2), 16–19.

Bratley, Paul, Bennet L. Fox, and Linuse Schrage (1983), *A Guide to Simulation.* New York: Springer-Verlag.

Brenenstuhl, Daniel C. and Ralph F. Catalanello (1976), "An Analysis of the Impact Upon the Learning Effectiveness of Traditional Instruction, Simulation Gaming and Experiential Learning Teaching Methodologies: An Experimental Design," *Computer Simulation and Learning Theory,* Burnard H. Sord (ed.), 463–473.

Brenenstuhl, Daniel C. and Ralph F. Catalanello (1979), "Can Learning Styles Be Used as Curriculum Aids?," *Journal of Experiential Learning and Simulation,* 1, 29–37.

Brenenstuhl, Daniel C. and Ralph F. Catalanello (1979), "The Impact of Three Pedagogue Techniques on Learning," *Journal of Experiential Learning and Simulation,* 1, 211–225.

Brooks, L. D. (1975), *The Financial Management Decision Game,* Homewood, IL: Irwin.

Brooks, L. D. (1978), "An Evaluation of Financial Management Learning Simulations," *Journal of Financial Education,* 7, 63–68.

Brooks, L. D. (1982), *Financial Management Decision Game* (Second Edition), Homewood, IL: Irwin.

Broom, H. N. (1969), *Business Policy and Strategic Action: Text, Cases, and Management Game,* Englewood Cliffs, NJ: Prentice-Hall.

Bruner, S. (1961), "The Act of Discovery," *Harvard Education Review,* 31 (Winter), 21–32.

Bryant, N. and G. Corless (1986), "The Management of Management Games," *Simulation/Games for Learning,* 16 (Fall), 121–138.

Budner, S. (1962), "Intolerance of Ambiguity as a Personality Variable," *Journal of Personality,* 30, 29–50.

Bunker, D. R. (1965), "Individual Applications of Laboratory Training," *Journal of Applied Behavioral Science,* 1, 131–148.

Bunker, Kerry A. and Stephen L. Cohen (1978), "Evaluating Organizational Training Efforts: Is Ignorance Really Bliss?" *Training and Development Journal,* 32, 4–10.

Burke, H. L. and Warrin G. Bennis (1961), "Changes in Perception of Self and Others During Human Relations Training," *Human Relations,* 14, 165–182.

Burkov, Vladimir (1985), "The Theory of Organization Management and Business Games in the USSR," *Simulation and Games,* 16 (June), 229–230.

Burns, Alvin C. (1978), "The Extended Live-Case Approach to Teaching Marketing Research," *Exploring Experiential Learning: Simulations and Experiential Exercises,* Daniel C. Brenenstuhl and Samuel C. Certo (eds.), 245–251.

Burns, Alvin C. (1990), "The Live Case Approach," in *Guide to Business Gaming and Experiential Learning,* James W. Gentry (ed.), New York: Nichols/GP Publishing.

Burns, Alvin C. and James W. Gentry (1977), "Some Thoughts on a 'Theory' of the Use of Games and Experiential Exercises," *New Horizons in Simulation Games and Experiential Learning,* Carl C. Nielsen (ed.), Vol. 4, 187–194.

Burns, Alvin C. and James W. Gentry (1980), "Moving Toward a 'Theory' of the Use of Simulation Games and Experiential Exercises," *Experiential Learning Enters the Eighties,* Daniel C. Brenenstuhl and William D. Biggs (eds.), Vol. 7, 17–20.

Burns, Alvin C., James W. Gentry, and Joseph Wolfe (1990), "A Cornucopia of Considerations in Evaluating the Effectiveness of Experiential Pedagogies," in *Guide to Business Gaming and Experiential Learning,* James W. Gentry (ed.), New York: Nichols/GP Publishing.

Burns, Alvin C., Steven P. Golen, and James W. Gentry (1983), "Report on Programmatic Research on Perceived Learning Barriers with Simulation and Experiential Learning, *Developments in Business Simulation and Experiential Exercises,* Vol. 10, Lee A. Graf and David M. Currie (eds.), 147–151.

Burns, Alvin C. and Daniel L. Sherrell (1984), "A Path Analytic Study of the Effects of Alternative Pedagogies," *Developments in Business Simulation and Experiential Exercises,* Vol. 11, James W. Gentry and Alvin C. Burns (eds.), 115–119.

Burns, P. K. and W. C. Bozeman (1981), "Computer-assisted Instruction and Math Achievement: Is There a Relationship?" *Educational Leadership,* October, 32–39.

Burton, Gene E. (1987), "A Survey of Behavioral Labs Used by American Business Schools," *Developments in Business Simulation and Experiential Exercises,* Vol. 14, Lane Kelley and Patricia Sanders (eds.), 23–26.

Burton, Gene E. (1987), "The Acute Susceptibility of Nominal Grouping to Negativity," Lane Kelley and Patricia Sanders (eds.), *Developments in Business Simulation and Experiential Exercises,* Vol. 14, 16–19.

Butler, Richard J., Peter M. Markulis, and Daniel R. Strang (1985) "Learning Theory and Research Design: How Has ABSEL Fared?" *Developments in Business Simulation and Experiential Exercises,* Vol. 12, James W. Gentry and Alvin C. Burns (eds.), 86–90.

Butler, Richard J. and A. Parasuraman (1975), "Integrating Business Game Performance with the Grading Process," *Proceedings of the Midwest AIDS Conference,* 93–97.

Butler, Richard J., Thomas F. Pray and Daniel R. Strang (1979a), "An Extension of Wolfe's Study of Simulation Game Complexity," *Decision Sciences,* 10, 480–486.

Butler, Richard J., Thomas F. Pray and Daniel R. Strang (1979b), *DECIDE,* NY: Random House.

Byrne, Eugene T. (1979), "Who Benefits Most from Participation in Business Policy Simulations: An Empirical Study of Skill Development by Functional Area," in *Insights Into Experiential Pedagogy,* eds. Samuel C. Certo and Daniel C. Brenenstuhl, Tempe: Arizona State University, 257–260.

Campbell, Donald T. and Julian C. Stanley (1963), *Experimental and Quasi Experimental Designs for Research,* Chicago: Rand McNally and Co.

Campbell, John P. and Marvin D. Dunnette (1968), "Effectiveness of T-Group Experiences in Managerial Training and Development," *Psychological Bulletin,* 70 (no. 2), 73–104.

Campbell, John P., Marvin D. Dunnette, Edward E. Lawler, and Karl E. Weick (1970), *Managerial Behavior, Performance, and Effectiveness,* NY: McGraw-Hill.

Campbell, John P., Richard L. Daft, and Charles L. Hulin (1982), *What to Study: Generating and Developing Research Questions,* Beverly Hills, CA: Sage.

Cannon, Hugh and Fred W. Morgan (1985), "An Expert Systems Approach for Teaching Marketing Case Analysis," *Developments in Business Simulation and Experiential Exercises,* Vol. 14, Lane Kelly and Patricia Sanders (eds.), 31–33.

Carlson, E. (1966), "The Versatile Business Game: Its Growing Use in Industry," *The Wall Street Journal,* July 8, 1–2.

Carroll, Stephen J., Frank T. Paine, and John J. Ivancevich (1972), "The Relative Effectiveness of Training Methods—Expert Opinion and Research," *Personnel Psychology,* 25, 495–509.

Carter, Philip, James Hickman, Philip McDonald, Robert Patton, and Donald C. Powell (1986), *Memorandum on Applied and Experiential Learning Curriculum Development,* AACSB Task Force Report, March.

Certo, Samuel C. (1975), "Developing Interpersonal Skills Experientially and Transfer of Training," *Proceedings,* 35th Annual Meeting of the Academy of Management.

Chain Store Age (1986), "Computers as Classrooms: Testing Employees Skills with Video: What If . . .?" January, 128.

Chase, Michael and D. Sepehri (1986), "Interactive Simulation Model for Risky Financial Decision-Making" *Computers and Industrial Engineering,* 11, (1–4), 416–420.

Chen, Henry C. K. (1977), "A Non-computerized Marketing Planning and Strategy Game," *New Horizons in Simulation Games and Experiential Learning,* Carl C. Nielson (ed.), Vol. 4, 254–262.

Chiesl, Newell (1978), "A Pedagogical Exercise Utilizing Computer Simulation," *Proceedings: Winter Simulation Conference.*

Chiesel, Newell (1986), "Simulation With Discrete and Continuous Mathematical Modeling," in Alvin C. Burns and Lane Kelley (eds.), *Developments in Business Simulation and Experiential Exercises,* Vol. 13, 239–240.

Chiesel, Newell E. (1987), "The Use of a Simple Forecasting Technique During an Interactive Computerized Business Game," in Lane Kelley and Patricia Sanders (eds), *Developments in Business Simulation & Experiential Exercises,* Vol. 14, 39–42.

Churchill, Geoffrey (1979), "Games Within Games: The Role of the Glitch," *Insights into Experiential Pedagogy,* Samuel C. Certo and Daniel C. Brenenstuhl (eds.), 112–114.

Clegg, William H. (1987), "Management Training Evaluation: An Update," *Training and Development Journal,* 11, 65–73.

Clement, Ronald W. and Eileen K. Aranda (1982), "Evaluating Management Training: A Contingency Approach, *Training and Development Journal,* 36, 39–43.

Coats, William D., and Uldis Smidchens (1966), "Audience Recall as a Function of Speaker Dynamism," *Journal of Educational Psychology,* 57, 189–191.

COGITATE: A Time-Shared Management Simulation Exercise (1983), Lexington, MA: Temple, Barker & Sloane.

Cohen, A. R. (1976), "Beyond Simulation: Treating the Classroom as an Organization," *The Teaching of Organizational Behavior,* 2 (no. 1), 13–19.

Cohen, Kalman J., et al (1960), "The Carnegie Tech Management Game," *Journal of Business,* 33 (October), 303–326.

Cohen, Kalman J. and Eric Rhenman (1961), "The Role of Management Games in Education and Research," *Management Science,* 7 (January), 131-166.

Colley, Russell H. (1961), *Defining Advertising Goals for Measured Advertising Results,* New York: Association of National Advertisers.

Cook, M. H. (1981), "Are You Game?," *Training and Development Journal,* 35 (No. 1), 405.

Cooke, Ernest F. (1986), "The Dilemma in Evaluating Classroom Innovations," in *Developments in Business Simulation and Experiential Exercises,* Vol. 13, eds. Alvin C. Burns and Lane Kelley, Stillwater, Oklahoma State University, 110-114.

Coote, Alan (1987), "Management Simulation and Business Gaming: An Introduction," *Simulation-Gaming in the Late 1980s,* in David Crookall, et al. (eds.), Oxford, England: Pergamon Press, 193-194.

Cosenza, Robert, Louis E. Boone, and David L. Kurtz (1985), "Integrating Microcomputers in the Marketing Curriculum Through the Use of Marketing COMUPROBS," *Developments in Business Simulation and Experiential Exercises,* Vol. 12, James Gentry and Alvin C. Burns (eds.), 54-55.

Cotter, Richard V. (1985), *The Business Policy Game,* Englewood Cliffs, NJ: Prentice-Hall.

Cotter, Richard V. and David J. Fritzsche (1986), *The Business Policy Game,* Second Edition, Englewood Cliffs, NJ: Prentice-Hall.

Couch, P. D. and Lee A. Graf (1981), "In Support of Experiential Learning: Results of a Follow-up Survey," *Developments in Business Simulation and Experiential Exercises,* William D. Biggs and David J. Fritzche (eds.), Vol. 8, 255-259.

Cougar, J. Daniel (1972), "Computers and the Schools of Business," *Decision Line,* 6 (no. 5), 23-28.

Courtney, J. F. Jr. and Ronald L. Jensen (1981), *Slim: System for Information Management,* Plano, TX: Business Publications, Inc.

Couvillion, L.J., Thomas F. Pray and Daniel R. Strang (1979), "A Statistical Analysis of Game Users: Relationships Between Stress and Human Subjects Guidelines," in *Insights Into Experiential Pedagogy,* Vol. 6, eds. Samuel C. Certo and Daniel C. Brenenstuhl, Tempe: Arizona State University, 141-144.

Cox, S.R. (1974), "Computer-Assisted Instruction and Student Performance in Macroeconomic Principles," *Journal of Economic Education,* 6, 29-37.

Crino, Michael D. (1979), "Computerized Business Simulations and Experiential Learning Exercises: An Instructional Interface," *Insights into Experiential Pedagogy,* Samuel C. Certo and Daniel C. Brenenstuhl (eds.), Vol. 6, 315-317.

Curran, Kent E. and Robert W. Hornaday (1987), "An Investigation of the Relationship Between Formal Planning and Simulation Team Performance and Satisfaction," in Lane Kelley and Patricia Sanders (eds), *Developments in Business Simulation & Experiential Exercises,* Vol. 14, 43-46.

Cyert, Richard M. and James G. March (1963), *A Behavioral Theory of the Firm,* Englewood Cliffs, NJ: Prentice-Hall.

Dale, A. G. and C. R. Klasson (1964), "Business Gaming: A Survey of American Collegiate Schools of Business," working paper no. 43, Bureau of Business Research, The University of Texas.

Davies, I. K. (1981), *Instructional Techniques,* New York: McGraw-Hill.

Davis, Keith and John W. Newstrom (1985), *Organizational Behavior: Readings and Exercises* (7th ed.) New York, NY: McGraw-Hill Book Company.

Davis, M.S. (1971), "That's Interesting! Toward a Phenomenology of Sociology and a Sociology of Phenomenology," *Philosphy of Social Science,* 309–344.

Davis, Samuel, Gary Kochenberger, Edward Reutzel, and John Tyworth (1986), "Demonstrating the Role of Simulation in Strategic Operations Planning: A Case Study in Bank Check Processing Location in Analysis," *Developments in Business Simulation and Experiential Exercises,* Vol. 13, Alvin Burns and Lane Kelly (eds.), 166–169.

Dawson, Peter P. (1985), *Fundamentals of Organizational Behavior: An Experiential Approach,* Englewood Cliffs, NJ: Prentice-Hall, Inc.

Day, Ralph (1968), "Beyond the Marketing Game—New Educational Uses for Simulation," *Marketing and the New Science of Planning,* No. 28, Robert L. King (ed), 581–588.

Day, Ralph L. (1974), "Growing Emphasis on Implementation," *Simulations, Games and Experiential Learning Techniques: On the Road to a New Frontier,* James Kenderdine and Bernard Keys (eds.), 314.

Day, Ralph L. (1986), "A Sales Management Simulation for the PC: An Integrative Tool for Sales Management Courses," *Developments in Business Simulation and Experiential Exercises,* Vol. 13, Alvin Burns and Lane Kelly (eds.), 63–65.

Day, Ralph L. and Thomas E. Ness (1962), *Marketing in Action: A Decision Game,* Homewood, IL: Irwin.

deBono, Edward (1985), *Six Thinking Hats,* Boston: Little, Brown, and Company.

Decker, Ronald, James LaBarre, and Thomas Adler (1987), "The Exponential Logarithm Function as an Algorithm for Business Simulation," in Lane Kelley and Patricia Sanders (eds.), *Developments in Business Simulation & Experiential Exercises,* Vol. 14, 47–49.

Deep, Samuel D., Bernard Bass and James A. Vaughan (1967), "Some Effects on Business Gaming of Previous Quasi-T Group Affiliations," *Journal of Applied Psychology,* 51, 426–431.

DeHayes, D.W., and J.E. Suelflow (1971), *Logistics Simulation Exercise— LOGSIMX.* Bloomington, IN: Indiana University (manuscript).

De los Santos, Gilberto and Thomas D. Jensen (1985), "Client Sponsored Projects: Bridging the Gap Between Theory and Practice," *Journal of Marketing Education,* Summer, 45–50.

Dennis, T. and Thomas Pray, (1982), "Nine Topic Oriented Mini-simulations: Descriptions, Purposes, and Observations," *Developments in Business Simulation and Experiential Learning,* David J. Fritzsche and Lee A. Graf (eds.), Vol. 9, 28–32.

Dewey, John and Evelyn Dewey (1915), *School of Tomorrow,* New York: E.P. Dutton and Company.

Dickinson, John R. (1986), "An Experiential Exercise in Bayesian Decision-Making," *Developments in Business Simulation and Experiential Exercises,* Vol. 13, Alvin C. Burns and Lane Kelley (eds.), 178–182.

Dill, William R. (1961), "The Educational Effects of Management Games," in *Proceedings of the Conference on Business Games,* eds. William R. Dill, James R. Jackson and James W. Sweeney, New Orleans: Tulane University, 61–68.

Dill, William R., W. Hoffman, Harold J. Leavitt and Timothy O'Mara (1961), "Experiences with a Complex Management Game," *California Management Review,* 3, 38–51.

Dill, William R., and Neil Doppelt (1963), "The Acquisition of Experience in a Complex Management Game," *Management Science,* 10, 30–46.

Di Vesta, Francis J. and Steven T. Peverly (1984), "The Effects of Encoding Variability, Processing Activity, and Rule—Examples Sequence on the Transfer of Conceptual Rule," *Journal of Educational Psychology,* 76 (no. 1), 108–119.

Dolich, Ira J. (1984), "Interacting Mainframe Computer Simulations and Microcomputer Information Systems," *American Marketing Association Educators' Proceedings,* 121–126.

Dommeyer, Curt J. (1986), "A Comparison of the Individual Proposal and the Team Project in the Marketing Research Course," *Journal of Marketing Education,* Spring, 30–38.

Downey, H. Kirk (1982), "Symposium: Business Policy Teaching Methods." Paper presented, Academy of Management, New York.

Durling, Allen (1974), *Computational Techniques: Analog, Digital and Hybrid Systems.* New York: Intext.

Edge, Alfred G., Bernard Keyes and William E. Remus (1985), *The Multinational Management Game* (2nd ed.), Plano, TX: Business Publications, Inc.

Edwards, W. F. (1987), "Learning Macroeconomic Theory and Policy Analysis Via Microcomputer Simulation," *Developments in Business Simulation and Experiential Exercises,* Vol. 14, Lane Kelley and Patricia Sanders (eds.), 50–52.

Einhorn, Hillel J. and Robin M. Hogarth (1981), "Behavioral Decision Theory: Processes of Judgment and Choice," *Annual Review of Psychology,* 32, 53–88.

Eldredge, David L. and Donald L. Bates (1980), *The Business Strategy and Policy Game,* Dubuque, IA: Wm. C. Brown.

Eliason, Alan L. (1972), "A Study of the Effects of Quantitative Training." *Academy of Management Journal,* 15, 147–158.

Emery, Douglas R. and Francis D. Tuggle (1976), "On the Evaluation of Decisions," *MSU Business Topics,* 24 (no. 2, Spring), 42–48.

Emshoff, J. R. and R. L. Sisson (1970), *Design and Use of Simulation Models,* New York: Macmillan.

Enderton, Herbert B. (1972), *A Mathematical Introduction to Logic,* Orlando, FL: Academic Press.

English, C. W. (1985), "Internships: New Uses for an Old Tool," *U.S. News & World Report,* 99 (July 1), 66.

Estes, James E. (1979), "Research on the Effectiveness of Using a Computerized Simulation in the Basic Management Course," in *Insights Into Experiential Pedagogy,* Vol. 6, eds. Samuel C. Certo and Daniel C. Brenenstuhl, Tempe: Arizona State University, 25–28.

Estes, James E. and C. Brian Honess (1973), *Mads-Bee: Managing a Dynamic Small Business,* West Columbia, SC: Wentworth.

Estes, W. K. (1972), "Reinforcement in Human Behavior," *American Scientist,* 60, 723–729.

Estes, W. K. (1976), "The Cognitive Side of Probability Learning," *Psychological Review,* 83, 37–64.

Falster, Peter (1987), "Planning and Controlling Production Systems Combining Simulation and Expert Systems", *Computers in Industry,* 8 (April), 161–172.

Faria, Anthony J. (1980), "Marketing Games: An Evaluation," in R. E. Horn and A. Cleaves (eds.), *The Guide to Simulations/Games for Education and Training.* Newbury Park, CA: Sage, 177–186.

Faria, Anthony J. (1986), "A Test of Student Performance and Attitudes Under Varying Game Conditions," in *Insights Into Experiential Pedagogy,* Vol. 13, eds. Alvin C. Burns and Lane Kelley, Stillwater: Oklahoma State University, 70–74.

Faria, Anthony J. (1987), "A Survey of the Use of Business Games in Academia and Business," *Simulation & Games,* 18 (No. 2), 207–225.

Faria, Anthony J. and Marc Schumacher (1984), "The Use of Decision Simulations in Management Training Programs: Current Perspectives," *Developments in Business Simulation & Experiential Exercises,* Vol. 11, David M. Currie and James W. Gentry (eds.), 228–232.

Faria, Anthony J., and Ray O. Nulsen (1978), "The New Research Focus: An Analysis of the Simulation Game User," in *Exploring Experiential Learning: Simulations and Experiential Exercises,* Vol. 5, eds. Daniel C. Brenenstuhl and Samuel C. Certo, Tempe: Arizona State University, 25–31.

Faria, Anthony J. and Ray O. Nulsen (1979), "Game Administration: A Life Cycle Analysis," *Insights into Experiential Pedagogy,* Vol. 6, Samuel C. Certo and Daniel C. Brenenstuhl (eds.), 220–225.

Faria, Anthony J., Ray O. Nulsen, and D. Roussos (1984), *COMPETE: A Dynamic Marketing Simulation.* Dallas, TX: Business Publications, Inc.

Feldt, Allan G. and Frederick Goodman (1975), "Observations on Design," in Cathy Greenblat and Richard D. Duke (eds.), *Gaming-Simulation,* New York: Halsted Press.

Fels, R. (1968), *Manual: Test of Understanding in College Economics,* New York: Psychological Corporation.

Field, Anne R. (1985), "Software for the Common Man," *Business Week,* (March 18), 95.

Finn, David (1987), "Teaching About Sampling in a Marketing Research Class," *Developments in Business Simulation and Experiential Exercises,* Vol. 14, Lane Kelly and Patricia Sanders (eds.), 57–62.

Fischer, William A. and Joseph B. Mazzola (1987), *FISCHTALE Enterprises,* Glenview, IL: Scott, Foresman and Company.

Fisk, Jamie T. and Raymond P. Fisk (1986), *Airways: A Services Marketing Game,* New York: John Wiley.

Francis, D. W. (1987), "The Competent Player: Some Observations on Game Learning," in David Crookall et al. (eds.), *Simulation-Gaming in the Late 1980s,* Oxford, U. K.: Paragon Press, 201.

Frazer, J. Ronald (1978), "Educational Values of Simulation Gaming," *Exploring Experiential Learning: Simulations and Experiential Exercises,* Daniel C. Brenenstuhl and Samuel C. Certo (eds.), 269–275.

Frazer, J. Ronald (1983), "BANKRUPT - A Deceptively Simple Business Strategy Game," *Developments in Business Simulation and Experiential Exercises,* Vol. 10, Lee A. Graf and David M. Currie (eds.), 98–100.

Frazer, J. Ronald (1985), "Advantages of a Multigame Simulation Course," *Developments in Business Simulation and Experiential Exercises,* James W. Gentry and Alvin C. Burns (Eds.), Vol. 12, 177–183.

Frazer, J. Ronald (1986), "Simulation—Indoctrination or Learning," *Developments in Business Simulation and Experiential Exercises,* Vol. 13, Alvin C. Burns and Lane Kelley (eds.), pp. 108–109.

Friend, Kenneth E. (1985), "Microcomputer Demonstration Exercises for a Course on Creativity and Problem Solving," *Developments in Business Simulation and Experiential Exercises,* Vol. 12, James W. Gentry and Alvin C. Burns (eds.), 135–139.

Fritzsche, David J. (1975), "Operational Problems and Solutions of Business Gaming: A Primer," *Simulation Games and Experiential Learning in Action,* Richard H. Buskirk (ed.), 41–47.

Fritzsche, David J. (1977), "Changing Perceptions of Learning in a Simulated Environment," *New Horizons in Simulation Games and Experiential Learning,* Carl C. Nielsen (ed.), 101–109.

Fritzsche, David J. (1978), "Let's Simplify the Administrative Requirements of Computerized Educational Simulations," *Exploring Experiential Learning: Simulations and Experiential Exercises,* Daniel C. Brenenstuhl and Samuel C. Certo (eds.), 39–43.

Fritzsche, David J. (1979), "A Data Entry and Retrieval System for a Computer Simulation (DERS)," *Insights Into Experiential Pedagogy,* Samuel C. Certo and Daniel C. Brenenstuhl (eds.), 291–294.

Fritzsche, David J. (1987), "The Impact of Microcomputers on Business Educational Simulations," *Simulation & Games,* 18, 176–191.

Fritzsche, David J., Grover W. Rodich, and Richard V. Cotter (1987), "Integrating Decision Support Systems and Business Games," *Developments in Business Simulation and Experiential Exercises,* Vol. 14, Lane Kelly and Patricia Sanders (eds.), 63–66.

Fry, Louis, Aryeh Kidron, and Chester Schriesheim (1975), "The Effectiveness of Experiential Methods in Training and Education: A Review," *Behavior and Attitude Review,* 365–373.

Fuhs, F. Paul (1988), "Event-Extended Entity-Relationship Diagrams for Understanding Simulation Model Structure and Function," in Patricia Sanders and Tom Pray (eds.), *Developments in Business Simulation and Experiential Exercises,* Vol. 15, 41–45.

Garvey, D. M. (1971), "Simulation: A Catalogue of Judgements, Findings and Hunches," in T. J. Tanscy (ed), *Educational Aspects of Simulation,* London: McGraw-Hill, 94–107.

Gass, Saul I. (1975), *Linear Programming: Methods and Applications* (4th ed.), New York: McGraw-Hill.

Gasser, Leslie G. (1987), personal communication, Los Angeles: University of Southern California.

Gassner, S., J. Gold, and A. M. Snadowsky (1964), "Changes in the Phenomenal Field As A Result of Human Relations Training," *Journal of Psychology,* 58, 33–41.

Gaynor, P. (1981), "The Effect of Feedback Delay on Retention of Computer Based Mathematical Material," *Journal of Computer Based Instruction,* Autumn, 28–34.

Gentry, James W. (1979), "Teaching PERT Experientially in Marketing Research," *Insights into Experiential Pedagogy,* Samuel C. Certo and Daniel C. Brenenstuhl (eds.), 175–177.

Gentry, James W. (1980), "Group Size and Attitudes Toward the Simulation Experience," *Simulation & Games,* 11, December 4, 451–460.

Gentry, James W. (1981), "What Is Experiential Learning?", *ABSEL News and Views,* 1 (no. 3), p. 4.

Gentry, James W. (1990), "What is Experiential Learning?" *Guide to Business Gaming and Experiential Learning,* James W. Gentry (ed.), New York: Nichols/ GP Publishing.

Gentry, James W. and Alvin C. Burns (1981), "Operationalizing a Test of a Model of the Use of Simulation Games and Experiential Exercises," *Developments in Business Simulation and Experiential Exercises,* Vol. 8, William D. Biggs and David J. Fritzsche (eds.), 48–52.

Gentry, James W. and Alvin C. Burns (1983), "Do We Learn From Experience?", *Developments in Business Simulation and Experiential Exercises,* Vol. 10, Lee A. Graf and David M. Currie (eds.), 139–142.

Gentry, James W. and Alvin C. Burns (1984), "The Effects and Consequences of Megatrends on Simulation Gaming: One View," *Developments in Business Simulation and Experiential Exercises,* Vol. 11, David M. Currie and James W. Gentry (eds.), 97–100.

Gentry, James W. and Gary A. Giamartino (1989), "Duel (sic) Views of Internships as Experiential Learning," *Developments in Business Simulation and Experiential Exercises,* Vol. 16, Tom Pray and John Wingender (eds.), 128–132.

Giamartino, Gary A. and van Aalst, F. D. (1986), "Experiential Learning About the World of Work: A Program for Primary and Secondary School Educators," *Developments in Business Simulation and Experiential Exercises,* Vol. 13, Alvin C. Burns and Lane Kelley (eds.), 270–272.

Gibson, Jane W. and Richard M. Hodgetts (1985), *Readings and Exercises in Organizational Behavior,* Orlando, FL: Academic Press, Inc.

Gill Stephen Joel, Carl F. Berger, and George L. Cogar (1983), "Evaluating Microcounseling Training," *Evaluation Review,* 7 (April), 247–256.

Gitman, L. J., A. Robana, and William D. Biggs (1980), *PORT-STRAT: A Portfolio Strategy Simulation,* New York: John Wiley.

Glass, Robert L. (1983), *Real-Time Software.* Englewood Cliffs, NJ: Prentice-Hall.

Gold, Steven C., and Thomas F. Pray (1983), "Simulating Market and Firm Level Demand—A Robust Demand System," in *Developments in Business Simulation and Experiential Exercises,* Vol. 10, eds. Lee A. Graf and David M. Currie, Normal: Illinois State University, 101–106.

Gold, Steven C. and Thomas F. Pray (1984), "Modeling Non-Price Factors in the Demand Function of Computerized Business Simulations," in *Developments in Business Simulation and Experiential Exercises,* Vol. 11, eds. David M. Currie and James W. Gentry, Stillwater: Oklahoma State University, 240–243.

Golden, Peggy A. (1988), "Matching a Strategy Simulation to the Business Policy Literature: A Black-Box Approach to Simulation Development," Patricia Sanders and Tom Pray (eds.), *Developments in Business Simulation and Experiential Exercises,* Vol. 15, 153–156.

Goldstein, A. P. and M. Sorcher (1973), *Changing Supervisor Behavior,* New York: Pergamon Press.

Golen, Steven P., Alvin C. Burns, and James W. Gentry (1984), "An Analysis of Communication Barriers in Methods of Teaching Business Subjects," *Journal of Business Communication,* 21 (No. 3, Summer), 45–52.

Gomolka, Eugene G. and Joanne L. Mackin (1984), "Individual vs. Group Grade: An Exercise in Decision Making," *Developments in Business Simulation and Experiential Exercises,* Vol. II, David M. Currie and James W. Gentry (eds.), 128–132.

Gooding, C. (1976), *Decision-Making under Environmental Constraints: A Management Simulation,* Ph.D. Dissertation, University of Georgia.

Gooding, C. and T. W. Zimmer (1980), "Use of Specific Industry Gaming in the Selection, Orientation and Training of Managers," *Human Resource Management,* 19 (no. 1), 19–23.

Goosen, Kenneth R. (1973), *Introduction to Managerial Accounting: A Business Game,* Glenview, IL: Scott, Foresman.

Goosen, Ken R. (1976), "An Analysis of ABSEL: Its Past Achievements and Future Prospects," *Computer Simulation and Learning Theory,* Vol. 4, Burnard H. Sord (ed.), 207–214.

Goosen, Kenneth R. (1981), "A Generalized Algorithm for Designing and Developing Business Simulations," in *Developments in Business Simulation and Experiential Exercises,* Vol. 8, eds. William D. Biggs and David J. Fritzsche, Normal: Illinois State University, 41–47.

Goosen, Kenneth R. (1981), "Editor's Notebook," *ABSEL News and Views,* 1 (no. 3), pp. 6, 11.

Goosen, Kenneth R. (1982), *A Comprehensive Guide to ABSEL'S Conference Proceedings (1974-1981).* Published by Ken Goosen, University of Arkansas at Little Rock.

Goosen, Kenneth R. (1986), "An Analysis of ABSEL Conference Papers (1974–1985)," *Developments in Business Simulation and Experiential Exercises,* Vol. 13, Alvin C. Burns and Lane Kelley (eds.), 97–101.

Goosen, Kenneth R. (1986), "An Interpolation Approach to Developing Mathematical Functions for Business Simulations," in Alvin C. Burns and Lane Kelley (eds.), *Developments in Business Simulation and Experiential Exercises,* Vol. 13, 248–245.

Gordon, J. (1985), "Games Managers Play," *Training,* 36 (No. 3), 30–47.

Gordon, R. A. and J. E. Howell (1959), *Higher Education for Business,* New York: Columbia University Press.

Goretsky, M. Edward (1984), "Class Projects as a Form of Instruction," *Journal of Marketing Education,* Fall, 33–37.

Gosenpud, Jerry (1982), "Who Gains and Who Does Not From Experiential Learning," *Developments in Business Simulation and Experiential Exercises,* David J. Fritzsche and Lee A. Graf (eds.), 9, 135–140.

Gosenpud, Jerry (1986), "Personality Variables on Group Cohesion, Team Participation and Total Learning," *Developments in Business Simulation and Experiential Exercises,* Vol. 13, Alvin C. Burns and Lane Kelley (eds.), 115–118.

Gosenpud, Jerry and Paul Miesing (1982), "Determinants of Performance in Computer Simulations," *Developments in Business Simulation and Experiential Exercises,* Vol. 10, Lee A. Graf and David M. Currie (eds.), 53–56.

Gosenpud, Jerry, Paul Miesing, and Charles J. Milton (1984), "A Research Study on the Strategic Decisions in a Business Simulation," in *Developments in Business Simulation and Experiential Exercises,* Vol. 11, eds. David M. Currie and James W. Gentry, Stillwater: Oklahoma State University, 161–165.

Gosenpud, Jerry, and Joseph Wolfe (1988), "Strategy Design, Process and Implementation in a Stable/Complex Environment: An Exploratory Study," in *Developments in Business Simulation and Experiential Exercises,* Vol. 15, eds. Patricia Sanders and Thomas F. Pray, Stillwater: Oklahoma State University, 147–152.

Graf, Lee A. and P. D. Couch (1984–5), "A Program for Managing Student Groups: An Applied Organizational Behavior Experience," *The Organizational Behavior Teaching Review,* 1 (no. 4), 34–40.

Graf, Lee A. and Calvin E. Kellogg (1986), "Justifications for and Problems in Developing and Using Computerized Experiential Activities," *Developments in Business Stimulation and Experiential Exercises,* Alvin C. Burns and Lane Kelley (eds.), Vol. 13, 119–121.

Graham, Robert G. and Clifford F. Gray (1969), *Business Games Handbook,* New York: American Management Association.

Grater, M. (1959), "Changes in Self and Other Attitudes in a Leadership Training Group," *Personnel and Guidance Journal,* 37, 493–496.

Gray, Clifford F. (1972), "Performance as a Criterion Variable in Measuring Business Gaming Success: An Experiment with a Multiple Objective Performance Model," Paper presented at the Southeastern AIDS Conference.

Graybeal, Wayne J. and Udo W. Pooch (1986), *Simulation: Principles and Methods,* Cambridge, MA: Winthrop Publishers, Inc.

Greenblat, Cathy S. (1973), "Teaching with Simulation Games," *Teaching Sociology,* 1 (October), 62–83.

Greenblat, C.S. and R.D. Duke (1981), *Principles and Practices of Gaming Simulation,* Beverly Hills, CA: Sage.

Greene, Scott, C. (1981), "Computer-Based Simulations: Overcoming Instructor Misgivings Through Effective Planning," *Journal of Marketing Education,* 4, Fall, 13–18.

Greenlaw, Paul S. and William D. Biggs (1979), *Modern Personnel Management,* Philadelphia: W.B. Saunders.

Greenlaw, Paul S. and M. W. Frey (1967), *FINANSIM: A Financial Management Simulation,* Scranton, PA: International Textbook.

Greenlaw, Paul S., M. W. Frey, and I. R. Vernon (1979), *FINANSIM: A Financial Management Simulation,* St. Paul, MN: West.

Greenlaw, Paul S. and M. P. Hottenstein (1969), *PROSIM: A Production Management Simulation,* New York: Harper & Row.

Greenlaw, Paul S. and F. W. Kniffin (1964), *MARKSIM: A Marketing Decision Simulation,* New York: Harper & Row.

Greenlaw, Paul S., W. H. Lowell, and R. H. Rawdon (1962), *Business Simulation in Industrial and University Education,* Englewood Cliffs, NJ: Prentice-Hall.

Greenlaw, Paul S. and F. Paul Wyman (1973), "The Teaching Effectiveness of Games in Collegiate Business Courses," *Simulation and Games,* 4 (no. 3, September), 259–293.

Gruendemann, Paul A. (1967), "The USC Management Strategy Simulation," Los Angeles: University of Southern California. (Mimeographed.)

Gruendemann, Paul A. (1987), personal communication, Los Angeles: University of Southern California.

Guin, Larry and John McGregor (1987), "An Expert System for Financial Planners," *Developments in Business Simulation and Experiential Exercises,* Vol. 14, Lane Kelly and Patricia Sanders (eds.), 80–83.

Hafer, John C. (1984), "A Comparison of the Effectiveness of the Small Business Institute Case Method," *Journal of Marketing Education,* Spring, 43–49.

Hai, Dorothy M. (1986), *Organizational Behavior: Experiences and Cases,* St. Paul, MN: West Publishing Co.

Hambrick, Donald C. (1983), "Some Tests of the Effectiveness and Functional Attributes of Miles and Snow's Strategic Types," *Academy of Management Journal,* 26 (no. 1), 5–26.

Hand, Herbert H., Max D. Richards, and John W. Slocum Jr. (1973), "Organizational Climate and the Effectiveness of a Human Relations Training Program," *Academy of Management Journal,* 16, 185–195.

Hand, Herbert H. and Henry P. Sims Jr. (1976), "Statistical Evaluation of Complex Gaming Performance," *Management Science,* 21, 708–717.

Harris, Catherine L. (1985), "Information Power," *Business Week,* (June 24), 108.

Harris, R. D. and M. J. Maggard (1977), *Computer Models in Operations-Management: A Computer-Augmented System,* New York: Harper & Row.

Harrison, R. and B. Lubin (1965), "Personal Style, Group Composition, and Learning," *Journal of Applied Behavioral Science,* 1, 286–301.

Hayes, James L. (1979), "A New Look at Managerial Competence: The AMA Model of Worthy Performance," *Management Review,* November, 2–3.

Hayes-Roth, B. (1985), "A Blackboard Architecture for Control," *Artificial Intelligence,* 26 (no. 2), 251–321.

Hegarty, W. H. (1976), "Contextual and Pedagogical Differences in Teaching Business Policy Among Academicians," *The New Role of the Marketing Professional,* Vol. 40, Peter J. LaPlaca (ed.), 125–129.

Helper, M. L. (1977), *Conduit Catalog of Reviewed and Tested Curriculum Materials,* Iowa City, IA: Conduit.

Henshaw, Richard C. and James R. Jackson (1978), *The Executive Game,* Third Edition, Homewood, IL: Richard D. Irwin, Inc.

Henshaw, Richard C. and James R. Jackson (1984), *The Executive Game,* Homewood, IL: R. D. Irwin.

Herron, L.W. (1960), *Executive Action Simulation,* Englewood Cliffs, NJ: Prentice-Hall, Inc.

Hinton, Roy W. and Daniel C. Smith (1985), *STRAT-PLAN,* Englewood Cliffs, NJ: Prentice-Hall.

Hoffmeister, J. Ronald and Nicholas J. DiMarco (1977), "Influence of Personality on Performance in a Financial Management Simulation," *Simulation & Games,* 8, 385–394.

Hofstetter, Fred T. (1985), "Perspectives on a Decade of Computer Based Instruction, 1974–1984," *Journal of Computer Based Instruction,* Winter, 1–6.

Holzman, T. G. and R. Glazer (1977), "Developing a Computer Literacy in Children: Some Observations and Suggestions," *Educational Technology,* August, 5–11.

Hoover, J. Duane (1974), "Experiential Learning: Conceptualization and Definition," *Simulation, Games and Experiential Techniques: On the Road to a New Frontier,* James Kenderdine and Bernard Keys (eds.), 31–35.

Hoover, J. Duane (1977), "A 'Live-Case' Approach to the Business and Society Course," *New Horizons in Simulation Games and Experiential Learning,* Carl C. Nielsen (ed.), 159–165.

Hoover, J. Duane and Carlton Whitehead (1975), "An Experiential-Cognitive Methodology in the First Course in Management: Some Preliminary Results," *Simulation Games and Experiential Learning in Action,* Richard H. Buskirk (ed.), 25–30.

Hoover, J. Duane and Carlton J. Whitehead (1979), "An Experimental Evaluation of a Cognitive-Experiential Learning Methodology in the Basic Management Course," *Journal of Experiential Learning and Simulation,* 1, 119–125.

Horn, Robert E. and Anne Cleaves (1980), *The Guide to Simulations/Games for Education and Training,* Beverly Hills, CA: Sage.

House, Robert J. (1979), "Experiential Learning: A Sad Passing Fad?" *Exchange: the Organizational Behavior Teaching Journal,* 4 (no. 3), 8–12.

Hummel, John W. (1985), "A Proposed Interactive Inventory Control Simulation", *Developments in Business Simulations and Experiential Exercises,* Vol. 12, James W. Gentry and Alvin C. Burns (eds.), 131–134.

Humphreys, Marie Adele (1981), "Client-Sponsored Projects in a Marketing Research Course," *Journal of Marketing Education,* Fall, 7–12.

Humphreys, Patrick and Dina Berkeley (1986), "Organizational Knowledge for Supporting Decisions," in E. R. McLean and H. G. Sol (eds.), *Decision Support Systems: A Decade in Perspective,* Amsterdam: Elsevier.

Hunsaker, Phillip L. (1978), "Debriefing: The Key to Effective Experiential Learning," *Exploring Experiential Learning: Simulations and Experiential Exercises,* Daniel C. Brenenstuhl and Samuel C. Certo (eds.), 3–4.

Info Corp (1985), "The Changing Face of Computer Demand," *Business Week,* (June 24), 77.

Ingersoll, V. (1973), "Role Playing, Attitude Change and Behavior," *Organizational Behavior and Human Performance,* 10, 157–175.

Ireland, R. Duane and J. Duane Hoover (1979), "Experiential Processing of Different Managerial Perspectives: The Use of A Game Show Format," *Insights Into Experiential Pedagogy,* Samuel C. Certo and Daniel C. Brenenstuhl (eds.), 63–65.

Jackson, George C. (1982), "SIMCOM I: A Computer Based Simulation Model for Evaluating Physical Distribution Strategies Involving Order Consolidation," *Developments in Business Simulation and Experiential Exercises,* Vol. 9, David Fritzsche and Lee Graf (eds.), 120–123.

Jackson, George C., James W. Gentry, and Fred Morgan (1985), "A Computerized Logistics Game for Micros," *Developments in Business Simulation and Experiential Exercises,* Vol. 12, James W. Gentry and Alvin C. Burns (eds.), 111–113.

Jackson, George C. and Fred Morgan (1983), "Business Logistics Game," *Proceedings,* Southwestern Marketing Association, Houston.

Jackson, James R. (1959), "Learning from Experience in Business Decision Games," *California Management Review,* 1 (no. 2), 23–29.

Jackson, James R. (1959), "UCLA Executive Decision Game," *Proceedings of the National Symposium on Management Games,* Center for Research in Business, The University of Kansas, VI-9-VI-15.

Janis, I. and B. King (1954), "The Influence of Role Playing on Opinion Change," *Journal of Abnormal and Social Psychology,* 49, 211-218.

Janis, L. and L. Mann (1965), "Effectiveness of Emotional Role Playing in Modifying Smoking Habits and Attitudes," *Journal of Experimental Research in Personality,* 1, 84-90.

Jaruga, Alicia and Andrzej Kisiel (1985), "Gaming and Simulation in Education and Research: The Polish Case," *Simulation and Games,* 16 (June), 230-232.

Jenkins, H. M. and W. C. Ward (1965), "Judgment of Contingency Between Responses and Outcomes," *Psychological Monographs: General and Applied,* 79 Whole No. 594.

Jenkins, T. M. and E. J. Dankert (1981), "Results of a Three Month PLATO Trial in Terms of Utilization and Student Attitudes," *Educational Technology,* March, 44-47.

Jensen, Ronald L., and David J. Cherrington (1984), *The Business Management Laboratory,* Plano, TX: Business Publications, Inc., Third Edition.

Johnson, L.E. and D. Loucks (1980), "Interactive Multiobjective Planning Using Computer Graphics", *Computers and Operations Research (UK)* 7 (1-2), 89-97.

Jolly, Laura D. and Ann E. Fairhurst (1986), "International Buying: An Experiential Exercise," *Developments in Business Simulation and Experiential Exercises,* Vol. 13, Alvin C. Burns and Lane Kelley (eds.), 233-234.

Kagel, Richard (1985), "Using the Computer as a Planning Aid in an Applied Marketing Course," *Developments in Business Simulation and Experiential Exercises,* Vol. 12, James Gentry and Alvin C. Burns (eds.), 50-53.

Kanter, Rosebeth M. (1983), *The Change Masters: Innovation and Productivity in One American Corporation,* New York: Alfred A. Knopf.

Kaplan, R. E. (1985), "What One Manager Learned in the Looking Glass and How He Learned It," *The Journal of Management Development,* 5 (no. 4), 37-45.

Kassarjian, Harold H. (1965), "Social Character and Sensitivity Training," *Journal of Applied Behavioral Science,* 1, 433-440.

Kaufman, Frank L. (1976), "An Empirical Study of the Usefulness of a Computer-Based Business Game," *Journal of Educational Data Processing,* 13, 13-22.

Keeffe, M. J. and C. J. Cozan (1985), "General Management Policy Simulations: Which Games are Popular and Why Do Professors Stop Using Games," in James W. Gentry and Alvin C. Burns (eds.), *Developments in Business Simulation and Experiential Exercises,* Vol. 12, 101-106.

Keen, Peter G. W. (1986), "Decision Support Systems: The Next Decade," in E. R. McLean and H. G. Sol (eds.), *Decision Support Systems: A Decade in Perspective,* Amsterdam: Elsevier.

Kelly, George A. (1955), *The Psychology of Personal Constructs,* Vol. 1, New York: N. W. Norton and Co.

Kelley, Lane (1979), "An Experiential Evaluation of a Didactic-Experiential Approach for Teaching Personnel Management," *Journal of Experiential Learning and Simulation,* 1, 39-44.

Kelley, Lane and Jeffrey Easton (1981), "Problems in Evaluation of Experiential Learning in Management Education," *Developments in Business Simulation and Experiential Exercises,* 8, William D. Biggs and David J. Fritzsche (eds.), 137–141.

Kelley, Lane and Arthur Whatley (1979), "The Teacher-Student Relationship in Experiential Classes and the Student's Perception of Course Effectiveness," in *Insights into Experiential Pedagogy,* Vol. 6, eds. Samuel C. Certo and Daniel C. Brenenstuhl, Tempe: Arizona State University, 235–238.

Kelley, Lane and Arthur A. Whatley (1987), *Personnel Management in Action: Skill Building Experiences* (4th Ed.), St. Paul, MN: West Publishing Co.

Kennedy, John L. (1971), "The System Approach: A Preliminary Exploratory Study of the Relation Between Team Composition and Financial Performance in Business Games," *Journal of Applied Psychology,* 55, 46–49.

Keys, J. Bernard (1976), "A Review of Learning Research in Business Gaming," in B. H. Sord (ed.), *Computer Simulation and Learning Theory,* 173–184.

Keys, J. Bernard (1977), "Total Enterprise Games: Computerized," in R. E. Horn (ed.), *The Guide to Simulations/Games for Education and Training,* Cranford, NJ: Didactic Systems, Inc.

Keys, J. Bernard (1977), "The Management of Learning Grid for Management Development," *Academy of Management Review,* 2, 289–297.

Keys, J. Bernard (1980), "Total Enterprise Business Games: An Evaluation," in R. E. Horn and A. Cleaves (eds.), *The Guide to Simulations/Games for Education and Training,* Newbury Park, CA: Sage, 277–285.

Keys, J. Bernard (1987), "Total Enterprise Business Games," *Simulation & Games,* 18, 225–241.

Keys, J. Bernard and Robert R. Bell (1977), "A Comparative Evaluation of the Management of Learning Grid Applied to the Business Policy Learning Environment," *Journal of Management,* 3, 33–39.

Keys, J. Bernard and Howard Leftwich (1977), *The Executive Simulation,* Dubuque, IA: Kendall/Hunt Publishing Company.

Keys, J. Bernard and Howard Leftwich (1985), *The Executive Simulation,* Dubuque, IA: Kendall/Hunt Publishing Company.

Keys, J. Bernard and Howard Leftwich (1985), *The Executive Simulation,* (3rd ed.), Dubuque, IA: Kendall/Hunt.

Keys, J. Bernard and Robert Wells (1987), *Microtronics,* New York: John Wiley.

Keyt, John C. and Ernest R. Cadotte (1981), "CHIPS: A Marketing Channels Management Game," *Developments in Business Simulation and Experiential Exercises,* Vol. 8, William Biggs and David Fritzsche (eds.), 242–246.

Kibbee, J. M., C. J. Croft, and B. Nanus (1961), *Management Games,* New York: Reinhold Publishing.

Kidron, A. G. (1977), "The Effectiveness of Experiential Methods in Training and Education," *The Academy of Management Review,* 2, 490–495.

King, B. and I. Janis (1956), "Comparison of the Effectiveness of Improvised Versus Non-Improvised Role Playing in Producing Opinion Changes," *Human Relations,* 9, 177–186.

Kinnear, Thomas C. and James R. Taylor (1982), *Exercises in Marketing Research,* New York, NY: McGraw-Hill Book Company.

Klein, Ronald D. (1984), "Adding International Business to the Core Program," *Journal of International Business Studies,* 15 (no. 1), 151–159.

Kleppner, Otto (1985), *Advertising Procedure,* 9th Edition, Englewood Cliffs, NJ: Prentice-Hall.

Knowles, A. S. (1974), "New Patterns of Learning and Work: An American Viewpoint," *Universities Quarterly,* Summer, 296.

Kolb, David A. (1974), "On Management and the Learning Process," in *Organizational Psychology: A Book of Readings,* Second Edition, David A. Kolb, Irwin M. Rubin, and James M. McIntyre (eds.), Englewood Cliffs, NJ: Prentice-Hall.

Kolb, David A. (1984), *Experiential Learning: Experience as the Source of Learning and Development,* Englewood Cliffs, NJ: Prentice-Hall.

Kolb, David A., I. M. Rubin, and J. M. McIntyre (1974), *Organizational Psychology: An Experiential Approach,* Englewood Cliffs, NJ: Prentice-Hall.

Kotler, Philip (1984), *Marketing Management: Analysis, Planning, and Control,* Englewood Cliffs, N.J.: Prentice-Hall, Inc., 612.

Krathwohl, D. R., Benjamin S. Bloom, and B. B. Masia (1964), "Taxonomy of Educational Objectives: The Classification of Educational Goals," *Handbook II: Affective Domain,* New York: David McKay.

Kulik, J., C. Kulik, C., and P. Cohen (1980), "Effectiveness of Computer-Based College Teaching: A Meta-Analysis of Findings," *Review of Educational Research,* Winter, 525–544.

Kulik, J. A., R. L. Bangert-Downs, and G. W. Williams, (1983), "Effects of Computer-Based Teaching on Secondary School Students," *Journal of Educational Psychology,* 75, 19–26.

Kulik, J. A., R. L. Bangert-Downs, and G. W. Williams (1983–84), "Effectiveness of Technology in Pre-College Mathematics and Science Training," *Journal of Educational Technology Systems,* 12, 137–158.

Kuzmits, Frank E. (1986), *Experiential Exercises in Personnel* (2nd ed.) Columbus, OH: Merrill Publishing Co.

Lamb, Steven W. and Samuel C. Certo (1985), "An Investigation of the Validity of a Recommendation for Experiential Exercise Debriefing," *Developments in Business Simulation and Experiential Exercises,* Vol. 12, James W. Gentry and Alvin C. Burns (eds.), 163–167.

Lambert, Nancy and David R. Lambert (1985), "A Reactive Microcase Pedagogy," *Development in Business Simulation and Experiential Exercises,* Vol. 12, James Gentry and Alvin C. Burns (eds.), 172–176.

Lambert, Nancy E. and David R. Lambert (1988), "Advertising Response in the Gold and Pray Algorithm: A Critical Assessment," Patricia Sanders and Tom Pray (eds), *Developments in Business Simulation and Experiential Exercises,* Vol. 15, 188–191.

Larreche, Jean-Claude and Hubert Gatignon (1977), *Markstrat,* Palo Alto, CA: The Scientific Press.

Larreche, Jean-Claude and David Weinstein (1988), *Industrat,* Englewood Cliffs, NJ: Prentice-Hall.

Lau, James B. and Mariann Jelinek (1984), *Behavior in Organizations* (3rd Ed.), Homewood, IL: Richard D. Irwin, Inc.

Lavidge, Robert J. and Gary A. Steiner (1961), "A Model for Predictive Measurement of Advertising Effectiveness," *Journal of Marketing,* 25 (October), 59–62.

Law, Averill M. and David W. Kelton (1982), *Simulation Modeling and Analysis,* New York: McGraw-Hill.

Lee, Ronald M. (1987), "A Logic Programming Approach to Building Planning and Simulation Models," in H. G. Sol et al. (eds.), *Expert Systems and Artificial Intelligence in Decision Support Systems,* Norwell, MA: D. Reidel Publishing.

Leenders, Michael R. and James A. Erskine (1973), *Case Research: The Case Waiting Process,* London, Ontario: University of Western Ontario School of Business Administration.

Lewin, Kurt (1951), *Field Theory in Social Science,* New York: Harper & Row.

Liebowitz, Burt H. and John H. Carson (1985), *Multiple Processor Systems for Real-Time Applications,* Englewood Cliffs, NJ: Prentice-Hall.

Lipstein, Benjamin and William J. McGuire (1979), *Evaluating Advertising,* New York: Advertising Research Foundation.

Locke, Thomas P., Glenn M. Johnson, Kathryn Kirigin-Ramp, Jay D. Atwater, and Meg Gerrard (1986), "An Evaluation of a Juvenile Education Program in a State Penitentiary," *Evaluation Review,* 10 (no. 3), 281–298.

Lombardo, Michael M., Morgan W. McCall, Jr., and David L. DeVries (1983), *Looking Glass,* Glenview, IL: Scott, Foresman and Company.

Lombardo, Michael M., Morgan W. McCall, Jr., and David L. DeVries (1987), *Looking Glass II,* Glenview, IL: Scott, Foresman and Company.

Loveluck, Clive (1983), "The Construction, Operation, and Evaluation of Management Games," in *Management Development and Training Handbook,* eds. Bernard Taylor and Gordon Lippitt, London: McGraw-Hill, 307–327.

Low, C.R. (1985), *Transportation Management: The Cunning Simulation,* New York: McGraw-Hill.

Low, James T. (1980), "Guidelines for the Use of Business Simulation Games," *Journal of Marketing Education,* 3, April, 30–37.

Lubatkin, M. and M. Pitts (1983), "PIMS: Fact or Folklore?" *Journal of Business Strategy,* 3, 38–43.

Lucas, Henry C., Jr. (1979), "Performance in a Complex Management Game," *Simulation & Games,* 10, 61–74.

Macmillan, Ian and Thomas Ference (undated), *Simmons Simulator,* Unpublished Proprietary Game, Columbia University.

Madden, C. S., D. H. Robertson, and Daniel C. Brenenstuhl (1983), "The Use of Videotaped Cases in Teaching Information Acquisition and Decision-Making Skills," *Developments in Business Simulation and Experiential Exercises,* Lee A. Graf and David M. Currie (eds.), Vol. 10, 42–44.

March, James G. and Herbert A. Simon (1957), *Organizations,* New York: Wiley.

Markulis, Peter (1985), "The Live Case Study: Filling the Gap Between the Case Study and the Experiential Exercise," *Developments in Business Simulation & Experiential Exercises,* Vol. 15, James W. Gentry and Alvin C. Burns (eds.), 168–171.

Marston, G.F., and K.S. Lyon (1975), "Learning and Attitude Change of Students Subjected to a National Income Simulation Game: Some Further Evidence," *Journal of Economic Education,* 7, 20–27.

Mathis, A. G. (1958), " 'Trainability' as a Function of Individual Valency Pattern," in *Emotional Dynamics and Group Culture,* D. Stock and H. A. Thelen (eds.), Washington, D. C.: National Training Laboratories-National Education Association.

McAfee, R. Bruce (1979), "Using A Case As the Basis for A Modified Debate," *Insights Into Experiential Pedagogy,* Samuel C. Certo and Daniel C. Brenenstuhl (eds.), 11–12.

McAfee, R. Bruce (1981) "The Test Preview Game: Applying the Game Show Format," *Developments in Business Simulation and Experiential Exercises,* Vol. 8, William D. Biggs and David J. Fritzsche (eds.), 99–101.

McAfee, R. Bruce and Paul J. Champagne (1987), *Organizational Behavior: A Manager's View,* St. Paul, MN: West Publishing Co.

McAfee, R. Bruce and Alex Hawryluk (1986), "The Assessment Center As A Teaching/Learning Device," *Developments in Business Simulation and Experiential Exercises,* Vol. 13, Alvin C. Burns and Lane Kelley (eds.), 260–264.

McAllister, Daniel W. (1987), "Testing the Page Technique: Results and Further Developments," *Developments in Business Simulation and Experiential Exercises,* 14, Lane Kelley and Patricia Sanders (eds.), 133–134.

McCain, Gary and Douglas J. Lincoln (1982), "Choice Criteria Model for Selecting Live-Case Marketing Research Class Projects," *Journal of Marketing Education,* Fall, 47–53.

McCune, Joseph T. (1987), "Computers in the Classroom," *MED Newsletter,* Vol. 14, No. 1 (November), 6.

McGuire, William J. (1978), "An Integrative Model of Advertising Effectiveness," in Harry C. Davis and Alvin Silk (eds.), *Behavior And Management Science In Advertising,* New York: Ronald Press, 156–180.

McNair, Malcolm P. (1954), *The Case Method at the Harvard Business School,* New York: McGraw-Hill.

McRaith, J. R. and C. R. Goeldner (1962), "A Survey of Marketing Games," *Journal of Marketing,* 26 (no. 3), 69–72.

McKenney, James L. and William R. Dill (1966), "Influences on Learning in Simulation Games," *American Behavioral Scientist,* 10, 28–32.

McLaughlin, Frank S. and Glenn M. Bryant (1987), "A Comparison of Student Perceptions with Accepted Expectations for Business Simulations," in Lane Kelley and Patricia Saunders (eds.), *Developments in Business Simulation & Experiential Exercises,* Vol. 14, 135–137.

McLuhan, Marshall (1973), "The Medium is the Message," C. D. Mortensen (ed.), *Basic Readings in Communication Theory,* New York: Harper & Row, 390–406.

Malone, T. W. (1981), *What Makes Things Fun to Learn,* Palo Alto, CA: Xerox Corporation Research Center.

Meier, R. C., W. T. Newell and H. L. Pazer (1969), *Simulation in Business and Economics,* Englewood Cliffs, NJ: Prentice-Hall.

Miesing, Paul (1982), "Group Processes, Decision-Making Styles and Team Performance in a Complex Simulation Game," in *Developments in Business Simulation and Experiential Exercises,* Vol. 9, eds. David J. Fritzsche and Lee A. Graf, Normal: Illinois State University, 228–231.

Miles, Mathew B. (1965), "Changes During and Following Laboratory Training: A Clinical-Experimental Study," *Journal of Applied Behavioral Science,* 1, 215–242.

Miles, Robert H. and W. Alan Randolph (1985), *The Organization Game: A Simulation,* Glenview, IL: Scott, Foresman and Company.

Mills, Janet (1988), "Six Thinking Hats: An Exercise to Combat Confusion and Develop Thinking Skills," *Developments in Business Simulation and Experiential Exercises,* Vol. 15, Patricia Sanders and Tom Pray (eds.), 201–204.

Mintzberg, H. (1973), *The Nature of Managerial Work,* New York: Harper & Row.

Mitroff, Ian I. and James R. Emshoff (1979), "On Strategic Assumption Making: A Dialectic Approach to Policy and Planning," *Academy of Management Review,* 4 (no. 1), 1–12.

Moberg, Dennis J. and David Caldwell (1988), *Interactive Cases in Organizational Behavior,* Glenview, IL: Scott, Foresman and Company.

Moskowitz, Joel M., Eric Schaps, and Janet H. Malvin (1982), "Process and Outcome Evaluation in Primary Prevention," *Evaluation Review,* 6 (no. 6), 775–778.

Neuhauser, John J. (1976), "Business Games Have Failed," *Academy of Management Review,* 1, 124–129.

Newgren, D.E., R.M. Stair, and R.R. Kuehn (1980), "The Relationship Between Group Size and the Learning Curve Effect in a Gaming Environment," in *Experiential Learning Enters the 80's,* Vol. 7, eds. Daniel C. Brenenstuhl and William D. Biggs, Tempe: Arizona State University, 203–205.

Ness, Thomas E. and Ralph L. Day (1984), *Marketing in Action: A Decision Game,* Homewood, IL: Irwin.

Nii, H. Penny (1986a), "Blackboard Systems, Part 1," *AI Magazine,* 7 (no. 2), 38–53.

Nii, H. Penny (1986b), "Blackboard Systems, Part 2," *AI Magazine,* 7 (no. 3), 82–106.

Nkomo, Stella, McAfee, Bruce, and Myron Fottler (1988), *Personnel: Innovative Cases, Exercises, Incidents, and Skill Builders,* Boston, MA: PWS Kent Publishing.

Nordstrom, Joseph (1972), "Top Management Decision Game," Hewlett-Packard BASIC Contributed Program DECSM A606-36065B, 1–22.

Nordstrom, Richard D. (1982), "Replication: A Goal and Guidelines," *ABSEL News & Views,* 2, 3ff.

Nordstrom, Richard D. and Charles S. Sherwood (1984), "A Marketing Plan Exercise: Development of Interteam Cooperation Using a Coordinated Experiential Approach," *Developments in Business Simulation and Experiential Exercises,* Vol. 11, David M. Currie and James W. Gentry (eds.), 133–138.

Norris, Dwight R. (1986), "External Validity of Business Games," *Simulation and Games,* 17 (no. 4, December), 447–459.

Norris, Dwight R. and Robert E. Neibuhr (1980), "Group Variables and Gaming Success," *Simulation & Games,* 11, 301–312.

Norris, Dwight R. and C. K. Snyder (1982), "External Validation of Simulation Games," *Simulation and Games,* 13 (no. 1, March), 73–85.

Ord-Smith, R. J. and J. Stephenson (1975), *Computer Simulation of Continuous Systems,* London: Cambridge.

Panitz, Eric (1986), "Restructuring the University," *Developments in Business Simulation and Experiential Exercises,* Vol. 13, Alvin C. Burns and Lane Kelley (eds.), 130–134.

Parasuraman, A. (1978), "A Framework for Determining the Pedagogical Value of Simulation Gaming: Implications for Future Simulation Gaming Research," *Exploring Experiential Learning: Simulations and Experiential Exercises,* Daniel C. Benenenstuhl and Samuel C. Certo (eds.), 127–132.

Parasuraman, A. (1980), "Evaluation of Simulation Games: A Critical Look at Past Efforts and Future Needs," *Experiential Learning Enters the 1980's,* Daniel C. Brenenstuhl and William D. Biggs (eds.), 192–194.

Parasuraman, A. (1981), "Assessing the Worth of Business Simulation Games," *Simulations and Games,* 13, 189–200.

Patton, Carol (1987), "Game Fires Managers for Bad Business Moves," *InfoWorld,* (December), 21, 25.

Patz, Alan L. (1981), *Strategic Decision Analysis: A General Management Framework,* Boston: Little, Brown.

Patz, Alan L. (1986), "Managing Innovation in High Technology Industries," *New Management,* 4 (No. 1), 54–59.

Patz, Alan L. (1987), "Open System Simulations and Simulation Based Research," in Lane Kelley and Patricia Sanders (eds.), *Developments in Business Simulation and Experiential Exercises,* Vol. 14, 159–164.

Patz, Alan L. (1988a), "Integrating Simulations: A Model for Business Policy Success," Patricia Sanders and Thomas Pray (eds.), *Developments in Business Simulation and Experiential Exercises,* Vol. 15, 15–19.

Patz, Alan L. (1988b), "The Quality of Business Policy Research," Los Angeles: University of Southern California. (Mimeographed)

Pearce, John A. (1979), "Developing Business Policy Skills: A Report on Alternatives," *Journal of Educational Technology,* 7, 361–371.

Penley, Larry E. and Yolanda E. Penley (1988), *Human Resources Simulation: Using Lotus 1-2-3,* Cincinnati, OH: SouthWestern Publishing Company.

Pepper, Jon (1986), "With New Training Method, Users Learn Fast," *PC Week,* November 25, 91–92.

Peterson, Robin T., Wilbur W. Stanton, and Arthur A. Whatley (1978), *Marketing in Action: An Experiential Approach,* St. Paul, MN: West Publishing Co.

Petre, P. (1984), "Games That Teach You to Manage," *Fortune,* 110, No. 9, 65–74.

Pfeiffer, J. William (1985), *Reference Guide to Handbooks and Annuals,* San Diego, CA.

Pfeiffer, J. W. and Jones, J.E. (1987), *A Handbook of Structured Experiences for Human Relations Training,* San Diego, CA: University Associates Press.

Philippatos, George C. and Donald R. Moscato (1969a), "An Empirical Study of the Learning Aspects of Experimental Business Game Playing," *AIIE Transactions,* 1, 343–348.

Philippatos, George C. and Donald R. Moscato (1969b), "Experimental Learning Aspects of Business Games Playing with Incomplete Information About the Rules," *Psychological Reports,* 25, 470–486.

Philippatos, George C., and Donald R. Moscato (1971), "Effects of Constrained Information on Player Decisions in Experimental Business Simulation: Some Empirical Evidence," *Journal of the Association for Computing Machinery,* 18, 94–104.

Philippatos, George C., and Donald R. Moscato (1972), "Laboratory Experiments with Large-Size Business Games," Working paper, College of Business Administration, Pennsylvania State University.

Piaget, J. (1973), *Psychology and Epistemology,* New York: Viking.

Pierfy, David A. (1977), "Comparative Simulation Game Research—Stumbling Blocks and Stepping Stones," *Simulation and Games,* 8 (no. 2, June), 255–268.

"PLANETS II—PLanning and NETwork Simulation II Manual" (1975), Paul W. Marshall, et al. (eds.), *Operations Management: Text and Cases,* Homewood, IL: Irwin.

Porter, Lyman W. and Lawrence E. McKibbin (1988), *Management Education and Development: Drift or Thrust into the 21st Century,* Hightstown, NJ: McGraw-Hill Book Company.

Porter, Michael (1980), *Competitive Strategy,* New York: The Free Press.

Potter, G.B. (1965), *An Exploratory Study of Psychological Factors in Business Simulation Games,* Master's Thesis, University of Illinois.

Pray, Thomas F., and Steven C. Gold (1982), "Inside the Black Box—An Analysis of Underlying Demand Functions in Contemporary Business Simulations," in *Developments in Business Simulation and Experiential Exercises,* Vol. 9, eds. David J. Fritzsche and Lee A. Graf, Normal: Illinois State University, 110–115.

Pray, Thomas F., and Steven C. Gold (1984), "Two Algorithms for Redistribution of Stockouts in Computerized Business Simulations," in *Developments in Business Simulation and Experiential Exercises,* Vol. 11, eds. David M. Currie and James W. Gentry, Stillwater: Oklahoma State University, 247–252.

Pray, Thomas F. and Steven C. Gold (1987), "Goal Setting and Performance Evaluation with Different Starting Positions—The Modeling Dilemma," Lane Kelley and Patricia Sanders (eds.), *Developments in Business Simulation & Experiential Exercises,* Vol. 14, 169–174.

Pray, Thomas F., Daniel R. Strang, Steven C. Gold and D. E. Burlingame (1984), *Decide-P/OM: An Integrative Computer Simulation for Production/Operations Management,* New York: Random House.

Priesmeyer, H. Richard (1987), *Strategy: A Business Unit Simulation,* Cincinnati, OH: SouthWestern Publishing Company.

Pritsker, A. Alan B. (1986), *Introduction to Simulation and Slam II* (3rd ed.), New York: Wiley.

Quinn, James Brian, Henry Mintzberg and Robert L. James (1988), *The Strategy Process: Concepts, Contexts, and Cases,* Englewood Cliffs, NJ: Prentice-Hall.

Purdue Industrial Administration Decision Simulation: Participant's Manual (Multilith; n.d.).

Raia, Anthony P. (1966), "A Study of the Educational Value of Management Games," *Journal of Business,* 39, 339–352.

Ray, Michael L. (1982), *Advertising and Communication Management,* Englewood Cliffs, NJ: Prentice-Hall.

Remus, William E. (1977), "Who Likes Business Games?" *Simulation & Games,* 8, 64–68.

Remus, William and Steven Jenner (1979), "Playing Business Games: Attitudinal Differences Between Students Playing Singly and as Teams," *Simulation & Games,* 10, No. 1 March, 75–86.

Remus, William E., and Steve Jenner (1981), "Playing Business Games: Expectations and Realities," *Simulation & Games,* 12, 480–488.

Ricciardi, Franc M. (1957), *Top Management Decision Simulation: The AMA Approach,* New York: American Management Association.

Richardson, Neil A. and John H. Summey (1980), "Experiential Live-Case Projects: Some Potential Legal Issues Affecting Instructors and Colleges," *Journal of Experiential Learning and Simulation,* 2, 29–37.

Richardson, Neil and Sion Raveed (1980), "A Live-Case Program For Teaching Marketing Research," *Journal of Marketing Education,* April, 38–42.

Ritchie, J. B. and Paul Thompson (1988), *Organization and People: Readings, Cases, and Exercises in Organizational Behavior,* Minneapolis, MN: West Publishing Co.

Ritchken, Peter H. and Gregory B. Getts (1985), "A Portfolio Risk-Management Simulation Game," *Simulation and Games,* 16 (March), 49–62.

Robana, A. (1980), "What Business Students Learn from Finance Simulations," in D.C. Brenenstuhl and W.D. Biggs (eds.), *Experiential Learning Enters the Eighties,* 177–179.

Roberts, R. M. and L. Strauss (1975), "Management Games in Higher Education 1962 to 1974—An Increasing Acceptance," *Proceedings of the North American Simulation and Gaming Association,* Vol. 13, Nancy Roberts (ed.), 381–385.

Roman, D. (1987), "Packaged Authors and Videodisks," *Computer Decisions,* January 2, 72–73.

Rogers, Carl (1969), *Freedom to Learn,* Columbus, OH: Charles E. Merrill Publishing Co.

Roland, Kendrith M. and David M. Gardner (1973), "The Uses of Business Gaming in Education and Research," *Decision Sciences,* 4, 268–283.

Rosenshine, Barak (1970), "Enthusiastic Teaching: A Research Review," *School Review,* 78 (August), 499–514.

Ross, Steven M., Thomas M. Hughes, and Richard E. Hill (1981), "Field Experiences As Meaningful Contexts for Learning about Learning," *Journal of Educational Research,* 75 (no. 2), 103–107.

Rothstein, Michael F. (1970), *Guide to the Design of Real-Time Systems,* New York: Wiley-Interscience.

Rowe, Alan J. (1972), The Task Simulation, Los Angeles: University of Southern California. (Mimeographed)

Rubin, Ronald S. (1987), "The Gamesmanship of Pricing: Building Pricing Strategy Skills Through Spreadsheet Modeling," *Developments in Business Simulation and Experiential Exercises,* Vol. 14, Lane Kelley and Patricia Sanders (eds.), 175–178.

Sahal, Devendra (1981), *Patterns of Technological Innovation,* Reading, MA: Addison-Wesley.

Sanchez, Peter M. (1980), "Common Errors in Using Marketing Management Games," *Journal of Marketing Education,* 3 April, 25–29.

Sanders, Patricia (1985), "Enthusiasm Awareness in the Experiential Classroom," in *Developments in Business Simulation and Experiential Exercises,* Vol. 12, eds. James W. Gentry and Alvin C. Burns, Stillwater: Oklahoma State University, 41–44.

Sanders, Patricia and Jerry Gosenpud (1986), "Perceived Instructor Enthusiasm and Student Achievement," in *Developments in Business Simulation and Experiential Exercises,* Vol. 13, eds. Alvin C. Burns and Lane Kelley, Stillwater: Oklahoma State University, 52–55.

Sawyer, T. A. (1985), "Human Factors Considerations in Computer-Assisted Instruction," *Journal of Computer Based Instruction,* 12, No. 1 (Winter), 17–20.

Schellenberger, Robert E. (1965), *MANSYM,* Dubuque, IA: Brown.

Schellenberger, Robert E. (1981), "Critical Variables in Research on the Educational Value of Management Games," *Developments in Business Simulations and Experiential Exercises,* Vol. 8, William D. Biggs and David J. Fritzsche (eds.), 70.

Schellenberger, Robert E. and Lance A. Masters (1986), *MANSYM IV: A Dynamic Management Simulation with Decision Support System,* New York: John Wiley.

Scherer, F. M. (1980), *Industrial Market Structure and Economic Performance* (2nd ed.), Boston: Houghton-Mifflin.

Schneier, Craig E. (1977), "Experiential Learning: Toward the Development of a Theoretical Base and the Identification of Variables and Hypotheses to Guide Research," *New Horizons in Simulation Games and Experiential Learning,* Carl C. Nielsen (ed.) 166–173.

Schreier, James W. (1977), "The Role of the Administrator in Experiential Learning and Simulations, *New Horizons in Simulation Games and Experiential Learning,* Carl C. Nielsen (ed.), 177–186.

Schreier, James W. (1978), "Measurement of Administrator Role for Feedback on Structure and Goals," *Exploring Experiential Learning: Simulations and Experiential Exercises,* Daniel C. Brenenstuhl and Samuel C. Certo (eds.), 139–145.

Schreier, James W. (1981), "Research Questions for Cases," *Developments in Business Simulation and Experiential Exercises,* Vol 8, William D. Biggs and David J. Fritzsche (eds.), 71.

Schreier, James W., J. R. Smith, and I.D. Donalinger (n.d.), *The Human Resources Simulation.*

Schroeder, David L. and James W. Gentry (1987), "Teaching MRP Experimentially Through the Use of Lotus 1-2-3," *Developments in Business Simulation and Experiential Exercises,* Vol. 14, Lane Kelly and Patricia Sanders (eds.), 179–182.

Schutz, William C. (1958), *FIRO: A Three Dimensional Theory of Interpersonal Behavior,* New York: Holt, Rinehart, and Winston.

Sciglimpaglia, Donald (1983), *Applied Marketing Research,* New York: Dryden Press.

Scott, C.R. Jr. and A.J. Strickland III (1984), *Tempomatic IV: A Management Simulation,* Third Edition, Boston, MA: Houghton Mifflin.

Scott, Timothy W. and Alonzo J. Strickland III (1985), *Micromatic: A Management Simulation,* Boston: Houghton Mifflin.

Seligman, Daniel (1985), "Life Will be Different When We're all On-Line," *Fortune,* (February), 68.

Selvidge, Lewis R. (1987), "Business Simulation Through Activities of a Manufacturing Company," in Lane Kelley and Patricia Sanders (eds.), *Developments in Business Simulation & Experiential Exercises,* Vol. 14, 183–185.

Sensbach, Paul R. and Roy D. Adler (1986), "Advertising Courses Should Simulate Real Life," *Journal of Marketing Education,* 8 (Spring), 66–70.

Shannon, Robert E. (1975), "Simulation: A Survey with Research Suggestions," *AIIE Transactions,* 7 (September), 289-301.

Sharda, Ramesh, Keith Willett, and Shen An Cheng (1986), "A Water Quality Management Simulation," *Developments in Business Simulation and Experiential Exercises,* Vol. 13, Alvin Burns and Lane Kelly (eds.), 146-151.

Sherman, J. Daniel (1988), *Interactive Cases in Management,* New York: Harper & Row, Publishers, Inc.

Sherrell, Daniel L., Kenneth R. Russ, and Alvin C. Burns (1986), "Enhancing Mainframe Simulations Via Microcomputers: Designing Decision Support Systems," in Alvin C. Burns and Lane Kelley (eds.), *Developments in Business Simulation and Experiential Exercises,* Vol. 13, 207-211.

Shirts, R. Garry (1975), "Notes on Defining Simulation," in Cathy Greenblat and Richard D. Duke (eds.), *Gaming-Simulation,* Halsted Press, 300-304.

Shubik, Martin (1959), In an invited speech and quoted in the *Proceedings of the National Symposium on Management Games,* Center for Research in Business, University of Kansas, 8-12.

Simon, Herbert A. (1957), *Administration Behavior* (2nd ed.), New York: Macmillan.

Simonetti, Jack L. (1987), *Experiential Exercises and Cases for Human Resource Management,* Boston, MA: Allyn and Bacon, Inc.

Sims, Henry P., Jr. and Herbert H. Hand (1975), "Performance Tradeoffs in Management Games," *Simulation & Games,* 6, 61-72.

Smedslund, J. (1963), "The Concept of Correlation in Adults," *Scandinavian Journal of Psychology,* 4, 165-173.

Smith, J. (1987), "Will You Ever Use Interactive Video?" *Computer Based Training,* October, 17-20.

Smith, Jerald R. (1987), *The Manager* (2nd ed.), Boston: Houghton Mifflin.

Smith, Jerald R. (1984), *MANAGER: A Simulation,* Boston, MA: Houghton Mifflin.

Smith, Jerald R. (1985), *MARKETER: A Simulation,* Boston, MA: Houghton Mifflin.

Smith, Jerald R. (1986), "Marketer: A Microcomputer Simulation in a High Tech Industry," *Developments in Business Simulation and Experiential Exercises,* Vol. 13, Alvin Burns and Lane Kelly (eds.), 157-158.

Smith, Jerald R. (1988), "Minimizing Startup Anxiety: Case Studies of Two Simulation Experiences," *Developments in Business Simulation & Experiential Exercises,* Vol. 15, Patricia Sanders and Tom Pray (eds.), 246-247.

Smith, Jerald R. and Peggy A. Golden (1987), *Airline: A Strategic Management Simulation,* Englwood Cliffs, NJ: Prentice-Hall.

Smith, P. B. (1964), "Attitude Changes Associated with Training in Human Relations," *British Journal of Social and Clinical Psychology,* 3, 104-113.

Smith, Susan R., Michael Szabo, and Cecil R. Trueblood (1980), "Modes of Instruction for Teaching Linear Measurement Skills," *Journal of Educational Research,* 73, 151-153.

Spuck, D. W. (1981), "An Analysis of the Cost Effectiveness of CAI and Factors Associated with Its Successful Implementation in Higher Education," *AEDS Journal,* Fall, 10-12.

Stacy, James E. (1988), "Employee Rights-Student Rights: A Classroom Exercise," *Developments in Business Simulation and Experiential Exercises,* Vol. 15, Patricia Sanders and Tom Pray (eds.), 129–131.

Starbuck, William H. and Ernest Kobrow (1966), "The Effects of Advisors on Business Game Teams," *American Behavioral Scientist,* 10 (November), 28–30.

Steinberg, E. R. (1977), "Review of Student Control in Computer-Assisted Instruction," *Journal of Computer Based Instruction,* Spring, 84–90.

Stevens, George E. (1986), *Cases and Exercises in Personnel/Human Resource Management* (4th ed.), Plano, TX: BPI.

Stewart, L. (1960), "A Survey of Business Games," *Proceedings of the American Management Association,* Vol. 24, Jack Belkin (ed.), 138–144.

Stewart, L. (1961), "A Survey of Business Games," *Simulation and Gaming: A Symposium,* AMA Management Report No. 55, New York: American Management Association, Inc., 16–26.

Stone, Eugene F. (1982), "Research Design: Issues in Studies Assessing the Effects of Management Education," in *Management Education: Issues in Theory, Research, and Practice,* eds. Richard D. Freedman, Cary L. Cooper and Stephen A. Stumpf, Chichester, England: John Wiley, 87–132.

Strickland, Alonzo J., III, and Timothy W. Scott (1985), *Micromatic: A Management Simulation,* Boston: Houghton Mifflin.

Stumpf, Steven (undated), *Financial Services Industry,* Unpublished Simulation, New York University.

Sugges, Peter R. (1980), "New Technology for Business Games," *Experiential Learning Enters the Eighties,* Daniel C. Brenenstuhl and William D. Bigg (eds.), Vol. 7, 69–71.

Sugges, Peter R. Jr. (1981), "Designs for Research on Simulation Games, Cases, and Other Experiential Exercises," *Developments in Business Simulation and Experiential Exercises,* Vol. 8, William D. Biggs and David J. Fritzsche (eds.), 67.

Suits, Bernard (1967), "What is a Game?" *American Philosophy of Science,* 34 (June), 148–156.

Summers, Irvin and Charles Boyd (1982), "Corporation Executives' Ratings of Policy Learning Techniques," in *Developments in Business Simulation and Experiential Exercises,* Vol. 9, eds. David J. Fritzsche and Lee A. Graf, Normal: Illinois State University, 69–72.

Summers, Irvin and Charles Boyd (1983), "Professors' Ratings of Business Policy Learning Methods," in *Developments in Business Simulation and Experiential Exercises,* Vol. 10, eds. Lee A. Graf and David M. Currie, Normal: Illinois State University, 32–34.

Summers, Irvin and Charles Boyd (1984), "Comparisons of Practitioners' and Professors' Perceptions of Business Policy Content and Learning Methods," in *Developments in Business Exercises,* Vol. 11, eds. David M. Currie and James W. Gentry, Stillwater: Oklahoma State University, 148–151.

Summers, B. I. and C. W. Boyd (1985), "Comparison of Practitioners' and Professors' Perceptions of Business Policy Content and Learning Methods," *Simulation & Games,* 16 (no. 1), 7–22.

Swierczek, Frederic W. and Lynne Carmichael (1985), "The Quantity and Quality of Evaluating Training," *Training and Development Journal.*

Talarzyk, W. Wayne (1987), *Cases and Exercises in Marketing,* New York: Dryden Press.

Tanimoto, Steven L. (1987), *The Elements of Artificial Intelligence: An Introduction Using LISP,* Rockville, MD: Computer Science Press.

Taylor, D., P. Berry, and C. Block (1958), "Does Group Participation When Using Brainstorming Facilitate or Inhibit Active Thinking?" *Administrative Science Quarterly,* 3, 23–47.

Teach, Richard D. (1984), "Using Spatial Relationships to Estimate Demand in Business Simulations," in *Developments in Business Simulation and Experiential Exercises,* Vol. 11, eds. David M. Currie and James W. Gentry, Stillwater: Oklahoma State University, 244–246.

Teach, Richard D. (1986), "Building Microcomputer Business Simulations," in Alvin C. Burns and Lane Kelley (eds.), *Developments in Business Simulation and Experiential Exercises* Vol. 13, 239–240.

Teach, Richard D. (1987a), "Profits: The False Profit," in Lane Kelley and Patricia Sanders (eds.), *Developments in Business Simulation and Experiential Exercises,* Vol. 14, 205–207.

Teach, Richard (1987b), "Desirable Characteristics and Attributes of a Business Simulation," David Crookall, et. al. (eds.), *Simulation-Gaming in the Late 1980s,* Oxford, UK: Pergamon Press, 229–234.

Teach, Richard D. (1988), "Designing an Intercultural Business Simulation," Presented to the International Simulation and Gaming Association's 19th annual meeting, Utrech, The Netherlands.

Teach, Richard D. (1989), "Using Forecasting Accuracy as a Measure of Success in Business Simulations," in Tom Pray and John Wingender (eds.), *Developments in Business Simulation and Experiential Learning,* Vol. 16, 103–107.

Teach, Richard and Gita Govahi (1988), "The Role of Experiential Learning and Simulation in Teaching Management Skills," in Patricia Sanders and Tom Pray (eds.), *Developments in Business Simulation and Experiential Learning,* Vol. 15, 65–71.

Thavikulwat, Precha (1988), "Simulating Demand in an Independent-Across-Firms Management Game," in Pat Sanders and Tom Pray, *Developments in Business Simulation and Experiential Exercises,* 183–187.

Thierauf, Robert J. and Richard A. Grosse (1970), *Decision-Making Through Operations Research.* New York: John Wiley and Sons.

Thistlethwaite, Paul C. and Belle M. Zimmerly (1978), "Experiential Learning in Marketing: Student Consultants," *Exploring Experiential Learning: Simulations and Experiential Exercises,* Daniel C. Brenenstuhl and Sam C. Certo (eds.), 252–258.

Thompson, Arthur A. Jr. and A. J. Strickland III (1987), *Strategic Management Concepts and Cases,* Fourth Edition, Plano, TX: Business Publications, Inc.

Thorelli, Hans B., Graves, R. L., and Howells, L. T. (1964), *INTOP (International Operations Simulation),* New York: The Free Press.

Twelker, P. A. (1972), "Some Reflections on Instructional Simulation and Games," *Simulation & Games,* 3, 147–153.

Underwood, William J. (1965), "Evaluation of Laboratory-Method Training, *Training Directors Journal,* 19, 34–40.

Valiquet, I. M. (1964), *Contribution to the Evaluation of a Management Development Program,* Unpublished Master's thesis, Massachusetts Institute of Technology.

Vance, Stanley C. (1960), *Management Decision Simulation,* New York: McGraw-Hill Book Company, Inc.

Vance, Stanley C. and Clifford F. Gray (1967), "Use of a Performance Evaluation Model for Research in Business Gaming," *Academy of Management Journal,* 10, 27–37.

Vaughn Richard (1980), "How Advertising Works: A Planning Model," *Journal of Advertising Research,* 20 (October), 27–33.

Vaughn, Richard (1986), "How Advertising Works: A Planning Model Revisited," *Journal of Advertising Research,* 26 (February/March), 27–33.

Vroom, V. H. and P. W. Yetton (1973), *Leadership and Decision-Making,* Pittsburgh: University of Pittsburgh Press.

Walden, Gene (1984), "Interactive Video: The New Management Training Tool," *Managing,* January, 10.

Walters, G. A. and S. E. Marks (1981), *Experiential Learning and Change,* New York: John Wiley.

Ward, James C. and William Rudelius (1987), "Using Discovery Techniques to Teach Marketing: Evaluation and Prospects," *Proceedings,* 1987 AMA Educators' Conference, Susan P. Douglas et. al. (eds.), 214–219.

Ward, Sid (1981), "What Is Experiential Learning?", *ABSEL News and Views,* 1 (no. 3), p. 2.

Ward, W. C. and H. M. Jenkins (1965), "The Display of Information and the Judgment of Contingency," *Canadian Journal of Psychology,* 19, 231–241.

Wason, P. C. (1960), "On the Failure to Eliminate Hypotheses in a Conceptual Task," *Quarterly Journal of Experimental Psychology,* 12, 129–140.

Wasson, Chester R. (1974), *Product Management: Product Life Cycles and Competitive Marketing Strategy.* St. Charles: Challenge Books.

Watkins, Larry E. (1987), "The Application of Spreadsheet Software Technology to Complex Taxpayer Elections," *Developments in Business Simulation and Experiential Exercises,* Vol. 14, Lane Kelly and Patricia Sanders (eds.), 219–222.

Watson, H. J. (1981), *Computer Simulation in Business,* New York: John Wiley & Sons.

Watson, H. J. and D. P. Christy (1982), "The Evolving Use of Simulation," *Simulation & Games,* Vol. 13 (no. 4), 351–364.

Wheeler, Kenneth, Wallace, Jr., Marc J., Crandall, N. Fredric, and Charles H. Fay (1982), *Practicing Human Resources Administration: Cases, Issues, and Experiences in Personnel/Industrial Relations Decisions,* New York: Random House.

Widmeyer, George (1987), personal communication, Los Angeles: University of Southern California.

Williams, E. L. (1987), "Business Simulation in the Business Policy Course: A Survey of American Assembly of Collegiate Schools of Business," *Developments in Business Simulation and Experiential Learning,* Vol. 14, Lane Kelley and Patricia Sanders (eds.), 235–239.

Wilson, Harold K. (1974), "Administration: The Key to Successful Gaming Experience," *Simulations, Games and Experiential Learning Techniques: On the Road to a New Frontier,* James Kenderdine and Bernard Keys (eds.), 174–181.

Wilson, H., and Hickman, R. (1982), *The World of Business Games,* New York: John Wiley and Sons.

Winer, Leon (1965). "Are You Really Planning Your Marketing?" *Journal of Marketing,* 29 (January), 3.

Wingender, John and Jack Wurster (1987), "Oil and Gas Well Investment Analysis Using the Lotus 1-2-3 Decision Support System," *Developments in Business Simulation and Experiential Exercises,* Vol. 14, Lane Kelly and Patricia Sanders (eds.), 245–249.

Winston, Patrick Henry (1984), *Artificial Intelligence* (2nd ed.), Reading, MA: Addison-Wesley.

Wolfe, Douglas E. and Eugene T. Byrne (1975), "Research on Experiential Learning: Enhancing the Process," *Simulation Games and Experiential Learning in Action,* Richard H. Buskirk (ed.), 325–336.

Wolfe, Joseph (1975a), "A Comparative Evaluation of the Experiential Approach as a Business Policy Learning Environment," *Academy of Management Journal,* 18, 442–452.

Wolfe, Joseph (1975b), "Effective Performance Behaviors in a Simulated Policy-Making Environment," *Management Science,* 21, 872–882.

Wolfe, Joseph (1976), "Correlates and Measures of the External Validity of Computer-Based Business Policy Decision-Making Environments," *Simulation & Games,* 7, 411–438.

Wolfe, Joseph (1976), "Comments on the Perception, Identification, and Measurement of Learning from Simulation Games," *Computer Simulation and Learning Theory,* Burnard H. Sord (ed.), 288–292.

Wolfe, Joseph (1977), "An Evaluation of a Simulation-Based Business School Curriculum Integration Effort," *Journal of Business,* 50, 343–355.

Wolfe, Joseph (1978), "Correlations Between Academic Achievement, Aptitude, and Business Game Performance," in *Exploring Experiential Learning: Simulations and Experiential Exercises,* Vol. 5, eds. Daniel C. Brenenstuhl and Samuel C. Certo, Tempe: Arizona State University, 316–324.

Wolfe, Joseph (1978), "The Effects of Game Complexity on the Acquisition of Business Policy Knowledge," *Decision Sciences,* 9, 143–155.

Wolfe, Joseph (1981), "Research on the Learning Effectiveness of Business Simulation Games—A Review of the State of the Art," *Developments in Business Simulation and Experiential Exercises,* Vol. 9, William D. Biggs and David J. Fritzsche (eds.), 72.

Wolfe, Joseph (1985), "The Teaching Effectiveness of Games in Collegiate Business Courses: A 1973-1983 Update," *Simulation & Games,* 16, 251–288.

Wolfe, Joseph, Donald D. Bowen and C. Richard Roberts (1989), "Team Building Effects on Company Performance: A Free Simulation Study," Working paper, University of Tulsa.

Wolfe, Joseph and Thomas M. Box (1986), "Relationships between Team Cohesion Dimensions and Business Game Performance," *Developments in Business Simulations and Experiential Exercises,* Alvin C. Burns and Lane Kelley (eds.), Vol. 13, 11–16.

Wolfe, Joseph and Thomas M. Box (1987), "Team Cohesion Effects on Business Game Performance," *Developments in Business Simulation and Experiential Exercises,* Vol.. 14, Lane Kelley and Patricia Sanders (eds.), 250–255.

Wolfe, Joseph and Thomas M. Box (1988), "Team Cohesion Effects on Business Game Performance," *Simulation & Games,* 19, 82–98.

Wolfe, Joseph and Thomas I. Chacko (1981a), "The Effects of Different Team Sizes on Business Game Performance," *Developments in Business Simulation and Experiential Exercises,* Vol. 9, David J. Fritzsche and Lee A. Graf (eds.), 232–236.

Wolfe, Joseph and Thomas I. Chacko (1981b), "Mean Size Effects on Business Game Performance and Decision-Making Behavior," *Decision Sciences,* 14 (no. 1, January), 212–233.

Wolfe, Joseph and Jerry Gosenpud (1989), "Strategy Design, Process, and Implementation in a Stable/Complex Environment: A Second Exploratory Study," *Developments in Business Simulation and Experiential Exercises,* Vol. 16, Thomas Pray and John Wingender (eds.), 111–116.

Wolfe, Joseph and Ralph Jackson (1989), "An Investigation of the Need for Algorithmic Validity," Working paper, University of Tulsa.

Wolfe, Joseph and C. Richard Roberts (1985–1986), "The Effects of Different Grade Weights on Business Game Learning Levels," *Journal of Educational Technology Systems,* 14, 307–316.

Wolfe, Joseph and C. Richard Roberts (1986), "The External Validity of a Business Management Game: A Five-Year Longitudinal Study," *Simulation & Games,* 17 (no. 10, March), 45–59.

Wolfe, Joseph and Richard Teach (1987), "Three Down Loaded Mainframe Business Games: A Review," *Academy of Management Review,* 12, 181–192.

Wynne, A James, J. Michael Klosky, and Charles A. Snyder (1979), "Computer-Aided Project Performance Control Simulation: An Interactive Experiential Gaming Technique for Managerial Decision-Making," *Insights Into Experiential Pedagogy,* Samuel C. Certo and Daniel C. Brenenstuhl (eds.), 299–300.

Zenger, John H. and Kenneth Hargis (1982), "Assessing Training Results: It's Time to Take the Plunge!" *Training and Development Journal,* 36, 10–16.

Zigli, R. M. (1981-2), "College of Business Internships: A Second Look," *Collegiate News & Views,* Winter 1981–1982, 21–25.

Zinkhan, George M. and James R. Taylor (1983), "RETSIM: A Simulation Model that Highlights Decision Making Under Conditions of Uncertainty," *Simulation and Games,* 14 (December), 401–416.

Zuckerman, D. W., and Robert E. Horn (1973), *The Guide to Simulations/Games for Education and Training,* Lexington, MA: Informational Resources.